Chinese Geopolitics in the 21st Century

A Post Pandemic Perspective

Chinese Geopolitics in the 21st Century

A Post Pandemic Perspective

Brigadier Anand Tewari (Retd), Ph.D.

PENTAGON PRESS LLP

Chinese Geopolitics in the 21st Century: A Post Pandemic Perspective

Brigadier Anand Tewari (Retd), Ph.D.

ISBN 978-93-90095-40-7

First Published in 2021

Published by
PENTAGON PRESS LLP
206, Peacock Lane, Shahpur Jat
New Delhi-110049
Phones: 011-64706243, 26491568
Telefax: 011-26490600
email: rajan@pentagonpress.in
website: www.pentagonpress.in

Printed at Aegean Offset Printers, Greater Noida

Dedicated to my parents

Contents

Preface

China quite often avows 'Peaceful Rise' or 'Heping Jueqi' in its diplomatic pronouncements. However, the very aphorism of highlighting the 'Peacefulness of the Rise' creates a doubt in the minds of China watchers especially when used during an aggressive strategic behaviour demonstrated by China. The expression indicates as if China's peacefulness is 'conditional' to say the least. Thankfully, nothing has gone beyond a limit so far.

This phrase was evolved by Chinese strategists during the times of Hu Jintao and is the most used phrase to assure the world of China's egalitarian strategic behaviour. But are people ready to believe it? What does it demonstrate of Chinese strategic behaviour? This being the most classic phrase in the Post-Cold War world used by China, if analysed for its validity, meaning and applications, can truly give away the Chinese strategic mind.

Also, China's conditioning to have every behaviour, especially the strategic behaviour, structured, is the right area of study where the answer to such disbeliefs can be found. Therefore, the Chinese frame work of strategic behaviour is the prime focus of the book brought out through exploration of temporal evolution of China's human geography and its metaphysical and geo-economic dispositions. These elements have also been explored in depth to fathom out the geopolitical imperatives for China.

However, the Covid-19 pandemic first traced in China and now making the world reel under a human and economic catastrophe, makes world rethink China. Is there need to rethink? China's astonishing recovery makes people think so. Countries may for now show civility to refrain from any blame game, but, there is certainly a trace of 'real-geopolitic' turning into 'cruel-geopolitic' and whether despite all this, 'Heping Jueqi' can still sustain is the big question. Reasons for the doubt can be found in the changing world geopolitical structures. The book takes this perspective earnestly to gaze the future responses of China.

Brigadier Anand Tewari (Retd), Ph.D.

Acknowledgements

This book is fruition of a very long academic journey of mine in the field of area study and international relations. I, being an ardent student of geopolitics and political geography, cherished a dream to research China way back in 1985 as a Junior Research Fellow in the University of Allahabad. Even after joining the services, the destiny played its part as I studied Chinese language, hence began reading about China in original Chinese language literature. Thus, came out the research '**The Chinese Geopolitics in the 21st Century**', a topic very well-conceived and useful for our times for the geopolitical upheavals created by this emerging power. However, it is the expert guidance which made things better and therefore, I immensely thank Prof A S Dalvi and Prof Shrikant Paranjape for their contributions.

I also received tremendous help and encouragement from the other institutes and departments. I am deeply thankful to the library staff of JNU, Mr M K Jha of IDSA library, New Delhi, Institute of Chinese Studies, New Delhi, Delhi University Library, Jaikar Library and NISDA Library at Pune University for providing me with all the intellectual resources I needed.

I am highly obliged to Dr V S Kale, Prof and Head of the Department of Geography, University of Pune for providing the GIS facilities to create and customise maps and in this effort, services of Mr Nilesh Susware can never be forgotten.

However, there is no parallel for resources provided to me by the Southern Star Library, Pune without which it would have been impossible to sustain the expensive research programme which I undertook. Therefore, I sincerely thank Col A K Sharma and his staff from the core of my heart. I also do not forget the services of typing my manuscript provided by Mr Sanjeeb Mohapatra and will remain ever grateful. I am also thankful to Mr. Sirajuddin Salim Sayyed for his whole-hearted efforts in editing work.

I cannot fail to recognise the anchorage provided by my wife Sudha, without whom, I could not have thought of undertaking this project. She withstood in all the trials and tribulations I faced. I also thank Prof (Dr.) Rameshwaram Tiwari, Prof (Dr.) Kalpana Tiwari, Prof (Dr.) Ajeet Tiwari, Akhilesh and Avinash who are not only my relatives but academicians par excellence and their advices in bringing out this book have been priceless. I also bless and thank Aditya and Divya, my son-in-law and daughter, for standing by me with full faith in this project.

In the end, my special thanks to my friend Mr Rajan Arya, who had more faith as publisher in my project than I had as author when the book was just conceived in the year 2015 and kept persuading me to bring it out at the earliest.

I wish this effort finds its right place and becomes a good read full of insights and logic, and helpful in assessing the Chinese geopolitics of the future correctly.

Brigadier Anand Tewari (Retd), Ph.D.

List of Maps and Charts

MAPS

CHARTS

Abbreviations

AD & CVD	Anti Dumping and Countervailing Duties
AMS	Academy of Military Science
ASBM	Anti-Ship Ballistic Missile
AVIC	Aviation Industry Corporation of China
BCE	Before the Common Era
BCIM	Bangladesh–China–India–Myanmar
BPD	Barrel Per Day
CASS	Chinese Academy of Social Sciences
CBM	Coal Bed Methane
CCP	Chinese Communist Party
CELAC	Community of Latin American and Caribbean States
CHINALCO	Aluminium Corporation of China
CIA	Central Intelligence Agency
CIC	China Investment Corporation
CMC	Central Military Commission
CNOOC	China National Offshore Oil Corporation
CNP	Comprehensive National Power
CNPC	China National Petroleum Corporation
CNPC	Chinese National Petroleum Company
COD	Control Organisation Department
CTG	Coal To Gas
EEU	Eurasian Economic Union
EEZ	Exclusive Economic Zones
EIA	Energy Information Administration

EPC	Engineering, Procurement and Constructions
ETIM	East Turkistan Islamic Movement
ETLO	East Turkistan Liberation Organisation
ETPRP	East Turkistan People's Revolutionary Party
ETR	East Turkestan Republic
EU	European Union
EW	Electronic Warfare
FDI	Foreign Direct Investment
FIE	Foreign Invested Enterprises
FOCAC	Forum on China Africa Cooperation
GA	Group Armies
GDP	Gross Domestic Products
GDs	General Departments
GE	General Eclectrics
GOES	Grain Oriented Electrical Steel
GSD	General Staff Department
GSH	General Staff Headquarters
ICBM	Inter-Continental Ballistic Missiles
IMF	International Monetary Fund
IOR	Indian Ocean Region
IR	International Relations
KMT	Kuo Min Tang
LAC	Latin America and Caribbean
LACM	Land Attack Cruise Missiles
MIRV	Multiple, Independently Targetable Re-Entry Vehicles
MNC	Multinational Corporations
MOOTW	Military Operations Other Then War
MRBM	Medium Range Ballistic Missiles
NAFTA	North American Free Trade Agreement
NATO	North Atlantic Treaty Organisation
NEG	New Economic Geography
NPC	National People's Congress
OPEC	Organisation of the Petroleum Exporting Countries
PAPF	People's Armed Police Force
PBOC	People's Bank of China

PLA	People's Liberation Army
PLAA	PLA Army
PLAAF	People's Liberation Army Air Force
PLAN	People's Liberation Army Navy
PLASAF	PLA Second Artillery Force
PPP	Purchasing Power Parity
PRC	People's Republic of China
ROC	Republic of China
SAC	Second Artillery Corps
SAM	Surface-to-Air Missiles
SASAC	State-owned Assets Supervision and Administration Commission
SCO	Shanghai Cooperation Organization
SLOC	Sea Lanes of Communication
SNG	Synthetic Natural Gas
SNOC	Sudan National Oil Company
SOCB	State Owned Commercial Banks
SOE	State Owned Enterprises
SSBN	Ship Submersible Ballistic Nuclear
TCF	Trillion Cubic Feet
TRA	Taiwan Relations Act
UN	United Nations
UNCLOS	UN Convention on the Law of Sea
UNCTAD	United Nation Conference on Trade and Development
UPRET	United Revolutionary Front of East Turkestan
US	United States
USD	US Dollar
USSC	US-China Security Risk Revival Commission
WTO	World Trade Organisation
XPCC	Xinjiang Production and Construction Corps

1

Introduction

In the world of geopolitics today, China is inadvertently drawing maximum attention of the countries and the international relations policymakers. In 1971, when US decided to normalise its diplomatic relations with the People's Republic of China (PRC) through the backdoor negotiations by its Foreign Secretary, Henry Kissinger, the Bamboo Curtain was supposed to have lifted. However, it was only after the courageous measures taken by Deng Xiaoping to open the economy within the centralised rule of the Communist Party starting in 1979 that China opened to the world in real terms. In fact, this opening aroused more curiosity about China than the one behind the Bamboo Curtain. Mao's China was kept guarded from the rest of the world during which the continuous revolutions propelled by him, kept the people on the brink at all times and caused much death and destruction in the name of implementing his philosophies and principles like the Great Leap Forward, the Hundred Flowers Campaign and the Cultural Revolution.[1] Mao's dream was of a new China, entirely purged of its past, as well as from the other international communities to make its people a blank slate on which a superior form of modernity could be inscribed.[2] The Bamboo Curtain was so incommunicable that nobody outside China could actually realise that around 5,000,000 leading intellectual cadres had been arrested and sent to labour camps during the Hundred Flower Campaigns; 20–30 million died of the all-pervasive famine between 1958 and 1960; about 90 million peasants, that is, about one quarter of the working population at that time, was mobilised to work in the primitive iron foundries and 4,00,000 people died due to various degrees of tortures and purging in the name of the Great Proletariat Cultural Revolution. This was mainly executed on the ground by the Red Guards established in 1966 comprising of the university youth, who were largely the children of the elite party officials and intellectuals.[3] This China was more of a mystery than a concern for the world because it did not affect the others' lives as much.

China caught on to the common consciousness only after Deng Xiaoping came to power in 1977, re-emerging from his second exile, after Mao succumbed to his illness on September 9, 1976. In his May 1977 speech, Deng appealed to the people of China to transcend the present backwardness through modernisation and achieve a glorious future.

> "The key to achieving modernisation is the development of science and technology, and unless we pay special attention to education, it will be impossible to develop science and technology. Empty talks will get our modernisation nowhere; we must have knowledge and trained personnel. Now, it appears that China is fully 20 years behind the developed countries".[4]

With this, the process of reform began and that could not have been possible without the interaction with the West. In a total turnaround from the ways of Mao, Deng Xiaoping declared in 1978:

> "To make revolution and build socialism we need large number of path breakers who dare to think, explore new ways and generate new ideas".[5]

Once China realised the follies of its recent past, interaction with rest of the world began. The rest of the world also required to interact with the enclosed nation that is China. However, the task before China was gigantic, as was put forward by the *People's Daily*, commenting on the political reforms that ensued:

> "A gigantic social system engineering project which involves straightening out the relationship between the party and the government, power and judicial organs, mass organisations, enterprises and institution, and between central, local and grassroots organisations; it concerns hundreds of millions of people. This is an arduous and protracted task."[6]

This was the first step towards China subsequently becoming the manufacturing backyard of the world in general and of the multinational companies in particular. The common man realised the gravity of existence of China when the unrealistically low priced goods pervaded the Western as well as the South-East Asian markets and destroyed the indigenous manufacturing, rendering thousands jobless, and heralding the development of a bipolar world order. But this is a very generic, perceptually populist and tip-of-the-iceberg variety of aspects for which we must avoid discussing China. Instead, more reasons why we must undertake China as a subject of study is discussed in the subsequent paragraphs. Now, since China has jockeyed the tide of reforms and has become the second largest economy in the world, it has not hesitated to claim a position of a world power in competition to the US unabashedly, espousing bipolarity.[7] Whether, this is a little premature ambition or a well-founded and geopolitically conceived concept, remains one of the main objectives of exploration of this book.

CHINA: A COUNTRY OF MAMMOTH SCALES

The geography of China, especially the Human Geography, is of such a mammoth scale that the geopolitical tremors of any politico-economic decisions taken by China can never be ignored or dealt with summarily. The huge mass of its land, population and economics have to be blamed squarely for the ripples that it generates in the world geopolitics. Therefore, understanding the geography of China becomes the steppingstone for a deep understanding. China is a huge country with a land mass of 9.33 million square kilometres (excluding waters), the third largest after Russia and Canada.[8] That renders China to be greater than even the US with a land mass of 9.16 million square kilometres. Some geopolitical experts argue that the continental size countries like China have potential to become superpowers. Although it is still a matter of analysis, because in the times of antiquity, the Roman Empire, the Spanish and the Ottoman Empires were world powers without having the size of a continent themselves, but certainly they won over a geography of continent size to become world powers. Even in the recent modern history, Great Britain, France and Germany became superpowers in the 19th and 20th Centuries, despite being small countries. However, they did win over large tracks of land mass or countries to become superpowers. Therefore, extensive territories do matter in making a nation a superpower and China does have that potential.[9]

Similarly, the other element of mammoth scale under the possession of China is its population, which is the largest in the world at 1,392,730,000 (World Bank, 2018) out of which 53.73 per cent live in the urban areas, which clearly shows that China is in the middle stage of its development, and that 67.6 per cent are below the working age of 60.[10] This will be discussed in detail subsequently. Of course, in the coming future, it is likely to become a negative phenomenon effecting

China's growth. China has also become the second largest country after the US in terms of GDP and contributing more than the US towards the growth of the global GDP with 27.1 per cent.[11] Presently, at more than 13.608 trillion dollars (2018) at nominal rate, China is extremely happy to surpass the US in terms of PPP rate.[12] China also prides itself on the mammoth size of its military being the largest in the world in terms of number and second only to the US in terms of expenditure. Ye Zicheng, a professor of international politics in Beijing University, posits that China with the mammoth scale of these four elements of national power, possesses the attributes of a great power.[13] He further argues that any country having territory more than 1 million square kilometres, population above 50 million and a GDP exceeding US$ 200 billion has a potential to grow as a superpower.[14]

Furthermore, as per these yardsticks, China in two aspects, i.e., area and population and GDP (at PPP), is already ahead of the US, the present superpower. Therefore, it is, in a way, already in the category of a world power heading on to become a superpower. However, further analysis is required as the resources, population, economy and security tell us a different story that is not as simple to comprehend as it appears. Therefore, there is a need to study the geography of China in detail in order to give us a perspective for further analysis.

CHINA'S GEOGRAPHY

In his article 'The Geography of Pivot of History' Halford Mackinder conjoined the vast Chinese land mass with the Pivot Region by saying that China (read the Chinese land mass what was there at the end of 19th Century and the beginning of the 20th Century) "...might constitute *the yellow peril to the world's freedom*, just because they would add an accessible frontage to the resources of the great continent an advantage as yet derived to the Russian tenants of the pivot region".[15]

Mackinder was certainly circumspect about the success of his concept of pivot that though seeming impregnable, at the same time, did not have the edge of having an all-weather ocean front, that too at the time of the dominance of naval power. Therefore, the pivot remained a defensive notion rather than becoming an offensive launch pad. China, with its physical connection to the pivot in the west and an ocean front to its east, removed that flaw for Mackinder. Such is the importance of the physiological expanse of China that it requires an analysis from an entirely fresh geopolitical point of view due to effects of its reach to the Central Asian Republics, and to the energy corridors of the Caspian Sea and the Middle East. It is now highly visible that while the ocean routes remain in use as a matter of routine, the alternative routes and sources of energy through this north-west corridor (the old Silk Route) will give a distinct advantage to China.[16] Therefore, first let us analyse the geographical deposition in order to carry out a geopolitical analysis in the subsequent chapters.

Location and Expanse

Spread over an area of 9.6 million square kilometres (including waters), China, the third largest country after Russia and Canada, is in almost the same latitudes as the US which it is trying to compete geopolitically. China is situated between the latitude 53° 30′ N from the centre of the Heilongjiang River (Amur river), north of Mohe to latitude 18.09° North to Hai'an Island, spanning approximately 5,500 km. From west to east, the expanse spans from the Pamirs from the longitude 73° 40° E to the confluence of Heilongjiang and Wu Suli rivers at the longitude of 135° 25° E for a total of 5,200 km. China has a land border of over 22,000 km surrounded by 14 contiguous countries: North Korea to the east, the People's Republic of Mongolia to the north, Russia to the north-east, Kazakhstan, Kyrgyzstan, Tajikistan, Afghanistan, Pakistan, India, Nepal and Bhutan to the west and south-west, Myanmar, Vietnam and Laos to the south. The Chinese mainland is flanked by the Bohai, Yellow, East China and South China Seas in

Map 1: China's Newfound Centrality in the Map of the World

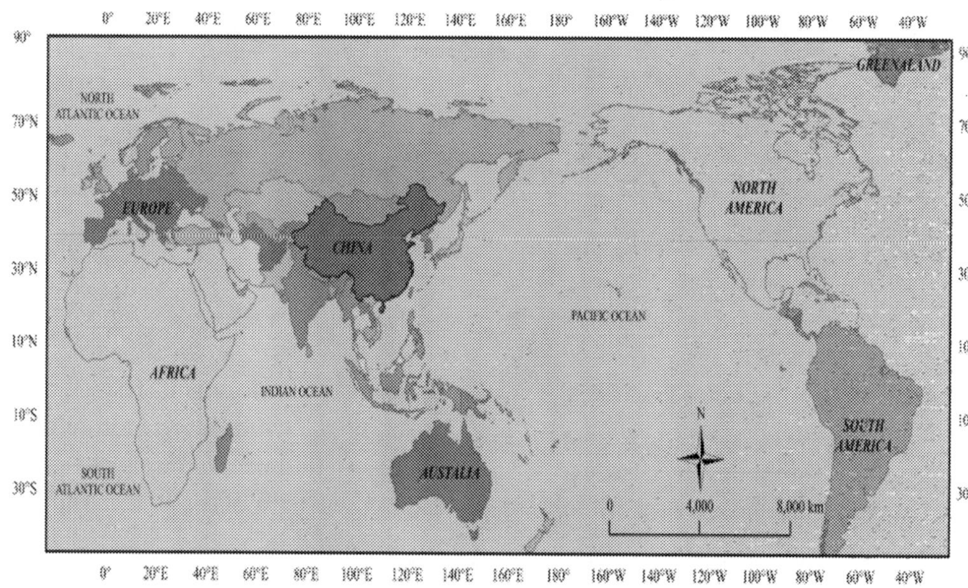

the Pacific. Across the sea in the east and the south, South Korea, Japan, Taiwan, the Philippines, Brunei, Malaysia and Indonesia surround China.

Physiographical Construct

Since the physiographical construct is a constant in the development of Chinese civilisation, polity and economics, it is pertinent to understand the role the different geographical regions playing as internal determinants of external geopolitics of China. Based on its physiological conditions, China has immense environmental diversities which have influenced the human development. Broadly, China can be divided into the following geographical regions.

Map 2: China's Geographical Regions

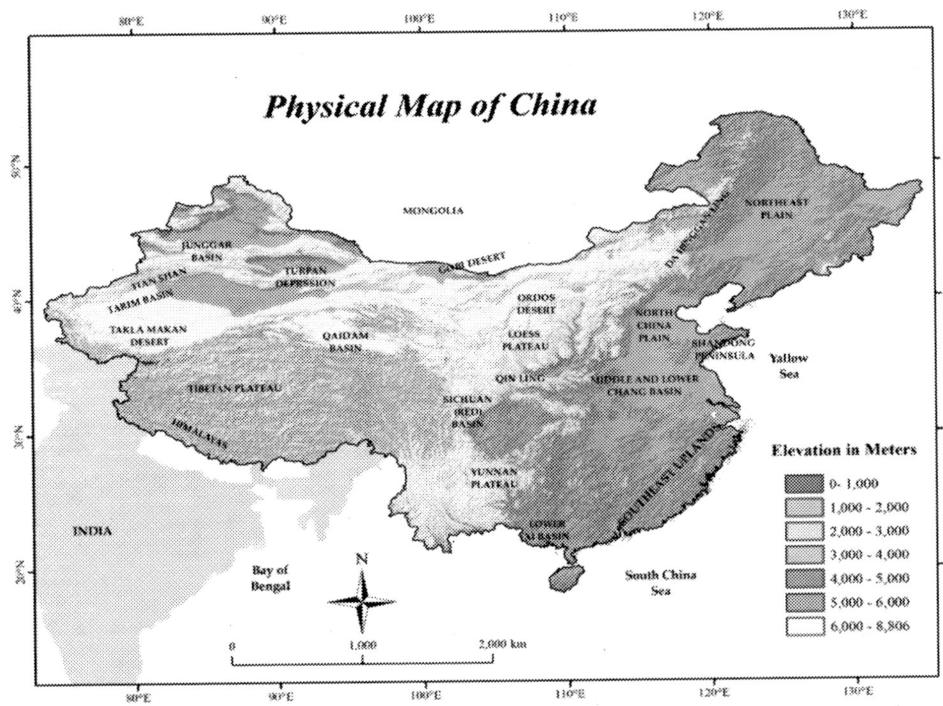

Loess Plateau: Loess Plateau in the north, adjacent to Inner Mongolia (Nei Meng Guo[17]) is a deposition of yellow dust-like fine soil by the winds blowing from the plains of Mongolia (the province of China) over a period of thousands of years. The soil is layered over the undulating plateau at the height of 4,300 feet and in the thickness range of 60 to 150 feet. Since the wind-deposited material is a phenomenon of dry climatic conditions, it lacks binding and consolidation of earth unlike in the case of a hot and humid climate. Therefore, though very fertile, the soil is prone to very high rates of erosion and weathering, compelling the farmers to terrace their fields for farming. The Huang He (Yellow) river derives its name from this phenomenon of taking a yellow hue from the yellow silt caused by the high rate of erosion in this region. The loess does not experience the summer monsoons but certainly, the dry winds with clear and bright days broken by occasional snowfalls. These geographical conditions allow the cultivation of a single crop, spring wheat, in Inner Mongolia and double crops of millet and corn with winter wheat in the lower loess.

North China Plains: Downstream from the Loess Plateau is a plain expanse of flood deposition by the Huang He, brought from Loess Plateau. Stretched up to the delta of the Huang He, the plain is very fertile but prone to frequent floods due to silting. Extensive levies and dikes have been made to check floods, but these often break and inundate the catchment. Up north-east, in the region of Manchuria, is the Northeast plain adjacent to the Russian Siberia and North Korea in the valleys of the Songhua and Liao rivers on a higher plateau. The climate in the region is cold and semi-dry to dry, only supporting autumn wheat and coarse grains. The North China plains suffered severe flooding 1573 times and 26 channel changes between 602 BC and 1950 AD. The most recent one occurred in 1936 and resulted in 8,90,000 deaths and also left 12 million people homeless.[18] Hence, the Huang He is called the "Sorrow of China".

Sichuan Basin: Surrounded by the Qin Ling Mountains in the north and the Chang Jiang (river) in the south, the Sichuan Basin is surrounded by high mountains and plateaus adjacent to the high Tibetan Plateau in the west. The main occupation being agriculture, the population is concentrated in the Chengdu plains. Enclosed by the mountains and plateaus from three sides, the Sichuan experiences relatively cool but humid winters and warm and humid summers. Therefore, maximum days in the year remain foggy. The area is prone to severe earthquakes as was witnessed in May 2008 in which more than 80,000 people were killed, more than 374,000 people were injured and millions left homeless.[19] When the Chang Jiang enters South-Central China, it is forced to pass through the Three Gorges region located near the town of San Douping in the Yuling district of the Hubei province to create the world's largest power station with a capacity of 22,500 MW, completed in May 2012. The dam has caused inundation of 13 cities, 140 towns and more than 1,600 villages displacing 1.3 million people.[20] By 2014, the Three Gorges dams' waterways projects with a capacity to handle maximum 10,000 ton of ship from Shanghai to Chongqing, were completed with water locks and ship lifts. Such has been the obsession with this gigantic project, which was originally fancied by Sun Yatsen, planned by Chiang Kai-shek but ultimately put into action by Mao Zedong cutting across the political ideologies, that they have been unmindful of the environmental hazards created. The emotions overriding sensibility about the dam is expressed by Mao Zedong in his poem titled 'Swimming':

> "*Walls of streams will stand upstream to the west.*
>
> *To hold back Wushan clouds and rains.*
>
> *Till a smooth lake rises in the narrow gorges.*
>
> *The Mountain Goddess if she is still there will marvel at a world so changed.*"[21]

Middle and Lower Chang Jiang Basin: After the Three Gorges Dam, the Chang Jiang descends towards a flattish surface dotted by many shallow meandering lakes acting as flood reservoirs during the summer monsoon. As the river approaches the East China Sea, the lower plain remains less than 10 feet above the sea level. The discharge volume of the Chang Jiang is 17 times greater than the Huang He, mainly due to the heavy monsoon rains. The climate remains hot and humid during summers but also experiences harsh winters with periodic frosts and occasional light snow. While Sichuan conditions support rice and dry grains, the middle and lower Chang Jiang basin is suitable for rice, winter wheat and tea.

The Yunnan Plateau and South-East Uplands: The high Tibetan Plateau when descending towards the south-east creates a transition zone which dissects itself into ranges and spurs that present a fascinating landscape at a height descending from 15,000 feet to 9,000 feet with the mountain ranges dotted with deep river gorges and small villages. The height causes moderate temperature with rains lashed by both Indian as well as the Pacific monsoons. The physical features and temperate and wet climate present a stunning visual impact for the tourists. The plateau while descending towards the ocean, graduates to rugged hills and low mountains up to maximum height of 1,200 metres, presenting China with many deep-water harbours along the South China Sea facing Taiwan. The Yunnan and the South-Eastern uplands remain suitable for intense rice cultivation throughout the year.

Tibetan Plateau and Xinjiang Desert: These two physiographic regions are territories in contrast. While Tibet is a plateau averaging a height of 4,000 metres above sea level, Xinjiang is made up of two basins: Tarim Basin in Taklimakan Desert and the steppe Junghar Basin and Turpan Depression at its extremity is 154 metres below sea level. Areas in Tibet situated more towards the eastern side experiences warmth and precipitation of the summer monsoon while the rare oxygen and bitter cold at such a height in the west renders the region a designation as the rooftop of the world and the Third Pole. Cultivation is possible only in the eastern half whereas, the western half witnesses a short autumn cultivation along the river channels. Therefore, animal husbandry is the main occupation. Xinjiang, on the other hand, is a lowland desert with surrounding oasis cities along with the rivers flowing from the surrounding mountains disappearing into the deserts and the Turpan Depression. Imagine this comparatively new inclusion of territories in China comprising 40 percent of the total area, which makes China look like a continent-sized country, reaching out to the core of Mackinder's World Islands.

Geographical Analysis

For the purpose of assessing any country geopolitically, it is important to analyse its geographical potential. Ever since China has openly aspired to become a superpower, the US international relations analysts have started comparing China with the US, the undisputed superpower. This could be one tool to measure the geographical potential of China. The US Scholar Nicholas John Spykman has listed ten elements of comprehensive national strength. These are territory, border characteristics, population, raw material, economy, national homogeneity, political stability and public morale.[23] We shall discuss only the geographical elements which are constant. The remaining requiring independent analysis will be dealt with subsequently, because more defining elements like the GDP, per capita GDP, military preparedness, industrial capacity, etc., have also been added to assess national power by the modern geopoliticians.[24] Making a comparison between the geographies of US and China, Robert D. Kaplan considers China to be less of a continent because of the advantage that the US has because of a spread between two oceans and the Canadian Arctic.[25]

Otherwise, if the maps are superimposed, the distribution of China's natural environment is found to be similar to that of the United States. China and the US are third and fourth largest countries, respectively, in terms of total land mass.

Map 3: Overlap Maps of China and USA

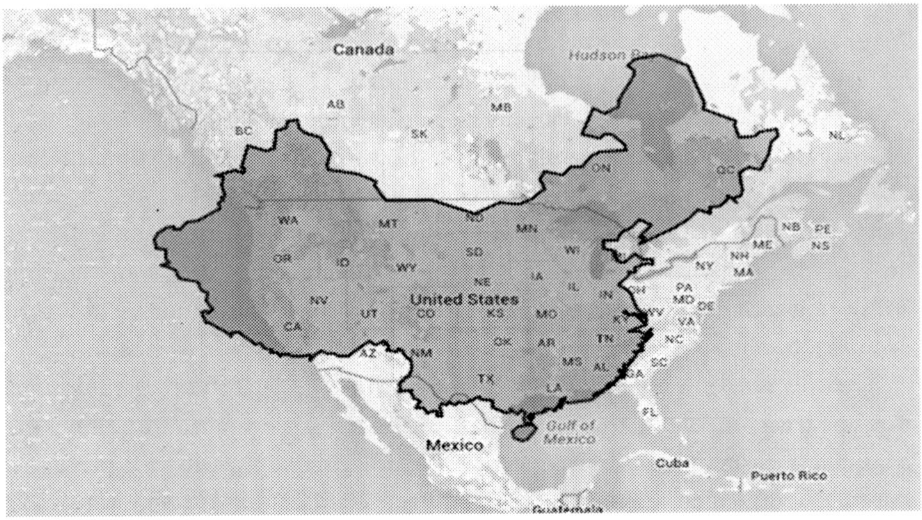

Source: http://overlapmaps.com/index.php

Both the countries share similar latitudinal dimensions. The topographical map, on the other hand, reveals the differences between China and the US. Only about one-third of the US is covered by mountains and deserts against half of China. This has a telling effect on the land available for cultivation in China, which is only 12 per cent as against 18 per cent of the US.[26] Also contributory to this is the fact that the western half of China is generally drier than the American west because China does not receive the most westerly maritime air masses that bring rain or snow to the upper elevations of the western United States. Although not comparable, but in a relative sense of internal dimension of the distribution of population, the west is less populated than the east in both the countries, but extremely less in the case of China. Two factors override all others in determining the population distribution. One is that China is primarily a riverbank civilisation as compared to the US, and second, 15 inch isohyets (380 mm) divide China clearly into two civilisations: one, a dense agricultural civilisation southeast of the 15 inch-isohyets and the other, a rarefied nomadic pastoral civilisation northwest of these isohyets (refer map). In China, actually the great rivers—the Wei, Han, Yellow and Yangzi—running from west to east, from the high and dry uplands of the Eurasian interiors to the moist agricultural lands closer to the Pacific Seas, define the main Chinese geography.[27] However, the geopolitical outcome of the lay of geography is brought out clearly as John King Fairbank writes, strengthening the argument of the 15 isohyets as the dividing line between pastoral China and agricultural China:

> "The contrasts between North and South China are superficial compared with those between the pastoral nomadism of the plateau of Inner Asia and the settled villages based on the intensive agriculture of China.[28]

But in his further analysis, the Harvard Professor Fairbank considers pastoral China to be culturally more akin to and part of "the wide arc running from Manchuria through Mongolia and Turkistan to Tibet". The ethnic geography therefore also reflects this core–periphery constitution with the core being the arable central plains (*zhong Yuan*) or Inner China (*neidi*) and the periphery being the pastoral frontiers (*bian jiang*) or Outer China (*waidi*).[29]

This purview, in fact, indicates the positive and negative aspects of geography of China. In a classical sense, it satisfies Mackinder's demand of an oceanic opening to the Pivot and makes China 'a hydraulic civilization' which has capped its potential so far.[30] But the wasteland in the west may become a burden. The population also raises many questions and along with it. The natural resources available to sustain growth requires a detailed discussion that will be carried out in the subsequent chapters. The position of the three seas and their shared and divisive legacy also needs a detailed analysis and exploring of eventualities, more in a geopolitical than in geographical terms.

Map 4: 15 Inch Isohyets (380 mm): also Denote the Cultural Divide

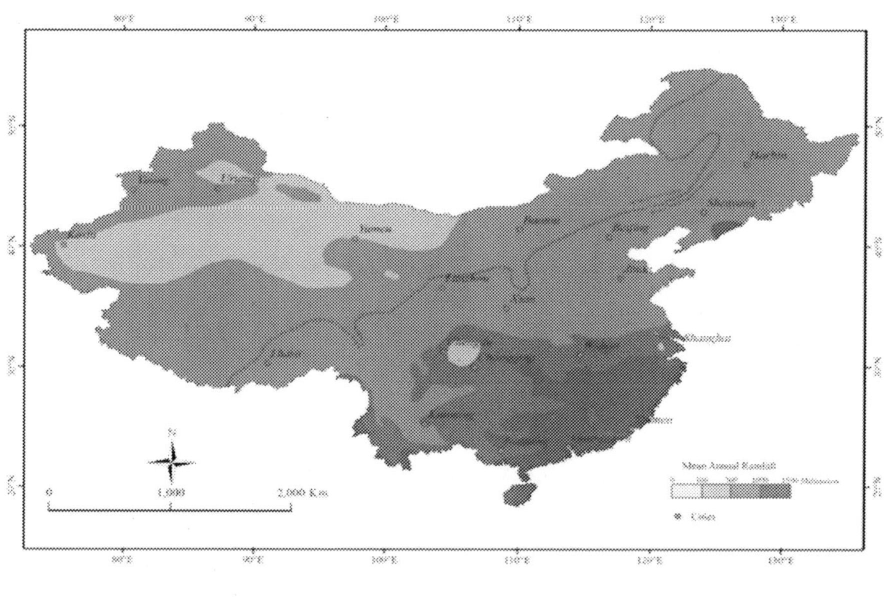

Another peculiarity of the Chinese geography in pure economic term is that the more favourable climatic condition supporting an intensive agricultural region lies in the further south-east due to a heavier rainfall. In contrast, the US agricultural land is almost equally distributed across the geography. The population density, therefore, is in conformity with the agricultural intensity in China, mainly concentrated towards the south-east. The biggest contrast, of course, is the population itself. With an equal land mass, but with one-and-half times more arable land, the US has to sustain only approximately 33 million people, whereas China has to sustain approximately 1.4 billion. This is one of the main reasons why the GDP per capita of the US was 62794.59 dollars as against only 9770.84 dollars of China as per 2018 World Bank data.

Energy resources and raw materials are more evenly distributed across China in comparison to agricultural land. A substantial quantity of coal is found across the eastern half of the country and in Xinjiang. The main oilfields are in Gan Sa, Xinjiang, Shan Xi, Sichuan and Heilongjiang. Today, 64.1 per cent of electricity is produced from coal, 17.6 per cent from hydroelectricity projects, 3.1 per cent from natural gas, 4.2 per cent from nuclear plants, 1.9 per cent from oil, 5.2 per cent from wind and 2.5 solar projects. Coal being low in quality and highest in consumption, is the greatest contributor to the pollution in China. In the US, only 38.31 per cent of electricity is produced from coal, that too of a higher quality coal, whereas natural gas contributes 29.83 per cent of electricity, and nuclear energy contributes 18.67 percent of electricity— thus, causing least pollution in the US.

In the light of China's ultimate desire to stand up as second power before the US, this comparison leads us to the ultimate question whether China will be able to bring up the per capita GDP to the level of the US. If yes, then how much resources and energy will China consume which it has not been endowed with for the volume of population it has?

UNDERSTANDING CHINA'S SOCIETY AND GOVERNANCE

China is a proclaimed communist country. But anyone visiting China does not think so as he or she does not come across the symbol of communist way of governance as imprinted on one's mind through historical communist anecdotes of the former USSR and its allies. In fact, it has been reduced to only a reminiscence now. What Mao Zedong started the governance in the Marxist-Leninist mode by tearing apart Chinese traditions as a deliberate act of state policy in order to usher in the communist way of life, has now turned into glittering capitalist culture.

Map 5: Population Density

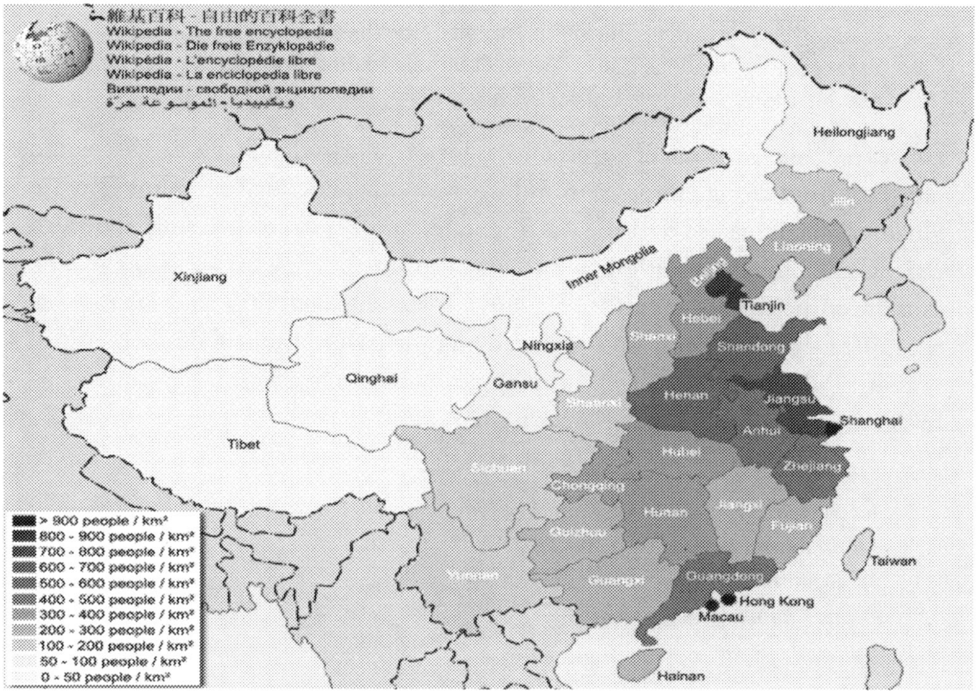

Source: http://www.worldofmaps.net/en/asia/map-china/map-population-density-china.htm

Mao Zedong had used violent ways to dismantle China's ancient heritage of Confucian ways of governance and he governed through various revolutions starting from his Hundred Flowers to Cultural Revolution, as he once himself said:

> "The thoughts, culture and customs which brought China to where we found her must disappear and the customs and culture of proletarian China, which does not yet exist, must appear.... Thoughts, culture, customs must be born of struggle and the struggle must continue for as long as there is still danger of return to the past."[31]

This was the essence of governance in China during the Mao regime and continuous revolution was the method. Mao was so captivated with the thoughts of revolution as a tool working behind governance that he talked of the nation to be smashed like an atom to carry tremendous power, in order to do things that he could not do before, as he says:

> "Now our enthusiasm has been aroused. Ours is an ardent nation, now swept by burning tide. There is a good metaphor for this: our nation is like an atom...when this atom's nucleus is smashed, the thermal energy released will have really tremendous power. We shall be able to do things which we could not do before."[32]

However, China's culture of governance is historically so rich that even Mao could not resist from citing examples from history, specially the first Emperor Qin Shi Huang who triumphed over the warring states, unified China in a single polity in 221 BC and brought in authoritarian ways of governance. It was in stark opposition to the Confucian ways of great harmony. In fact, he liked Qin Shi Huang more because of the Emperor's ways of destroying the past to bring about his utopian system— while doing so, even burying 460 Confucian scholars alive. Mao had full praise for Qin Shi Huang Di as he says.

> "*Please don't slander Emperor Qin Shi Huang, sir*
> *for the burning of the books should be thought through again.*
> *Our ancestral dragon, though dead,*
> *While on its spirit,*
> *While Confucians, though alive*
> *was really no one.*
> *The Qin Order has survived from age to age.*"[33]

Mao in a way discarded Confucianism to embrace Qin but could not expel Chinese history from his ways to govern. This was a clear diversion from the laid-down path of communism. Further, a dilemma in governance was created by Deng Xiaoping when he brought in sweeping reforms in 1979 after the death of Mao and his rehabilitation in 1977. In this first wave of reforms, several special economic zones were established along the south-eastern seaboard and local governments were given total freedom to facilitate industry. An agricultural reform also ensued; peasants were given control of land on long-term lease and allowed to sell their produce in markets. This was another dilemma as Deng himself was 'seeking truth from the facts'. The fact remains that Deng himself had been idealising Zhou En Lai's concepts of national modernisation during his younger days, but never had a chance during Mao's extremist policies of running the country. He did notice the will of the people to have economic liberty, but when they demanded civil liberties, he went on to crush them in 1989 epitomized by Tian Anmen Square. Partly, the student movement had also been motivated by Gorbachev's Perestroika. This was certainly caused by an internal governance dilemma as the scholar Andrew J. Nathan puts it eloquently:

> "The students did not act out to pose a mortal challenge to what they knew was dangerous regime. Nor did the regime relish the use of force against the students. The two sides shared many goals and much common language. Through miscommunication and misjudgment, they pushed one another in to positions in which options for compromise became less and less available. Several times a solution seemed just within reach only to dissolve at the last moment. The slide to calamity slowed at first but then accelerated as divisions deepened on both sides. Knowing the story with a sense of horror that we receive from true tragedy".[34]

It is a clear indication of a dilemma of the internal kind, already sown in the minds of the people and the government, or as we may call it, 'the Party'. The further reforms and growing aspirations along with a faster communication with the outside world must have compounded the agony of this dilemma. How much this dilemma will play behind every geopolitical behaviour of China is a constant factor in our discourse.

Alongside these two internal dilemmas in governance, there is an external dilemma of governance that manifests in the international relations of China. Why are these termed as dilemmas because the first two are in contradiction with the philosophy and tenets of communism and the third one is in contradiction with the perception of the West through which we tend to see Chinese governance and the Chinese international behaviour. The first two dilemmas take their inspiration from the history of China, whereas the third one comes from the Western ideals and standards of acquiring knowledge, understanding and propagating democracy.

Nationalism and Role of National Humiliation

Nationalism is the first phenomenon that is often evoked in the minds of the Chinese masses. Nationalism has become one of the tools to captivate the common people's minds at various times, under the republicans as well as the communist rule. And to the surprise of the rest of the world, nationalism is evoked through reminding the people of the humiliation that they supposedly suffered in the past which is denoted as the '100 Years of National Humiliation'. It began with the first Opium War and was considered to have ended in 1927 with the Nationalists asserting state sovereignty and quickly declaring May 9—the day Chinese President Yuan Shikai accepted most of the 21 demands of Japan's claims—as National Humiliation Commemoration Day. Making it an official holiday in an attempt to construct a different kind of reactive citizenship and national identity against Japan, Great Britain and other imperialist powers, China has deepened the scar in the minds of its citizens.[35] To initiate this, first the Nationalist party issued an official calendar of twenty-six National Holidays that were being observed at that time throughout the year in which government officials consolidated China's various locally observed National Humiliation Days. As William A. Callahan says:

> "...the state thus sought to mirror and contain popular practices by nationalising the local customs in order to buttress its particular patriotic national identity through national time".[36]

By 1928, the month of May became very bad as it got crowded with six such days. One Chinese author of that time sarcastically said:

> "May has become a sad month. We should follow the English pronunciation 'May' which in Chinese is 'mei', meaning 'out of luck'. May is the unlucky month".[37] Subsequently, May 9, the holiday, was terminated in 1940 and replaced with July 7, the day of the War of Resistance against the Japanese invasion. But the National Humiliation day resurfaced during the Communist regime in 2001 as the National Defence Education Day. There were several other regional National Humiliation Days declared to commemorate incidents like the Nanjing Massacre. The government's policy to evoke national pathos from the Nationalist to the Communist regimes has been the same. The inspiration was also drawn from the US's commemoration of the Japanese attack on Pearl Harbour, although wrongly perceived as national humiliation day of the US by the Chinese. However, an uncanny obsession towards establishing a National Humiliation Day to evoke nationalistic feelings is well summed up in the comments of Chen Yunjie:
>
> "The shame of history cannot be forgotten, forgetting the past is a betrayal. Establishing "National Humiliation Day" would make an alarm bell ring out in the hearts of every Chinese and arouse the national spirit."[38]

Ultimately, the National People's Congress (NPC) deliberated on the demand and reached a conclusion to commemorate the National Humiliation Day as National Defence Education Day on the third Saturday of September. In addition, the September 18 History Museum in Shenyang is entirely dedicated to display the elements of national shame in order to arouse nationalist passion. Then, there are efforts to teach schoolchildren the maps of China's different regimes in the history to show greater territories to have been in possession of China at various points of time and how various borders, which appeal to people's imagination has been shrunk and that China as a great civilisation is now being victimised in the modern times.

Map 6: One of the Popular Maps of Propagated as 'Lost Territories' causing National Humiliation

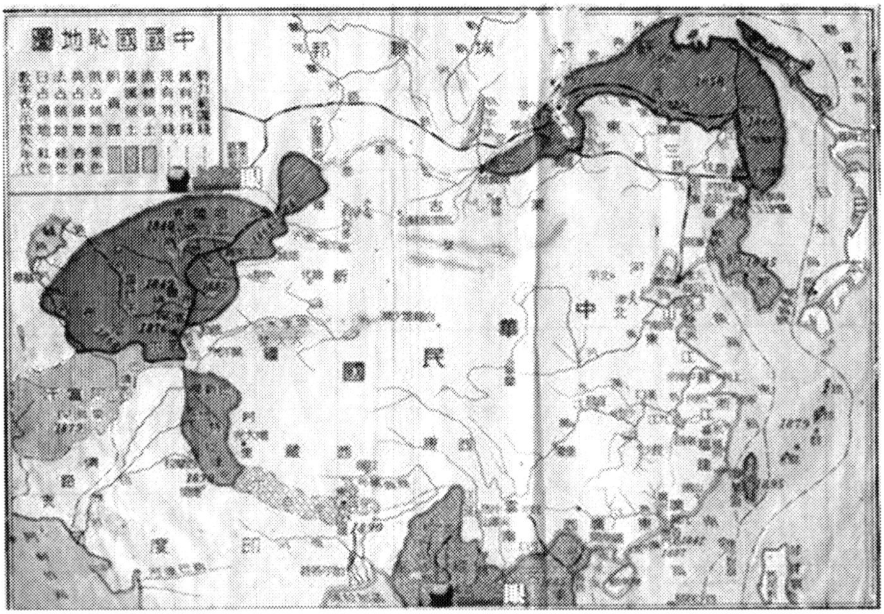

Source: https://forums.bharat-rakshak.com/viewtopic.php?f=1&t=6580&start=440

The discovery of a map of Zheng He from 1418, suggesting voyages to Africa and the so called discovery of America before Columbus, appears to be part of such a nationalistic propaganda policy. This certainly is a gradual alienation from the policy of Communism prevalent during Stalin's times. The collapse of the USSR also has been responsible for nationalism being the most popular way to enchant the people in the times of economic liberalisation. China, in fact, does not lose an occasion to drum up such fervour. Nationalistic feelings were in fact best evoked in the form of the conduct of Olympic games and specially the conduct of the Olympics' ceremony on August 8, 2008, which encapsulated the emancipation of China from national humiliations through the showcasing of various positive events of history, starting from demons chanting the opening lines of 'Confucian Analects': "It is glorious to receive friends from afar". For the Chinese it was a dream come true, nurtured over a hundred years. After the Hundred Years of Humiliation, the games became a kind of emancipation to a proud nationalist Chinese, who would no more succumb to the West as Ye Hailan says:

> "The games proved not only the existence of the China model, but also its success. At the opening and closing ceremony of Beijing Olympics, athletes,

> volunteers, the audience and even the residents all sent one clear message that the Chinese people act according to their own mode of conduct and will not succumb to any allegedly superior Western values."[39]

These thoughts certainly get the international relations theorist perplexed as a successful conduct of the games has also been exploited to derive national/ international power. The same sentiments also manifest itself in the various curbs that China employs on the media, internet and sources of governmental and non-governmental info, especially when it comes to giving an information or opinion about China's imperial past, the neighbouring countries with which they have border disputes and geopolitical rivals. This attitude colours their vision towards international news in the home media. The Party's ability to control information that reaches the public is declining, but it still provides a flashpoint for more lethal action by the military if any upsurge takes place.[40] Nationalism per se does not go well with communism, compounded with the misinformation through which the citizens are intellectually prepared against the foreign powers. This leaves the scholars and diplomats guessing. This also becomes prohibitive to an apt reaction and adds on to the enigma that China has become to the rest of the world. This is another area worth examining in further details as to how best we can eliminate national fervour from diplomacy to understand China's international behaviour more pragmatically.

Mysticism in Governance

When it becomes extremely difficult to explain one's conduct, we need to explore the wisdom of the person and decipher how and what kinds of knowledge dispositions he/she is made of. As we have already discussed, China, despite being officially a communist regime, draws heavily from its history, culture and traditions. In fact, it is often said that the modern Chinese regime still draws its power from the concepts of the 'Son of Heaven' and the 'Mandate of Heaven' to rule, more than the communism as such. It is often argued that the present Chinese regime is in the same line of approximately 4000 years of history under the rule of about 25 different dynasties. Today, the feudalism of the past has converted itself into conventional forms of political, social, economic and ideological constructs but the essence and aspiration remain the same.[41] Communism may have come, but the wisdom on which it draws the conclusions and decisions, whether political or economic, remains deep-rooted in the culture, history and traditions of China. That is why Chen Yuan of the China Development Bank could safely say:

> "We are the communist party, and we shall decide what communism means."[42]

As described earlier, even Mao derived his authority from the Qin Emperor Qin Shi Huang rather than Lenin and Stalin, and the Intercom concept he already abandoned during the times of Nikita Khrushchev. It was this authority for which he went on to inflict millions of casualties on the Chinese people through continuous revolutions, purges and destruction of assets. Although some people today say that he had, due to these excesses, lost the 'Mandate of the Heaven' to rule, but it was only after his demise that a new form of communist liberalism could come to the fore for sure. What is derived as China's theoretical foundation from its history, culture and tradition, requires greater examination. The Western political scientist Samuel P. Huntington purports in his proposed clash between the Western civilisation and the Islamic civilisation of the Middle East that the Confucian civilisation of China will be on the side of the latter than the former.[43] However, it remains a matter of debate whether China as a civilisation will align with the Islamic civilisation just because it has been opposed to the Western values historically, for it is doubtful in the modern perspective. This, however, adds on to the enigma that is China, which is one of the research questions of this book.

CHINA'S ECONOMIC POWER

Why China has become a subject of constant research is because of its dualism, revisionism, nationalism and communism in vogue at the same time or sometimes at different times of its modern history used for different purposes, especially, by the communist regime. Evident is the fact that what Mao denounced in the early 1960s to be a 'goulash communism' was what Nikita Khrushchev had said about Chinese communism of that time:

> "To follow their line of thinking, it transpires that if a people walk in rope sandals and eat watery soup out of a common bowl that is communism, and if a working man lives well and wants to live even better tomorrow that is almost tantamount to the restoration of capitalism".[44]

The above observation was remarkably adopted in 1979 when Deng Xiaoping rationalised his economic reforms when he said:

> "Socialism means eliminating poverty. Pauperism is not socialism, still less communism. The superiority of the socialist system lies above all in its ability to develop the productive forces and to improve the people's material and cultural life."[45]

Whatever Deng Xiaoping might have said, it was a recipe laced in contradictions of sweet with bitter, as he himself had kept the Party's control as supremo as he surmised that the reform measures were legitimate till the time they did not weaken the Party's control of the political system, and that everything else was subject to compromise. Ever since China shed its Stalin-style central planning and adorned the cloak of market economy, it has been the most dynamic economy growing at an average of over 9 per cent and today is the second largest economy in the world. China has become the manufacturing workshop of the world. It can comfortably compare with the industrial revolution of Great Britain. Today, 21.2 per cent of consumer goods that the US buys are produced in China.[46] The Chinese economy in the past 20 years with low-end manufacturing has given competition to many economies and has destroyed some. This phenomenon can be judged by the impact of the Chinese exports on various geographies. Take the example of the impact of Chinese cheaper imports in Latin American countries and on their exports to intra-regional countries and the US and the EU in the nineties. In the bargain Latin American countries lost their exports by 25 per cent to the US, with Mexico losing the US exports by 93 per cent. As a study by Osvaldo Rosales brings out, even in the intra-regional industry, the share of exports had gone down to 12 per cent due to the Chinese imports and had specially hit the manufacturing industries of Brazil, Mexico and Argentina which together constitute a total share of 94 per cent of the Latin American manufacturing.[47] In Argentina, Brazil, Mexico and Columbia, the Chinese imports had hit industries like textile, clothing, footwear, industrial machinery and equipment, etc., in the domestic market. This raised anti-dumping investigations against the Chinese imports. The trade disputes with China became a common feature the world over. But, in reality, it is only the US which was able to give China a challenge of the reverse kind in the WTO. The greatest example was of the US Grain Oriented Electrical Steel (GOES) which is used as a high-value magnetic specialty steel in the power-generating machinery in China. China imposed Anti-Dumping and Countervailing Duties (AD&CVD) to block the US from China which had caused further trade deficit with China. The US has effectively challenged the Chinese blocking of exports in the WTO.[48,49] We are aware that China is exporting cheap steel to all over the world after processing the raw material drawn from across the globe by providing subsidies to manufacturing units and export subsidies, and grants for research and development. Thus, making the Chinese steel dirt-cheap, despite the imported raw material and destruction of the auto and auto-parts industries abroad. But, no one except the US could block China effectively in the

WTO.[50] On the contrary, when it comes to exporting raw material out of China, China blocks such material to preserve its raw material for its heydays, especially when it comes to rare earth. China produces 90 per cent of the world's rare earth, key to the defence industry and modern technologies like iPhones, disk drives and wind turbines. This gives China an undue advantage by making items produced outside China very costly. The case was again challenged years ago by the US in the WTO and the verdict was given in favour of the US and EU.[51] It is a fact that China has reached down to every nook and corner of the world to satiate its huge appetite for raw material and market for manufactured products. The hunger for further industrialisation and enhancement of production is most likely to get accelerated, as China must go a long way to bring its per capita GDP to minimum number seventh position (held by the US) from the present 72th position in the world, despite being second in GDP (total) only to the US. These factors indicate strife and confrontations with China and lead to a larger geopolitical ramification the world over, which is another research question in this study.

CHINA'S TERRITORIAL DISPUTES AROUND ITS LAND AND OCEAN BORDERS

Over a period of 4000 years with more than 25 regimes, China's map has been altered many a times due to external forces and internal compulsions. Today's China has a land boundary of over 22,000 kilometres and a coastline of about 14,500 km. It can be safely said that somewhere between 15 to 21 countries in different period of times have had a contiguous boundary with China and as John Vasquez says, "contiguous states have opportunities to have fight over territory than the non-contiguous states"[52], China has behaved in the past in no different manner. Today, China has progressed economically in a most dramatic fashion. The neo-rich mentality and the confidence overlook many untouched aspects which are yet to progress and assume many others—those have been kept on the backburner for the sake of economic progress. The Chinese economic progress has led to the second next area of progress that is military, which has been taken up as a natural consequence of economic progress. The Chinese people have been made to understand that the nation can take on the issues of territoriality and reactions on the border issues and territorial waters boldly. The transfer of Hong Kong to China on July 01, 1997, was a perfectly timed event that bolstered these sentiments. After the end of the Cold War in 1991, there was a cooling period of about 10 years in which the US enjoyed a unilateral hegemony while China, by matter of policy, wished to peacefully execute its economic pursuits. Now that China thinks it is ready economy-wise and with the US trying to disengage itself from its unilateral hegemonic pursuits like in Iraq and Afghanistan, the Asia-Pacific region has begun to feel the heat of strategic flux mainly manifested in the East and South China Seas and the heightened activities on the Indo-China border. It is in this background that the rise of China is directly responsible for consequent irredentist claims and thus the peace in the region may become a direct outcome of China's domestic fervour of nationalism and which may or may not be as the ability of the China's foreign policy response. The threat to the peace and stability of the region around China over territorial issues becomes imminent only when negotiations give way to the use of force, and negotiations fail, not because of the inability to accommodate the details of give-and-take, but due to a gross change of perception which makes the government/citizens feel the gap between the ascribed and desired international status becoming large and growing.[53]

On the other hand, there is a growing economic stature of China the world over, which is still in need to be nurtured because growth has still not reached where it desires to and has a long way to go. Torn between the two, on the present situation of Chinese territoriality, China will persist on pragmatism for some more time or will leave the present status prematurely. Whether China will be sucked in by the domestic compulsions of nationalistic fervour that the establishment itself has been fomenting as a matter of state policy to drum up support for the legitimacy of the one-party government, or that it will be guided more by larger national interest and geopolitical imperatives, will be examined through different discourses in this book.

CHINA'S MILITARY MODERNISATION

One of the reasons why China qualifies for a study of geopolitical responses in the 21st Century is its military and its modernisation that clearly indicate China's realist approach to attain international hegemony. As China has grown in its economy to become the second in the world, its national interests have expanded beyond the immediate borders. For this, China has charted out new missions and visions for security strategy and military strategy, as Hu Jintao committed the PLA to these "new historic missions" beyond an immediate focus on China's territory, sovereignty, unity and security.[54] The vision entailed that the implementation of such plans would require expanded military capabilities and a new Chinese proficiency in a variety of areas including information warfare, trans and extra-regional mobility, long-distance maneuverability, effective counter-terrorism, extended maritime depth, strategic air projection and a robust strategic nuclear deterrence, as brought out clearly in China's 2006 White Paper on the military.[55] There has always been a mismatch and contradiction in the facts given by the Chinese sources and the independent sources. Therefore, an overview of the PLA's new developments is most necessary at this stage. The official view of the PRC is explicitly spelt out in the Chinese white papers, published from time to time. These White Papers of the recent past if examined sequentially will show the ideological development for the modernisation. A sequential linkage can be established in these white papers to seek for the reasons justifying the military expenditure and modernisation in the Chinese military.

The 2010 Chinese White Paper highlighted the following:[56]

(a) The whole world remains peaceful and stable.
(b) Steady progress is being made in the establishment of mechanisms for the management of global economy.
(c) International military competition remains fierce. Major powers are stepping up the realignment of their security and military strategies, accelerating military reforms (read modernisation and expansion) and vigorously developing new and more sophisticated military technologies.
(d) Some powers have worked out strategies for outer space, cyber space and the Polar Regions, developed means for global strikes, accelerated development of missile defence systems, enhanced cyber operations capabilities to occupy new strategic commanding heights.

Analysing the above narrative of the world military and strategic affairs, in fact, the PRC reveals its own intentions and the directions in which its development is oriented. As the title of the White Paper of 2013 "The Diversified Employment of Chinese Armed Forces" indicates, it gives out an overview of the quantum of its various forces and their employment propositions and modernisation. However, before that, the White Paper also gives out its strategic concerns given as under, as reasons for its new strategies and commensurate modernisation.[57]

(a) The world is still far from being tranquil. There are signs of increasing hegemonism, power politics and neo-internationalism. Local turmoil occurs frequently. Hotspot issues keep cropping up. International issues are growing more abrupt, interrelated and comprehensive.
(b) The Asia-Pacific region has become an increasingly significant stage for world economic development and strategic interaction between major

powers. The US is adjusting its Asia-Pacific security strategy, and regional landscape is undergoing profound changes.

(c) China has seized and most of this important period of strategic opportunities for its development and its modernization and its achievements have captured world attention.

But the paper does not conclude the section 'New Situation, New Challenges and New Mission' and ends without solutions highlighting fluidity, saying that

"However, China still faces multiple and complicated security threats and challenges. Some country has strengthened its Asia Pacific military alliances, expanded its military presence in the region, and frequently makes the situation there tenser. On the issues concerning China's territorial sovereignty and maritime rights and interests, some neighbouring countries are taking action that complicate or exasperate the situation, and Japan is making trouble over the issue of Diaoyu islands. The threats posed by three forces, namely, terrorism, separatism and extremism are on the rise. The 'Taiwan Independence' separatist forces and their activities are still the biggest threat to the peaceful development of cross-straits relations."

The above security situation narrative however only highlights the eastern seaboard as the main military concern. The diversified employment of China's Armed Forces mainly serves the objectives of safeguarding national sovereignty, security, territorial integrity and supporting the country's peaceful development. Basing the military preparedness on the conditions of internationalisation, China wishes to intensify the joint employment of different services and arms and enhance the war-fighting capabilities based on information systems. Two additional objectives, i.e. formulating the concept of comprehensive security and effectively conducting Military Operations Other Than War (MOOTW) and providing reliable security support for China's interests overseas, have also been envisaged.[58] The first signs of reforms were seen in the changes made in the Central Military Commission which the White Paper called as the "intensification of the strategic administration of the Central Military Commission". In the hierarchy of the command-and-control system of the Communist Party of China (CPC), most of the career military officers are made CPC members. Units at the company level and above are posted with political officers responsible for decisions related to the personnel, propaganda and counterintelligence, whereas the operational aspects are controlled by career officers. The major documents at all levels are made by the CPC committees led by the political officers and commanders.[59]

In order to bring more professionalism into PLA, the CPC has given fewer positions in the key political bodies to the PLA. This has taken place as China's revolutionary generation has retired or exhausted itself from serving in the PLA and thus career military officers have taken their place at the higher echelons. In fact, the Politburo standing committee has not had any uninformed officers as members since 1997 till 2014 out of the 25 Politburo members, only 4 had any kind of military experience.[60] However, because of the CMC's special bureaucratic construct with a majority of the office-bearers being from the military stream but under the Chairman who invariably holds the position of President as well as the Chairman of the CPC, the Party's control over the PLA becomes absolute. These perceptible changes were brought through the 18th Party Congress in 2012. There has also been a debate on nationalising the PLA in terms of more professional and less political control down to the unit level. As the drive gained momentum, General Li Jinhao, a member of the CMC and Director of the PLA General Political Department in an editorial of the *PLA Daily* said:

> "We must resolutely reject these false political ideas (of PLA dissociating itself from the party) and unswervingly listen to and follow the party."[61]

In fact, the demand for a national army meant an apolitical army answerable to government of the day and not the Party. However, the 2015 White Paper "China's Military Strategy" asked for CPC's absolute control over PLA which did not necessarily means Party control but Leader's control which is reflected in the new construct of the CMC and the reforms and the modernisation that ensued. The white paper enumerated following responsibilities which also indicates a shift towards more objectively defined aims than the previous papers and it was enlarged in scope as PLA took upon itself to credibly respond to the new requirement arising from the Worldwide Revolution in Military Affairs (RMA)[62]:

- To deal with a wide range of emergencies and military threats, and effectively safeguard the sovereignty and security of China's territorial land, air and sea.
- To resolutely safeguard the unification of the motherland;
- To safeguard China's security and interest in new domains;
- To safeguard the security of China's overseas interests;
- To maintain strategic deterrence and carry out nuclear counterattacks;
- To participate in regional and international security cooperation and maintain regional and world peace;
- To strengthen efforts in operations against infiltration, separatism and

terrorism so as to maintain China's political security and social stability; and

- To perform such tasks as emergency rescue and disaster relief, rights and interest protection, guard duties, and support for national economy and social development.

To achieve these aims few key measures were indicated in the White Paper that can be enumerated as under.

- The CPC's absolute leadership over military must be upheld.
- PLA Army to equip for trans theatre mobility.
- PLA Navy to shift its focus from "offshore water defense" to a combination of "offshore water defense" to open sea protection".
- PLA Airforce to shift its focus from territorial air defense to both defense and offence and build an air-space defense force to meet the requirement of informationised operation.
- PLA Second Artillery will strengthen itself for strategic deterrence and nuclear counterattack, and medium and long-range precision strike.

In the latest White Paper on defense released on 24 July 2019 "China's National Defense in the New Era", there is a clear shift towards preparation for Great Power Competition. The paper first raises alarms like China facing "diverse and complex security threats and challenges" and that "International strategic competition is on the rise" then indirectly tries to answer the US documents " National Security Strategy" 2017 and "National Defense Strategy" 2018 which bring forth China as the sole competitor. To achieve this China sets the following aims[63]:

- to deter and resist aggression;
- to safeguard national political security, the people's security and social stability;
- to oppose and contain "Taiwan independence";
- to crack down on proponents of separatist movements such as "Tibet independence" and the creation of "East Turkistan";
- to safeguard national sovereignty, unity, territorial integrity and security;
- to safeguard China's maritime rights and interests;
- to safeguard China's security interests in outer space, electromagnetic space and cyberspace;
- to safeguard China's overseas interests; and
- to support the sustainable development of the country.

Therefore, a clear direction is seen on modernisation on two fronts. First on total political control over PLA which is being beautifully done in the name of making PLA a professional force totally under control of the political masters (or master i.e. CMC Chairman Xi Jinping). And the second, reorganising the PLA with double aim, one, to disrupt the well-entrenched command and control running since Jiang Zemin's time and, two, to make the PLA a force capable of joint operations. Effects of these measures are evident in the reorganised structures from Central Military Commission to lowest units in PLA.

Central Military Commission (CMC): As Mao has been professing that 'power runs out of barrel of gun', control over CMC has always been considered true control over power. In the past, when tall leaders like Mao had no insecurity, could allow vice -chairman Lin Biao to do day to day work of the CMC. Then there was the time of dual control on the PLA by Party CMC and National Defence Council. Consequent to Cultural Revolution in 1975, National Defence Council was abolished and the Party CMC had absolute control over PLA. It was then that leaders like Deng Xiaoping who had confidence to institutionally separating Party and state created State CMC. The influence of Deng over PLA was so great that he held the chairmanship of CMC even after retirement. Jiang Zemin also tried to hold on as Chairman of CMC but was opposed by PLA. However, he held on to influence during Hu Jintao chairmanship through two generals Xu Caihou and Guo Boxing whom he had appointed vice chairmen of CMC through accelerated promotions. Realising this, Xi purged them in an anti-corruption drive when he took over as President and CMC chairman in 2012. Xu died of gallbladder cancer in 2015 before getting sentenced and Guo was sentenced to life imprisonment in 2016.[64] This was also the time of 'vice-chairman responsibility system' which now Xi has changed to 'chairman responsibility system' leaving no scope for any vice-chair to wield power. Xi further went on to reduce the number of Members of CMC from 11 to only 7 announced on 25 Oct 2017 during the 19th Party Congress. The lack of confidence in PLA leadership which was being steered towards making it a national army has now been turned into Chaiman PLA as the Party as well as State CMC both have identical membership under chairmanship of Xi turning it into one identical institution under two different names called *yige jigou, liangkuai paizi.* Hence, Xi is 'purportedly' has total control over the power of barrel of guns. The present CMC now has following make-up with their other concurrent appointments:

Chairman: Xi Jinping – He is also General Secretary of CPC, President of the

PRC and Leader of the CMC Leading Group for National Defence and Military Reforms.

> **Vice Chairmen – 2**
> **Xu Qiliang** – General from PLAAF, Member of 19th Politburo, Executive Deputy Leader of the CMC Leading Group for National Defence and Military Reforms.
> **Zhang Youxia** – General from PLAA, Member of 19th Politburo, Deputy Leader of the CMC Leading Group for National Defence and Military Reforms.
> **Members – 4**
> **General Wei Fenghe** – State Councillor and Minister of Defence.
> **General Li Zuocheng** – Chief of Joint Staff.
> **Admiral Miao Hua** – Director of Political Work Department.
> **General Zhang Shengmin** – Secretary of the CMC Central Commission for Discipline Inspection.

All the above names are pure Xi loyalists to say the least. Out of the Vice Chairmen, Xu Qiliang has shown ardent loyalty supporting Xi's policies in the first tenure, while Zhang Youxia is son of Zhang Zongxun, who served with the father of Xi (Xi Zhongxun) during the civil war in 1940s. Wei Fenghe, Miao Hua and Zhang Shengmin, all were given *Rocket Type Promotion* by XI in Chinese parlance while Li Zhoucheng was brought out of oblivion sent by Jiang Zemin and given several promotions. Therefore, it is simpler now to deduce that the call for loyalty to party has now clearly been redefined as loyalty to Xi jinping.

There are three dimensions of the sweeping modernisation of PLA evident from analysis. One, that Xi, though has taken upon him the mantle of Mao to rule lifelong but not being as popular and confident of the PLA leadership, not even as Jiang, had to change the conventional setup that gave strength to old guards. Two, breaking the lead of ground forces i.e. PLAA which led the four General Departments thus held the true power. Three, fulfil the ambition of creating a force capable of conducting joint operations and at least become a preeminent power in Indo Pacific Region. This had necessitated method of 'modernisation by total disruption'.

Organisational Reforms: Disruptive measure has taken place in the way four General Departments have been abolished and replaced with fifteen organs to include seven departments, three commissions and five offices. Out of these fifteen organs three are concurrently headed by the members of the CMC to have direct control. Joint Staff Department being the key to operations is headed by General Li Zuocheng. Political Works Department key to Party control over PLA is headed by Admiral Miao Hua. The Discipline Inspection Commission most critical to use as instrument of anti-corruption drive is headed by General Zhang Shengming.

Ministry of National Defence: The Ministry of National Defence in China is not equivalent to the defence ministries in other countries. With the entire decision-making powers vested with the CMC, the Ministry of National Defence merely carries out the tasks where an overlapping of the responsibilities between the civilian government and the Armed Forces, including foreign military relations, mobilisation, recruitment, national defence, education and civil support to military operations, is involved. General Wei Fenghe who is also member of CMC is heading the Minisrty of National Defence.

Changes In Services Structure: While PLAA, PLAAF and PLAN have retained the old versions of the name, Second Artillery Force has a changed name as PLA Rocket Force (PLARF). The Second Artillery Force which was not a full service has now been given equal status to Army, Navy and Air Force as PLARF. A new service branch, The PLA Strategic Support Force (PLASSF) has been created. As the White Paper 2019 talks about 'Optimising Size, Structure and Force Composition', the main effect has been on the services brought into effect by optimising structure, developing new type forces, adjust proportion and reduce sizes. The impact on services can be explained for each service separately.

PLA Army (PLAA): The most impact has been on the PLAA. The PLAA did not have a separate headquarters and rather was omnipresent and had its total control over PLA by heavily populating previous four General Departments. After abolition of four General Departments PLAA has been given a new Army Headquarters and therefore been brought as co-equal to any other service. The majority of reduction planned out of 300000 personnel has come out of Army to maintain it at a level of one million. To achieve that, 18 Group Armies have been reduced to 13. To achieve mobility and capability to fight three dimensional war, China has created Corps - brigade - battalion structure and integrated mobile, modular units of all arms like artillery, aviation, logistic support, air defence, electronic counter measure units and of course armour and infantry to make a combined arms brigades, an effective fighting formation capable of independent operations. PLAA now is made up of 13 Army Groups (Corps) having 78 Combined Arms Brigades, 15 Artillery Brigades, 13 Army Aviation/ Air Assault

Brigades and 1 Mechanized Infantry Division.[65] Although operationally PLAA has become more sharp but structurally it has been demoted due to resistance from its corrupt leaders to any structural change as they had always enjoyed the power to be behind any regime. Their businesses or 'paid commercial services' as called so in the White Paper 2019 involving 15 sectors like real estate lease, agriculture and associated products and hospitality, were the main source of corruption in the PLAA which has been done away with. Even Peoples Armed Police (PAP) which was part of PLA and therefore indirectly controlled by the PLAA has now been placed directly under CMC. Thus PLAA's teeth has been further smothered.

The PLA Navy (PLAN): The loss of PLAA has become gain of PLAN because the PLAN has to now become a military instrument for offshore defence and open seas protection of SLOCs and other open seas interest, an aim declared for PLAN in the White Paper "China's Military Strategy" May 2015. The operational control has been taken away from PLAN, three fleets each in ETC (Donghai Fleet), STC (Nanhai Fleet), NTC (Beihai Fleet) and the PLAN Marine Corps are under control of the PLAN headquarters for development purposes. These fleets form of naval bases, submarine flotillas, surface ship flotillas and aviation brigades. The development of PLAN is a work in progress to improve its capabilities to exercise strategic deterrence and counterattack, maritime manoeuvre operation, maritime joint operations, comprehensive defence and integrated support, so as to build a strong and modernised naval force.[66] To further elaborate upon the expansion in PLAN, the main import from the PLAA is in the form of troops trained in amphibious/special operations to enhance the strength of PLAN Marine Corps (PLANMC) from present 10000 personnel to 20000 by 2020 and further raise the PLANMC troops level to 100000 contributing roughly 43 percent of the total PLAN strength of 235000.[67] Although it appears that by trying to make PLAN an expeditionary force China can carry out operations in the far seas like Indian Ocean and the Pacific, but in reality China can only go little beyond protecting its interests in the East and South China Sea and at the most will deploy PLAN/MC in Djibouti and Gwadar. In addition There are China Coast Guard (CCG) and Peoples Armed Forces Maritime Militia (PAFMM) who work on behest of the government for initial enforcement of maritime laws and early armed engagements with PLAN to follow.

The PLA Air Force (PLAAF): In the scheme of sweeping reforms PLAAF troops l have been kept at same level. It comprises of aviation, airborne, ground-to-air missile, radar, ECM and communications forces. There are 5 Air force Commands for each Theatre Command and since 2017 in accordance with the restructuring plan by reorganising regiments into brigades have been relocated and resubordinated them to different theatre commands. The PLAAF has therefore carried out major organisational readjustments for operational purposes for its transition of its task from territorial air defence to both offensive and defensive joint operations.

PLA Rocket Force (PLARF): The PLA Second Artillery has been converted to PLA Rocket Force which of course comprises of nuclear missiles, conventional missiles, and other support forces. It was given a full status of a service and inaugurated on 1 January 2016 along with PLA Strategic Support Force and new command and control organ of PLAA in Beijing as reported by Xinhua. PLARF comprises of all land based nuclear and conventional missiles and is a critical component of China's deterrence strategy. They are responsible for development and testing of new missiles, upgradation of older versions and forming of new missile units.

PLA Strategic Support Force: PLASSF is a newly created service supporting battlefield environment, information, communications, information security, and new technology testing. But besides the white paper testing this force is basically created to provide PLA with cyber, aerospace, electronics and information warfare capabilities. This, therefore, will support joint operations with reconnaissance, early warning, communications, command, control and navigation involving all services. In July 2017, the force units participated in PLA's 90th anniversary parade with its electronic reconnaissance formations. However, with its space related missions, the ambition of PLAAF to control the Chinese military aerospace has been dashed.

PLA Joint Logistic Support Force (PLAJLSF): As the 2015 military modernisation schemes were set on course, the corrupt General Logistics Department was abolished and the PLAJLSF came into existence in September 2016. The role spelt out in the White Paper 2019 is common inventory and warehousing, medical services, tranport, force projection, oil pipelines, engineering and construction management and procurement. For this purpose five joint logistic centres have been created in Wuxi, Guilin, Xining, Shenyang and Zhengzhou to look after theatre-wise supply operations while service branches retain services-specific supply responsibilities. The headquarters is stationed at Wuhan. The greatest strategic direction of the new logistic system is to integrate civilian-controlled assets by developing uniform military and civilian standards for infrastructure, technologies of production, training military personnel in industries, outsourcing logistic support to industries and carrying out civil-military joint exercises for seamless operation in war. In the wake of this, it will never be easy to estimate how much civil resources can be appropriated for military purposes.

People's Armed Police: The reorganisation of PAP takes its motivation from the Tian Anmen episode of Jun 1989 where the dual control of PAP causing unprofessional handling called for ruthless intervention by PLAA. Thereafter, reforms in the policing system were in the offing where central leadership do not have to look towards the provincial leadership to quell any civil unrest and is compelled to call PLA and be accused of use of disproportionate force. Reforms also aimed at misuse of police by provincial leadership due their partial control over this central police established in 1982. Hence PAP has been brought directly under CMC with China's Coast Guard and Maritime Militia under it. This makes Xi Jinping in full control of internal security as well which I argue to be his ultimate concern. Professionally PAP has been now calibrated by the standards of PLAA. It's all low intensity law enforcement and protection activities like border defence, forestry and natural resource protection, firefighting and hydropower etc have been taken away to give it more focused security responsibilities as deemed fit by the CMC. Therefore, PAP is made up of Mobile Force and Internal Security Force. Mobile Force comprises of two division level force transferred from PLAA which can be pressed in service if Internal Security Force fails but still the force will be called 'Police'. These two divisions are responsible north and central China and eastern and southern China respectively. The Internal Security Force has 32 Commands to cover the entire internal security spectrum. PAP has also been made highly capable of surveillance and intelligence using new technologies like Uninhabited Air Vehicles.[68]

Changes in Operational Command Structure: The new command control system has fulfilled the aspirations of China spelt out in the White Paper 'China's Military Strategy' 2015.[69]

> "In the implementation of the military strategic guideline in the new situation, China's armed forces must closely centre around the CPC's goal of building a strong military, respond to the state's core security needs, aim at building an informationised military and winning informationised wars, deepen the reform

> of national defence and the armed forces in an all-round way, build a modern system of military forces with Chinese characteristics, and constantly enhance their capabilities for addressing various security threats and accomplishing diversified military tasks."

Therefore, the modernisation has moved towards joint operation command system by creating five Theatre Commands (TC) replacing seven Military Regions made up of all required services integrated with PLA's command control, communication, computers, intelligence, surveillance and reconnaissance (C4ISR) system necessary to fight a modern war with command and control directly under CMC.

Map 7: Theatre Commands: China

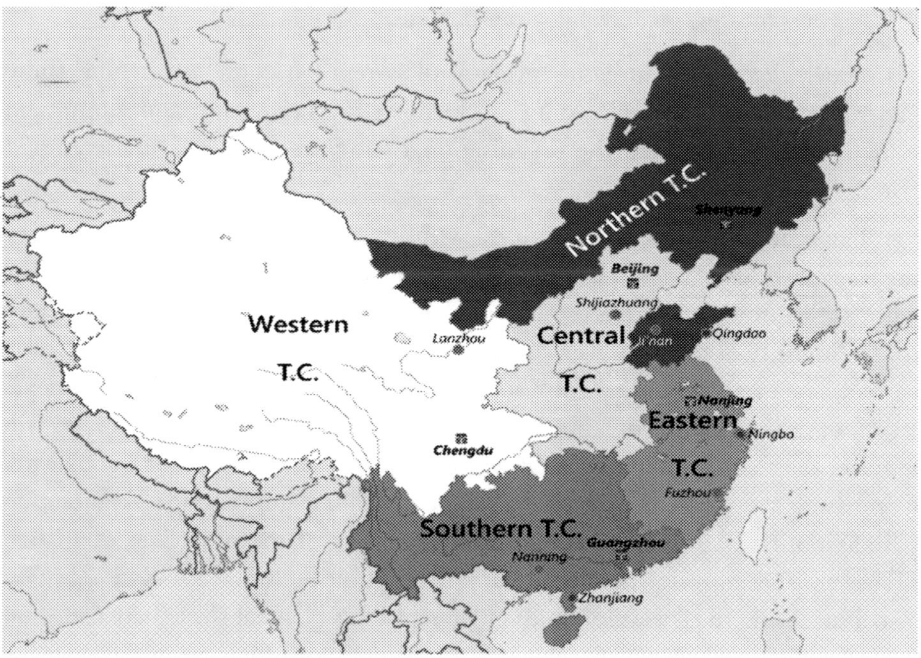

Source: http://en.wikipedia/org/wiki/theatre_commands

Analysing the Modernisation: Not discussing details of modernisation in terms of acquisitions and development of modern armament which is the general trend, analysing the intent and direction of the power accumulation to be is more important. To that regard I would like to quote Xi Jinping what he said in October 2017 Nineteenth National Congress of the Party:

> "We will upgrade our military capabilities, and see that, by the year 2020, mechanisation is basically achieved, IT application has come a long way, and strategic capabilities have seen a big improvement....We will make it our mission to see that by 2035, the modernisation of national defence and our forces basically completed; and that by the mid-21st century our people's armed forces have been fully transformed into world class force."[70]

To put in place such a fighting machine first the mixed command was required to be sorted. For example, the service headquarters also had control over operations in which PLAA had the lead, whereas joint operations needed a centralised strategic planning and theatre specific tactics and development of forces accordingly. Thus the division of work was formulated as under:

> "CMC exercising overall leadership, the TCs direct military operations and services focusing on developing capabilities."[71]

The above clarity in command and control system has come out in the White Paper 2019 under the subheading ' Reforming the Leadership and Command system. This has dictated the organisational structure for the Chinese Armed Forces (Chart 1)

The modernistion has more to do with independently projecting power to the respective adversaries in the given theatre and be able to fight and win the war without disturbing any other theatre. The magnitude of deployment also indicates to the intensity of threat perceived. And the Central Theatre in any case is ready to mobilise in any eventuality. With PAP made more military like, it relieves PLAA of the earlier role of a power to quell internal unrest. However, PLAA still remains the main source of internal power as till the time four of the Theatre Commands are commanded by PLAA Generals. This augurs well for "maintaining China's political security and social stability," one of the objectives of PLA.[72] However, one exception taken in 2017 by appointment of Vice Admiral Yuan Yubai as Southern Theatre Commander replacing General Wan Jiaocheng, 64 who was still left with one year of service. This development when China faced stiff opposition from the South China Sea littorals for developing artificial islands there indicates to China's objective to prepare Southern Theatre Command for operations in the 'far seas'. Also, with assigning PLARF and PLASSF to each TC China has challenged the adversaries in all possible dimensions of warfare.

The security challenges faced by China are of numerous varieties and dimensions. While most of them are in the east and south east, there are a few in the west and southwest and almost none in the north. In the east PLA has to deal

Chart 1: Organisation: Central Military Commission

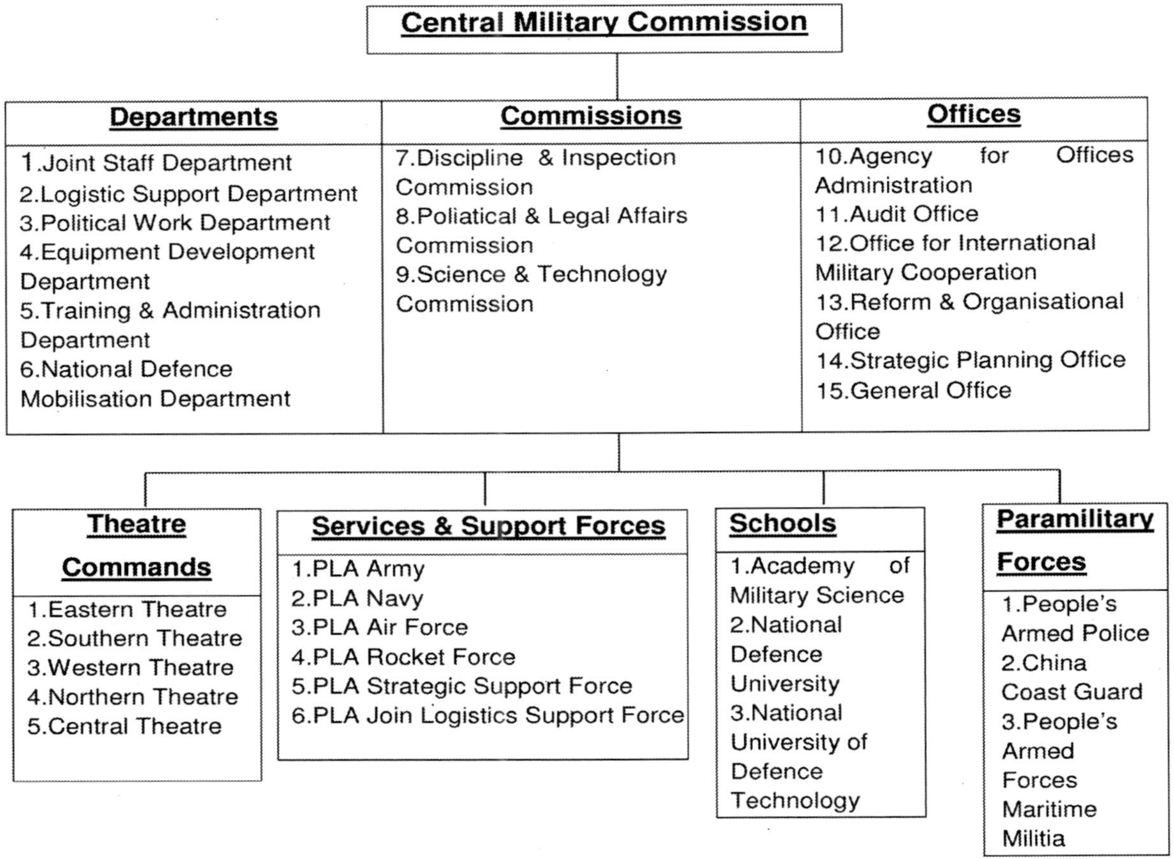

with the Terminal High Altitude Area Defence (THAAD) deployed in South Korea by the US, which China considers having undermined regional strategic balance in favour of the US and its littoral allies in the East and South China Seas. China's military issues with Japan are historical as well as contemporary. The Chinese dream to annex Taiwan getting farther as the US consolidates its commitment to protect Taiwan by passing new Taiwan Allies International Protection and Enhancement Initiative (TAIPEI) which was passed in the US Congress and signed as law by President Trump on March 27, 2020. It has tried to create a protective shield against China peeling away countries having diplomatic relations with Taiwan as Republic of China. This act ostensibly encouraged countries like India, Japan and Australia to further warm up their relations with Taiwan. It has thus, hardened military options for China against Taiwan. The East Turkistan movement in the Xin Jiang and Tibetan freedom movement along with border disputes with India are the other military challenges. Hence the modernisation of PLA has to be discussed more in strategic and geopolitical terms than in terms of hardware.

Anti-Access/Area Denial Strategy (A2/AD)

Today, the US hegemony in the Indo-Pacific has become the main concern for China. It has become an impediment in its territorial ambitions in the East China Sea with the non-achievement of accession of Taiwan, the claim on the Diaoyu/ Senkaku islands and the conflict with Japan and the claim of the nine-dot line as an EEZ. China' has made all-round efforts to include a variety of air, sea, undersea, space and air counter-space, information warfare systems and operational concepts to deny the US any access to China's 'near seas' as a counter to the US hegemony in the region. The US Department of Defence has termed this strategy as the development of 'Anti Access and Area Denial' capabilities by China. This concept was first reflected by China in its 2008 Defence White Paper, which laid down the objectives of modernisation as an instrument to increase the country's capabilities to maintain maritime, space and electromagnetic space security.

The QUAD: The Quadrilateral Security Dialogue, popularly known as 'The Quad' was signed in 2007 as an informal security dialogue between the US, Japan, Australia and India as a response to increased military and economic power of China in Asia Pacific. It has progressed haltingly for the inhibitions on part of countries like Australia and India because of their bilateral entanglement with China and trade and border repercussions respectively. While Australia withdrew in 2007 itself but rejoined in 2017 during the ASEAN Summit but then India, post Doklam, began to balance between Shanghai Cooperation Organisation and Quad which China considers as Asian NATO. As an indicator to China, India has not allowed Australia to participate in Malabar Naval Exercise to keep is low key. However, now the situation has again changed for China post Corona pandemic, as Quad Plus meeting on March 20th 2020 telephonic was held to discuss methods to deal with the pandemic, which included like-minded countries like New Zealand, South Korea and Vietnam and it is further trying to engage ASEAN countries to make Indo -Pacific strategy more acceptable and effective against China.[73] Therefore, China is running out of diplomatic options against Quad and resorting to military options as incase of India. Therefore, its geopolitical implications have far reaching effect on China's options.

COVID-19 Pandemic: China is also faced with a new situation wherein it is being squarely blamed for spread of Corona virous from its city of Wuhan taking toll on millions of lives and trillions of dollar worth economy of the world. It has led to lockdowns of economies to save lives and the countries are now resorting to protectionism. The role of WHO in this whole episode has been questioned for favouring China and an Australia sponsored evaluation of the reasons has been ordered by the WHO of which India is Chairman of the Executive Board. This portrays China in negative light. This besides, the world is reorganizing itself and dealings with China will have far reaching implications which will be examined in detail.

CONCLUSION

With Chinese hegemonic conditions on the rise and the United States hegemony on the decline, it is also a pertinent question whether the US is still willing to reinvigorate its global leadership post Covid-19 pandemic or will allow space to China to keep filling the void. Evident is the fact that in the war on Iraq and in Afghanistan, the US despite remaining a stronger power than it is now, has eased itself out due to a lack of will of its people to bear the cost of its global power projection. It has also proved that local wars are unsustainable for a distant power like the US. While China is projecting itself as a global power, it is first going to test the US capability to fight a war in its own waters. That is going to be tougher for the US to handle when coupled with the economic reasons like China being the highest foreign buyer of its securities.[74]

For China, in the backdrop of probable intervention of the US on the behalf of Taiwan, Japan, Philippines, and other littorals, its economic ambition to bring up its citizens to a fair level of prosperity which has not been achieved so far, will keep lingering in the minds of Chinese strategists while considering any military option east and south of China.

Therefore, China must think about the geographical compulsions of resource acquisition and military operability for the effectiveness of its polity and economic prosperity because the flip side is, what if a military action spirals out of control? This makes China an intriguing, enigmatic and complex country for a researcher as China remains trapped in a vicious circle for a rising power as described by the historian Paul Kennedy:

> "Wealth is usually vested to underpin military power, and military power is usually needed to acquire and protect wealth."[75]

Therefore, this book will examine the geopolitical evolution of China based on geographical, economic and metaphysical elements to establish a geopolitical pattern in the international relations responses and to establish a model for the future predictions valid for this century.

While China has emerged as the second most important world power after the US, riding on the wave of the US-led market economy and globalization. however, its geographical configuration and historical experiences are different and unique, thereby leading to unique geopolitical imperatives.

These unique geopolitical imperatives will call for unique responses in China's foreign affairs, depending mostly on its ability to balance between the gains versus risks of economic hegemony as well as military hegemony.

China, as a country of research, has always maintained its insulation and impregnability on two counts: one, its geographical desolation from the West and the second, its linguistic and cultural steadfastness. Although, under the modern system of communication, China is no more physically unapproachable but the linguistic and cultural understanding still remains pivotal to know China from the Chinese perspective, as the scholars on China say:

> "Language skills and familiarity with China strike us as remaining the core prerequisites for scholars wishing to make sense of any given aspect of Chinese Politics."[76]

However, this limitation is significantly offset with sourcing information from original Chinese literature. Owing to a rich and abundant historical and cultural wealth of China and the availability of resources and publications, now there is a problem of selection of material which has been written with objectivity and impartial approach. The majority of the literature has been written from the perspective of the country of the authors specially the US. Therefore, efforts have been made to keep an independent perspective. It will not only create unbiased information and a knowledge bank to make correct deductions but also give an untainted perspective as well.

China is a one-party nation. Therefore, internally, there is hardly any independent agency to evaluate the reliability and validity of the state-generated data. This phenomenon has led to the creation of upstream and downstream flawed data. As the economic boom accentuates competition among the regional governments of China in order to show their performance better than the others, it causes the reliability and validity issues of the data generated by these states. To offset this limitation, data by other agencies like the World Bank, IMF, SIPRI and many such independent bodies has been used in addition to the state-generated Chinese data if it has comparability with these agencies.

The uniqueness of its history and an open economy under the controlled governance of the Communist Party of China do not make a valid comparison with any other country because of the inherent dissimilarities. However, comparative studies have been resorted to on an absolute premise where the type of governance, ethnicity and culture do not significantly influence the results. In addition to a comparative study in the international sphere, comparative studies within China between various regions have been resorted to in order to bring about an understanding and to prove an argument. This method has been used especially in the chapter related to the geo-economic evolution of China.

Another problem with China's concurrent publications, especially the government media and at times the articles by a think tank, is that either they reproduce the rhetorics of the government or propagate and instill in our common psyche, a government agenda or a motive. The use of results of new technology like 'Yoshicoder' have been successfully used by researchers world over to gauge this influence and we hope that such influences are therefore, warded off.

One conceptual and three evolutionary test beds have been used to examine the Chinese geopolitics, besides a common method of research in the general social science researches; a conceptual framework of geopolitical theories, the historical evolution of China as a nation-state, the metaphysical evolution of Chinese Strategic minds and its geo-economic evolution for the development and nurturing of the Chinese polity.

The temporal element is conspicuous in all the four test beds. Spatial distribution of the elements of Chinese geopolitics have also been used in the first two. The philosophical and cultural elements, social norms to be adopted by citizens and a strategic philosophy behind the interstate relations in the third test bed have been used extensively. The fourth test bed uses the global linkages of Chinese economy to derive geo-economic imperatives for China. These four elements will enable us to extrapolate the present geopolitical conditions, out of which we can then derive the geopolitical imperatives for China, and then evolve a model for future responses to various countries, group of countries and regions in the perspective of the effects of ongoing pandemic.

NOTES

1. Kissinger, Henry, *On China,* USA: Penguin Press, 2011, pp. 107-108.
2. Westand, Odd Arne, *Restless Empire: China and World since 1750*, London: Random House, 2012, p. 334.
3. Heath, John, 'Tibet and China in the Twenty First Century' *SAQI*, 2005, pp. 117-126.
4. Deng Xioping, 'Respect Knowledge, Respect Trained Personnel: May 24, 1977', in *Selected Works of Deng Xiaoping*, Vol. 2, p. 53.
5. Gittings, John, *The Changing Face of China*, Oxford: Oxford University Press, 2005, p. 156.
6. *People's Daily*, 1 July 1987, quoted in ibid., p. 186.
7. Yan Xuetong, Professor, Qing Hua University, Beijing, and from an eminent think tank believed to be closer to the establishment, expressed these views during a conference while presenting his paper *'The Bipolarisation in East Asia'*. IDSA, New Delhi, 19 Feb 2014.
8. *World Development Indicators,* World Bank www.databank.worldbank.org/, Accessed on 03 Apr 2014.
9. Ye Zecheng, *Development of Land Rights and Rise and Fall of Great Powers: Geopolitical Development and Geostrategic Choice of China's Peaceful Development*, Beijing: New Star Press, 2007.
10. *Statistical Communiqué*, National Bureau of Statistics of China, 24 Feb 2014, www.stats.gov.in/english/statistics, Accessed on 04 Apr 2014.
11. Jacques, Martine, *When China Ruled the World*, NY: Penguin, 2012, p. 231.
12. Haishan Fu & Nada Hamadeh, *New results from the International Comparison Program shed light on the size of the global economy.* May 19, 2020. https://blogs.worldbank.org/opendata/new-results-international-comparison-program-shed-light-size-global-economy. Accessed on 16 Jun 2020.
13. Ye Zecheng (trans. From Chinese by Steven I Lavine and Guoli Liu), *Inside China's Grand Strategy: Perspective from the People's Republic*, New Delhi: KW Private Ltd, 2013, p. 14.
14. Ibid., pp. 14-17.
15. Mackinder, HJ, 'The Geographical Pivot of History', *The Geographical Journal*, 1904.
16. Win, Christina Y., 'China's Strategic Shift towards the Region of the Four Seas: The Middle Kingdom arrives at the Middle East', *Middle East Review of International Affairs (MERIA)*, 17 (1), 2013, www.gloria-centre.org, Accessed on 25 Mar 2013.

17. *Nei Meng Guo* means the 'inner Meng (Mongolian)' country in Mandarin.
18. Johnson, Douglas L., Viola Haarmann, Merril L. Johnson and David L. Clawxon (eds), *World Regional Geography: A Developmental Approach*, New Delhi: PHI Learning Pvt Ltd, 2012, p. 508.
19. Thomson Reuters Foundation, www.trust.org/spotly/China-earqukes-2008 8/4/14.w..business, Accessed on 12 Feb 2014.
20. 'Three Gorges Dam: 2010', *Business Insider*, www.businessinsider.com. Accessed on 12 Feb 2014.
21. Mao Zedong, 'Swimming', *Selected Works of Mao Zedong, Swimming*, 1956, www.marxists.org/reference/archive/mao/selectedwork/poems/poems23htm. Accessed on08 Apr 2014.
22. Kaplan, Robert D., *The Revenge of Geography*, NY: Random House, 2012, p. 205.
23. As given in Nicholas John Spykeman, *The Geography of Peace*, NY: Harcourt Brace, 1944.
24. Morgenthau, Hans J., *Politics among Nations: The Struggle for Power and Peace*, NY: Knopf, 1978, and Ye Zicheng, *Inside China's Grand Strategy: The Perspective from the Peoples Republic*, New Delhi: KW Publishers, 2013, p. 8.
25. Kaplan, op. cit., p. 189.
26. *World Development Indicators*, www.databank.worldbank.org, Accessed on03 Apr 2014.
27. Keay, John, *China: A History*, London: Harper Collins, 2008, p. 13.
28. Fairbank, John King and Merle Goldman, *China: A New History*, Cambridge: Harvard University Press, 2006, pp. 23.
29. Fravel, M. Taylor, *Strong Border, Secure Nation: Cooperation and Conflicts in China's Territorial Disputes*, Princeton: Princeton University Press, 2008, pp. 41-42.
30. Kaplan, Robert D., 'The Geography of Chinese Power', Foreign Affairs, www.foreign affairs.com/articles/06205/robert-d-kaplan/the geography of Chinese power. Accessed on 16 Dec 2013.
31. Malraux, André (trans. by Kilmartin Terrance), *Anti Memoirs*, NY: Henry Holt, 1967, pp. 373-74.
32. Mao Zedong, 'Speech at the Supreme State Conference', in *Mao Zedong Unrehearsed: Talks and Letters: 1956-71*, Harmondsworth: Penguin, 1975, pp. 92-93.
33. Macfarquhar, Roderick, Timothy Cheek and Eugene Liu (eds), *The Secret Speeches of Chairman Mao: From the Hundred Flowers to Great Leap Forward*, Cambridge: Harvard University Press, 1984, p. 405.
34. Nathan, Andrew J., *Introduction*, in Zhang Liang, Andrew J. Nathan and Perry Link (eds), *The Tian Ammen Papers*, NY: Public Affair, 2001, p. viii.
35. Chiang Kai-shek, *China's Destiny*, NY: Roy Publishers,1947, pp. 44-75.
36. Callahan, William A., *China: The Pessoptimist Nation*, Oxford: Oxford University Press, 2010, pp. 69-70.
37. Cheng Zhizheng, " *Wuhu Wuyue*" (Alas, May), *Shenbao*, May 9, 1928, p. 21. (Source: Callahan, op. cit.).
38. Yunjie Chen, "*Qing Shi 'Gouchi Ri*' " (Please Establish National Humiliation Day), *Jiaoyu Yu Zhili*, 4, 1999, p. 22.
39. Ye Hailan, 'Games Prove Validity of the China Model', *China Daily*, September 23, 2008.
40. Shirk, Susan L., *China: Fragile Super Power*, Oxford: Oxford University Press, 2007, p. 104.
41. Ching, Julia, *Mysticism and Kingship in China; The Heart of Chinese Wisdom*, Cambridge: Cambridge University Press, 1997, p. 264.

42. McGregor, Richard, *The Party: The Secret World of China's Communist Rulers*, NY: Harper Collins, 2010, p. 34.
43. 'The Clash of Civilization?' *Foreign Affairs*, Vol. 72, Summer, 1993, pp. 22-49.
44. Starr, John Brayan, *Understanding China*; NY: Hill and Wang, 2001,p. 72.
45. Ibid.
46. Office of the United States Tread Representative. *The People's Republic of China: U.S. China Trade Facts.* https://ustr.gov/countries-regions/china-mongolia-taiwan/peoples-republic-china Accessed on 17 Apr 2020.
47. Rosales, Qsurldo, 'Trade Competition from China, Global Rise: Implications for the Americas', Winter 2012, www.americasquarterly.org/Rosales. Accessed on 13 Apr 2014.
48. 'The United States Challenges China's Non Compliance in WTO Steel Dispute', Press Release of the Office of United States Trade Representative, www.ustr.gov/about.us/press release/2014/ January accessed on 13/4/14.
49. 'Remarks by United States Trade Representative Michael Froman announcing Compliance Action in China-Goes Dispute', www./ustr.gov/abouus/press release/2014/January, Accessed on 13 Apr 2014.
50. 'Fact Sheet: WTO Case Challenging Chinese Subsidies', www.ustr.gov/about-us/press-official/ fact-sheets/2012/September, Accessed on 13 Apr 2014.
51. 'China Loses Trade Dispute over Rare Earths Exports', www.reuters.com/march 26.2014,Accessed on 13 Apr 2014.
52. Vasquez, John, 'Why do Neighbours Fight: Proximity, Interaction, Territoriality', *Journal of Peace Research*, 32 (2), 1995, pp. 277-294.
53. Johnston, Alistari Jain, 'China's Militarized Interstate Dispute Behaviour 1949–1992: A First Cut at the Data', *China Quarterly March*, No. 153, 1998, p. 29.
54. Mulvewon, James, 'Chairman Hu and PLA's New Historic Mission', China's Leadership Monitor, No. 27, 2009, www.medi.hoper.org/sites/default/files/ docus/clm/27June. Accessed on 17 Apr 2014
55. Information office of the Council of the People's Republic of China, 'China's National Defence in 2006' Beijing, December 2006.
56. White Paper on Defence 2010.
57. 'The Diversified Employment of China's Armed Forces' (White Paper), The Information Office of the State Council, China's Cabinet, PRC, Beijing, April, 2014, www.news.xinhuanet.com/ english/China/2013-04/16/C- 32312681.htm. Accessed on 17 Apr 2014.
58. Ibid.
59. 'Annual Report to Congress: Military and Security Developments Involving the People's Republic of China', www.defense.gov/pubs/2013 China-report-final.polf. Accessed on 17 Apr 2014
60. Ibid, p. 25.
61. Singh Mandip, 'The ChineseMilitary in 2012', China Year Book 2012,Institute for Defence and Strategic Studies, New Delhi, 2013,pp.29-30.
62. Defence White Paper 2015: *China's Military Strategy*, http://english.www.gov.cn/archive/ white_paper/2015/05/27/content_281475115610833.htm, Accessed on 18 Jun 2020.
63. Defense White Paper 2019: *China's National Defence in the New Era*, 24 July 2019, Xinhhua/ Eng.news.cn. Accessed on 07 June 2020.
64. The Diplomat, Dan Tse, *Why China's Central Military Commission Got Down Sized*, httpp://

the diplomat.com/2017/11/why-china-military-commission-got-downsized. Accessed on 30 May 2020.

65. Defence Intelligence Agency, *China Military Power: Modernizing a Force to Fight and Win*, 2019, p. 58.
66. Defence White Paper 2019: *China's National Defence in the New Era*, 24 July 2019, Xinhhua/ Eng.news.cn. Accessed on 07 June 2020.
67. GlobalSecurity, *People's liberation Army Navy – Marine Corps*, https://www.globalsecurity.org/ military/world/china/plan-mc.htm. Accessed on 07 June 2020.
68. Henry Boyd, Meia Nouwens, *China's People's Armed Police: Reorganised and Refocused.* http:// iiss.org/blogs/military -balance/2019/06/chin-pap. Accessed on 09 June 2020.
69. :Defence White Paper 2015 *China's Military Strategy*, http://english.www.gov.cn/archive/ white_paper/2015/05/27/content_281475115610833.htm, Accessed on 18 Jun 2020.
70. Xi Jinping, *"Secure a Decisive Victory in Building a Moderately Prosperous Society in All Respects and Strive for the Great Success of Socialism with Chinese Characteristics for a New Era."* Delivered at the 19th National Congress of the Communist Party of China October 18, 2017. http:// www.xinhuanet.com/english/download/Xi_Jinping's_report_at_19th_CPC_National_ Congress.pdf. Accessed on 13 June 2020.
71. Defense White Paper 2019: *China's National Defence in the New Era*, 24 July 2019, Xinhhua/ Eng.news.cn. Accessed on 07 June 2020
72. Defence White Paper 2015: *China's Military Strategy* http://english.www.gov.cn/archive/ white_paper/2015/05/27/content_281475115610833.htm Accessed on 18 Jun 2020.
73. Rajeswari Pillai Rajgopalan, *Towards a Quad - plus Arrangement*, http://www.orfonline.org/ research/towards-a-quad-plus-arrangement-65674/ Accessed on 15-06-2020.
74. Tellis, Ashley J, 'Uphill Challenges: China's Military Modernisation and Asian Security', in *Strategic Asia's and China's Military Challenges*, Ashley J. Tellis and Travis Tanner (eds), Washington DC: National Bureau of Asian Research, 2012, p. 8, www.carnegoendowment.org and www.google.co.in,Accessed on 17 April 2014.
75. Kennedy, Paul, *The Rise and Fall of Great Powers*, NY: Vintage, 1989, p. xvi.
76. Carlson, Allen, Mary E. Callaghan, Kenneth Liberthal and Malivic Manion (eds), *Contemporary Chinese Politics: New Services, Methods and Field Strategies*, Cambridge: Cambridge University Press.

2

A Conceptual Framework for Chinese Geopolitics

WHY A GEOPOLITICAL APPROACH?

It will be apt to begin by quoting Sir Halford J. Mackinder (1861-1947) what he said in 1890:

> "The course of politics is a product of two sets of forces, impelling and guiding. The impetus is from the past in the history embedded in a people's character and tradition. The present guides the movement by economic wants and geographical opportunities. Statesmen and diplomats succeed and fail pretty much as they recognise the irresistible power of these forces."[1]

Against the American idealists who had rubbished geopolitics as a straitjacket, self-serving edifice of the theoretical justification of expansionism, the modern-day revival of the use of the geopolitical approach is a dynamic interaction between the opportunities provided by the geographical configuration and the historically predisposed mindset of the policymakers and politicians. While the impelling force are the lessons from the historical past, the guiding forces are the geographical opportunities those have come up in the concurrent period. Therefore, one cannot remain embedded in the historical justification of a policy or remain independent of dynamic geographical realities. As Grey and Sloan say:

> "This relationship between the geographical environment and the decision-making process is dynamic one; it is dependent upon changing levels of transport and weapons technology. This dynamic aspect is one of the most important links between geopolitical theory, geography, and strategy. It

illustrates the pivotal nature of the continuing exchange between theory and history."[2]

In the case of China, that is what happened when Mao the policymaker ignored the opportunities provided by the geographical configuration. He never paid attention to the importance of certain geographical patterns in political history and the theories of spatial relationship and historical causation. Therefore, Mao insulated China as a location and did not allow it to interact with other locations in a complementary fashion. This led to a great famine, abstinence from learning from the historical experiences and interpretation of its geographical configuration, causing destruction of vast knowledge and experience of the use of location, space, and interaction between them and the geographical opportunities they provided. China confronted both superpowers: the US on the Taiwan issue and subsequently the former USSR on a border issue that had started with a clash on the Zhenbau Island in the Ussuri River. At this juncture, Nixon had decided to define his foreign policy by geopolitical considerations and declared that the US had a strategic interest in the survival of a major communist country. The former USSR was conveyed that the US was not indifferent and would not be passive. With back-channel diplomacy by Henry Kissinger, Mao understood the deficits of standing alone and the providence of an interaction between locations or countries in this case. Nixon visited Beijing and the CPC Central Committee issued a communiqué describing Nixon's visit as an instance of "China utilising contradictions, dividing enemies and enhancing ourselves".[3] Although the interests of both countries were not congruent, the interaction was certainly forced upon both by the geopolitics that provided the geographical opportunities to the policymakers to take a strategic decision beneficial to both. Subsequently, Deng Xiaoping took a unilateral decision in 1979 to open the economy, take advantage of China's own geographical opportunities, explore geographical opportunities of the world, and prosper. This consolidated the 'geopolitical guiding' of the Chinese Polity.

Geography is a Reality that will Never leave the Space

After World War II, there has been a tendency among the political scientists led by the US scholars to deny geopolitics its reasonable place in explaining as a cause to the effect or in the decision-making of a policymaker during war and peace mainly because of its association with Nazi ambitions. Even Richard Hartshorne, the political geographer, called 'geopolitics as an intellectual poison despite him working in the office of the strategic services of the CIA and helped generate geographical intelligence for the US military.[4] What he actually however did was assessing the geographical suitability for political and military strategies. He, in the end, could not get away from geography as such. Actually, in the bargain to obliterate geopolitics from the process of strategic decision-making, no one could ever forget geography for long. As Spykman, the great Dutch American strategist of the early World War II era wrote in 1942:

> "Geography is the most fundamental factor in foreign policy of the state because it is most permanent. Ministers come and go, even dictators die, but mountain ranges stand unperturbed. George Washington, defending thirteen states with ragged army, has been succeeded by Franklin D Roosevelt with the resources of continent at his command, but the Atlantic continues to separate Europe from the United States and the ports of St Lawrence River are still blocked by winter ice. Alexander I, Tzar of all Russians, bequeathed to Joseph Stalin, a simple member of the communist party, not only his power but also his endless struggle for access to the sea, and Maginot and Clemenceau have inherited from Caesar and Louis XIV anxiety over the open German Frontier".[5]

How logically he has explained that geographical conditions are so deterministic in nature that they do not change with the change of political situations! He said in the same book that "Geographies don't argue. It simply is".

I am taking the argument of geopolitics from the backyards of the adversarial exponents against the term to posit that even the US strategies could not deny the usefulness of geographical considerations which never leaves the map as the map is a mere representation of geography. That was the reason why President Roosevelt in the aftermath of the Japanese attack addressed the US citizens to bring home the importance of maps and places in the common consciousness and in fact, he brought out the importance of geographies and their relevance to the making of strategy.

> "Look at your map. Look at the vast area of China, with its million fighting men. Look at the vast area of Russia, with its powerful armies and proven military might. Look at the British Isles, Australia, New Zealand, the Dutch Indies, India, the Near East and the continent of Africa, with their resources of raw material, and of peoples determined to resist axis domination. Look too at North America, Central America, and South America... I ask you to look at your maps, particularly at that portion of the Pacific Ocean lying west of Hawaii. Before this war even started the Philippines Islands were already surrounded on three sides by Japanese power. On the west, the China side, the Japanese were in possession of the coast of China and the coast of Indo-

> China, which had been yielded to them by the Vichy French. On the north are the islands of Japan themselves reaching down almost to northern Luzon. On the east are the mandated islands-which Japan had occupied exclusively and had fortified in absolute violation of her written word on 23 February 1942.
>
> The islands that lie between Hawaii and the Philippine...these islands, hundreds of them appear only as small dots on most maps. But, they cover a large strategic area. Guam lies in the middle of them – alone outpost which we have never fortified."[6]

The strategic compulsion which made him exalt his countrymen to look at the map made him say, "we must all understand and take the hard fact that our job now is to fight at distances which extend all the way around the globe." And in modern times the Americans understand importance of Guam against China no better than ever.

The primary aim of maps is to enhance visualisation of the geographies in which strategic and political operations take place. Agnew seeks for global visualisation before the development of a modern geopolitical imagination in order to pursue politics.

> "World politics was invented only when it became possible to see in its totality (in the imagination) as whole and pursue goals in relation to that geographical scale."[7]

Therefore, visualisation only became possible with the development of modern maps. These maps only enable the IR theorists and practitioners of geopolitics to see the world as a unitary whole. In fact, all ground strategies and tactics are planned first on maps, initiating from global to local. Therefore, maps become a fundamental assumption of geography and geopolitics.

Why the geopolitical approach to studying China's international relations behaviour becomes important is because China has been endowed with such geographical characteristics that it has an overbearing effect on its IR advantages and limitations. In fact, Robert D. Kaplan brings out this significance explicitly: "The fact that China is blessed by geography is something so basic and obvious that it tends to be overlooked in all the discussion about its economic dynamism and national assertiveness over recent decades. Thus, a look at the map through the prism of history is in order."[8]

Therefore, what Mackinder said about the map that at one glance a whole series of generalisation is 'conveyed by the maps', has never been truer. No history can be gauged without a backdrop of geography. Historically, however these generalisations at times, are plagued by cartographical distortions. But they are those elements that reveal the long-range geopolitical intentions of the governments releasing them.[9] There are many such evidence that maps have not only been used for the representation of geographies but also for plotting the later ambitions of the rulers, governments and policymakers. That is the reason why the British geographer John Brian Harley said that cartography could be a "discourse of power" and it was this discourse of power that led to the making of Mercator projections which tend to show Europe larger than it really is.[10] Bold colouring and other specifications given on the maps naturally do not reveal reality—rather, they hide it.

Maps have been an instrument in the hands of those pursuing a realist agenda. Realism has been at the base of the Chinese policies of international relations through history. That is why Kaplan says:

> "Realists from the ancient Greeks and Chinese right up through the mid twentieth century French Philosopher Reymont Aaron and his Spanish contemporary Jose Ortega Y Gusset believe war is naturally inherent in the division of humanity into states and their groupings."[11]

The geopolitical approach to study China's IR responses in the 21st Century, therefore, becomes important as China has historically used cartography and mapping extensively in the past and present to further its geopolitical aims and objectives. In 2001, China discovered a map dated to 1418 AD which charted the Ming Dynasty voyages of Admiral Zheng He to South East Asia, South Asia and Africa. It went on to assert that Zheng He had actually discovered America before Columbus![12] The projection on which the map is made showed China as a bigger territory than it is at present. This certainly was a ploy to project inherently a great power and not a power recently discovered after its economic boom. Then there are hosts of other maps which have been introduced as showing the intentions of the Western world as to how it intends dividing China as was given on the back cover of the book *China's Road: Under the Shadow of Globalization* (1999). Although these have been unofficial sources, but they do have great currency in China for raking up nationalist fervour. However, it is not that the official version of Chinese maps has not been showing distortion of the international imagination. China has been issuing aspirational maps in which it records Taiwan as a province of China and also shows Outer Mongolia as part of Republic of China. These distortion-raising aspirations occur in the background of the fact that on the foundation of Republic in 1912, China, for the first time, made a national map to know what it was actually ruling.[13] Here, William Callahan brings up the concept of 'Geo-body' propounded by Thongchai Winichakul and replaces the well-defined maps with Chinese Geo-body and posits that

> "...remembering of territories that have been dismembered (fen ge) is a keyway of imaging and then managing China's geo-body in a way that combines symbolic politics and geopolitics and integrates soft power with hard power."[14]

The geopolitics of cartography is one such issue that requires elaborate discussion to assess China's interactions with others that will guide its geopolitical behaviour in the 21st Century. In the latter part of this research, we shall trace and explore the geopolitics of changing shape of China as it became a modern nation, from a pre-modern, unbounded understanding of space and territory to a bounded understanding of space and territory, as well as a shifting of the geo-body in different periods. A geopolitical approach to analyse China's international relational behaviour in the 20th Century is also relevant from the point of view of looking at China from the perspective of human geography that has developed through history, covering varying places and spaces. It gives us the opportunity as Knox and Marston say "systematic study of what makes places unique and the connection and interaction"[15] between places, basically to be able to characterise the regions of China from the weather pattern, the physical settings, settlements, resources and transport system. It gives us the opportunity to study the spatial organisation of power relations. The human geographical approach towards geopolitics of China also allows us to study the distribution of power and weaknesses within the country and its geopolitical impact outside China in its international relations policies because power is never present in an equal magnitude all over the country nor felt equally at all spaces internationally. In its course, the we shall be able to define important places in China as a combination of location, locales and sense of place as postulated by John Agnew who gives a place a character. However, the character of the places within China and the character of China itself has been changing over different periods of history. Therefore, it becomes imperative to trace these patterns of change for which the geopolitical approach of study of a country is an apt tool. As Gray Colins says:

> "In essence, geopolitics is an attempt to draw attention to importance of certain geographical patterns in political history."[16]

In the final assessment as to why a geopolitical approach is necessary for studying China's future international politics is that the policymakers will certainly try to give coherence to their political aims by paying attention to the geographical configurations of land and sea. The policymakers will have to develop an outlook that may not conservatively be based upon geopolitical theories in a classical sense but certainly they will require developing a global sense of wisdom and understanding out of how man and his environment (read geography) have interacted historically. What Mackinder said in 1942 remains relevant in the 21st Century to underpin the need for a geopolitical approach in policymaking when he desires the policymakers to have certain capabilities and attributes:

> "They must have a global outlook and guide readiness to meet emergencies, for it was never more than this newly closed world that our stability is but balance, and wisdom lies in masterful administration of the unforeseen; they must also have a trained power of judging values for the future; and they will, of course, still need an understanding of the momentum with which both man and his environment come to the present from the past."[17]

A Conceptual Framework for Chinese Geopolitics

So far we have emphasised geography, and above all, the Human Geography that analyses the human interaction with the physical elements of the habitat, the earth, and in that interaction either the human overpowers geography by technology and endurance demanded by the conditions or the geography overpowers the human minds. Perhaps, that was the case when Sir Halford Mackinder talked about the Pivot Area and the Heartland and the German geographer, General Haushofer really took it to heart and got it implemented by an invasion of Russia in World War II. Actually, it was the human geography much more in action then the physicality of the geography as the geography of Russia first interacted assumedly strongly with the German soldiers' minds and they lost the battle first in the mind as geography overpowered the humans. Today, when technology, air power and space power have progressed so much, perhaps, as a strategic necessity, the mind could overpower geography. A study of war on the Eastern front narrates it explicitly:

> "The history of Panzer Corps Grossdeutsch...records, how very early in the first campaign (1941) many men of the regiment, as it then was, were over with depression at the immensity of the task involved in subduing the Soviet Union and of the war which they were committed to fighting.
>
> The same thought occurred to many: that extending from the German front line and reaching as far as Vladivostok, there-existed a vast area of enemy territory wherein their regiments, indeed the whole German Army, could vanish without trace."[18]

There is also a case of oversimplification of the geopolitical theories and the implementation of such formula everywhere. There is a danger in such omnipotence of theorising. More so, in the modern world of globalisation and proliferation of techno-scientific risks where politics has transcended the formal territoriality of geopolitics as much as some have started suggesting that this mark 'the end of geopolitics. But Gearoid O Tuathail says that such arguments have a narrow Cold War conception.[19] Therefore, an approach to the application of geopolitics on China's 21st Century responses must save itself from both the extremities while discussing the theories of geopolitics hereafter.

Geopolitics

In gross terms of reference, when we analyse the geographical factors underlying international relations and gauge political interactions, it only presents a desirable direction and enables the decision-makers to foresee the likely impact on the relations in the bilateral as well as multilateral spheres. Geopolitics has evolved itself over a period while being used implicitly and explicitly. While spatial and geographical factors were already considered for propounding theories guiding political and military decisions, the term geopolitics was only implicit. It was coined explicitly by Rudolf Kjellen only in 1899 when he defined geopolitics as:

> "...the theory of the state as a geographical organism or phenomenon in space."[20]

Karl Haushofer, the father of German geopolitics defines it as:

> "Geopolitics is the new national service of the state... a doctrine on the spatial determinism of all political processes, based on the broad foundations of geography especially of political geography.[21]

As evident, two elements of his determination to be a 'national service' and 'spatial determinism' in fact became tools of justification of the German expansionism. However, the definition by the *Encyclopaedia Britannica* takes geopolitics to a more plausible and inclusive domain.

> "Geopolitics is the analysis of the geographic influence on power relationships in international relations."[22]

In the initial stages before 1899, when the term geopolitics was in use, geopolitics was studied under political geography. It was evident when Napoleon argued that every state pursues the politics of its own geography. It in fact deals with concepts like space, place, territory, policy, politics, power and equilibrium. Now, geopolitics has transcended the realm of political geography as it concerns the spatial requirements of a state. Whereas, political geography only examines its spatial conditions.[23] Therefore, geopolitics has often been applied from the national perspective or even bias of the originator as Taylor says:

> "...in the case of geopolitics, it has been very easy to identify the nationality of an author from the content of his or her writings."[24]

However, in the course of our discourse on geopolitics, we are likely to be overpowered by the dimensions, facets, intent and scales of geopolitics and defining the terms is restricting the fluidity of geopolitics as such, which invents and reinvents itself, for as Colin Flint says:

> "Why are we so focused on trying to define such a fluid and complex term when what makes it so interesting is that the definition is contested? I try to emphasize that Geopolitics (broadly the mutual construction of space and power relations) is both matter of practice (doing) and representation (justifying the doing)."[25]

It was evident in the case of the German Geopolitik of Haushofer and the Macedonisation and Balkanisation of South-East Europe by the US and NATO.

CLASSICAL GEOPOLITICS AND CHINA

When we trace the classical geopolitics, it can actually be traced back to Aristotle, Strabo, Montesquieu and Kant and travel up to the American political scientists like Edmund Walsh who revived the element of international justice in geopolitics and in establishing the role of the international justice system when he termed geopolitics to be:

> "...a combined study of human geography and applied political science... dating back to Aristotle, Montesquieu and Kant."[26]

Leaving out the precursors and searching for bold etchings of the founders of geopolitics, we can easily name Ratzel, Mackinder, Kjellen, Bowman, Mahan, Haushofer and Spykman effectively exercising geopolitical principles for strategizing the furthering of their own national interests.

Friedrich Ratzel (1844–1904)

Considered as the father of German Political Geography, he was a national scientist who based his geopolitical law on the 'organic' theories of state growth which befitted the future German expansion of what Cohen calls a youthful, aggressive, capitalist 'giant state' already unified by Bismarck and victorious over Austria and France.

As the geopolitical laws at that time remained confined to serving the national purpose and affected relations with most of the neighbouring countries, Ratzel's law also focused on the space of the nation (*raum*) its location (*lage*) that made it unique and the frontiers (*skins*) that either showed growth or decline. In accordance, with a new powerful fleet, Germany had posed a serious threat to Britain and France and had acquired territories expanding 'skins' in East and West Africa and the Western Pacific. His theorising of geopolitics however remained restricted to a nation's strategy to expand it like an organism. However, the space, location and *Lebensraum* (living space) came in active use of geopolitical determinism of that time. This has been expressed in a similar expansion of the Qing Emperors in the 19th Century to occupy Tibet and Xinjiang and during the nationalist period that will be discussed later in detail.

Halford J. Mackinder (1861–1947)

Halford J. Mackinder (1861–1947), foresaw a threat to the guarantee of the British world hegemony through its naval power and growing influence of land mass to accumulate and command resources and move them from one place to other with the advent of railroads like the Union Pacific (1861), Berlin–Baghdad (1896), and Trans-Siberian Rail (1905). He realized the futility of sea power and the immunity of deeper land masses from sea powers, specially the Eurasian lowland and theorised that land as a pivot area in 1904.[27] He was in awe of the superiority of rail over ships in terms of time and reach and was also in awe of the advantages he visualised for countries with a great land mass at that time like Germany, Russia and even China. And he therefore believed that the land powers will outmaneuver the maritime powers. Slowly, the influence of land mass power grew on the minds of the geographers of maritime countries. After 11 years, an English geographer, James Fairgrieve, expanded the Pivot Area into the Heartland and found that China had the advantage of a deep land-based immunity and a maritime trade flexibility over Eurasia.[28] Impressed by the inclusiveness of the term Heartland and compounded by the advances in land transport, industrialisation, population growth and availability of natural resources, Mackinder included larger areas around the Pivot Area in his book *Democratic Ideals and Realities* (1919), which included Eastern Europe as well.[29] Juxtaposing the power of the Heartland, he feared the British colonial power diminishing and called for North America and Europe to unite to evolve a North Atlantic Community to rebalance the power.

He also propagated to unite the Atlantic Community and the Asian Heartland (mainly Russia and subsequently, the USSR) to come together to check the German ambitions.[30] He also talked of 'Mantle of Vacancies', akin to what Cohen calls these days as 'Shatter Belts' and 'Compression Zones' starting from the Central Asian region to the Sahara and the Amazon. He categorised India and China as a monsoonal belt and third balancing region in what he called as 'Asiatic Monsoonal Land' which in the concurrent period is geopolitically the most active region.

Map 8: An Expression of Mackinder's Pivot Area

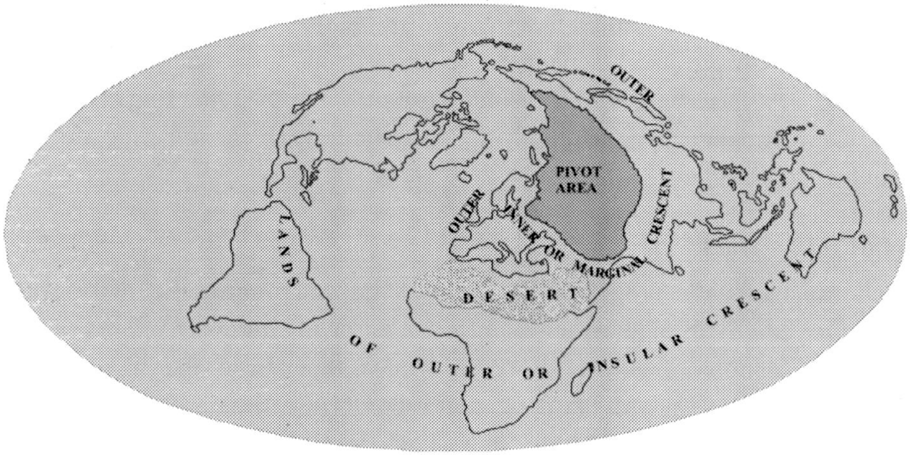

In his overall assessment Mackinder who gave the dictum in 1919 that 'who rules the Eastern Europe commands the Heartland, who rules the Heartland commands the world', gave an ideological justification to Haushofer to propound the expansionist German Geopolitik to seek 'Lebensraum'. But by 1943, with the advent of air power and the vulnerability of the Heartland, Mackinder in an article 'The Round World and Winning of Peace' discarded the Heartland as key to commanding the world and rather asked the entire world island to command the world—an unwitting similarity between his theorising of 1919 and the Cold War and his 1943 views and post-Cold War American policy of balance of power goals. Mackinder's geopolitics was very fluid in nature. Though it looks rigid due to its adoption by the German Geopolitik, but it did have influence over world affairs for nearly seventy years with intensity and still has relevance as a foundation for theorising power relations in the new world order that is emerging. With regard to China's place in his scheme of things, he in fact feared that one day China would conquer Russia and if Eurasia conjoined with Africa to form the world Island, then China as Eurasia's largest continental nation and with a coastline in both the Tropics and the Temperate Zone would occupy the globe's most advantageous position.[31] Mackinder says in 'Democratic Ideals and Realities' that along with the United States and Great Britain, China would eventually guide the world by building for a quarter of humanity, a new civilisation—neither quite Eastern nor quite Western.[32] He certainly saw no leading role for Great Britain—a country deriving power out of the US. However, he gives a definite hint for China to emerge as a superpower not then, but later. The changing world of Mackinder elucidates so in the future, as given below:

Map 9: Mackinder's Ever-Expanding Heartland

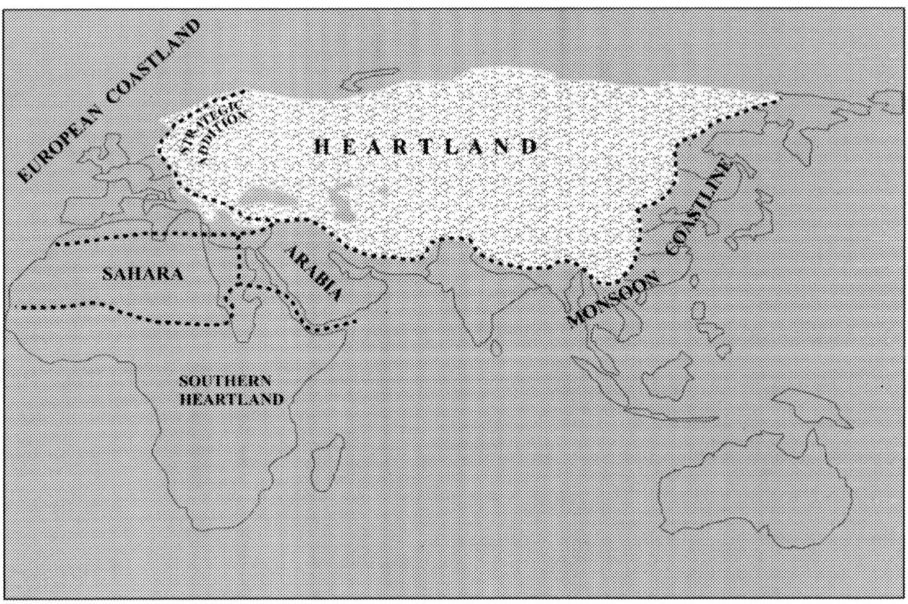

Admiral Alfred T. Mahan (1849–14)

A naval officer and president of the United States Naval War College, he saw geopolitics from a naval-accessibility point of view and remained focused on Eurasia. He recognised access through Panama and Suez as the key to world power and Russia as unassailable. His prediction about the Anglo-American alliance surrounding Eurasia has been near-true, of course, with the help of Germany and Japan post-World War II. He avowed the US as a Trans-Atlantic extension of European civilisation and interests. He propagated to extend the area of influence of European culture across the Pacific and come to the Eurasian shores on the east. Therefore, he strongly supported the US annexing the Philippines, Hawaii,

Guam and Puerto Rico along with the control of the Panama Canal Zone. For this, he espoused "a blue water strategy'" and strong navy which was endorsed by President Roosevelt.[33] Mahan considered China as the eastern half, i.e. as a part of his two-fold global framework—one on the outer side of Asia and the other of Europe and America. It was actually his initiative that we see China contained from the east through what China calls the first and second chains of islands—of Taiwan, Philippines, Indonesia, Japan, Korea and Guam. He actually pre-empted the importance of Eurasia or mainly Asia that Mackinder brought out in the form of the Pivot and Heartland.

Rudolf Kjellen (1864–1922)

Kjellen considered five major elements and their study in order to understand the state. These were econo-demo-souo and crato (power) politics. As all these elements were to occur in geographical space, the geopolitics that Kjellen discovered in 1899 subsumed all these five elements. He considered that political processes were spatially determined. He considered geopolitics to be a science of state in which the state's natural environment provided the framework for the power unit's pursuit of "inexorable law of progress".[34] Also, a giant state in Europe could only be created by war. He has viewed geopolitics as primarily a science of war.[35]

Although he was Swedish and a conservative member of the Swedish Parliament, he viewed geopolitics as a science of war and believed that Germany's emergence as a great power was inevitable as well as desirable, thus giving the first whip to the emergence of German Geopolitik. Germany did become a giant state but was divided in World War I and humiliated in the Treaty of Versailles, and thus made a fair ground for Karl Haushofer to revive the concept. He however did not have a vision for China as such.

Karl Haushofer (1869–1946)

Karl Haushofer led a group of German geopoliticians like Otto Maull, Erich Obst, Evald Lanse, Richard Henning, Colin Ross and Albert Haushofer and propounded the concept 'Geopolitik' for Germany, actually based upon the postulates of Kjellen, Ratzel and Mackinder. Haushofer posited his 'official' definition of 'Geopolitik' as:

> "The doctrine of the earth's relations of political developments... based on the broad foundations of geography, particularly political geography, as the doctrine of political space organisms and their structures."[36]

Although Mackinder's Heartland was the main allurement for Haushofer's German Geopolitik, the five major elements were originally to his credit, on which we can examine even the present Chinese geopolitical patterns and positions.

First is the concept of LEBENSRAUM—a term for ample space and resources for the people of a nation—as a right and duty of the nation to provide for. The growing population meant a growing demand for space and resources, thus a growing friction among the nations leading to a changing power structure. He considered it a duty of the state to provide for space and resources and a stronger nation does that at the cost of the weaker ones. For Haushofer, the growth of a state was like the growth of an organism based on biological laws and in order to obtain Lebensraum, a state may resort to expansion by direct or indirect methods or a 'just war'.[37] From China's perspective, the sovereignty claims on the South China Sea with its Nine Dash Lines and subsuming Xinjiang and Tibet is appearing exactly the same ploy to expand the territory to muster more resources for a growing population with an ambition to bring them out of poverty. Militarily, China is poised against the weaker nations around the South China Sea. In addition China is using direct (Just War) and indirect economic hegemony and political relations, to exploit the resources of the world.

'Autarky' was Haushofer's second element of Geopolitik—a geographical construct of economic self-sufficiency. It posited that a state must produce everything it needs in order to attain an independence from imports. In that term, only Mackinder's notion of Heartland stands out. But how far Chinese land mass only considered an eastern extension of Heartland stands out in terms of its potential to attain 'Autarky' will be examined in another chapter of this book when we discuss the economic evolution and its imperatives. However, at this stage it can be safely said that in the backdrop of the WTO regime and present international order, China will move towards 'Autarky' through different courses or routes based not on independence but dependence on other countries.

The most interesting concept of 'Pan-region' by Haushofer brings out the longitudinal pan-regions, i.e. any nation to have become a region due to related geographical needs and realities of cooperation or conflict. Cooperation and conflict mainly depend on firstly, similar speech and culture and secondly, people of related speech and culture. In China, this factor has been a source of cooperation as well as conflict. As for the outside world, the East Asian culture or in broader terms, the culture of Asia-Pacific appears similar if not the same. But it has enough differences within China, and outside China to cause conflict. And that is why what Haushofer has given Pan Asia as a region, has a striking similarity with the present-day Asia-Pacific region that has become the centre of attention for world geopolitics.[38]

Map 10: 'Pan Regions' by Haushofer

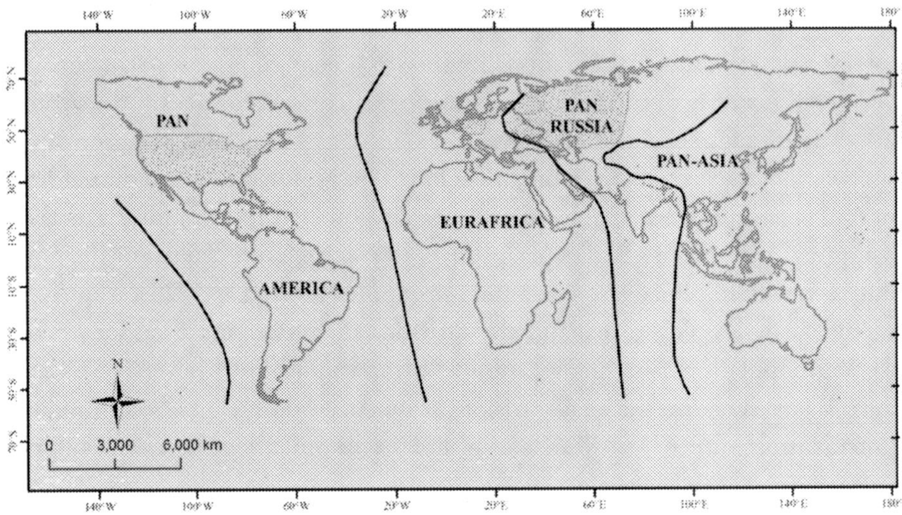

Haushofer further expanded the pivot to the entire land mass of Eurasia and Africa and considered it as the centre of gravity and sufficient land mass for the fulfilment of 'Autarky'. In his idea of land powers versus sea power, a notion adopted from Mackinder, he also visualised a crescent around this land mass as sea power like the British Isles and the Japanese Archipelago as great sea powers due to their location to contain the exit to the seas. America, Australia and New Zealand were considered as sluggish out-crescents. Although he undermined the continentality of the Americas, especially North America and the US, he brought out Japan adequately, for causing a geopolitical choking to China on its eastern fringes and that remains a key component in the containment of China in the Asia-Pacific till date.

The fifth concept of Haushofer is the '**Frontier**' that for him always remains fluid and dynamic, and which does not guarantee permanency by legal means of any treaty or international regulators or by the confines of natural physical obstruction considered as borders. For him, they merely remain a temporary halt and a breathing spell in a nation's march to his adequate Lebensraum and Autarky. What can we call the Chinese expansion or the inclusion of Tibet and Xinjiang? What can we call China's claim across the watershed of Himalayas into Arunachal

Pradesh of India, where China does not accept natural hurdles of Himalayas as boundary and the region across as untenable if acquired and persists on its claim?

Nicholas Spykman (1893-43)

While there was a clear trend emerging in the US to repudiate the German Geopolitik after Haushofer justified the expansionist designs of Germany and gave Hitler an geopolitical framework for capturing the Heartland, the Office of the Chief Counsel of the US on September 7, 1945 derogating geopolitics, declared it to be driving the dynamic plan for German conquests and Hitler's territorial ambitions.[39] It was in this tinted US perception of geopolitics as a subject that Spykman reflected upon the views of Mahan and propounded his 'Rimland' theory and posited that the Eurasian coastal lands including of those Maritime Europe, the Middle East, India, South-East Asia and China were key to Eurasia (Heartland) and could control the destiny of the world. Spykman's 'Rimland' was in fact akin to Mackinder's marginal crescent and his offshore regions of American continents and other islands were actually Mackinder's outer crescent and sought to arouse the US against his fear of Germany controlling the European 'Rimland' and then controlling the world alone and this was therefore, required to be checked by the US, British and Soviet Alliance.[40]

To make the 'Rimland' and its control too crucial by Spykman was a fault as it was never possible from the beginning for a country or an alliance of a country to control the entire 'Rimland'. Moreover, countries like China had a rim as well as the interiors reaching up to the heartland of Eurasia and the offshore powers could be only a strategic advantage to continental powers like the US. That is why when the US attacked North Korea and North Vietnam, it got defeated by the continental power China using the depth of its land to attack the seaboard. However, combined with Mahan's maritime power and choke points of the concentrated sea routes, the 'Rimland' countries do become very important along with the role of Mackinder's outer crescent islands, what Spykman called offshore continents and islands. Although China is itself a part of the Rimland, it faces the constriction of various choke points for its sea trades going west and a total blockage condition while going east by the second island chain.

Geopolitics in the Cold War period and China

The phrase 'Cold War' basically denotes a forty-year period of ideological confrontation escalated by a commensurate military built-up starting from the end of World War II and ending with the fall of the Berlin Wall in 1989. The term 'Cold War' was first used by an American journalist Walter Lippmann in 1947.[41] But some attribute the term to the famous English writer George Orwell who had predicted the post-World War II period to be period of nuclear stalemate between the United States and the former USSR, perhaps indicating to the growing cold feet towards any direct action by both against each other. 'Geopolitics' per se had become a taboo during the Cold War period and put out of the use in the US as well as in the former USSR due to its association with the Nazi regime. However, on a closer examination, geopolitics always appeared lying under its skin as Brzezinski says:

> "... the contest between the United States and the Soviet Union represented the fulfilment of the geopolitician's fondest theories: it pitted the world's leading maritime power, dominant over both the Atlantic and Pacific Oceans, against the world's leading land power, paramount on the Eurasia heartland (with the Sino-Soviet bloc on composing a space reminiscent of the scope of the Mongol Empire). The geopolitical dimension could not have been clearer: North America Vs Eurasia, with the world at stake. The winner would truly dominate the globe. There was no one else to stand in a way, once victory was finally grasped."[42]

The above comment sums up the probable outcome of the cold war which was reversed by the collapse of the USSR, but it certainly underpins the classical geopolitical theories working in the subconscious minds of the policymakers like the American diplomat George F. Kennan, who played a crucial role in the making of American policies against the former Soviet Union. Kennan, who was trained on Russia in Germany, certainly had moorings in the German School of Geopolitik and had adopted this vision when he was posted to the US embassy in Moscow between 1944 and 1946. He sent a report to the US, bringing out the expansionist tendencies of the former USSR and opposed the wartime marriage of convenience with the former USSR.[43] He also highlighted the need for containment of expansionist tendencies of the Soviet Communism around every point of Heartland in his article 'The Source of Soviet Conduct'.[44] He also presented the former Soviet Union as the main enemy of the US and said that the US must continue to regard it as a rival and not a partner in the political arena and that the policy with regard to the former Soviet Union should be a 'long term, patient, but firm and vigilant containment of Russian expansionist tendencies'.[45] Thus, the concept of containment was first introduced. There were many other such political strategic concepts like 'Domino theory', 'Balance of Power Linkages' and 'Linchpin States' that were introduced into the lexicon of the Cold War geopolitics. The communism as an ideology was spreading not only around former USSR in East Europe and China but also across the Atlantic in the US and Cuba. Kennan's policy paradigms against the former USSR were adopted in the Truman Doctrine in 1947. In 1950, John McCarthy headed a committee to investigate the spread of communism. The instigating of the people to make Intercom under the influence of the Soviet Union possible was termed as creating a 'domino effect' within the world as a biological organisation.[46] In this context, China was one prominent country that became communist under this 'domino effect' that will be analysed while discussing the evolution of Chinese polity.

Under the Truman Doctrine, NATO came into existence against the threat from the Soviet aggression, considering that the world was body and the former Soviet Union was a disease and the USA was its protector. Thus, the world was divided into friendly and unfriendly spaces in purely binary terms.[47]

The communist geopolitical view which saw all the hitherto existing human history as the history of class struggle, argued that

> "Nation states were managed by the capitalist class to promote their collective interest against their workers, against capitalist of other countries and sometimes, in self-restraint to shorten the longer term viability of the system in face of its self-destructive anarchy."[48]

There was no obvious IR theory in it but an ideological framework, the acceptance of which became a virtual inclusion of a country into the communist fold with the former Soviet Union as its head, creating a kind of loose confederation around the heartland first, and then as far and vide as the Caribbean and the South America—clearly, a 'domino effect' and a result of latent geopolitical intent as was brought out by Brzezinski. However, the US policymakers did not overtly recognise the geopolitics playing any role in their policymaking. Rather, they credited their policies to various IR theories—only in a denial mode. The containment of the former USSR against the 'domino effect' became the main stay of their IR policy but the line of containment always conformed to Mackinder's East Asia and Spykman's Rimland to position the NATO forces, and seeking for allies in these peripheries became a geopolitical compulsion. William Bullit who propounded the 'Domino Theory', feared that the Soviet Communist Power would spread through China to South-East Asia and elsewhere through other Third World countries. Therefore, the US intervention in Vietnam was considered as a measure to save the rest of South-East Asia from the Russia–China axis.[49] the 'Domino Effect' subsequently became an alibi for the containment policy to be implemented in the Middle East, the Horn of Africa, Sub-Saharan Africa, Central America and Cuba.

A spatial interrelation between two places of the world otherwise faraway, means that they have a cause and effect linkage geopolitically. This principle of linkage was introduced by Henry Kissinger on the premise that all the troubled spots of the world had a direct linkage with the former USSR and espoused that any win or loss by the US anywhere in the world would have an impact upon the overall superpower balance and erode the credibility of the US in the other parts of the world. Therefore, the linkage was actually a geopolitical linkage.[50] Linkage was also applied to a detente with the former Soviet Union and accommodation with China to maintain a balance of power. The linkages were well established before the US and China decided to come close as Henry Kissinger describes the impelling geopolitical situation well:

> "By the time the impossible pair of Richard Nixon and Mao Zedong decided to move towards each other, both of their countries were in the midst of upheaval. China was nearly consumed by turmoil of the Cultural Revolution; America's political consensus has strained by the growing protest movement against the Vietnam War. China faced the prospect of war on all its frontiers – especially its northern borders, where actual clashes between Soviet and Chinese forces were taking place."[51]

The effect of this 'anti-domino' policy of the US was that the balance of power tilted in favour of the US and with the playing of China against the former Soviet Union, the US could bring about Moscow on the issues of strategic arms limitation and mutual nuclear deterrence. China's coming closer to the US however caused Brezhnev to espouse the doctrine that used military power to hold on to the socialist countries of Eastern and Central Europe.[52]

Whatever may be the cover-up till the arrival of Kissinger and Brzezinski, who brought back geopolitics to the US as factor for determining the US foreign policy, the US was always considered as a maritime power against the former USSR, a land-based power. Therefore, to contain the land-based powers, the US under Brzezinski decided to control places on the maritime routes and access points to the Heartland defined by their geographical positions, and to exert economic/military influence. These states containing these places were termed as linchpin states. By controlling the linchpin states of South Korea, Japan and Philippines, and the Malay Straight, the US actually ensured that China could not be controlled by the former USSR.[53] However, in order to pursue its own policies of superpower balance of power politics, which involved the superpowers and their allies, neither of them took care of other geographically potential powers like China and India which were not part of the NATO or Warsaw Pact and also weak and unstable allies, especially of the communist bloc.

As with Henry Kissinger reviving geopolitics for his balance of power politics and its dynamics, the geographers moved from the bipolar to different approaches, applied to the discourse of geopolitics. As per Cohen, three approaches dominated the latter part of the Cold War period: polycentric international power system, economically ordered system and socially ordered system. While Mackinder rejected his own proposition in his last writing of 1943, looking with hindsight, the Cold War geopolitics followed his geographical pattern of geopolitics in the control of the Heartland by the former USSR and the containment of the former USSR by the USA by control of Rimland. This was challenged by the geographers who engaged themselves in dealing with geopolitics through a polycentric and multi-nodal/multilevel approach. Although they evolved their theories in the latter half of the Cold War period itself, however, we shall discuss them in brief under the next heading because they emerged as a rejection to the Cold War-period geopolitics.

GEOPOLITICS IN THE POST-COLD WAR PERIOD AND CHINA

Geopolitics in the post-Cold War era has a global perspective instead of the West vs. Communist and land power vs. maritime power perspective. A Basic fault line emerged as these two superpowers could no more sustain the unproductive expenditure on their global efforts to maintain the balance of power—perhaps the geopoliticians had foreseen the non-viability of that kind of world order. Therefore, economic integration had been taking place regionally despite political divisions. The world moved towards free commerce for sustenance. Therefore, the controlled economies collapsed. The political collapse followed the economic collapse. The geopolitics reinvented itself from the geopolitical structure of the country itself, to the regions around and then to the global linkages. This simple explanation of structure also did not survive for long as communication and information started moving long distances in the entire globe faster than to the next village. The space and place appeared more virtual then actual. It appeared to some that territory and international borders had become less significant in shaping human affairs and commentators like Richard O'Brian referred to 'the end of geography' as a new dictum.[54] The communication speed also gave connectivity and spread of own presence based on religious lines. Samuel Huntington declared that the politics of the new era will be played along the civilisation fault lines and did not give much credit to economic linkages in his article, 'The Clash of Civilisations' published in 1993 in Foreign Affairs.[55] Then there were other thought processes like Cohen's new structures of global geopolitics, GR Chrome's Ten Regional Groupings, Peter Taylor's World Systems Approach, Wallenstein's Single Global Society based on economic inter-dependence, and Georg Modelski's Model of Cycles of World Power. These theorisations do require a little elaboration to put China in the perspective of modern geopolitical dynamics of globalised, informationised space age.

Cohen's Geopolitical Structure

Over a period of time, geographical and political forces have interacted in a certain fashion leading to a hierarchal geopolitical structure in which the entire space of the globe can be organised.[56]

Cohen's structures are primarily based on two major physical and human geographical settings; maritime and the continental realm. Both are considered complimentary to each other, with the ability of the land near the sea having the potential to progress faster. These structures are also carried out with a balance in centrifugal and centripetal forces. At a national level, both are linked to territoriality.[57] These structures are shaped by a balance or equilibrium between the forces of separation (centrifugal) and the forces of integration (centripetal). While centrifugal forces may be manifested in the desire of people of a geographical space to maintain a different linguistic, cultural and religious identity and eventually wanting to establish a different political system while at the same time, centripetal forces may compel these geographical spaces to remain united against a danger of even greater linguistic, cultural and religious differences. Such forces of unity are manifested in national actions in the areas such as commerce, communication, military defence and foreign affairs and even in the regional action of confederation with another state. At a global level, the balance between these forces of integration and separation was affected by the imperialist system, destroyed by World War II and again balanced by the Mutually Assured Destruction between the US-led capitalist realm and the Soviet–Chinese led communist realm. It was then followed by the Chinese delineation from Soviet-led realm due its nationalist geopolitics taking over idealist geopolitics. After the demise of the Soviet Union, China was provided with an opportunity to emerge as an independent strategic realm. In this background, it becomes relevant to discuss Cohen's structures of the world. Cohen divides the globe into multilevel structures based on the maturity of regional cohesion. The geostrategic realm, the geopolitical regions and the nation states have no sacrosanct guarantee of unity forever, but each hierarchal structure has common geopolitical features.

(a) **The Geostrategic Realm**: At the top of the spatial hierarchy of the global structure these realms have been constructed by either conditions of 'maritimity' or 'continentality' or a combination of both. Cohen divides the globe in to three realms; Atlantic and Pacific trade-dependent maritime realm, Eurasian Continental Russian Heartland realm; and a mix of continental East Asia with China in the pivot and emerging South Asia realm with India in the centre.[58] China, in the perspective of a mixed realm, has been oscillating between the continental and maritime geostrategic dispositions historically. Now after Mao, China has clearly tilted in favour of a positioning itself as a maritime realm due to economic and commercial reasons, but we cannot assume a permanency in this tendency. Therefore, this structural oscillation of China will be discussed in detail when we discuss geospatial and geo-economic evolution China.

(b) **The Geopolitical Region:** It is a subdivision of the geostrategic realm at a meso-level region based on geographical contiguity and political, cultural, economic and military interaction and migration and intermixing of people and shared heritage. The East Asian Realm, therefore, has been divided into two regions: Mainland China and Indochina (Vietnam, Cambodia and Laos).

(c) **Nation States:** Nation states are highly autonomous regions; quasi-states and territorial sub-divisions within and across the states have been kept at the lowest end or micro-level. This division within delimited international political boundaries is of much relevance to China as it does recognise several regions as autonomous regions due to the presence of centrifugal forces. This will attract a detailed discussion in the next chapter.

(d) **Shatter-belts:** Cohen finds that there are certain areas of the globe, big or small, that cannot be at present unified by the force of integration and thus remain scattered like shattered glass. He defines Shatter Belts as the 'strategically oriented' regions that are both deeply divided internally and caught up in the competition between great powers of the 'geostrategic realms'.[59] These areas because they are not organised, fall prey to a power play of the geostrategic realm and regions which have equal opportunity to exercise their hegemony over these. These regions in a way absorb a lot of shock emerging from these power plays, manifested in resource exploitation and military interventions because of a lesser degree of cohesiveness but due to an internal power of independence, do not succumb to this power but do succumb to diplomacy. Such shatter belts of lesser magnitude have been termed by Cohen as Conversance Zones or Compression Zones. China did start the power play in the Middle East shatter belt, Sub-Saharan Compression Zone and the Eurasian Convergence Zones of Central Asia due to its resource imperatives that will be discussed in the subsequent chapters.

Map 11: Cohen's Convergance Zones, Compression Zones and Shatter Belts

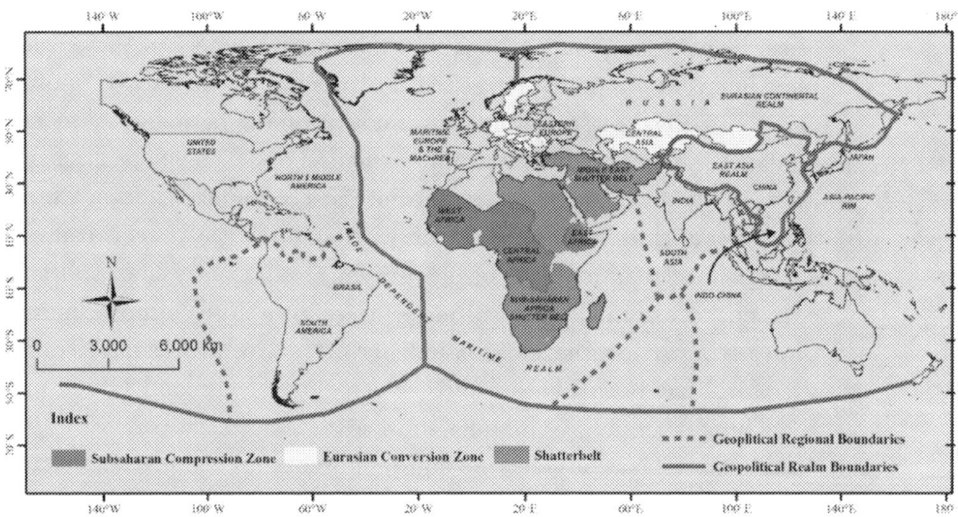

Geopolitical Features Common to Hierarchical Structures

Cohen has described several features of verifying functions and scales that are common to all structures and more relevant to analysing the internal structure of the nation state and more relevant as a parameter for analysing a country of continental size like China. These conceptual parameters are good to analyse the geopolitical evolution of China through history and the concurrent geopolitical layout and the implications thereof.

Historic and Nuclear Core: A nation germinates at a particular place or area and expands around it due to an interaction between the physical environment of this core and the political–cultural system. This process subsequently shapes the national and regional identity. The same is equally true of China, as China has one of the most clearly defined cores which evolves itself around Xian and in the Loess plains and the Huang He basin historically.

Capital or Political Centre: Every politically defined structure has capitals or centres which become focus of activities. These may be selected due to geographical centrality, defensive quality, being a commanding location of the frontiers or as spring boards for territorial acquisition. China's capitals through its history have been shifting owing to these reasons and have become a curious element of analysis.

Ecumenes: Evolved for the reasons of most intense interactions between peoples and their geographical environment, the ecumenes of Cohen manifest in the population growth and concentration and are now flustered with fast telecommunication. However, concrete benefits are ultimately accrued to these ecumenes of the structure. China's development of ecumenes closer to South and East China is therefore will also be analysed in this book.

Effective National Territory and Effective Regional Territory: These are the areas of favourable resource bases but moderately populated having a potential for expansion and growth. It applies very well to China as the distribution of resources is such that the hinterland is now being developed after the potential of the coastal areas has been fully exploited and the communication to the hinterland developed.

Empty Area: With least prospect for dense population settlements, these areas may provide defensive depth, space for weapon testing and an important source of certain minerals. The territorial expanse of China in the west will be analysed on these parameters subsequently.

Boundaries: The marking of boundaries is basically a kind of linear delimitation of national space wherein the consent of the country across is imperative, otherwise it leads to conflicts. For China, historically, this becomes a major issue of discourse for the reason of conflict with its neigbhours.

Non-Conforming Sectors: These are the areas inhabited by minorities, which do not conform to the rules and aspirations of the majority. If these areas are situated on the periphery, the problem automatically gets compounded. With abetment from across the border, China has full potential for the growth of such problems around its boundary with more intense potential in the west due to the distance from the core and therefore, this will be analysed in detail to bring out the imperatives for China in this regard.

Cohen propounded these concepts by modelling, like the plat tectonic theory of the earth's evolution and posits that these structural realms, regions and states are fluid and dynamic in nature, therefore keep mending fences as the overall geopolitical environment develops and new imperatives emerge. Shatter belts, compression zones and convergence zones act as a buffer stock, including certain areas and excluding others.[60]

GEOSTRATEGY IN THE ELECTRONIC AND SPACE/ AEROSPACE AGE AND CHINA

What we have discussed so far is the two-dimensional space of the globe and the influence of the land and marine power in determining the balance of power or the lack of it. During the Cold War, the strategic deployment of air power and long-range bombers with a nuclear payload made the air power a dominant force. The strategists began to look at the globe, cartographically from a polar projection perspective and with the development of the Inter-Continental Ballistic Missiles and their capacity to carry a nuclear payload through the shortest trajectory. Again, the air power was relegated to theatre-specific tactical weaponry. It was only in the 1991 Gulf War that observers realised the predominance of conventional missiles and bombers as the RAF Air Vice Marshal Tony Mason observed: -

> "The Gulf War marked the apotheosis of twentieth century air power".[61]

These developments in coordinated air power strikes to neutralise the enemies before the ground forces capture and hold the ground, has demonstrated the relative leverage of an advanced air weapon in comparison to the advanced land forces. However, despite the air dominance, by no means the war could ever be won without the involvement of all forces in appropriately integrated fashion. Moreover, we did not see the involvement of space technology that was in the nascent stage but was used in the form of the Navstar Global Positioning System that came of age by providing a real-time navigation system used for targeting by all the coalition forces in the undistinguishable Iraqi desert terrain. GPS was the first cross-over enabler from space and a small step towards information, a task carried out by only 16 satellites in orbit, short of the number required for full coverage and 8 short of a complete network including 3 spare satellites.[62] The outer space also came into play when the Defence Support Programme's constellation of infrared sensing satellites began to detect the heat of the Scud rocket exhaust fume within 30 seconds of launch. Though originally not designed to detect a launch of short-range ballistic missiles, it did provide information about the Scud launch sites and its near-real-time coordinates to the F-15 E and Patriot missile defence crew.[63]

By then, the strategists had realised the potential of space leading to an astro-political analysis of space for evolving a geo-strategy at the onset of an air–space age. Jean Goldman argued that as the geography of the earth's surface led to the evolution of geopolitics, from space the earth becomes smooth like a billiard ball and loses its siginificance.[64] But what gains significance is the vital control of strategic space locations, pathways and choke points. The least any state can do if it wishes to remain sovereign or become a world power, is to prevent another state from gaining advantage by blocking its effort at control. It is actually similar to the geopolitics that is exercised on the earth's surface in classical terms.[65] Mahan had said regarding the oceans that they were, 'a wide common, over which men may pass in all directions but on which well-worth paths (emerge for) controlling reasons'.[66] And this is equally true for the space topology. For the control of these, competition is already on. Although going into technical details of territorial orbits, etc. is beyond the purview of this book, however, giving the four regions of space like that of Mackinder, control of which could dictate the political, military and economic fates of the territorial governments, will be relevant.[67] The key dynamics of air and space age geopolitics is in their fast transportational mode for information and military mobility used for access to and denial of access of adversaries. Space geopolitics also develops a true global perspective out of which new global geopolitical theories have emerged and will be discussed next.

Modelski's Model of World Leadership: From the perspective of geopolitical determinism, geographic size, internal make-up and location determine the power of a country, which manifests itself by economic, military and demographic elements. Such a powerful country is to set a global agenda that other countries more or less support. Modelski's cyclic model of world leadership is based on a power derived on global reach or else, the most potent naval power and its ocean-going capacity and the control of the oceans. His leader is not hegemonic, but he represents his followers. Although the basic premise is taken from classical geopolitics but the mainstay of power remains as the innovation of all kinds—whether ideas, practices or institutions—to establish a geopolitical agenda for the world in a most modern manner which appear convincing to all followers or by innovation in the field of material power for all to follow. The model is a dynamic one, which sets a cycle of world leadership of 100 years with four phases of 25 years each.[68]

(a) **Phase of Global War**: A new leader emerges and challenges the authority of the declining leader either as an enemy or in coalition in a condition of global war in which one country shows material capacity and ideological ascendency to impose a new global order.

(b) **Phase of World Power**: In this phase which comes after victory, the new leader implements the new agenda and ideological conduct is shaped during the first phase through new institutions.

(c) **Phase of Delegitimation**: Over a period of time, the world leader welcomes the new leader of the new order and appears self-serving, therefore is increasingly challenged. Alternative agendas crop up and new leaders emerge. However, the world leader still remains stronger than the challengers.

(d) **Phase of Deconcentration**: When the challenges and challengers become stronger, the material and ideological capacity of the world leader gets exhausted. On the other hand, as he is called upon to respond to the challenges more militarily than morally and ideologically, the world leader's legitimacy is questioned, and the challenge intensifies as a new leader emerges.

Modelski's model is clearly made deductively, tracing evidence from the history of the world leaders. He seeks his evidence from circa 1500 BC onwards and brings out the following cycles of world leaders:

World Leader	*Century*	*Global War Period*	*Challengers*	*Coalition*
Portugal	1500s	1494-1516	Spain	Northern lands
Netherlands	1600s	1580-1609	France	England
Great Britain	1700s	1680-1733	France	Russia
Great Britain	1800s	1792-1815	Germany	US plus allies
United States	1900s	1914-1945	Soviet Union	NATO/Coalition

Courtesy: Colin Flint.

Here, Modelski's model still considers the former Soviet Union as a Cold War challenger, now turned into Russia, still challenging the US on its moral ascendency and authority over the Iran, Syria and Ukraine imbroglio. The al-Qaeda remains a challenger despite Osama bin Laden being killed by the US in Pakistan. But I would argue that China has now emerged from its peaceful development and has challenged the US authority in the Asia-Pacific as this theatre emerges as a centre of global geopolitical attention. It is also evident that the US has not been able to cleanly resolve the problems for which it had militarily intervened in Iraq, Afghanistan and is now focusing all its energies in the Asia-Pacific or Indo-Pacific. China's economy is on an ascendance while the US economy is on decline; both the countries are in the Fourth Phase of Modelski's model. But how potent is the new emerging power that is China, to put up a credible challenge to the US is a serious matter of discourse of this book which evaluates China's capacity to sustain a global war and emerge as a world leader. Else it will accept a second place and allow the US to have a second cycle as world leader as it happened for the Great Britain for which Colin Flint seems more positive.[69] The application of this model is going to be of immense benefit in our subsequent analysis of China as an emerging power specially when China is losing its credibility morally and ideologically post Corona Pandemic when it had a chance to come up better against the US for its access of military use.

Wallenstein and Peter Taylor's World System Theory

It is pertinent to discuss in brief this theory here as it has a similarity with Modelski's model wherein it posits that a power emerges in a global conflict, but it is not one country that is all important as a leader. Rather, it is a system that shapes the society which overpowers the other types of societies. In this case, they consider the capitalist world economy that has created a peculiar social system that has become a world system. This world system has benefited certain countries which exercise hegemonic power out of the benefits accrued and the US has certainly led this system. Since it is an economic system, it always tries to achieve a selfish goal or profit and is not aimed at benevolence by the world leader as Modelski argues. There is no outright leader, if there is one, like the US and it declines, there may come a period of world system without an outright dominant power or state.[70] This gives an optimism towards a non-conflict period ahead, and a multipolarity of the world system or order unlike Modelski's model, wherein a world leader has to emerge or reoccur to lead the world in a second cycle. But there is certainly no chance for a multipolar world in Modelski's system. China in the concurrent conflict of interest, with the US, is going to emerge as new leader or just another pole in a multipolar set-up as per Wallenstein. This will be analysed in the perspective of the direction that China and the US are taking.

Nationalism as a Tool of Geopolitics

Fluidity in geopolitics as discussed so far has been caused due to the globalisation of all kinds and opportunities and threats and leads us to discuss critical geopolitics which tries to sum up all the classical theories and their futilities in the face of globalisation, space-age informationisation and proliferation of techno-scientific risks. But it also does consider national identity as a goal as well as a tool of practising geopolitics. Therefore, there is a need to discuss nationalism as a tool for practising geopolitics. A nation has two aspects. At the very first instance it is identified with a state which is defined by its possession of sovereignty over a territory and its people and the state then becomes a primary political unit of the international system. This is the formal aspect of a nation. Then there is an informal aspect of the nation that is known as national identity which emanates from the desire of its people to weed out 'others' from 'us'. As the core element of conflict and struggle is difference, the identification of 'others' become identification of 'us' which is the group left out from the exclusion of 'others'. That is how the 'remaining' then organise themselves into a state, and homogeneity is thus created throughout and thus it becomes the national identity called 'us' differentiated from 'them'. More often than not, 'them' or 'others' are organised in a separate state and make up a different national identity and at times, are even regarded as an enemy. As Jenkins puts these phenomena:

> "...one of the things, 'we' have in common is our difference from 'others'. In the face of their difference, 'our' similarity comes in to focus. Defining, 'us' involves defining a range of 'them' also. When 'we' say something about 'others', we are often saying something about we discuss 'ourselves'.... At the boundary we discuss what 'we' are and what 'we' are no."[71]

This identification of 'us' from 'them' evolves over a period of time in a territory. Therefore, this identity of 'us' has a history and geography of its own. The interaction with the history and geography of 'others', becomes geopolitics in its primary stage. Therefore, the national identity governs the geopolitics with its immediate neighbourhood. Thereafter, the state's boundary becomes identical to the national boundary. At times, when the state's boundary shrinks, the national boundary remains where it was perceived to have been historically. This leads to the notion of nationalism when the sense of identity is focused upon the 'nation' rather than the state. But there is never a pure state which can become a pure nation or vice versa. Gurr T R says that nearly all states have such diverse groups which may define themselves as separate nations.[72] There are other cases where the national identity takes over other identities like linguistic or ethnic, like the US, and there are others which satisfy themselves with a reasonable autonomy within the state like in India.

Nationalism operates on two dynamics; one is the 'top down mode' and the other is the 'bottom up mode'. At times, both may work simultaneously for different group of peoples. In the top down mode, the state creates the sense of unity with equality, opportunity, symbols like the national flag and anthem and a cultural mythology of the nation.[73] Although today the US can be termed as the state governing nationality, but it was not without different cultural groups like the Chinese, Indians and African Americans suffering at the hands of the state.[74] In the bottom up mode, the desire of the larger group or ethnicity is to identify the factor of 'others' and their exclusion is stronger. Colin Flint terms these types of states as geopolitical anomalies and terms them as the nationalism of 'Ethnic Cleansing'. This ethnic cleansing is carried out either by expulsion or by eradication or ethnic expansion (if similar ethnicity is a minority across the contiguous border).[75]

All the above examples are available in the Chinese geopolitical overtures and are being used at different times for different purposes. The expulsion of ethnic Tibetans was carried out in the 1950s when the Dalai Lama had to flee to India. Eradication is a constant state process and a state policy to deal with ethnic extremism with a heavy hand. Ethnic expansion is a constant Chinese policy by which the state encourages the settling of the Han ethnicity into Tibet and Xinjiang and to render the Tibetans and Turks as a minority in their own region and expand the Han nationality's area. The state expansion method is used to claim areas across contagious borders like the Chinese claim over the Indian state of Arunachal Pradesh for which they use the premise of similar ethnicity that of the Tibetans Chinese, otherwise is making all efforts to render them as minority in their own region. What is most glaringly evident is that nationalism remains more concerned about territoriality and its expansion and becomes a realist tool of geopolitics of China. It is in this perspective that we should now discuss the theories and concepts of critical geopolitics in a globalised world because two things do not leave the space; the national interest does not leave the virtual and mental space, and the territoriality does not leave the geographical space of a nation. Especially in the case of China, it is a curious case of investigation as to how the state drums up nationality by propagating events of national humiliation to ramp up nationalism and in the bargain, keeps territoriality alive as unfinished agenda to obtain legitimacy for the communist government.

CRITICAL GEOPOLITICS AND CHINA

Critical geopolitics is aimed at revisiting the fundamental assumptions of classical geopolitics in the most modern perspective that helps the scholars to better understand the cultural origins, biases and theoretical limitations of classical geopolitics. As Simon Dalby articulated in 1991:

> "What is being argued for here is nothing less than a recognition of the importance of stating the political operation in terms of geographical understandings, recognising that geo-graphs are specifications of political realities, that have political effect. To construct critical political geographies is to argue that we must not limit our attention to a study of the geography of politics within pre-given, taken for granted, commonsense spaces but investigate the politics of the geographical specifications of politics. That is to practise critical geopolitics."[76]

It is clearly evident that in the modern world of prevailing chaos, proliferation of risks and pervasive disorder, there is a need to develop a critical perspective as the classical geopolitics have started to appear seductively oversimplistic and have counter-modern tendencies.[77] In the bargain, geography has also enlarged its scope of application as it has become inescapably social and political, geographing an earth and writing of cultural and political meaning about the world. Therefore, any discourse about Chinese geopolitics has to have this perspective more than any other. John Agnew has categorised geopolitics into three ages: civilisational geopolitics (the concept of Europe and British dominance), Naturalised geopolitics (of the inter-imperial rivalry) and ideological geopolitics of the Cold War period.[78] Critical geopolitics deconstructs the geopolitical traditions, makes these theories more pragmatic and relevant to the modern world, and brings out contemporary structures for relevant use. For heuristic research, critical geopolitics divides geopolitical studies into four types for analysis and critique.

Formal Geopolitics

It is considered as an arbitrary construct used for the motivated purposes of the state of originators in its political and cultural context, starting from Ratzel, Mahan, Kjellen, Mackinder, Haushofer, Spykman to the modern contemporary figures like Henry Kissinger and Zbignew Brzezinski. Critical geopolitics tries to use these theories in a most unorthodox fashion, detached from the context and purpose for which they made these theories. As Gearoid O Tuathail (Gerard Toal) says:

> "Critical geopolitics in other words sides to recover the geography and geopolitics of Geopolitical thought' while opposing any glib celebration of the so called 'timeless insights' of certain geopolitical masters."[79]

Mackinder did not realise the potential of the Americans especially the US and its continentality, maritimity of equal proportion and immunity as well as direct connectivity provided by the Pacific and Atlantic oceans. Similarly, the continentality of China with a limited maritimity was also not realised by him. He was rather more obsessed with the Pivot Area, connectivity to which with a sea opening in the east appeared more significant to him. In today's world order, a continentality and maritimity combination has become much more vital than mere continentality or mere maritimity. This argument will be used to explain China's geopolitical attributes in the subsequent chapters.

Practical and Popular Geopolitics

It utilises the implicit forms of inherited theoretical knowledge of geography and geopolitics and deploys the tacit cultural geographical discourses and reasoning for explaining and planning international political and military events based on informal everyday discourse and is described as commonsense geopolitics. This practical application of everyday geopolitics was manifested in Balkanisation as manifested in 'conditioning American foreign policy ambivalence towards the breakup of Yugoslavia and Bosnian War'.[80] Zbigniew Brzezinski took this ambivalence further by giving Bush an idea of the Global Balkans stretching from Turkey to the farthest reaches of Central Asia and down in to South and South-East Asia.[81] Ultimately, the Balkans have become a symbol of violence and instability due to a mixture of heterogeneous nationalities in one region. Although it is a part of Europe, it is not as much significant as the other parts of Europe were to Europe and the US. Therefore, the US could use the NATO forces for four years to settle a quagmire rather than to stabilise a geopolitically important region. It became a place to show a hegemon its force without any collateral geopolitical damage. Brzezinski when extended the Balkans up to Central Asia,[82] the NATO forces attacked Iraq and Afghanistan; the US could not create a decisive war and had to extricate itself without stabilising the areas because the geopolitical attributes were much more complicated. Critical Geopolitics, therefore, with its sensitivity to geographical difference and power of ethnocentric cultural construct in the era of technology-backed time–space compression, has given an opportunity for a different type of discourses for the different strategic value of places.

Structural Geopolitics

The basic premise being globalised economy dissolving the ability of any single country to control and manage its own economic destiny has led to a creative destruction of the Cold War international system. However, in 2008, a kind of 'economic domino' effect took place which took several emerging economies to the brink of failure without any forewarning, due to a dizzying pace because of which ascendance as well as crises take place. It has led to a structural process of informationisation based on international technology-enabled manufacturing and service sector, global telecommunication; transnational cultural experience through movement and media and has made the virtuality of space more significant then territoriality. Therefore, as Tauthail says 'Geopolitics is becoming postmodern'.[83]The third structure is made of a proliferation of risks created by a techno-scientific civilisation anywhere in the globe. Starting from nuclear proliferation to environmental poisoning, ozone depletion, global warming, breakdown and corruption of information systems and decapacitation of weapon systems, to the pervasiveness of risks, they all have gone beyond the rational calculation or imagination of humankind.

Omnipresence of three structures—globalisation, Informationisation and techno-scientific risks—have incited people to suggest that this marks the end of geopolitics, but critical geopoliticians do not subscribe to this notion as at the end of the process a place, space or states remains the ultimate target and not a void. Even if a virtual space is targeted, it certainly belongs to a civilisational group or state or religion which has flourished within its spatial dimensions. Cannot we say that if a server in India carrying information of the US is hacked, it is ultimately going to harm the US and affect the people in the US territoriality in the end? At the end of the discourse one aspect becomes amply clear that the more and more we travel into this modernity, the prevailing institutions and concepts of politics can neither grasp the situation nor can adequately respond. Therefore, the calculation of risk and loss is always a suspect. Therefore, the state is also always circumspect.[84] It is in this perspective that China's geopolitical options will be discussed.

About the Argument of the IR Theories vs. Geopolitical Theories

The 'versus' controversy began with Frederick Sondern writing articles in the *Reader's Digest* and *Current History* in 1941 about the Institute of Geopolitics:

> "The work of Major General Professor Dr Karl Haushofer and his Geographical Institute in Munich, with its 1000 scientists, technicians and spies (is causing great alarm).... These men are unknown to the public, even in the Reich. But their ideas, their charts, maps, statistics, information and plans have dictated Hitler's men from the very beginning."[85]

Clearly the alarmist reporting shrouded in mystery, created a public opinion against the German Geopolitik associated with invasion and mass murder. The American geographer Richard Hartshorne, who himself along with Isaiah Boman was associated with the office of the Strategic Service of the CIA to generate geographical intelligence for the US military, termed the entire concept of geopolitics as an intellectual power. This outright opprobrium led to a movement of sorts to discard geopolitical considerations in terms of the pure internaltional relations theories in determining the foreign policies. Interesting to mention is that International Relations (IR) became an independent academic discipline only in 1919, much after geopolitics as we reckon, to study and resolve the reasons of the 'unprecedented horrors of conflict', by the establishment of a Chair of International Politics at the university of Wales in Aberystwyth and subsequently in 1920, the first Department of International Relations was founded in the London School of Economics.[86] As it became evident, the IR gained currency as a 'discipline for conflict prevention' and against geopolitics, 'the discipline of war' in the US after the World War II. In the present discourse here, our aim is to discuss the IR theories and examine the assumptions and see if there is any convergence between IR and geopolitics.

IR is an incredibly broad field, the theories of which emerge from the debates; realism versus idealism, realism versus behaviouralism, realism versus pluralism globalism and neo-realism versus post-structuralism/post-modernism. Therefore, the discipline has always remained a loose assortment of distinct but related theories despite their aim for discovering the idealist plank of conflict prevention. The aftermath of World War I was dominated by liberal internationalism on the premise that the basic human nature was good and it will help in prevention of war by means of international law, treaties and negotiations through the League of Nations.[87] This Wilsonian premise subsequently fell flat as it could not prevent World War II. Post-World War II, idealism gave way to realism by a range of US-based writers, like E.H. Carr who presented a critique of idealism in his book *The Twenty-Two Years Crisis* and a subsequent book of Hans Morgenthau, who in 1948 propounded a grand theory of IR. Not denying the role of morality, law and diplomacy, the realists emphasise 'armed might as an instrument of peace'.[88] They argued that idealist values did require the threat of force for their maintenance. Going into details about the different theories within the discipline of IR, the stream of theories revolves around the argument put up by Fred Halliday:

> *"International Relation (IR) has occupied, often a marginal place in the study and teaching of Social Sciences. Yet its subject matter is in the simplest terms,*

> *clear enough, comprising three forms of interaction – relation between states, non-state or transitional relations across frontiers, and the operations of the system as a whole, within which states and the societies are main components. While they may vary in the stress, they lay on each of these forms of interaction; all theories of 'international relation' propose some explanation of each: indeed the major debates within IR revolve, to greater or lesser extent, around these three dimensions and primacy of one or the other.'*[89]

It is clearly seen that nowhere does geopolitics find any reference in any of the theories, premises and assumptions. However, realism is found to be the most practised with challenges thrown in from pluralists, transitionalists and globalists to ultimately say that states are no more an effective agent of power. But that is what is said by the critical geopolitics as well. However, realism in IR was reborn after World War I and developed on of its own after World War II, despite the US foreign policy persisting on following interventionist idealism during the Cold War period. Ultimately, it was the realist theory of IR followed by Henry Kissinger and Kenneth Waltz in the policymaking of the US that led to reinventing relations with China and consequently recognising the role of geopolitics in the US's IR policies.

Therefore, as the realism in IR recurs, geopolitics resurges on a parallel track and the IR policies take advantage of the understanding of both to get formulated. As we bring out the common assumptions of realism by Nicholson that are practised in everyday statecraft, we shall able to discuss their affinity with geopolitics:[90]

(a) States are dominant actors in international affairs.
(b) National interest justifies pursuance of power by the states.
(c) Relationship between and among the states does not depend upon the type of regime.
(d) Anarchy prevails in the inter-nation system due to lack of a central sovereign regulatory authority.
(e) National interest is collective interest of the human beings of the state which changes with realities and needs of time and space, thus causes conflict which becomes an ever-present reality.
(f) Order and security is a direct function of balance of power between and among the nations maintained by shifting alliances not allowing any one or a group to become so powerful that causes threat to peace and security.
(g) International laws and institutions are effective only when backed by force.

It has been prolifically evident that the 'states' in whatever notion, have been defined, have always existed despite the parallel existence and propagation of pluralism, trans-nationalism, globalism, idealising and hoping for national boundaries, whether actual or virtual, to end. Therefore, realism has always existed, even if it had to mellow down to a more popular perception of neo-realism. The use of power and force was used to address the issue of "how to maintain stability, how and why it breaks down: how to retain sovereignty: when and how to use force to maintain stability and sovereignty."[91]

Here, the state and power take centre stage in both the traditional geopolitics as well as classical realism. Ultimately, it is the power of a state that manifests itself, to the cognition of other countries, and power flows from the advantages of geopolitical location, size of population and natural resources and, power also reflects itself in an attempt to monopolise it in competition with other states.[92] We have already discussed that classical realism and traditional geopolitics have a state-centric approach to deal with other states; the scope of power is the only aspect that has developed from a narrow to more holistic span due to the dimensions of space the power has covered.

Geopolitics and realism in IR both recognise the primacy of the state as a hegemon and that it works to promote and maximise its national interest which becomes unique in accordance with the nationality or the cultural homogeneity the state holds from being recognised as territory. In the end, the utterance of only the capital adequately represents the whole state, exactly like in an organism its head and face represent and communicate the nature of the entire body and its potential—thus just saying Washington, Beijing and New Delhi is enough to represent the US, PRC and India and the power of the state. Ratzel had already propounded the theory of organic state in geopolitics and Hobbs's state as a self-interested individual is similar to the imagining of a state. Rather, Ratzel is more prolific in explaining the growth of a state as an organism. Geopolitical theorists and realists in IR like Morgenthau and Carr have insisted upon normative concerns in international relations and espoused that the law could only be respected as it was backed by force.[93] In the remaining discourses, realism and geopolitics will remain in the explanation of interstate relations and in the determination of imperatives and responses of a state.

The Framework for China

In studying the geopolitical imperatives and responses of China to the world, leaving out any of the classical, structural or critical geopolitics even the geopolitics of air, space and informationisation, will be erroneous and will not bring out the correct results about the Chinese geopolitical imperatives. As we have discussed and proved the centrality of the state and its power in the international affairs policies, the traditional geopolitics will remain the bedrock of our discourse, supported by the realism in international relations. We have also examined other theories of geopolitics that have expanded the horizon to include globalization, informationisation and proliferation of techno-scientific risk in entire time and space. However, we have also concluded that even if the international boundaries may appear blurred due to these proliferations and omnipresence of national elements, the interest of the state remains the last bastion of the national interest, and thus the nation. Every element of globalisation, informationisation and proliferation of techno-scientific risk can be considered at the most, a global outreach of the state agents to ultimately serve the national interest or an outreach of a purported nationality seeking or striving for a state and at present termed as 'non state actors'. Having briefly examined the international relations, it has been concluded that while idealism has fallen flat, as it could not prevent World War I, relying on the mere goodness of human nature is perilous to say the least. Other theories like behaviouralism, pluralism and post-modernism explain only the part effective at its relevant place. Holistically, it is only the realist theory which stands its ground which is closest to the traditional geopolitics in its basic philosophy.

Therefore, I argue that the traditional geopolitics will remain the mainstay of our analytical tool along with Cohen's structural theory and the critical geopolitics to determine the geopolitical direction and course of a state response of China, not forgetting that a state's response may not always be coterminous with the national aspirations as well as regional aspirations. China being a one-party state is also an element of examination throughout our discourse.

NOTES

1. Mackinder, H.J., 'The Physical Basis of Political Geography', *Scottish Geographical Magazine*, Vol. 6, 1890, p. 84.
2. Sloan, Geoffrey and Colin S. Gray, *Geopolitics, Geography and Strategy*, London: Frank Cass, 1999, pp. 2-3.
3. CCP Central Committee, 'Notice on the Joint Sino-American Communiqué 07 Mar 1972', as quoted in Yang and Xia (eds), *Vacillating between Revolution and Detente*, p. 395.
4. Dodds, Klaus, *Geopolitics: A Very Short Introduction*, Oxford: Oxford University Press, 2007, p. 22.
5. Spykman, Nicholas J., *American Strategy in World Politics: The United States and the Balance of Power*, NY: Harcourt Brace, 1942, pp. xv, 41 (2007 edition).
6. Dodds, op. cit., pp. 115-116.

7. Agnew, John, *Geopolitics: Revisiting World Politics*, London: Routledge, 1998, p. 2.
8. Kaplan, Robert D., *The Revenge of Geography*, NY: Random House, 2012, p. 189.
9. Mahan, Alfred Thayer, *The Problem of Asia and Its Effect Upon International Policies,* Marston: Sampson Low, 1900, p. 56 (Elibron Edition, 2005).
10. Black, *Maps and History: Constructing Images From the Past*, Haven: Yale University Press, 1997, pp. 58, 173.
11. Kaplan, op. cit., p. 27.
12. 'Chinese Cartography: China Beat Columbus to it, Perhaps', *The Economist*, 12 January 2006.
13. Chen Gaoji, Preface to *Zhongguo Xin Yutu (New Atlas of China),* Commercial Press Shanghai, 1925.
14. Callahan, William A., *China: The Pessoptimist Nation*, Oxford: Oxford University Press, 2010, p. 95.
15. Knox, P.L. and Marston S., *Places and Regions in Global Context: Human Geography in Practice*, NZ: Hall, p. 3.
16. Sloan and Gray, op. cit., p. 2.
17. Mackinder, H.J., 'Geography, an Art and a Philosophy', *Geography*, Vol. 27, 1942, pp. 129-130.
18. Lucas, James, *War on the Eastern Front 1941-95: The German Soldiers in Russia*, London: Janes, 1979, p. 33.
19. O Tuathail, Gearoid, 'At the End of Geopolitics? Reflection on Pluralizing Problematic at Century's End', in *Alternatives: Social Transformation and Humane Governance*, 22, 1997, pp. 35-58.
20. Kjellen, Rudolf, *Staten Som Lifsform, 1916,* Cited in Hans Weigert, *Generals and Geographers*, NY: Oxford University Press, 1942, pp. 106-9.
21. Henning, Richard, *Geopolitik: Die Lehre vom Staat als Lebenesen*, Liepzig, Hirjel, 1931, P-9, quoted in S Bernard Cohen, *Geopolitics of International Relations*, Lanham: Rowman & Littlefield, 2009, p. 11.
22. 'Geopolitics', Encyclopaedia Britannica Online, http://www.britannica. com/EBchecked/ topic/ 229932/geopolitics. Accessed on 24 April 2014,
23. Goodall, *Dictionary of Human Geography*, Puffin, 1987, p. 191.
24. Taylor, Peter J., quoted in Leonhardt Van Efferink, *The Definition of Geopolitics, Classic, French and Practical Traditions*, www.exploringgeopolitics.org/publication_ Efferink_ van_ leonhardt_ the_ definitionofgeopolitics_classical_french_critical.htm, Accessed on 24 April 2014.
25. Colin Flint speaking in an interview at the launching of the second edition of *Introduction to Geopolitics*, May 2012, www.exploringgeopolitics.org/H_geopolitics_geography.html, Accessed on 25 April 2014.
26. Walsh, Edmund, *Geopolitics and International Morals*, in *Compass of the World*, H.W. Weigast and V. Stefansson (eds), NY: Macmillan, 1944, pp. 12-39.
27. Mackinder, H.J., 'The Geographical Pivot of History', *The Geographical Journal*, 23 (4), 1904, pp. 421-44.
28. Fairgrieve, James, *Geography and the World Power*, London: University of London Press, 1945, pp. 329-46.
29. Mackinder, H.J., *Democratic Ideas and Realities Norton*, 1962, pp. 265-78.
30. Cohen, Saul Bernard, *Geopolitics: The Geography of International Relations*, Lanham: Rowman and Littlefield, 2009, p. 16.

31. Kaplan, op. cit., p. 189.
32. Mackinder, H.J., *Democratic Ideals and Reality: A Study in the Politics of Reconstruction,* as quoted in Kaplan, ibid.
33. Smith, Neil and Jan Nijman, *Alfred Thayer Mahan in Dictionary of Geopolitics,* John O' Loughlin (ed.) Westport: Greenwood, Westport, 1994, pp. 156-58.
34. Cohen, op. cit., p. 21.
35. Parker, Geoffrey, *Geopolitics: Past, Present and Future,* London: Printer, 1998, pp. 10-19.
36. Haushofer, Karl, *Bausteine zur Greopolitik, K Vowinckel,* 1928, pp. 23-4 as quoted in Herwig, Holger H. 'Geopolitik: Haushofer, Hitler and Lebensraum' in *Geopolitics, Geography and Strategy,* Colin S. Gray and Geoffrey Sloan (eds), London: Frank Cass, 1999, p. 219.
37. The term 'Lebensraum' was used first by Haushofer in the first volume of *Zeitschriftfur Geopolitik* and subsequently twice in the second volume of *Mein Kampf* and 11 times in Hitler's unpublished *Zweites Buch* in 1928, proving it to be the foundation stone of German expansionism. Herwig, op. cit. p. 226.
38. Haushofer, Karl, *Geopolitik der Pan-Ideen,* Berlin: Zentral, 1931.
39. Herwig, p. 218.
40. Spykman, Nicholas, *The Geography of Peace,* NY: Harcourt Brace, 1942, pp. 457-72.
41. Dodds, Klaus, 'Cold War Geopolitics', in *A Companion to Political Geography,* John Agnew, Katherine Mitchell, Gerard Toal (eds), Oxford: Blockwell, 2003, p. 207.
42. Brzezinski, *The Grand Chess Board,* NY: Basic Books, 1997, p. 6.
43. Kennan, George F., *Cold War Iconoclast,* NY: Columbia University Press, 1989, p. 21.
44. Kennan, George F., 'The Source of Soviet Conduct', *Foreign Affairs,* Vol. 25, 1942, pp. 566-582.
45. Ibid.
46. Klaus Dodds, op. cit., p. 209.
47. Ibid., p. 210.
48. Kearns, Gerry, 'Imperial Geopolitics: Geopolitical Vision at the Dawn of the American Century', in *A Companion to Political Geography,* John Agnew, Katherine Mitchel, Gerard Toal (eds), Oxford: Blackwell, 2003, p. 173.
49. O'Sullivan, Patrick, 'Anti-domino', *Political Geography Quarterly,* Vol. I, 1982, pp. 57-64.
50. Kissinger, Henry, *The White House Years,* Boston: Little Brown, 1979, pp. 127-38.
51. Kissinger, Henry, *On China,* NY: Penguin Books, 2012, p. 202.
52. Cohen, op. cit., p. 26.
53. Brzezinski, Zbigniew, *Game Plan,* Atlantic Monthly Press, 1986, pp. 52-65.
54. Dodds, op. cit., p. 52.
55. Huntington, Samuel P., 'The Clash of Civilizations?' *Foreign Affairs,* www.foreignaffairs.com, Accessed on 26 Sep 2013.
56. Cohen, op. cit., p. 33.
57. Ardrey, Robert, *The Territorial Imperative,* NY: Athenaeum, 1966, pp. 3-41.
58. Cohen, op. cit., p. 37.
59. Ibid., p. 44.
60. Ibid., p. 36.
61. Anson, Sir Peter and Group Captain Dennis Cummings, RAF (Retd), 'The First Space War: The Contribution of Satellites to the Gulf War', *RUSI Journal,* 136 (4), 1991, pp. 45-53.
62. Lambeth, Benjamin S., *Air Power, Space Power and Geography,* as explained in note 17, p. 82, in Gray and Sloan (eds), op. cit.

63. Ibid., p. 75.
64. Gottman, Jean (ed.), *Centre and Periphery*, Beverly Hills: Sage 1980, p. 1.
65. Dolman, Evert C., 'Geo-strategy in Space Age: An Astro-political Analysis', in Gray and Sloan (eds), p. 84.
66. Mahan, Alfred Thayer, *The Influence of Sea Power upon History, 1660-1783*, Boston: Little Brown, 1890, p. 25, as quoted in Dolman, op.cit., p. 93.
67. Ibid., p. 91.
68. Modelski, G. Long, *Cycles in World Geopolitics*, Seattle: University of Washington Press, 1987, as quoted in Colin Flint, *Introduction to Geopolitics*, London: Routledge, 2006, pp. 35-39.
69. Flint, op. cit., p. 39.
70. Taylor, Peter J., *Political Geography: World Economy*, London: Nation State and Locality, Longman, pp. 4-10, 53-58.
71. Jenkins, Richard, *Social Identity*, London: Routledge, 1996, pp. 80-81.
72. Gurr, T.R., *Peoples Against States*.
73. Billing, M., *Banal Nationalism*, CA: Sage, 1995.
74. Flint, op. cit., p.108.
75. Ibid., pp. 108-112.
76. Dalby, Simon, 'Critical Geopolitics: Discourse, Difference and Dissent', in *Environment and Planning: Society and Space*, No 9, 1991, p. 274, as quoted in Gerard Toal, *Critical Geopolitics: The Polities of Writing Global Space*, London: Routledge, 1996, p. 62.
77. O Tuathail, Gearoid, *Understanding Critical Geopolitics: Geopolitics and Risk Security*, in Gray and Sloan, (eds), op. cit., pp. 107-124.
78. Agnew, op. cit.
79. O Tuathail, op. cit., p. 111.
80. Ibid., p. 114.
81. Brzezinski, Z., *The Grand Chess Board: Americas Primacy and its Geo-strategic Imperatives*, NY: Basic Books, 1997.
82. Ibid.
83. O Tuathail, Gearoid, 'Post Modern Polities? The Modern Geopolitical Imagination and Beyond', in *Rethinking Geopolitics*, London: Routledge, 1998, pp. 15-38.
84. O Tuathail, in Gray and Sloan (eds), op. cit., pp. 118-123.
85. Dodds, op. cit., pp. 22-24.
86. Burchill, Scott, *Introduction*, in Scott Burchill, Andrew Linklater (eds), *Theories of International Relations*, NY: St Martin Press, 1996, p. 3.
87. Halliday, Fred, *Rethinking International Relations*, London: Macmillan, 1994, p. 10.
88. Ibid.
89. Halliday, op. cit., p. 1.
90. Nicholson, *International Relations: A Concise Introduction*, p. 95.
91. Zalenski, Marysia and Cyntia Enloe, 'Questions about Identity in International Relations', in Ken Booth, Steve Smith (eds), *International Relations Theory Today*, Cambridge: Polity, 1996, p. 294.
92. Agnew, op. cit., pp. 74-75.
93. Stean, Peltiford, *International Relations: Perspective and Themes,* Edinburgh: Pearson Education Ltd, 2001, p. 24.

3

Historical Evolution of China's Nation-State and its Implications on Chinese Geopolitics

Political science or international relations experts, especially in India, proclaim that China has always been a strong, unified state headed by a single power, may be an emperor, carried forward in the modern era by Mao Zedong and his successors. Therefore, its present occupation of space and the related geospatial advantages or disadvantages have been taken to have existed in the same way from the antiquity. This impression is further compounded by the ancient Chinese concept of Tian Xia ('All under Heaven') being ruled by the Emperor of the Middle Kingdom (*Zhong Guo*) under the 'Mandate of Heaven'. The Chinese people have also been made to understand that China has ever been what it is today and even more than that territorially.[1] But, it is a misnomer. China like any other civilisational state did evolve on this earth in the same geospatial manner from a nucleus to as it exists today. To understand China better, we need to deconstruct China's geospatial existence in a historical perspective, derive the geopolitical evolutionary processes and arrive at the geopolitical dimensions of the present geospatial form, devoid of any predisposed idealism and mysticism. Therefore, in this analysis, a historical approach has been adopted which gives an evolutionary narrative of present day Chinese geo-body.

It is not for the intention of geographical determination that the historical perspective is undertaken to explain the evolution of Chinese geopolitics. It has been undertaken to basically study the evolution of human settlements and political spaces at various times that will gives us the opportunity to demolish many such notions that predispose our vision and impression about China. During this historical analysis of geopolitical growth, many myths like China being a uniform civilisation, having no evolutionary phases of its geopolitics as it would have happened to any other civilisational nation state or having far reaching oceanic influence, would be busted. Therefore, to underscore these evolutionary phases, the explanation of the geospatial developments has been categorised in the time periods accordingly.

PREHISTORIC PERIOD

By the end of the Pleistocene Age, Loess was deposited by its cool and dry climate. Then, the climate became warmer and humid. The northern margins towards Mongolia remained drier but the Huang He which flowed seasonally, caused along with its tributaries, a new phase of erosion.[2] The climate became warmer and more humid comparatively during the Mesolithic and Neolithic periods. As the land was rising, the erosion also became more acute—more so in the Sichuan basin.[3] The evidence of fishing and hunting is found as the central Manchurian plain and the North China plain were well-wooded and humans lived in dry limestone caves in the North China Plains. As K.C. Chang says:

> "Nearby there were woods in which tigers, leopards, bears and wolves dwelt; there were steppes on which the Chinese deer, the red deer, and gazelles roamed about; and plains and lakes in which gigantic fish swam. The men hunted in woods, fished by the lakes, and made abundant bone and shell artefacts."[4]

During this time not only the Peking man (*Homo erectus pokinensis*) but also the Yuanmou man (*Homo erectus yuanmouanesis*) existed as evidence exists of the migratory trails of these humanoids in Zhoukoudian near Beijing (Peking), Yuanmou county in Yunnan province and in Lantian county in the Shanxi province.[5] Therefore, it is evident that besides the Peking man, there were other homo sapiens too who flourished in the nearby vicinities and "interaction and sustained migration between East Asian and European population prevailed over a long period of time".[6] This was the period when China was progressing from the stone age to new stone age of the Neolithic period (5000–4000 BC). A transition to agriculture marked the early Neolithic period and the domestication of more dogs and pigs and less sheep and goats, along with wooden hoes and digging tools suggested the practice of agriculture.[7] Later, the development of the Neolithic culture in China named after the sites of evidence, Yang Shao (5000–

Map 12: Neolithic China

Source: http://archive.artsmia.org/art-of-asia/history/chinese-dynasty-map.cfm

3000 BCE) and Longshan (3000–2000 BCE), developed in the Yellow River valley, extending from the modern province of Jiangsu in southern China to the north-western provinces of Qinghai and Gansu. Although going into details of the various prehistoric civilisations is beyond the scope of this book, however an established locational graph of the Neolithic cultures of China giving out overlaying chronological existence of geographical dimensions brings out the fact that there were several cultures that flourished in each other's' vicinity simultaneously, and therefore interacted.

It is also evident that during the Yang Shao and Longshan cultures, there were also cultures in different geographical domains like those in the Yang Ze Valley along the eastern seacoast, south-eastern seacoast and others, besides the northern and central plains, that coexisted. This fact contradicts the notion of only one Chinese culture and has brought forth the intermixing of other regional cultures during this time.

Yang Shao (5000–3000 BCE)

In 1921, the Swedish Geologist J.G. Andersson stumbled upon a site between the Huang He in the north and a tributary Lo He in the south and excavated a late Neolithic village near Yang Shao.[8] The evidence revealed that the Yang Shao farmers

Map 13: Various Cultures of Neolithic China

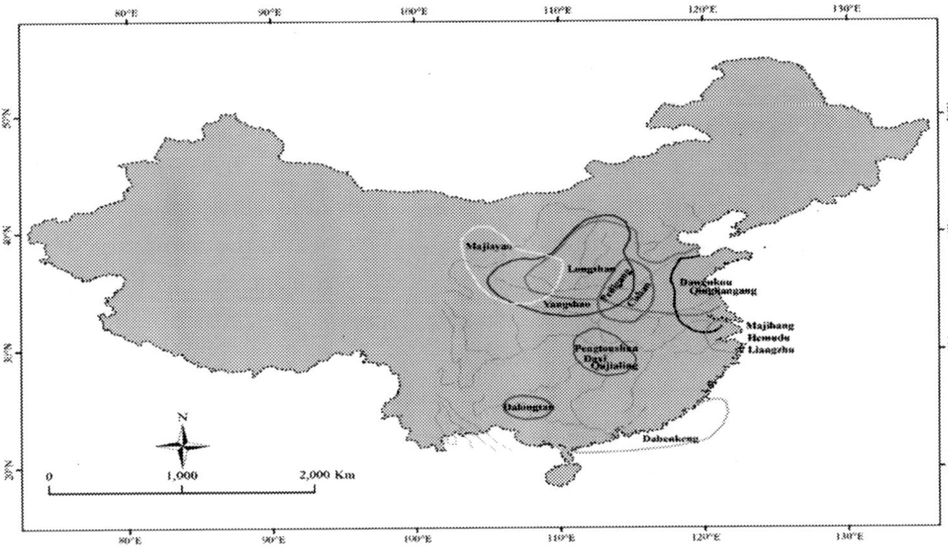

dug wells, made houses above the ground with wooden pillars and poles besides the cave houses in the limestone walls, cleared forests with fire and axe and tilled a stone-less soil with limestone hoes.[9] The Yang Shao culture had spread into the upper Huang He basin at the river's confluence with Dao He and developed terraced agriculture in the loess.[10] The size of villages, like the ancient site of Ban Bocun, had more than 200 houses with a population of 500 to 600 people. These villages were ringed by a ditch with a purpose of defence or grouped around a large commune house measuring 66 feet in length and 41 feet in width. In the north beyond the ditch, was a village cemetery.[11]

Longshan (3000–1000 BCE)

The Longshan culture was more advanced than the Yang Shao culture. The most remarkable change was the expansion of geographic area from an essentially upland setting of Huang He basin to an alluvial lower Huang He and in the south to the lower Chang Jiang and further down south to the regions of South China and Taiwan. To decide about a core area of the Longshan culture is difficult, but certainly this culture emanated from the Yang Shao and made its way from the upland to the plains of Hunan. It is also evident that the villages of the Longshan age in this core area were larger than the Yang Shao-age villages often found stratigraphically below them. Wherever possible, these villages were built within the sight of a hill which could provide refuge during the floods.[12] Tools made of stones were better like sickles of slate stone of a semi-lunar shape. Fishing, animal-rearing increased; among crops, millet in the north, wheat in the northern An Hui and rice in the Han Chiang, Huai He and Chang Jiang were predominant. Villages were surrounded by a stamped earth wall and a defensive ditch, which indicate more militant inter-regional/village relations.[13] The period up to the Longshan culture is assessed only on the basis of archaeological evidence but opens up to the recorded history of civilisation. As regards the civilisation of that time in China, human figurines found at several Neolithic sites with Caucasoid features like large noses, deep eyes and narrow faces are the evidence of the contacts with people outside the central plains.[14]

EARLY HISTORIC PERIOD

There is a transitory period between the prehistoric and early historic period which needs discussion before proceeding further. A period between 2000–1600 BCE is a period in which the Xia dynasty supposedly ruled the areas in the central and lower Huang He plains, especially between 1700 and 1500 BCE, preceded by the Erlitou period. The *Yu Gong* (The Tribute of Yu) written during the Han period by Sima Qian (206 BCE–200 BCE) talks about the greatness of the 'founder' of the Xia dynasty that he ruled China with a political system of nine provinces, carried out land reforms and took measures to check floods.[15] It was attributed to the great Yu that he opened the rivers of the nine provinces, improved the outlets of the nine marshes and improved the land conditions to the benefit of the succeeding dynasties. Earlier, he was considered a mythological god who separated land from water but was established as founder of the Xia dynasty during the later Zhan period.[16] This conception of the Xia dynasty though recorded by Sima Qian could not be supported for two reasons; one that the terminologies used for the regions were only of the later Zhan period and second, fundamentally it was narrated in an oral tradition, though even older archaeological history of the Neolithic period is available.[17] A parallel can be drawn from the Ramayana and Mahabharata of the Indian mythology in this regard when myth mixed with facts does become part and parcel of the evolution of any civilisation. However, the first recorded history with archaeological evidence draws us to the Shang dynasty, after which clear geospatial evidence is available along with recorded history for analysis.

Shang China (1766–1045 BC)

Bronze metallurgy had already preceded Shang through the Erlitou culture as is evident from the bronze vessels found at the Erlitou sites from circa 1700 to 1500 BCE. The technology was passed on to Erlitou from the neighbouring Qijia and Siba cultures in the west which themselves had acquired this technology from south-western Eurasia through Central Asia.[18] The Shang who were the first recorded dynasty of the bronze age, ruled the Huang He Valley, succeeding the mythical Xia dynasty. The major archaeological sites of the Shang have been found in the modern province of Henan; first near Anyang (Ruins of Yin) the last capital, in 1928 and then at the bend of the Huang He near the modern city of Chengzhou. As it appears, the northern Henan was the nucleus of the Shang culture and from there it spread to southern Hebei and Western Shang Dong of the North China plain and eventually created a whole cultural complex assimilating the northern part of Chang Jiang (Yangze) valley.[19]

Map 14: Shang China

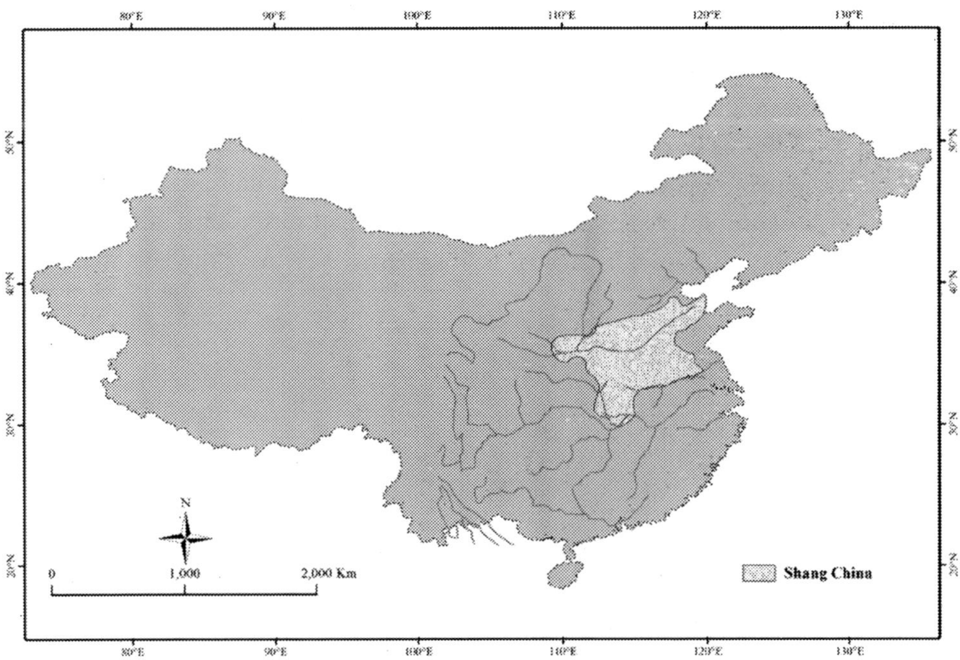

The Shang achieved great sophistication in bronze metallurgy and writing. Their capitals were larger than that of the prehistoric Longshan. They protected their cities with a pounded earth wall. The Shang capital of Cheng Zhen was an enclosed area of 1.3 square miles.[20] These areas were rectangular in shape and aligned with cardinal directions and gave an architectural foundation to the political layout of future cities and satellite villages. Outside the walled cities were bone factories for oracle bone writings, pottery kilns and bronze foundries. The farmers lived in pit houses, especially the foundry workers. Royal cities were a demonstration of elevated architecture and the mastery over humans as powerful machines. For example, the Shang City of Cheng Zhou used 10,000 workers for 330 days a year for 18 years to prepare the wall around. People were used as farm labourers under superintendents. Even human sacrifice was practised along with animal sacrifice by the king especially while building houses. These facts have been unsentimentally recorded on oracle bones found near An Yang. Their greatest contribution was a writing system of about 3,000 characters out of which 1,000 have been decoded so far.

The system of rule was through the hierarchical overlordship of the Shang over the vassal states. Chariots were first introduced during the Shang between 1600–1500 BCE taken from the Caucasus through Central Asia as evident from the remains of the rock drawings.[21] Horse-riding skills were developed much later in the 4th Century BCE.[22] What it does indicate is the fact that intercultural communications were open during the Shang period and the tools of mobility were used by the overlords for military purposes. However, the mobility of the chariots remained restricted due to terrain and wet agricultural and forest landscape. The polity during this period was mainly confined to the intrigue of the vassal states, mainly Zhou, whose leader subsequently overthrew the last Shang king, Di Xin.

Zhou (1045–256 BCE)

The Chinese history is full of legends. Even the first recorded history by Sima Qian also records many legends like the Yu of Xia as history. Likewise, the origin of the Zhou Dynasty which succeeded the Shang also remains shrouded in mystery, legend and fantasy. It is said that a man by the name Qi grew up as a farmer and served as agriculture minister under a sage-like king and went on to establish an agrarian-based tribal state by the name of Zhou under Shang suzerainty in the Wei River Region around modern Xi An. Over a period of time, other subordinate states of Shang allied with Zhou against the arbitrary imperial power. The influence thus grew over a geographical area of the Han River valley and the Yangzi (Chang Jiang) River valley, threatening the southern flank of the Shang Kingdom. The Zhou Chief Xibai was arrested by the Shang but released after taking ransom. He was, in any case, an ideologue of sorts who had mustered the support of many adjacent vassal states. It was his son Fa who actually mustered forces and attacked Shang and established the Zhou Dynasty. Therefore, among the Zhou kings, Xibai was proclaimed as King Wen (Cultured King) and the son Fa as King Wu (the Martial King).[23] This clan ruled China as Western Zhou as they had emerged from the western region of the Loess over the area as shown in the map, till 771 BC.

Map 15: Zhou China

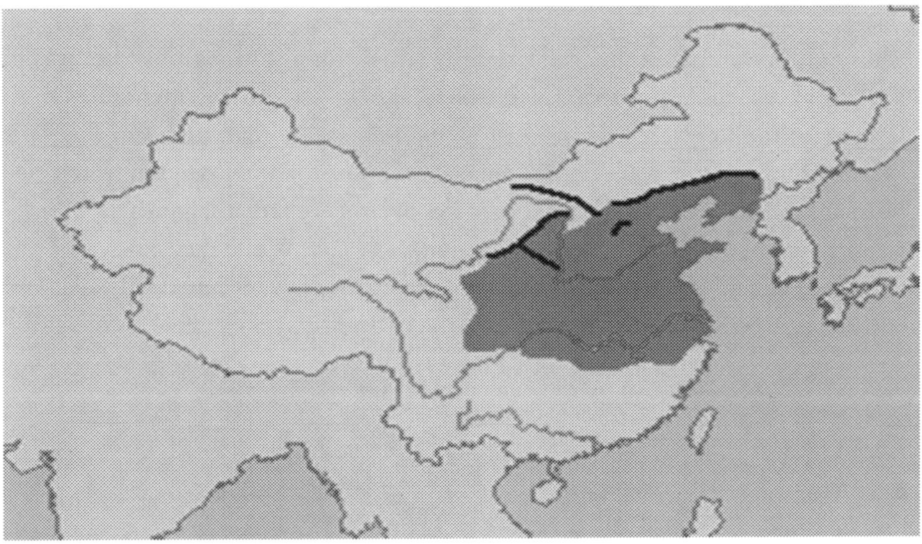

Source: https://taobabe.files.wordpress.com/2013/03/zhoumap.gif?w=600

The Zhou ruled the Huang He basin for nearly 800 years through some of the thirty-nine kings mostly in a father-to-son succession—the longest ever in the world for any dynasty.[24] It is estimated that population increased from ten million to as many as fifty million towards the end of the period. This demographic gain had commensurate reclamation of agricultural land from forests, innovation in agro-techniques like the use of iron in implements and the growth of commerce in new cities.[25] The Zhou kings followed a feudal system for ruling, called '*fengjian*'. The space of kingdom was occupied in an imaginary concentric nine squares by a hierarchy of five territorial lords selected from the kin of the royal houses, the descendants of the vanquished Shang, chief of the tribal states, who had been amalgamated. The royal capital stayed at the centre of these concentric squares. Though Xi An, the capital, was never at the centre of the Zhou Kingdom, but it was an idealistic concept of ruling the territory and state-building.[26] During the Western Zhou period, such domains that existed in these concentric squares were more than a thousand. The Zhou king during the Western Zhou period did not live in any house of architectural grandeur and the nobles lived with others, outside the walled premises. The common folks in the countryside still lived in subterranean dwellings or in loess caves as *Shijing*, 'the Book of Songs' suggests:

Of Old Tanfu the duke
Scraped shelters, scraped holes;
As yet they had no houses.[27]

Although in the spare time, collection by females and hunting by males was the livelihood, the main occupation remained agriculture, for the menfolk. On the terraces of the Loess, south and east-facing fields were preferred. On the flatter North China plain, a well–field system of cultivation was adopted in which eight peasant families occupied about forty acres of land each, divided into nine perfect squares—one in the centre and three on its each side. While they cultivated their own piece of land separately, the one in the centre was always cultivated collectively and the proceeds went to the king and the concept of public service emerged.[28]

Map 16: Well Graph And Its Realistic Expression

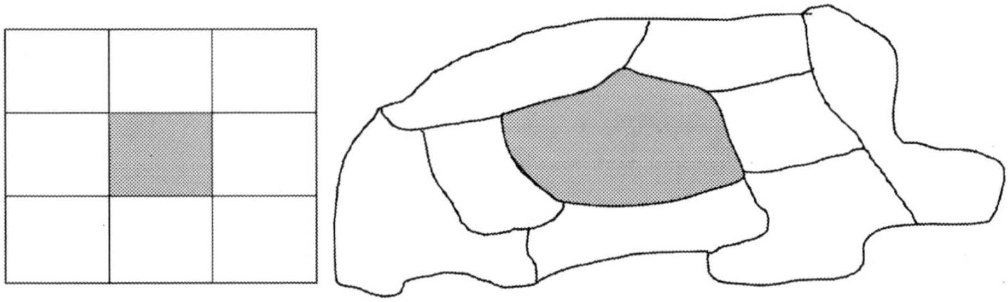

For 250 years or so, the Western Zhou expanded and controlled territories well, but the power of the royal family after the capital moved from Xi An in the west to Luoyi in the east, suffered a continuous decline because Xi An was attacked by a tribe in the west and the king was killed in 771 BCE. Hereafter, known as the Eastern Zhou, they conceded the western portion of the territory of the Wei He valley to Qin, nominally still a Zhou vassal. Due to a population growth and the introduction of taxes, the Zhou arrangement of limitation on every aspect of tillage became unviable and the peasants became freer to acquire land in the no man's land and more and more forests were cleared by the vassal states. This practice was condemned by Mozi (Mencius).[29] This period was known as the

Spring and Autumn period (722 BCE–481 BCE), named after the Chronicle of the State of Hu written by Confucius. The authority of the Zhou became nominal and boundaries of vassal states became contiguous—a cause of constant strife. Fragmented into 148 states, some of them of the size of a small city, 128 of them were absorbed by four larger states called Qin in the west, Jin in the centre, Shu in the south and Qi in the east. In 497 BCE, the nobles in Jin began a civil war. There were four regions in Jin. Three weaker regional clans defeated Jin and divide the Jin state between themselves. Now there were eight states in the former Zhou Empire: Han, Wei, Zhao, Qin, Chu, Qi and Yan with the Zhou remaining confined to the capital area of Luoyang. This marked the beginning of the Warring States period, spread between 475 to 221 BCE. The Chu in the south and Qin in the west were the largest regions controlling one-third of the area each, leaving the remaining one-third for the other states. Zhou's position of an overlord through the 'Mandate of Heaven' was also not recognised by other states. The disintegration of Zhou however had more to do with the influence of geography in the form of floods and draughts and survival of the fittest. Another factor was the attack on Zhou from the west by the nomadic tribes of Quanrong because of which the Zhou had to migrate to the east. This also marked the end of the centrally controlled rule of the Western Zhou period as well as the beginning of two geographically determined civilisations: nomadic versus sedentary. With regards to floods and famine control, the *Spring and Autumn Annals* discloses that in 651 BCE in the absence of Zhou, under the leadership of the powerful Duke of Qi, Quiqiu, a convention was concluded to ensure that no state would execute any water works that causes floods in other state and no one would impose a grain embargo during famine. On the other hand, the unpredictability of rains caused a serious crop failure every six years and a general famine every twelve years. Therefore, those on both banks of the Wei and Huang He had no respite. In the discourses of Mencius, it is mentioned that the King of Wei said to Mencius that due to his state being located on both sides of the Yellow River, he had no place to transfer his citizens in order to save them from floods. These reasons had actually led to war for the expansion of territories and attacks by nomad tribes and kings of the north and west of China on the farmers to take away their half-year's savings of grains. It is also evident from the geospatial analysis that a pastoral culture in the west and north took up the mode of transportation differently. Horse-riding, a faster mode of communication to traverse over the western stretch of flat arid land, was adopted by the nomad tribes, while the mode of communication taken up by the sedentary culture of agriculture in the Loess and the Central China plains, was wheeled carts and chariots—the main purpose of them being a better agricultural load carrier and prestigious conveyance for the kings and feudal lords. Although first acquired as booty from the adversaries of the north and northwest during the Shang period, chariots were used for warfare only in the Western Zhou period.[30] These chariots were more useful in the Central Chinese plains than in the Loess. However, the chariots ultimately proved difficult in the military manoeuvres against the nomad attacks in the west and the north.

Map 17: China during the Spring and Autumn Period

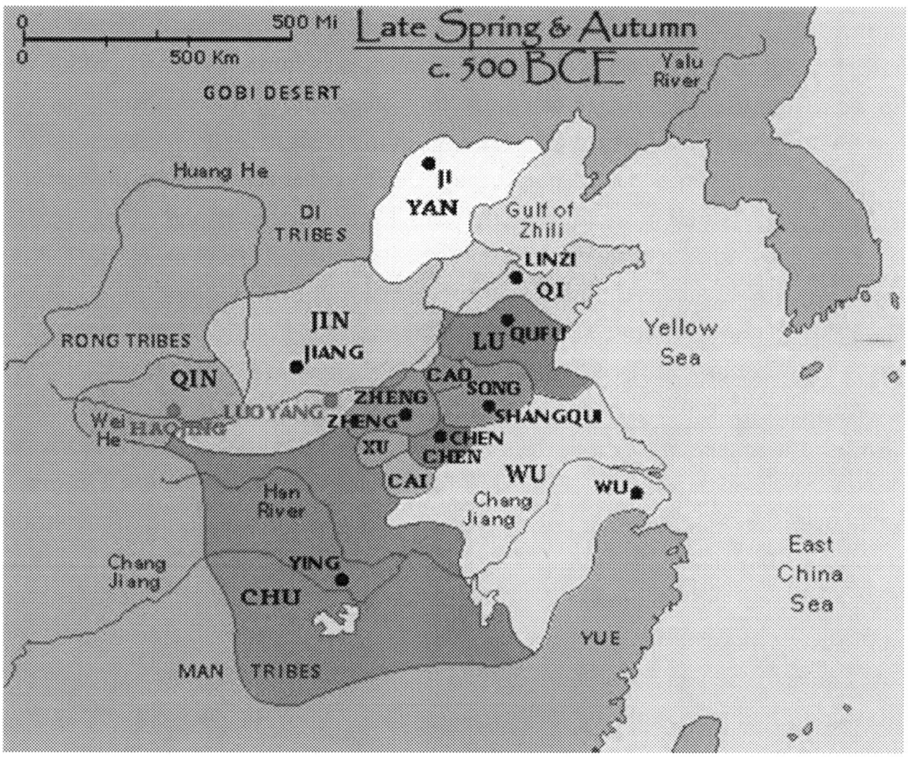

Source: http://www.globalsecurity.org/military/world/china/images/map-500bc.jpg||| China-History Map-Spring and Autumn Period.

Thus, came the mounted archers from the land of nomads in the west and the north that had become battle ground for warfare between the warring states in the Yellow River valley in the 4th Century BCE. It is, however, certainly not a coincidence that the dynasties which overpowered the existing one, always came from the west. But even if indigenous, they overpowered the existing one, with their sheer mobility. Like the Zhang who came from the west, who themselves experienced the onslaught of the nomads, overpowered the Shang and other states by their advantage of better chariots and mounted archers, learnt from the nomads, during the Warring States period.

Map 18: China during the Warring States Period

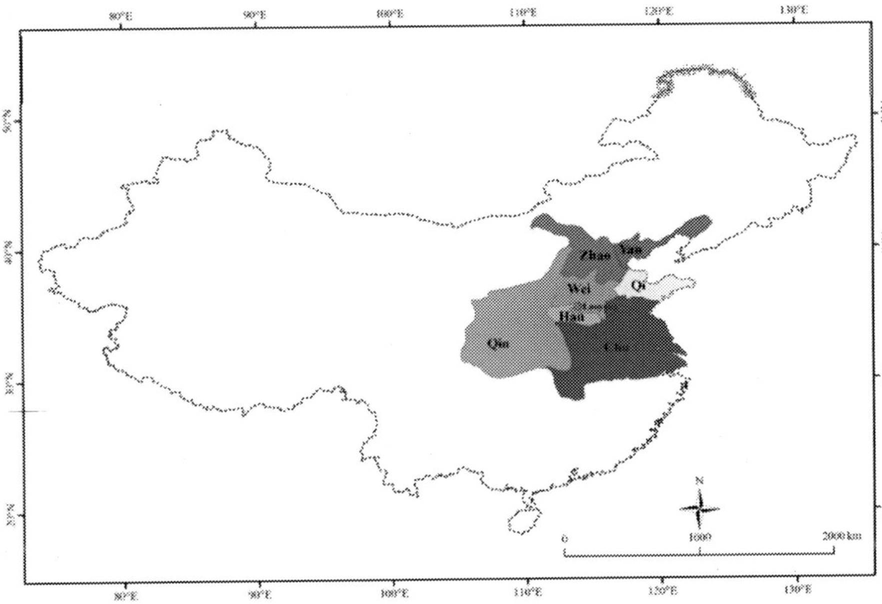

Due to the crop failures and inability to sustain the population of small states and the army, it was felt advantageous to have larger states, like the state of Lu, which expanded its territory by five times from its original authorisation by the Zhou overlord and the neighbouring Qi, by ten times its authorisation, during the Spring and Autumn period.[31] Perhaps this was the reason why Qin of the west went all-out for unification. The other reasons were his pioneering work in erecting earthen walls as barriers on the frontiers in the northwest exposed to the nomad tribes/barbarians. This barrier coincided with the 15-inch isohyets that also mark the climatic divisionary lane between the arid nomad and agrarian cultures. I also argue that the militancy by the vassals in the west against the kings whether Zhou against Shang or Qin against Eastern Zhou, may have been caused due to the influence of the nomadic people further to their west and north who believed in usurping others' earned assets by their sheer mobility and undefined, unregulated statecraft practised, that was diagonally opposed to the agriculturist kings of the Loess and Central China plains. However, the cavalry tactics and skills of the mounted bowmen could never become integral to the military acumen of the Zhou and its vassals. By the time of the warring states specially Qin in the west and Zhou in the north, these states had adopted two-fold strategies to counter the attacks of the nomadic tribes of Central Asia and Mongolia. The first was massed infantry by supplying hundreds of thousands of soldiers with metal weapons which was unthinkable during the Bronze Age.[32] The second was the erection of earthwork walls in the northwest (Qin) and in the north (Zhou and Wan) as a continuous barrier, under an understanding amongst these states to keep the external attacks away.[33] This act of initiative by Qin also justified his efforts towards the unification of China to great extent, which he took up subsequently. If we carry out a geopolitical sketching of these states of the later warring states, first before the Qin unification, we have evidence to support a pattern that influence on the north-western states like Qin and Zhou was predominantly nomadic to maritimic in the coastal regions of the Chu state. It greatly influenced their war-fighting tactics and strategies as well. There was more military in the northwest as compared to the southeast regions of the coast. As the northern and western states waged wars on mounted chariots and cavalry, the states in the southeast fought on water, in fleets of canoes. Their ways of handling water also reflected itself in the digging of an ancient canal by a king of Wu that connected the Yangzi and Huai rivers.[34]

EARLY EMPIRES

Qin Ascendency

From the period of the Western Zhou to the Eastern Zhou, the Zhou Dynasty declined from use of the title of king (*Wang*) in an actual sense, to only in a virtual sense by the end of the Warring States period. The leader of almost every state like Wei in 344 BCE, Qin and Han in 328, Zhao, Yan and Zhongshan in 323, declared themselves as kings. Even between 288–287, the kings of Qin and Qi briefly declared themselves as emperor or '*Di*' but reverted to king or '*Wang*' title. This only denoted the demise of the Zhou kingdom. However, Qin was always powerful since the beginning when the Zhou were driven out from the Wei valley in the west by the Quanrong, the Nomadic tribes.[35] Zhou had overlordship over Qin, and gave Qin the task to restore the Zhou authority in the West from the tribes in 771 BCE. The Western states always had advantage of aloofness from the states in east and its unnecessary interstate fights. Qin absorbed the Quanrong tribal areas, enforced administrative reforms to establish a centralised kingdom with a powerful military as prescribed by the legalist Shang Yang in his book *The Book of*

Lord Shang introducing meritocracy and devolving power from the nobility. By 260 BC, as described earlier, Qin had become as huge a state covering one-third area of China and disproportionately powerful compared to the remaining six states. This threat of Qin led to a Vertical Alliance propounded by the political strategist Su Qin who impressed upon the weaker states (located north to south, thus called Vertical Alliance) to collaborate against the Qin expansion, which worked for some time. But Qin revived with the Horizontal Alliance diplomacy of Zhang Yi to befriend the states of Vertical Alliance located west to east in accordance with the strategic norm of Han Feizi being "Vertical Alliance supporters encourage the weak multitude to attack the strong (Qin) side, whilst the Horizontal Alliance promote one strong side (Qin) attacking the weak multitude." In the bargain, Qin first conquered the weakest and adjacent Han state in 230 BCE, then Wei in 225 BCE. In 223 BCE, Qin attacked Chu, the largest in the south, conquered after a long and arduous battle in 222 BCE; then Qin conquered the northern states of Zhou and then Yan. In 221, Qin conquered the final unconquered state of Qi and the Qin Dynasty was finally established making Zhou Zheng (childhood name Ying Zheng, 259 BCE to 210 BCE) the emperor, who assumed the title Emperor Qin Shi Huang.[36]

Map 19: China during the Qin Rule

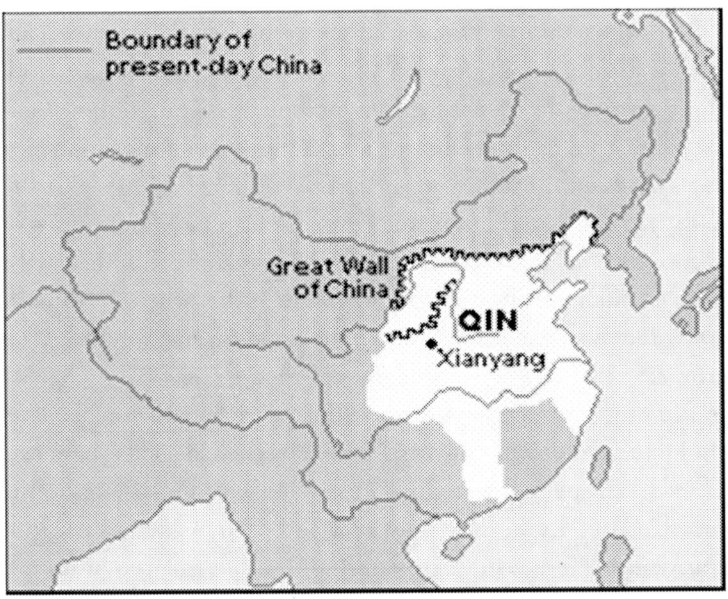

Source: http://classconnection.s3.amazonaws.com/569/flashcards/867569/png/qindynasty_map1365289325189.png

Geospatial Analysis: The geospatial analysis of this unification gives a different reason for Qin's success. Firstly, Qin was an outside power in the far western Wei He valley, protected by mountains and girdled by the Huang He and having barriers on all four sides.[37] Ray Huang says, '... a power from the far side with long range goals was bound to fare better than the central states caught in confusing and uncertain way of intrigues and rivalries with their neighbour.'[38] Another reason attributed to the success was Qin's expansion to the fertile and already developed plains and valley of the Sichuan basin. The extension of the irrigation work under Li Bing to the Chengdu plains made the Qin state even wealthier. The construction of the Chengguo canal reclaimed 4,50,000 acres of wasteland and increased the valley's agricultural productivity five-fold.[39] However, geographically speaking, there were two reasons as to why the Qin succeeded in conquering: one, they had a rich experience of dealing with the nomadic barbarians along their vulnerable north-western flanks and they themselves adopted their military techniques of conducting fast-paced warfare on horseback; two, as the attacks by the Xiongnu (Huns) increased at the northern and western frontiers, a need for unification grew stronger leading to a pro-Qin Horizontal Alliance as opposed to the earlier Vertical Alliance diplomacy that was being practised against the Qin. Preceding unification, states including Qin had started the practice of protecting frontiers with the aim to protect China from the nomadic barbarians. The Qin, thereafter, conjoined these walls to strengthen the defence, calling them as the Great Wall of China. Between 221–214 BCE, the Qin expanded south beyond the Yangzi basin to the regions of Pujian, Guangdong, Guangxi and Dongqing, considered as non-Chinese areas, and made great engineering works of link-canals between the Yangzi and Pearl rivers. The Qin made cart roads fifty paces broad; tree-lined, radiating out from the capital. The *Shiji* records 270 palaces within 200 *li* (Chinese mile) around Xienyang and linked with covered roads for nobles. Such was the density and grandeur that when the imperial palaces were burnt by the rebels in 206 BC, the flare lasted for three months.[40] However, the emperor Zhou Zheng (Qin Shi Huang) died in 207 BCE after drinking a mercury potion for immortality. His heir Fusu committed suicide. The younger brother Hu Hai seized power but was defeated by the Chu-led rebels, remnants of the Warring States period who had not been conquered, and the Empire disintegrated. Qin Shi Huang however left two legacies: the purging of Confucianism and a Terracotta Army of 8,000 soldiers placed around his tomb.

Han Ascendance (206 BCE to 200 AD)

Sima Qian who was an official historian of Han, recorded the causes of the decline of Qin Shi Huang, saying that he was "greedy and short sighted, dismissive of advice, leading whole world to violence and cruelty, having harsh laws and deceitful conduct and most of all not changing with times".[41] What may not have been officially liked about Qin during Han must be the former's dislike of Confucianism and the latter's unacceptability of Zhou Zheng, the first emperor of Qin, to have had a controversial inheritance from Lu Buwei, a trader and his concubine who became the Dowager Empress, causing the 'Mandate of Heaven" to have been taken away. However, within four years of the demise of Qin Shi Huang, the dynasty collapsed and got divided into 18 kingdoms after being defeated by Xiang Yu of the Chu state.

Map 20: The Disintegration of China after Qin

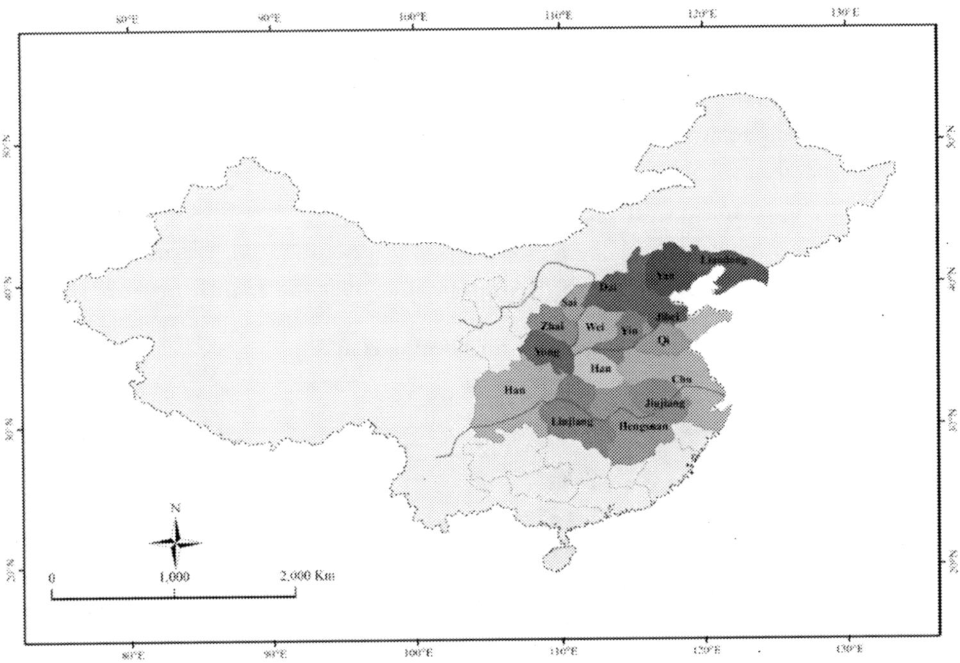

Later in a war to decide the hegemony in China, a battle with Liu Bang of Han ensued in which Xiang Yu was defeated (the Battle of Guixia, 202 BC) in modern Anhui. Liu Bang assumed the title of Emperor of reunited China and Chang An was made the new capital.[42] This was the foundation of the Western

Han which was divided into thirteen centrally governed commands and ten semi-autonomous kingdoms. Despite replacing these kings with his clan members, the 'Rebellion of Seven States' took place in 154 BC compelling the imperial court to restructure the territories and curtail their authority. Kingdoms did exist in the Western as well as Eastern Han.[43] However, there was a brief period between 9 AD to 23 AD in which Wang Mang, a nephew of the Empress Dowager Wang Zhenjun, seized the throne from the Liu family to establish the Xin Dynasty. He introduced several reforms which included the outlawing of slavery, nationalising land to equally distribute it among the peasants and a new currency and overwhelming flood control after the massive floods of 3 AD to 11 AD which dislodged thousands of farmers, causing unrest and the Red Eyebrows Rebellion against Xin. This resulted in the killing of Wang Mang and the overthrowing of the Xin Dyansty and the restoration of the Liu family's rule of Han.[44] This revival marked the beginning of the Eastern Han or later Han established in August 25 AD by Liu Xiu of the Han Dynasty who became Emperor Guang Wu. He shifted his capital to Luoyang, 335 kilometres east of the earlier capital of Chang An. Emperor Zhang's reign (75–88 AD) was the highest point of the Eastern Han.[45] Eunuchs and relatives of consorts and concubines of the emperors had always been crucial in the succession struggles of the Han. The role of the palace eunuch Sun Cheng in masterminding the enthroning of the actual heir, Prince Bao, as Emperor Shun of Han (125–144 AD) is well documented.[46] There was a time that the eunuchs had so much of stranglehold over the Han Emperors that the

Map 21: China during Han Rule

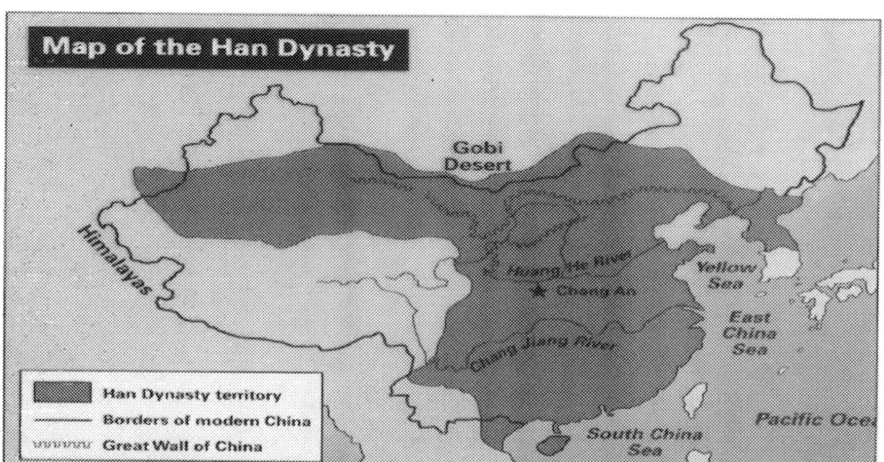

Source: http://easytalkchinese.com/images/info/history/han/han_dynasty.png

Confucian scholars/students who stood up against their corruption and domination of were purged, which was known as the Partisan Prohibition.[47] They were only excused because of the fear that they may join the Yellow Turban Rebellion, basically an agrarian uprising against over-taxation and low production, coupled with the Five Pecks of Rice Rebellion, a Taoist cult (142 CE) that later developed into a million-strong force. At the end, China got divided into three spheres of influence, under: Cao Cao (155–220 AD) in the north, Sun Quan (182–258 AD) in the south and Liu Bei (161–223 AD) in the west.[48] Cao Cao's son Cao Pi (187–226 AD) removed the last Han Emperor Wan of Wei. Thus, the Han dynasty was formally removed and a period of conflict between the three states of Cao Wei, Eastern Wu and Shu Han ensued.

The Geospatial Analysis of Han China

At the threshold between Qin and Han, two geospatial elements emerged. One, before the Qin period, there had been a practice to build defensive walls amongst the warring states that took a national turn for the first time when the Qin Dynasty reoriented the walls of Yan, Zhou and Qin themselves to consolidate them as defence against the foreign forces called the nomadic Xiongnu of the north and the north-west. It was in a way the first instance that the agrarian civilisations of the fragmented states collected themselves as a Chinese state to put up a brave front against nomadic civilisation and created a genuine distinction of 'us' and 'them'.[49] Second, the Qin dynasty did venture beyond the Yangzi but could not actually colonise the wet wildness of South-eastern China. Before the Han Dynasty, China's population was estimated to be 50 million. The first census taken up by the Western Han in the year 2 AD estimated the population at 58 million, of which 43 million lived in northern China, north of the line between the Jiuling and Yangzi Deltas.[50] Major population centres remained the same: the Huang He basin, the Sichuan basin and the Chengdu plains. The Western Han, despite an initiative taken by the Western Zhou, could not colonise the middle and lower Yangzi valley, despite being full of wealth of natural environment which as Sima Qian explains,

> "...in the region south of the Yangzi and Huai Rivers no one ever freezes or starves to death, but on the other hand there are no wealthy families."[51]

What Sima Qian actually indicates is the lack of commercial activities that made families richer in the north despite natural calamities rendering the remaining often poor. He did indicate the abundance of natural resources round the year.

However, out of these 43 million in the north, 35 million were concentrated in the alluvial plains of the Huang He. During the Western Han period, there was a greater shift of population from the Wei valley to the east of the Huang He passes into the alluvial plains and there developed five densely populated cities to the east of the Shan Xi uplands.[52] However, the densest population remained concentrated in and around Chang An, the capital and the ancient core area of the Chinese civilisation. Whether during the times of the Western Zhou around 1000 years before or in the times of the Qin and Western Han, this area always supported the core population and remained a base for troops but was never a battlefield. The development of the area was further emphasised by the construction of the Chengguo canal by the Qin and Emperor Wu of the Western Han for irrigation and transportation. Therefore, it proves that the two sharply delimited natural environments in North China, the Loess Uplands and the great alluvial plains, were developed first and became the cradle of the Chinese civilisation. The lower reaches of the Huang He were only ventured into with great care and for an achievement of control over floods by the dredging of Huang He. The Han Emperor Wu went further north-east and won the northern part of Korea in 188 BC and had a colony of approximately 3,15,000 people.[53] However, the most pronounced expansion of the Western Han was to the north-west. The Han power audaciously tried to terminate the problematic attacks by the nomadic kingdom of Xiongnu which was a confederation of twenty-four nomadic tribes which had influence over 1,500 miles of area north of the then smaller area of China from the fringes of Manchuria to the grasslands of Kokonor. In 200 BC, they besieged the Han Dynasty founder Liu Bang with 3,00,000 mounted warriors. The basic reason for their success was 'the coincidence of combat conditions with living conditions'. While Hans remained an infantry needing a cumbersome process of mobilisation, the Xiongnu fought the same way as they lived and did not require going through the steps of Chinese mobilisation of inducting peasants, training, equipping and transporting them to battlefields and then maintaining a harsh supply line behind them. Emperor Wu in his campaign of 119 BC and 99 BC, suffered 60 to 70 per cent casualties but did expand into the Tarim basin and western Asia. It is believed that some 6,00,000 garrison soldiers were mobilised including 1,00,000 cavalry who became settlers in the colonies of oasis in the Tarim basin.[54] This westward expansion also resulted in the establishment of a trade corridor famed as the Silk Route from China to the Mediterranean, spanning over 4,500 arduous miles. This Silk Route also brought in a continuous contact with the lands west of the Pamir, introduced in China the knowledge about breeding horses, grape wine, skins, wool and linen, etc.[55] But the continuous strife had always remained which was overbearing in the forms of the ravages of wars, arduous deserts, immense distances and cold north winds.

Because of these adventures to the north-west, civil wars, rebellions and the Xiongnu attacks, the population of the Han Empire which was approximately 50 millions in 2 AD got reduced to 40 to 45 million in 57 AD.[56] This was also a period of devastating floods besides political upheavals. Therefore, large movements of population took place. One was in the direction of the east, into the uplands of the Shandong peninsula and second was to the south Yangzi delta, the Boyang lake basin and the Gan river and then towards the Han river valley, the Dongqing lake basin and the Xiang river. By 40 AD, the Eastern or Later Han completed the unification of China and the population did recover slowly by 140 AD, but was still lesser by 8 million people compared to the Western Han in 20 AD. However, what was most significant was that while during the Western Han period at the end in 2 AD, the population was concentrated in the north; the significance of the north was lost during the Later Han as the Qin Ling mountains to the Yangzi delta gained some 9 million people and the population increased four-folds in the Hunan, Qiangxi and Guangdong regions and a new trade route was established through Yunnan to India.[57] It was a clear-cut shift of core towards the south and south-east which was geographically more amenable and allowed a greater sustenance of population by multi-cropping, less catastrophes and smoother communication to other civilisations like India through the land and sea routes.

The Later Han was a period of restoration, therefore similar aspirations as raised by Wang Mang were presented in a dynastic system which was considered more solid, better organised and responsible. It was basically the peasants and the local warlords whose aspirations were being represented by Wang Mang. Therefore, the actual appropriation of power was by these elements rather than Wang Mang. The Later Han also ensured a greater representation by the peasants and public through its tripartite governance system like the Qin with a chancellor as the head of the civil officials, the grand commandant as the chief of the army and the department of the colonel of censure, led by the imperial secretary. However, the Chief of the Army controlled the power in reality. Although the polity is not the purview of discussion of this chapter, it is pertinent to mention that the Han Dynasty did see the demise of the eunuchs' control over the imperial family and the capital after a showdown in 189 AD between the eunuchs and the military commander. This led China into a dark age from 220 AD till the rise of the Sui in 581 AD. The geopolitical space during this period signified the presence of non-

Chinese elements who became major players in the Chinese polity. These ethnic groups were called the 'five barbarians', four of which comprised the Tibetan peoples, the Altaic people, Proto-Mongols and Turkic war bands. They reigned in the north of the Yangzi from 204 AD to 439 AD, forming a total of sixteen small kingdoms. They were although nomads but once they got their domain, settled into an agrarian mode and settled into their kingdoms and even strengthened and made walls in the existing gaps to consolidate their defences against other nomads who had yet not got their own domain.[58] During this period, the traditional Chinese dynasties, in total four of them, namely Sang, Qi, Liang and Chin ruled in the south. They kept fighting the barbarian settlers in the north who as time progressed, had naturalised themselves into Chinese ways of agrarian culture and were themselves fighting the relatively greater nomadic tribes further north and west. This was a period in which the Chinese obsession with method failed itself and gave way to chaos accelerated by nomadic assimilation, giving way to warlordism which lorded over the fragmentation of the empire into about 300 self-defence units in 350 AD to about 3,000 by the end of 408 AD caused by the collapse of the Han due to a failure of its own governance system.

MEDIEVAL EMPIRES

Many historians posit that nations are a product of their unique spirit and any regime of substance therefore has to have a theoretical foundation of indisputable quality. The Han dynasty had the acceptance of all that is a repository of values that governed the vast territories, which were otherwise not governable in Machiavellian terms. This hereditary monarchy naturally assumed the 'Mandate of Heaven' which Cao Cao's dynasty asked them to pass on. The Cao Cao did assume the mantle but were not accepted as such. Therefore, the imperial control retreated to the palatial area of influence and was transferred to the south only after the imperials had been driven out south after the fall of the Xian and the Louyang in the north by the five barbarians. This was a period when there was a rapid turnover of dynasties and the restoration of imperial order in Jiankang in the south and a bureaucratic management was not a distant possibility. During these four hundred years of chaos, the five barbarians as mentioned earlier who had naturalised themselves into the Chinese ways in the north, contributed immensely towards the reunification of China, that will be discussed in detail for its importance to the geospatial development by the assimilation of non-Chinese people into China. The other important assimilation of the period of chaos was Buddhism and a renewed interest in Taoism. This happened due to a narrowed application of Confucianism by Han which was a purely social discipline. Thus, a great craving for the concept of Karma to bring in the cause and effect as revealed by the Natural Law emerged instead of the Han dogma of symmetry and balance which was already lost.[59]

The first legitimised assimilation of barbarians took place in 310 AD. The Tuoba, the overlords of the Xian Bei people migrated from Manchuria and helped a Jin general to drive out other nomads in the north. In turn, the Tuoba were authorised to settle 100 miles inside the Great Wall by the Jin and made an agricultural base inside China. After the Jin's short life, the Tuoba went into oblivion from the northern landscape. The 4th Century saw the ascendency of the Tibetans who commanded all non-Chinese groups which came into prominence. As they tried to occupy space in southern China in 383, they were defeated with the help of the Tuoba. But the Tuoba reasserted themselves and declared their leader as the emperor of Northern Wei by assimilating 16 kingdoms which lasted till 534. During this period, they crushingly defeated the Xiongnu tribes and compelled them to settle as agricultural workers around the Huang He bend. They were also responsible for bringing in the Xianbei tribes like the Koreans and the Murong in their capital district around Datong. In the process of consolidating their regime, they forced many nomad barbarians to settle in north China as agriculturists but under nationalised control. They civilised themselves totally and renamed themselves as the Yuan, and moved the capital to Luoyang in 494 AD, reintroduced Han Chinese institutions and took to Taoism and then Buddhism.[60] In 534, Northern Wei split into two. The Western Wei settled its capital in Xian and the Eastern Wei moved to Ye near Anyang leaving Luoyang. Before the split, the Tuoba king Yuan Hong who was threatened by his army officers fled to Xian in the west but was killed by the commander of the Xian. These army commanders divided the Northern Wei into Eastern Wei and Western Wei first and then installed puppet emperors and subsequently usurped the kingdom and established the Northern Qi dynasty in the Eastern Wei and the Northern Zhou dynasty in the Western Wei. These dynasties were of Xianbei ancestry, mixed with Chinese and Xiongnu blood. It is clear that by 557 the distinction between non-Chinese and Chinese was obliterated in the northern space. Now a well-organised and integrated peasantry was put in place by the Northern Wei, but the imperial rule stood divided. Yang Jian, the Duke of Sui under Northern Zhou, took advantage of this situation and after helping the Northern Zhou Emperor to conquer Northern Qi, he took over the Northern Zhou himself in 581 AD and proclaimed the Sui Dynasty. By 589 AD, he annexed Chen, the last of the transient dynasties in the south and unified China again. This was considered as the most autocratic rule which lived for a very short time from 581 to 618 AD but has significance in the Chinese history of cycles of disintegration and reunification and can be compared with what the first Emperor Qin did to Warring States period. Here it is very appropriate to quote the opening aphorism of the *Romance of the Three Kingdoms*: "The empire long unified must divide, long divided must unite," and the ending aphorism in reverse phrasing, "The Empire divided must unite: long united must divide" as an instinct of geopolitics of China in its long history.

Geospatial Analysis

The Sui followed the principles of the Han in terms of dealing with the 'domestic to foreign' span of territories in form of concentric circles beginning from the capital territory to subordinate territories to allied dependents to tributary states, rippling out in all directions. In the bargain, the Sui did reach out to Vietnam, Champa and Khmer kingdoms on the lower Mekong in the south but had no power to subjugate and retain them. While the Sui sensibly considered them as tributary states due to occasional exchanges of missions, but in no way were the Sui considered the suzerain by these states.[61] Similar wishful feelings were nursed by Sui Yangdi towards the Philippines, Taiwan and Rokokyu, but never ever could he send an expedition to Japan. Both did exchange religious–diplomatic missions. Though Sui Yangdi assumed Japanese acceptance of Sui suzerainty, the Japanese empress Yamato considered the Japanese emperor as the 'Rising Son of the Heaven' against the Chinese counterpart as 'Sunset Son of Heaven'—an equal denomination thereby. Sui's invasion of Korea remained unsuccessful, but he did win over a token acknowledgement for Chinese suzerainty.

As far as the domestic space was concerned, the population during this time was around 54 million—the main concentration was around the Wei-Fan valley having about 11 million people.[62] The remaining were located in the east and south. Despite the south of the Yang Zi being the grain bowl of China, it remained sparsely populated and was considered as one province only. In this short period of rule, Sui obsessively engaged himself in construction work. The great wall was fortified with the labour of 1 million people. Near Chang An, a capital of mammoth scale (around 31 square miles) was built as the western capital. The eastern capital of Luoyang was further expanded with 2 million labourers bringing timber from the Yang Zi valley.[63] Not satisfied with two capitals, the Sui Emperors constructed a third capital Qiangdu (Yangzhan) on the estuary of the Yang Zi in order to consolidate their hold on to the rich south, with its rice surpluses. They made canals by clearing the waterways made in the mid-4th Century which connected the Yang Zi and the Huai rivers. They further extended them to connect the Hai river (Tianxin) in the north with the Huang Zhou in the south, making a total of 800 miles of canals.[64] This trend of geo-spatial consolidation was proving too much for the well-organised peasantry. Even then, the Sui could not include Guangxi and Yunnan within China's sovereignty. The Sui was also a period in which the barbarians mixed with the Chinese, dominated the north in the Huang He valley and the pure Han remained confined to the south.

The Tang Period (618–907)

The Tang dynasty was founded by Liyuan of the Li family, belonging to the military aristocracy of the north-west, during the collapse of the Sui dynasty caused primarily by the failed Korean campaign.[65] First installing a puppet child emperor of Sui, he then relegated Emperor Yang of the Sui to the position of Tai Shang Huang (retired emperor) and ultimately declared himself as the Emperor of a new dynasty Tang, on June 18, 618 AD.[66] Lishi Min deposed his father and became the famous Tang Emperor Taizong. Taizong and Xuanzong were two prominent rulers during the Tang rule, under whom the Tang dynasty reached to golden period, especially during the 44-year rule of Xuanzong.

Map 22: Tang China and the 'Others'

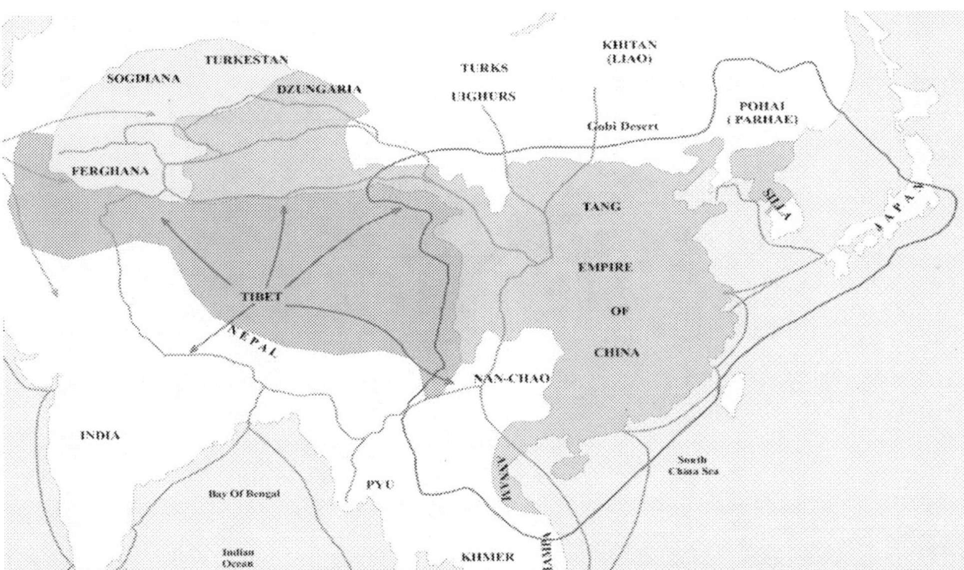

A Geospatial Analysis of China during the Tang Period

The Tang kept Chang An (Xi An now) as their capital which was the most populous city in the world during those days. Some estimated the population to be around 74 million that was achieved during the golden period of the Tang from 640 to 755 AD.[67, 68] In the initial stages of the Tang, the Tibetan empire gave Tang a tough fight over the control of the Tarim basin between 670–692 and ultimately captured Xinjiang and even captured Chang An during the An Shi Rebellion, for 15 days.[69] Thus China lost control over the western regions beyond the famous Jade Gate known in Chinese as the Yumen Guan,[70] 80 km ahead of Dun-Huang. It was the last outpost city of China's western territories under an effective control at the end of the geo-strategically most important Hexi corridor through which the Silk Road ran north-west and was key to China's trade to Central Asia, the Arab world and South Asia. During this time, in order to assuage the Tibetan ruler Songtsan Gampo, the Tang Emperor married Princess Wen Cheng to him, and it is claimed that she took Buddhism to Tibet along with her. This certainly has a counterclaim in the same king also being married to a Nepalese princess Bhrikuti Devi who brought Buddhist scripts along with her and Buddhism thus

Map 23: Hexi Corridor

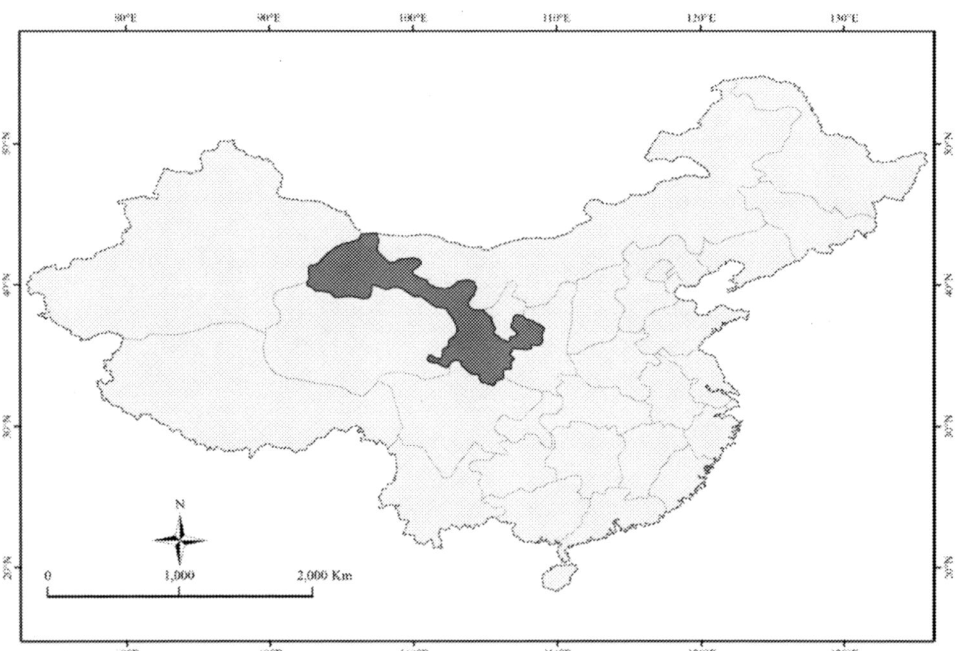

spread in Tibet. This narrative is not accepted by the Chinese historians who try to blame on modern Tibetans' over-anxiousness to relate themselves more to India and Nepal than to China.[71] However, by 751 AD the Tang lost control over the Tarim Basin to the Turks and Arabs and the landscape changed from Buddhist to Islamic.

The main movement of population and the consolidation of Tang to include the areas permanently under their realm was towards the subtropical and tropical regions in the south. The causes of migration were harassment from the Turks and Tibetans, famines, floods, heavy taxation to support the war expenses and a lack of land to cultivate for an increasing population in the north. Jiang Xu and Chejian were the main areas of occupation which extended into present-day northern Vietnam and then to Guandong, Fujian and Ziang Xu in the south-eastern coastal areas. The coastal areas were also engaged due to the Arab and Persian traders coming through the sea route and doing business with the Chinese traders. However, what China could not usurp was the Korean peninsula. The Tang had though attacked the Goguryeo and Backje kingdoms with the help of Silla kingdom by 668 AD, but due to the Tang assertion on their allied Silla kingdom, the Silla turned into an enemy of the Tang. Ultimately, the Silla expelled the Tang from the entire peninsula as well as from the areas south of the Bohai river by 676. This was the territory which saw a direct influence of the Yamato allies from Japan later.[72]

Geopolitically, Tang during Taizong expended its territories to make China bigger than Han. This was the beginning of the golden period of Tang which ended after the An Lushan rebellion in 756 and the Tibetan, Turk and Arab invasions. These territories were never a permanent feature for long as the claim of influence under the metaphysical concept of the 'Mandate of Heaven' to rule '*Tian Xia*' (All under Heaven) remained a mere conjecture of a bigger nation as it did not have as much support on ground as claimed by China.

China during the Song, Yang and Ming

China, after a prolonged reign of various regimes, has always fallen into a period of disarray. A similar trend took place when the Tang regime of about four hundred years (618–907) fell into the hands of Zhu Wen, a military governor of the Tang, leading to the Five Dynasties and Ten Kingdoms period of disintegration. The decline of the Tang can be attributed to the An Shi Rebellion, the weakened control of the ageing Emperor Xuanzong, the subsequent rebellion of Huang Chao and a greater autonomy to the regional military commanders to counter external threats as the Tang central power found itself incapable against these many odds. These regional military commanders became a challenge to the central power and the usurpation of the Tang regime by Zhu Wen who established later the Liang Dynasty, was followed by others to make themselves into independent realms of the Five Dynasties and Ten kingdoms.[73]

One geospatial difference that is clearly evident through these discussions so far is a geographical divide and the geopolitical pull of opposite directions between north and south China. Xi An in the west no more remained as capital after the Tang. Louyang in the east was taken as capital with the preference over the north-western arid region for Manchuria being a semi-nomad, semi-agricultural region and the bedrock of the northern dynasties. With pure nomadic threats from the Tibetans and Turks, this move achieved a strategic depth and closeness to the areas of economic benefit. Thereafter, the intensely agricultural south and commercially more vibrant south-east, due to the coastal commerce developing at a fast pace, changed the direction of struggle between the Chinese and the non-Chinese groups in the ensuing 400 years. The first manifestation of this geopolitical change became evident when China was demarcated between the north and the south with the Five Dynasties ruling north China and the Ten Kingdoms ruling south China. It was also a characteristic of north to have greater upheavals due to cultural differences compared to the south which looked more settled. Due to this cultural difference of being semi-nomadic in nature and being more prone to adopting violent methods to settle disputes, one of the Five Dynasties i.e. the Later Zhou, took upon itself to first annex all other dynasties north of the Yangzi between 956–959 AD and establish the Northern Song Dynasty and then winning all the Ten Kingdoms in South China, to establish a unified Song Dynasty in China by 918 AD. Besides the Five Dynasties of the north and the Ten Kingdoms of the south, we have also witnessed a similar divide in the period before and during the Three Kingdom period (220–280 AD), the Sixteen Kingdoms period (317–470 AD), the southern and northern dynasties of the Warring States (420–589 AD) and subsequently, the Southern Song (1127–1279 AD), the Jin Dynasty (1115–1234 AD) and the Warlord era (1916–1928 AD). This divide of the north and the south was basically a geopolitical manifestation of difference in climatic geography, culture and physical traits. Militarily, this divide manifested itself in a cavalry dominance in the north and that of river-based navies in the south.

Map 24: Song China

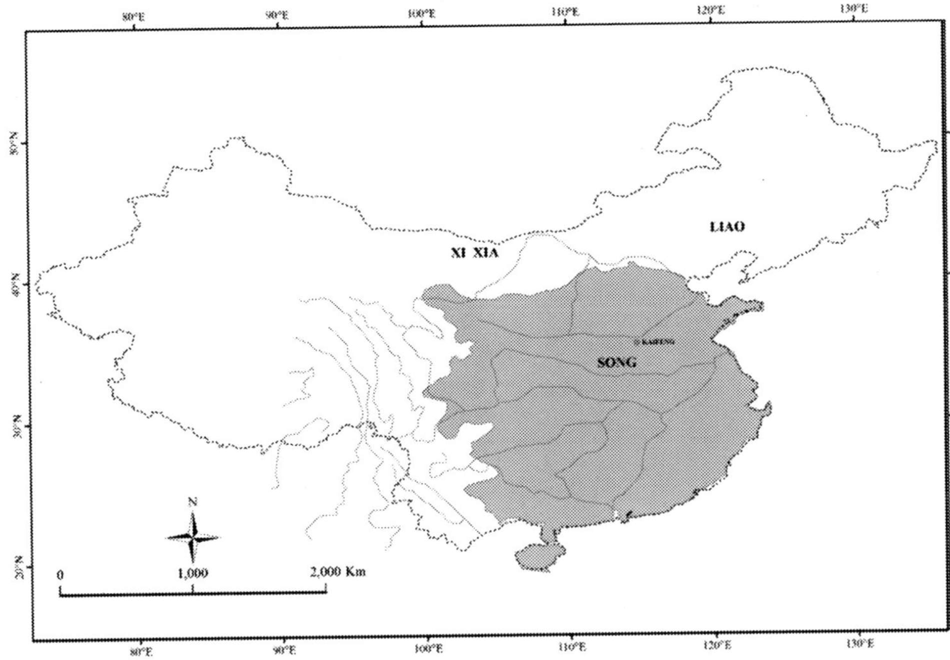

A Geospatial Analysis of the Song (960–1279)

Being attacked by the Jurchen from the north east, the Song capital was shifted from Kaifeng in the north to Hangzhou in the south of the Yangzi. The Jurchen established rule of Jin dynasty in the north and the Song established their rule south of Yangzi river by 1227 AD. Thereafter, the Southern Song period began which though remained confined to the areas south of the Yangzi was actually commanding 60 per cent of China's population and agricultural canals.[74]

The Southern Song remained peaceful till 1279 when the Great Khan of the Mongol Empire, Mongke Khan, overran the Jin in the north and captured Chonqing in the upper Yangzi. After his death, his son Kublai Khan proclaimed himself as the Emperor of China and conquered the Song Dynasty in 1279 unifying North and South China under the Yuan Dynasty (1271–1368) of Mongol origin.[75] Otherwise, during their heydays, the Song penetrated down south up to Hanoi in Vietnam by 1082, and exchanged each other's territories under an agreement. Besides these, they maintained diplomatic relations with the Cholas of India and Sirivijaya of Indonesia and Egypt through the sea route, but when the Khitans of the north once pushed the Jin to south and the Jin pushed the Song to further

Map 25: Jin Ascendance

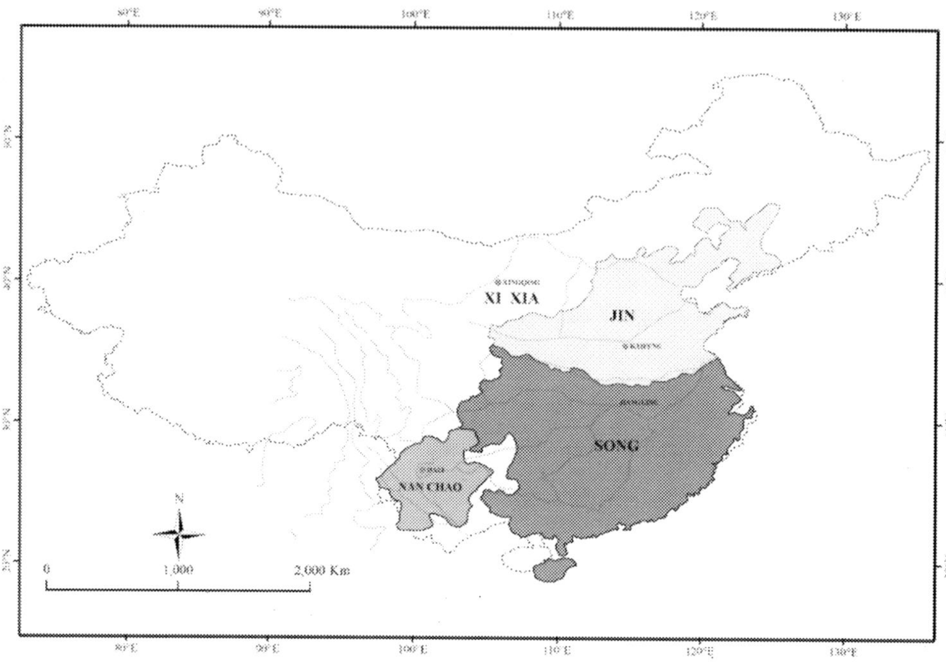

south, the Song did develop themselves into a naval power of the ocean and the rivers.

Yuan Dynasty: Mongolian China (1271–1368)

So far, we have seen the struggle of power between the nomadic forces and the Chinese agriculturist forces. The nomadic forces like those of the Scythians and Xiongnu had threatened the Chinese empire between 800 BC to 500 AD. Thereafter, the Rouran, Juan and Rudu tribes of Mongolia, the Gokturks of Central Asia, the Uyghur and Tibetan nomadic forces troubled China from the north-west to due east. But these nomadic forces could not be kept away from occupation of China for long as they had developed themselves into great expeditionary forces. By 1200 AD, Genghis Khan had founded the Mongol Empire which encompassed the territories of north-east Asia and eastern Europe. In this wake, Genghis Khan united the Mongols and Turkic tribes of the steppes and sent his third son Ogedei Khan to destroy the weakened Jin Dynasty in North China. The task was completed by capturing China north of the Yangzi by 1234. Genghis Khan died in 1227 and was succeeded by Ogedei Khan and then Mongke Khan to control the Chinese territories.[76] Mongke Khan died while campaigning against the Song in South China in 1259 without a successor. By now, there were four Khaganates of the Mongols encompassing most of the Eurasian continent. The Golden Horde controlled most of Russia including Moscow and Kiev. Chagdai Khan controlled most of Central Asia and Afghanistan, whereas the Ilkhanate controlled Iran, Iraq, Turkey and Armenia. After having conquered Southern Song, thereby entire China, Kublai Khan Younger brother of Mongke Khan and grandson of Genghis Khan was declared the Great Khagan presiding over all four Khaganates at Kaiping in Inner Mongolia.[77]

Map 26: China as a Mongolian Khaganate

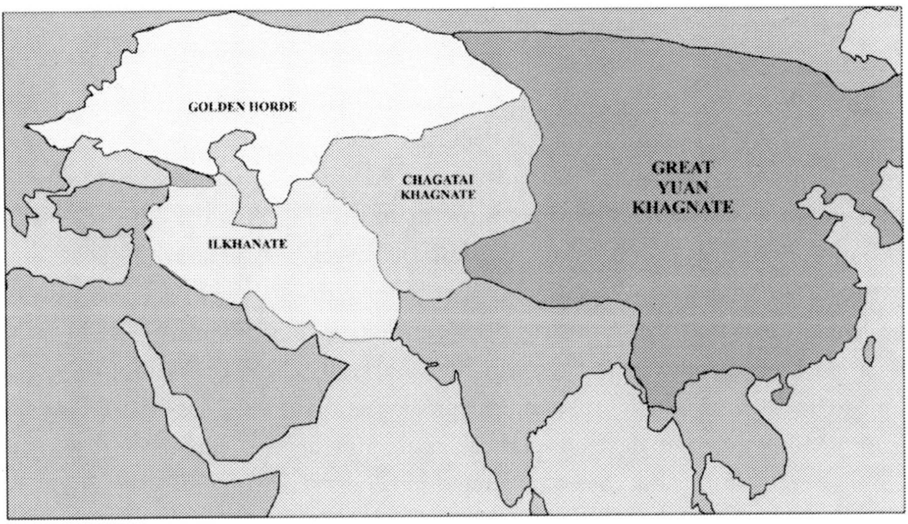

Geospatial Analysis

The great Yuan was the largest of the four Khaganates with its capital at Karakorum in Mongolia which was moved by Kublai Khan to Khanbaliq near Beijing (Zhongdu, the Jurchen Jin capital) in 1260. Kublai Khan by now had realised the greater importance of the Chinese territories over the Mongolian in terms of geographical resources and the dense agrarian population he had under control. Therefore, he adopted all Chinese traditions and claimed the 'Mandate of Heaven' to rule China in 1271 and declared the new dynastic rule of the Dayuan or Great Yuan in 1272. In 1278, he captured entire south China, uprooting the remnants of the Southern Song. However, his subsequent campaigns against Japan, Vietnam (Annam) Champa (Indonesia) and Burma (Myanmar) failed.

Since Kublai considered himself the Great Khan of all four Khaganates, the Yuan remained an occupational force throughout their reign despite modelling his government on the bureaucracy of the traditional Chinese dynasties and adopting the Chinese era, Zhongtong. During his time the geopolitical landscape of China was more Mongolian than Chinese; one because the map of the Yuan Empire was more a map of Mongolia than of China as it began from vast areas even north of Mongolia, and second, because it included Tibet which had been so far beyond the reach of any Chinese dynasty. Most of all, Kublai divided the Yuan society into four classes with the Han occupying the lowest rank.[78] Therefore, the Yuan geospatial aggregation remained alien to the imagination of the Chinese people or the majority Han; otherwise they would have loved to invoke the Yuan for the purposes of their modern-day territorial claims.

Ming China

There were several reasons for the decline of Yuan and the rise of the Ming. Foremost was the demise of Kublai Khan in 1294, followed by a succession of eight emperors in the next 26 years through coups and plots besides the general alienation of Chinese population. The last Yuan emperor ruled for 35 years, but by then Zhu Yuanzhang (also known as Ming Taizu, or "the great Ancestors of the Ming") had risen from dust to become the most formidable power to expel the Yuan towards north, and the northern parts of China including Mongolia came to be called as Northern Yuan. The proclamation of the 'Mandate of Heaven' on the Ming thus got delayed as there could not be two emperors as per the Chinese tradition. Zhu then conducted several waves of political purges to consolidate his ascendency and centrality of command and declared himself as Emperor Hong Wu. He went for an extreme centralisation of power, divided population into military and civil, organised them into platoons and companies, granted them parcels of land and assigned them military service obligation and administrative support obligations. The families obliged to render military service were not to pay any taxes.[79] In this way, the Ming decentralised the military with a centralised command, without any need to mobilise them and to support them with any long supply line. Of course, this strict control on the employment and movement of population had stalling effects on the polity and economy.

Map 27: Ming China

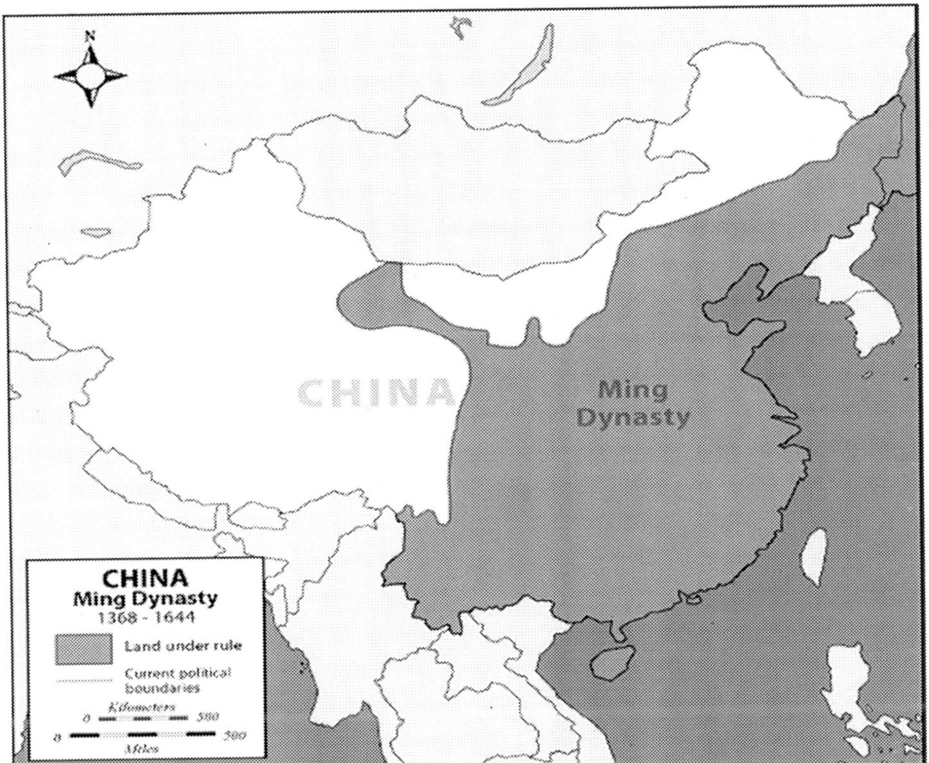

Source: http://archive.artsmia.org/art-of-asia/history/images/maps/china-ming-large.gif

Geospatial Analysis

Zhu Yuanzhang, the first emperor, was a rebel from the Yangzi river valley region who first made Nanjing his capital and then moved north to expel the Northern Yuan residual elements and razed the Yuan capital of Khanbaliq to establish the first capital of China by the name of Beijing (Beiping). The Yuan thus retreated to the other Central Asian steppes of Mongolia. Emperor Hong Wu (Zhu Yuanzhang) kept the country tightly enclosed. He did not venture out much. He did not allow his own people to take to the sea and when Japanese pirates encroached upon the coastline. Rather he shifted the local population inland. On top of that, he left permanent injunctions for his descendants against sending expeditions to 15 countries of the east, the south-east and south.[80] The sole reason which could be attributed to such tight central control of movement to any direction other than the north and west was that he remained paranoid with the Yuan rebels in the north and a drive to assimilate the Muslim population well, with cross-marriages with the majority Han, and by awarding of better positions. The Hui Salar and Uighur Muslims settled in Changde and Huinan. He also annexed the Kingdom of Dali in Yunnan, held by the Yuan-loyalist Mongols and Hui Muslims and colonised the state by sending 2,00,000 military colonists to Yunnan and Guizhou.[81] The sinification of the local people was his one of the main concerns. His strategy of central control is followed even today.

On the Tibetan front it is believed that Tibet remained largely cut off, but they did maintain a relationship of tea and horse trade and scholarship of the Lamas for the exchanges on Buddhism.[82] Unlike the Yuan, the Ming due to their highly restrictive and internalised strategies of domain consolidation, did not have garrisons in Tibet allowing a Mongol dominance via the Amdo region—one of the three regions of the Historical Tibet, now not part of the Tibetan Autonomous region. Therefore, the Mongols reached first when the 5th Dalai Lama of the Yellow Hat Sect asked for help, culminating into the establishment of the Khoshut Khanate with an understanding of power-sharing to dominate the rival religious sects in Tibet. The power of the Dalai Lama was recognised by the Qing Emperor even after the demise of the Ming Dynasty which had recognised the suzerainty of Tibet, as was recognised by the Mongolian Khans and the kings and the rulers of Ladakh, Nepal, India, Bhutan and Sikkim.[83] Similarly, Xinjiang also remained out of the political control of the Ming but it did pay tribute to the Ming Empire.

The most geopolitical activity of significance during the Ming period were the the Zheng He voyages, an activity which was not allowed by the first emperor. The second emperor Zhu Di, better known as Yongle Emperor, after seizing the throne reversed the injunctions of the first emperor. He sent expeditionary forces to Vietnam and incorporated Vietnam as a Chinese province and commissioned Zheng He, a eunuch, in 1405, to take the first voyage of 62 large ships and 225 small ships with 27,800 men on board. He took seven such voyages, the last being in 1432–33 during reign of the fifth Ming Emperor Zhu Zhang.[84] The fleet was more of a military envoy than being commercial in nature. Zheng He is said to have engaged in the local politics of Java, captured the King of Ceylon (Sri Lanka) and brought him to Nanjing as well as inducing a dozen of other states to pay tribute to Chinese Emperor. The fleets called upon the ports of Hormuz, Zanzibar, Aden and others.

The Chinese scholars immensely regard the discontinuation of the voyages a reason for setting China back on the ocean front, allowing the Japanese pirates to

Map 28: Zheng He Voyages

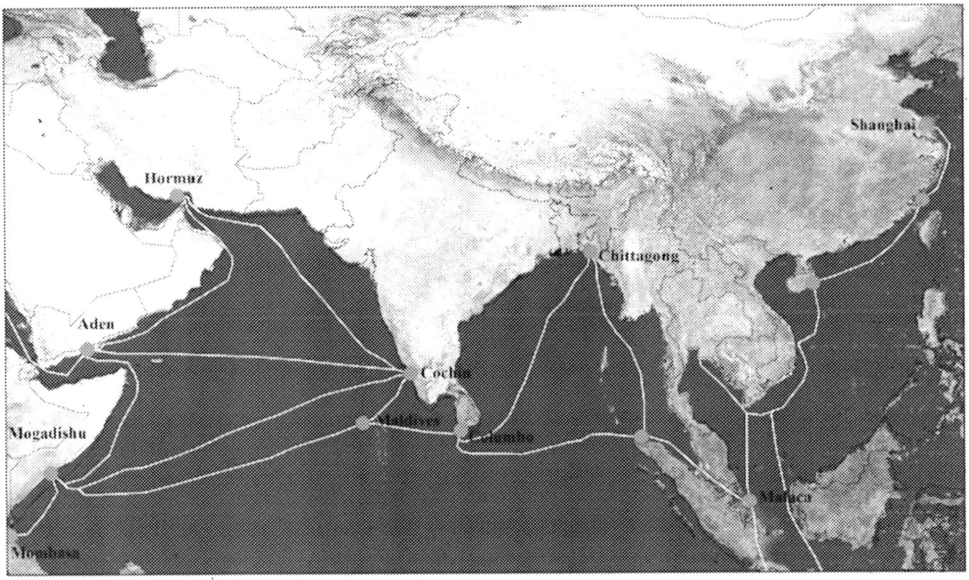

attack coastal China, disabling China from acquiring the modern seafaring techniques of the Europe, the capture of Ma Cao by the Portuguese and the 17th and 18th Centuries and humiliation of China by the naval powers in the absence of a credible naval force. Although the reasons for the discontinuation are not clear, they can be directly attributed to the revoking of the restrictive orders of the Hong Wu Emperor as Yongle Emperor's grandson Hong Xi Emperor considered that those voyages were contrary to the rules stipulated in the Huan Ming Zuxun, the dynastic foundation documents laid down by the Hong Wu Emperor.[85] However, the voyage of Zheng He was allowed for last time (the seventh) by the Xuan De emperor during which he died. The voyages of Zheng He have also become a symbol of invoking a nationalist pride for China as some sources even claim that Zheng He discovered the Americas even before Columbus.[86] In his book, Gavin Menzies claims that in the 18th Century, a copy of Admiral Zheng He's 1417 map was discovered by a Beijing Attorney, which supports that argument. He corroborates this with Chinese names of Peruvian villages and the Chinese genealogical strands in the Latin Americans, especially the Peruvians. The claim is still considered unfounded and premature and has no archaeological evidence in China. Nevertheless, it indicates either of the two: either the tall claims are part of the Chinese campaign to bolster nationalism through going back to history for claims ranging from territoriality to being a supreme civilisation or that the event was capped down by the reassertion of the existing Ming policy of the Hong Wu Emperor without much successes.

With this analysis, now there are a few deductions from the Ming Dynastic policies, those can be brought out. One is that the Ming were internally strong but externally restrictive and week. This led to an obstruction in the flow of the economy and technology leading to an overbearing cost of running a centralised governance system. This ultimately led to a collapse of the regime as, while outward expeditions were checked, the external threats loomed large. The Ming did not have resources at the end of their regime to support the counter-expedition because as Ray Huang says, a separation from the natural power of the national economy was a characteristic of the Ming administration. However, this self-administrated filter of territorial claims to reduce 'us' from 'others' (barbarians) by the Ming gives us the truest map of 'China proper' for the geopolitical analysis of China's imperatives for constructing its future geopolitical responses.

A MODERN PERSPECTIVE

The geopolitical elements from the history derived by the modern Chinese scholars and the establishment on majority of occasions for looking back into the 100 years of humiliation are to invoke a sense of revenge and another 100 years of glorious past before this period to revive nationalism among the common Chinese. Therefore, the Qing Empire has the most profound and indelible imprint of the imperial China on the Chinese minds in both a negative as well as a positive sense. The geographical history of the Qing Empire also becomes important because of the fact that Modern China's foreign relations began with the Qing Dynasty, albeit by force, which impacted the thinking of the Chinese mandarins and foreign policymakers alike. This is despite the fact that at the onset, Qing the Manchu themselves who were an original Jurchen Aisin Giioro clan ruling in the Northern China and more akin to the Mongols than the Han, were the rulers under whom the Han did experience humiliation. There are, therefore, two arguments convenient to modern China that will be our emphasis of discussion. One is that the Qing expanded China to more than a shape that it looks today and second that the Qing became one among the Chinese, in fact, both became complementary to each other. Hence, modern China becomes inseparable from the Qing China geopolitically in its historical perspective.

Early Qing and the Golden Period

Li Zecheng, leader of the peasant rebellion, had gained a lot of ground in Shan Xi in 1642 after the Kaifeng Floods in which 3,00,000 out its 3,70,000 citizens had died. The Ming were very weak at that time as they were also facing external threats on the Manchurian borders in the north-east. When in April 1644, Li Zecheng entered the capital Beijing, Wu Sangui, the Ming military commander defending against the Manchus (Qing) far from Beijing was called for help to protect Beijing. But the Ming fell before Wu Sangui could reach, and Li Zecheng declared himself emperor. Wu was about to surrender to Li being a domestic force but on learning that he had seized his favourite concubine Chen Yuanyuan, reversed his decision and colluded with the Qing, opening the gates of the Great Wall at the Shanhai pass and defeated Li Zecheng along with the Qing who in turn captured Beijing on 25 April 1644.[87] the Qing then implemented their Banner system, an administrative system under which several military colonies were supported by local resources. This military colonisation was carried out by bringing

Map 29: An Unfounded Map of Trouble that Fascinates the Chinese Consciousness Today

Source: https://upload.wikimedia.org/wikipedia/commons/c/ca/Qing_Dynasty_1820.png

in and settling down military families from Manchuria. A combination of military expedition and diplomacy enabled them to wipe out the remaining Ming resistance in the south. Once they won over the support of the Yangzi valley gentry by 1673, their conquest of China was complete

A Geospatial Analysis of Modern China

After a total control over the territories of Ming China, the Qing then till the end of the 18th Century, continued with their expansion plans slowly and steadily as they consolidated more and more power. After Kang Xi, the second emperor, completed the occupation of China Proper; the Qianlong Emperor (1735–1796) took ten campaigns to extend China into Central Asia. Kang Xi Emperor adopted a Neo-Confucian bureaucratic system of the earlier dynasties for governance and the centralised examination system for the selection of the bureaucrats as well. Secondly, the Qing kept their separate identity of the Central Asian heritage alive so that they could appear appealing to other nationalities like the Mongols, Tibetans, Uighur constituents of the Qing empire and their Khans and Buddhist sage rulers along with being the 'Son of Heaven' for the Han at the same time.[88] However, during their entire regime they crafted their identity to remain unique by several measures. Marriages between the Manchu and Han were forbidden. The Manchu under the Eight Banner System maintained separate Manchu garrisons which lived off the Han countryside and state resources. The status of Manchu was always higher in all the spheres. The Manchu started a separate examination system for the selection of the Manchu officials so as to avoid a fierce competition with the Han.

Qianlong Emperor completed the occupation of Xinjiang by 1759 and extended his reign up to the Balkhash Lake. His forces engaged Tsarist Russian forces in the north-east and got a great chunk of land surrendered to the Qing. Korea, already a protectorate of China, was joined with other protectorates like Siam, Burma, Vietnam, Bhutan and Mongolia. After Qianlong Emperor retired in 1796, his son Jiaqin Emperor (1796–1820) took over. But the problems to the throne had already emerged. The first was the population which ballooned from 100 million to 300 million during the 18th Century due to a diversified food production with the introduction of European crops like potatoes and peanuts. But even that was not sufficient for the rate of growth.

The geospatial expansion of the Chinese settlements during the Qing had three dimensions beyond the China proper which were exclusively marked by the drainage systems running to the east and the interspersed mountains between the river valleys. These were the high mountains and the river valley at the edge of Tibet, the broad steppe and deserts of Inner Mongolia and the grasslands and forests of Manchuria. The Chinese landmass during the Qing period went much beyond the present-day political boundaries. The reason of the subsequent shrinking basically lies in the manner these outside regions were held and governed. The Chinese concept of '*Nei*' (inner) and '*Wai*' (outer) did play a major role in holding these territories in relation to the '*nei guo*' which matched with the pre-Qing, Han territory. The map shows the region under active control and the outer regions under the passive control of the Qing. Ironically, Manchuria did remain an outer region even during the Qing period, along with Mongolia. Parts of Central Asia, adjacent to East Turkistan and Tibet claimed independence, some for a short while and others permanently. However, some Chinese historians like Zhao Gang do portray the territorial expanse of Qing China as the Historical Chinese people which includes Han, Manchu and Mongol subjects of the Qing, the Chinese language including Chinese, Manchu and Mongol languages and China or Zhong Guo equated to Qing China including the present day Manchuria, Xinjiang, Mongolia, Tibet and other areas.[89] Many such authors have invoked the territoriality of the Qing as evidence to the territorial claims of China in various border disputes.

China Proper and the Century of National Humiliation

The geospatial texture of China changed dramatically during these 100 years of National Humiliation, a term which was coined first in 1915 for invoking the Chinese nationalist feeling against the Twenty-One Demands put forward by the Japanese and accepted by the Qing representative to Japan, Yuan Shikai. The first inception was by the Guomin Dang, and subsequently the Chinese Communist Party, for gathering support—first against the Qing and the imperial forces, and then against the rest of the world as imperial forces.

The geopolitical ramifications of these 100 years have been so deep that the impact needs a detailed discussion as it still looms large in the minds of the policymakers in China.

The period of national humiliation is basically a reflection of a weak empire which had outgrown its capacity to uphold its integrity. It was further compounded by the simmering alienation felt by the Han against the Manchu although today the official mindset does not support this argument.[90] Yongzheng Emperor entered into an agreement with Russia for non-interference in Mongol affairs for an exchange of territory. This delegation purely made up of the Manchu was resented by the Han. Then the emperor turned to the Junghar rebellion in Mongolia and the Miao rebellion in the north-west. All these campaigns drained the finances.[91] Subsequently, Qianlong Emperor faced a revolt in Mongolia and Xinjiang and an uprising in Sichuan while expanding control over Tibet. Corruption by Qianlong Emperor's favourite official Heshen (estimated to have amassed 1,100 million Tael (40 grams silver each), which was estimated to be 15 years' revenue of the Qing government of that time), the population explosion especially in South China and the primitiveness of the Banner system of the Chinese army against any modern European Army were several other reasons making ground for the incidents of the next hundred years which was to be called as the period of humiliation.

The European trading companies had already consolidated their hold in India and Indonesia and began trading with China privately on the south-eastern coast. To deal with these traders, the Qing established a Canton System giving thirteen private merchants factories through which trade could be carried out through a single port only, for a fear of the internal situation aggravating if the southern citizens came into contact with the foreign traders like Flint Affairs, wherein the foreign companies violated restrictions for better commercial gains.[92] To resolve this issue of tight control by China on foreign trade, the East India Company under the permission of the King of Britain took a McCartney mission to the court of Qianlong Emperor to remedy the situation by seeking permission of the Qing Emperor to establish reciprocal and commercial access to other ports along the Chinese coast.[93] The mission was an initial failure due to McCartney's refusal to kowtow (bow down with the head to touch the ground) before the Emperor considering it to be a mark of subjugation of the King of Britain, accepting to kneel before him. But after the audience after a month and a half. while participating in the birthday celebrations of the emperor to win his sympathy, what McCartney got was the most humiliatingly worded letter to the King of Britain, not befitting an equal sovereign, dismissing any need to trade on other ports saying:

> "...should your vessels touch the shore, your merchants will assuredly never be permitted to land to reside there but will be subject to instant expulsion. In that event your barbarian merchants will have a long journey for nothing. Do not say that you were not warned in due time! Tremblingly obey and show no negligence! A Special Mandate."[94]

Henry Kissinger rightly says that McCartney's only achievement was to be allowed to kneel on one knee before Qianlong and then his letter as a reprisal. This failure of the mission was of one of the causes of the European powers taking up illegitimate means of trade in coastal China and the first Opium War which brought in great changes in the geospatial landscape of China as such.

China remained closed to the European 'barbarians', and despite the arrogant mandate of the emperor of the Celestial Empire (China) in the letter, the British envoys—Lord Amherst and Lord Napier— were sent as Britain was in more of a need of China's economy which was seven times greater than Britain at that time.[95] While other countries were engaged in a restricted business from Canton, the British East India Company offloaded opium from India in the greed of Chinese silver bullion through Chinese smugglers. This was a substance totally banned in China. The Qing Emperor decided to enforce a ban in Canton in 1839. Once having failed to stop the opium import, he blockaded all foreigners by sending the Chinese official Lin Zexu. While the cause was legitimate, the self-gratifying notion of the Chinese's military power or moral ascendency in the terms of considering themselves as a Celestial Empire under the 'Mandate of Heaven' was reflected in the letter of Lin Zexu sent to the British Queen saying that if the Chinese goods do not reach the Western Barbarians they would die, whereas the Chinese could do without theirs, therefore, the opium trade must stop.[96] It did not, as it was a counter-trading measure for gaining silver from China to square off the trade deficit in the payments of Chinese silk, porcelain and tea, in silver. Lin Zexu then destroyed 20,000 chests of opium and imposed the death penalty if any ships carrying opium docked at Canton. In fact, war was started by the British naval ships firing at their own ships carrying opium to sink them following the regulations of Chinese and the Chinese trying to save them and the British in turn blockading the Pearl River delta. In June 1840, the British Indian Army troops on 15 ships, 4 steam-powered gunboats and 25 smaller boats reached Canton. In a war that lasted for over two years, the British East India Company captured the Pearl River delta, Chusan, the Bogue Forts, Ningbo, Dinghai and Shanghai in 1842 and entered into the Treaty of Nanjing.[97] It was a treaty between the winner and the defeated. Therefore, highly unequal conditions against the wishes of the Chinese sovereign were accepted by the Qing like the opening of the additional four ports of Xiamen (Amoy), Fuzhou, Ningbo and Shanghai; to pay for the opium destroyed and to pay 21 million silver dollars as war reparations; to release all British prisoners and those Chinese who had aided and abated the British. The acquisition of Hong Kong as a Crown Colony was the most cherished success of the British, which remained under British in occupation till 1997. Considered as the most unequal treaty, the Chinese mark it as the first event of national humiliation. It exposed the Chinese Army, destroyed the Qing Dynasty's prestige and changed the Chinese coastline. It also forced China to look to the south militarily, which it had ignored so far.

The Taiping Rebellion (1850–1864): Led by Hong Xiuguan, who proclaimed himself as the younger brother of Jesus, the Taiping Rebellion was a manifestation of the Qing weakness against the Western imperial power. Therefore, it was said to be a Han rebellion against the Qing, seeking to replace Confucianism and Buddhism through an own form of Christianity. The rebellion became popular because of the equal right of property and equality for women. The rebels established the Taiping Heavenly Kingdom with its capital at Nanjing. Ultimately, the Qing government crushed the rebellion with the help of the French and British forces, killing not less than 20 million people.[98]

In addition, there were many other rebellions in China like the Nian Rebellion (1851–1868) in north China, the Muslim Rebellion known as the Panthay Rebellion (1853–1873) and the Dungan Revolt (1862–1877) that ran concurrently in order to topple the Qing. These rebellions weakened the Qing and invited a rapid growth of Western imperialism. This was a time for other Western colonial powers to expand their overseas market and attain more ports of call as was manifested in the French Treaty of Hengpu and the US Treaty of Wangxia. Although the British had the advantage of being the most favourite nation, they still could not access the inner China for trade and a permanent embassy in Beijing besides the request to legalising the opium trade along with the English language treaty text to be referred to in case of disputes. The request was rejected as its acceptance would have construed an equal status to the Barbarian West. However, though the Chinese did not check the British flagships, they did harass their Chinese native collaborators. One such flagship was the *Arrow* which flew the British Flag which was checked by the Chinese, upon which an apology was asked from the Chinese by the Hong Kong Governor. Seeing no apology coming, the British governor ordered an attack on Canton in 1856. The Second Opium war ensued with all other rebellions running concurrently. The Qing were unable to resist the West. The French joined the action with the British, over the execution of a French missionary. After capturing Canton, they marched north to Tianjin and captured the Dagu Fort and asked for negotiations with the Qing who were not ready to enter as an equal if not defeated, which was in fact a denial mode. Ultimately, the Treaty of Tianjin was drawn, and the British were allowed a permanent embassy in Beijing, travel up the Yangzi river, open additional ports for trade, the protection of Christian converts (despite suffering at the hands the Christian-leaning Taiping Rebellion). The French and Americans also drew their own negotiations separately. However, the treaty was not settled.

By now the Manchu and Han divide had become wider as was evident in the Mongolians being brought to defend the Dagu Fort which was held briefly in the First Opium War. When the Anglo-French envoys went via land route to establish respective embassies as per the Tianjin Treaty, they were not permitted to do so. They attacked the Dagu Fort and laid siege with the Americans also joining in. They captured Tianjin and marched ahead to Beijing in August 1860. In the meanwhile, Lord Elgin joined the battle with reinforcements from India. When they reached Beijing, Xianfeng Emperor of the Qing, fled Beijing. By now, all eight Western powers had joined in the onslaught. The summer palaces were burnt down on the orders of Lord Elgin. The Convention of Beijing was signed by the brother of the Emperor, Prince Gong, ratifying the Treaty of Tianjin and giving more benefits to the Western powers. These included opening Tianjin as a trade port, ceding Kowloon to Britain, the freedom of religion in China, the legalisation of the opium trade, and allowing the ships carrying indentured Chinese labourers with an indemnity to Britain and France by 8 million silver Taels. The Chinese also ceded their maritime provinces east of the Ussuri river to Russia where today the port of Vladivostok has been developed. This defeat by small firepower led to an introspection by the Qing and a self-strengthening movement and to the Yong Ying system of the army separate from the Eight Banner and the creation of a Green Standard Army based on the local unit system wherein the officers were never rotated.[99] The imperial family did realise the inadequacy of the imperial system and initiated the Tong Zhi Restoration to adopt the Western military technology with a new governmental system based on the Confucian philosophy to put up departmental interfaces to deal with the new-found affairs of necessities like foreign maritime trade and foreign affairs through the Zongli Yamen (Office in Charge of Affairs of All Nations) or simply said, an Office of Foreign Affairs and Chinese Maritime Customs Service, besides the opening of diplomatic missions by foreign nations.[100] These restoration measures were manifested in the self-strengthening movement led by the generals and diplomats like Zeng Guofan and Li Hongzhang.

Despite all these efforts, however, the geospatial deterioration of China continued. Russia, which was closer to China diplomatically, had already occupied Outer Mongolia through its dubious diplomacy of Count Nikolai Ignatieff, the

Tsar's brilliant but devious plenipotentiary in Beijing.[101] This was also a period when Empress Dowager Cixi along with Empress Dowager Cian ruled as regent for the Guangxu Emperor. After the death of Cian, Cixi alone ruled as regent, from 1881.[102] This was a clear weakness in the imperial rule. On the other hand, the Meiji restoration which began in 1868 in Japan became successful and restored the imperial rule of the Meiji (enlightened rule) in order to combine the Western advances with the traditional Eastern values.[103] By 1895, Japan had become militarily modern, whereas China could not keep up the pace. Therefore, Japan was ready to settle its rule over Korean peninsula from being a Chinese protectorate to a Japanese extension of one on the mainland. The *New York Times* appropriately carried a report then— 'Japan anxious for a Fight: The Chinese are Slow and Not in Good Shape to go to War'.[104] the Japanese were a modern naval power and moved freely with the Western-manufactured warships upto Taiwan. The Treaty of Shimonoscki was signed on April 17, 1895 to declare the independence of Korea and the cessation of the Liaodong peninsula, Taiwan and Penghu Island to Japan. A resistance by residual Qing officials, led to the declaration of the Republic of Formosa in May 1895 that was decidedly quelled in October 1895 by Japan. China had to pay 13,600 tonnes of silver Taels to Japan as war reparation—about six times the revenue of the Japanese government. This war, therefore, became one of the gravest symbols of the Century of the National Humiliation as a small Japan defeated a giant China. This was one power in the immediate East that the Chinese diplomat Li Hongzhang had recognised and considered as greater a threat for all times, as he summarised the threat geopolitically:

> "Her power is daily expanding and her ambition is not small. Therefore, she dares to display her strength in the eastern lands, despises China and takes action by invading Taiwan. Although the various European powers are strong, they are still 70,000 li away from us, whereas Japan is as near as the courtyard or the threshold and is prying into our emptiness and solitude. Undoubtedly, she will become China's permanent and great anxiety."[105]

Li Hongzhang, the lone modern Chinese strategist and diplomat who interfaced with the West, tried to use one power against the other as he said:

> "Since you are aware of the strength of your adversaries, use all possible means to divide them; go warily, use cunning – thus will you prove yourselves good strategists."[106]

Although this strategy caused a Triple Intervention by Russia, France and Germany forcing Japan to return the Liaodong peninsula, Russia in turn hoodwinked China to acquire the right to construct the Trans-Siberian Railways across Manchuria and usurp the adjoining land subsequently. Over the years, it consolidated control over the area Japan had vacated, thus significantly changing the geospatial make up of north-eastern Asia and it stays as such till date, giving a great opening to Russia in East Asia. This makes Russia a legitimate stakeholder and a player in any geopolitical game that ensues.

The Century of Humiliation may be an instrument of invoking nationalistic feelings through negative emotions and hatred towards the rest of the world for Chinese politician and thinkers, but a closer analysis of events establishes a cause-and-effect relationship between external aggressions and internal upheavals. Thinking at a macro level, China's sense of denial towards the rest of the world led to initial unregulated trade practices by the Western trading companies to develop into a forced later, realising the Chinese weakness at sea. The defeats in the Opium War gave the much-needed air to internal rebellions like the Taiping Rebellion. Then, China seeking the help of these very colonialist forces, further exposed the weakness of China inside its landmass underbelly as well. Then these colonial forces get emboldened and went deep north to occupy Beijing and force the most humiliating treaty on China after the Second Opium War. Then Japan attacked in the north-east and occupied Korea, parts of Manchuria and Taiwan. The weak China and its strategist Li Hongzhang then invoked a policy of divide and rule by using the old maxim of pitching one barbarian against the other. He failed to realise the cost of consideration when Russia was invited to intervene. A stage came when not only Japan occupied most of the north-east but the 'friendly barbarian' Russia also did not leave the outer Manchuria which it had forced Japan to leave. Then a stage came when the common masses felt most threatened by the weakness of the Chinese imperial power against the Western colonial powers and Japan and took up arms against all, including the Qing monarchy, called the Boxers Rebellion. In the next paragraph we shall see how the Boxers Rebellion was further used to control China by the foreign powers when they had not succeeded to do so politically.

Facing a defeat in the north-east compelled Emperor Guangxu to bring in sweeping reforms of polity and military, known as the Hundred Days Reforms (June 11– September 21, 1898). The conservative faction including Empress Dowager Cixi of the imperial household considered these reforms as a threat to their powers as the reforms intended to establish a formation of a federation of China, Japan, United States and the United Kingdom as proposed by the British missionary Timothy Richard.[107] Most of all, the Yong Emperors' reform edict had a Manchu to study foreign languages and travel abroad for studies. Timothy Richard also reveals that the Grand Councillor Kang Yi made it clear that it was the Chinese who were the obstruction to reform and not the Manchu and that they (the Chinese) were the ones who were 'incorrigibly anti-foreign'.[108] It is clearly evident that the Manchu were ready to accept the foreigners, whereas the Chinese were not. Therefore, in the circumstances which developed after the occupation of the north-east by Japan and Russia, the hurt pride of the Chinese who had become subject to the Manchu, further reeled under the fear of a greater occupation of foreign powers, both militarily as well as religiously. The Boxers (or Yihequan or Militia United in Righteousness) therefore, raised their heads in the Shangdong province in the North China plain against the Western imperialist powers spreading their influence through military occupation and proliferation of Christianity. It would not have taken its roots among the peasants if the Qing were found capable of resistance. The Chinese found the Manchu Qing collaborating with the foreign powers in the name of the modernisation of the country and in the concurrent situation, considered their rule as a foreign imposition in itself.[109] The Boxers being primitive in effort, as they were unsupported, rather resisted the Qing army by invoking courage amongst their cadre by claiming supernatural invulnerability towards the blows of cannons, bullet shots and knife attacks. It was indeed a resurrection and rebellion at the grass-root level by a society under stress for survival as the other natives or common citizenry had been practising in such situation to gather courage from the Taoist and Buddhist practices. Therefore, in the initial stages, they were indiscriminate about their attacks on Western offices, Chinese Christians, railroads, telegraph offices, Western schools and any other elements including the Qing establishment if they were perceived as collaborating with the foreigners. It was the fear of the onslaught reaching to the doorsteps of the Qing Monarchy and authority that brought Empress Dowager Cixi out of retirement to replace the reformist Guangxu Emperor and embrace the Boxers. This was a period of confusion wherein some Manchu generals like Rongli protected the foreign delegations in Beijing despite the siege, while Han Chinese generals like Dong Fuxian and his Muslim Ganxu Braves attacked these delegations alongside the Boxers.[110] Even the rail-road from Nanjing to Beijing was protected by Rongli which helped the Eight Nation Alliance of France, Britain, the US, Japan, Russia, Germany, Austria-Hungary and Italy to arrive in Beijing in August 1900 and relieve the Embassies after which another unequal treaty imposing a reparation of 450 million silver Taels (17,000 tonnes) was imposed, to be paid in 39 years, and a further occupation of the extended concessions.[111] Cixi fled to Xian, the Chinese capital of antiquity, under the protection of Muslim-dominated Ganxu Braves. It is an irony of geopolitics as we notice that so far while the foreign attacks came from the north-west before and the declining emperors fled to the east to Luoyang for protection, now the attack came from the south-east and the ruling class had to escape to the northwest—that too under the protection of the Muslims who were the main aggressors during the medieval period. Another element of geopolitics in the eight countries' alliance not pressing for a total occupation and colonisation of China was due to the vastness of the landmass, the governance of which was considered economically untenable due to the cost of controlling the huge rebellious population as the Boxer rebellion did create a fear among the foreigners. It was evident in a popular saying that a vicious circle of fear was present among all the stakeholders, as it says: 'the people are afraid of officials, the officials are afraid of the foreigners, and the foreigners are afraid of the people'. It is at times compared with the Indian Mutiny of 1857 and invites an equal amount of debate whether it was actually a Chinese Nationalist Revolution's seeds that were sown by this peasant class, or not.[112] Nevertheless, while the Western historians termed the rebellion as a myth, the violent and xenophobic Mao Zedong did use the Boxer Rebellion as the starting point of the revolution against the imperialist forces and due to its cultural obscurantism, the rebellion was used by Mao during the cultural revolution for xenophobic purposes in the text books in China in order to invoke nationalistic emotions.

The Boxers' war was a last-ditch effort by China to salvage its old-fashioned statecraft. A last ditch effort because after the failure of the state (read imperial power), the citizens took upon themselves to save the state of China which had moved over the synonymous with the imperial power which so far had had the 'Mandate of Heaven', considered to have been lost due to its prolonged failure of seventy to eighty years against the Western occupational forces. It was evident that while the Qing dynasty collapsed, there was no other clear-cut power to take over the mantle of a consolidating agent. Rather, in fact by now, there were many such power agents who had gathered together to consolidate the benefits of foreign technologies and commerce in their respective areas of influence by defying the decree of the Empress Dowager Cixi and did not join the Boxers for war against the foreign powers. These were the Qing officials or generals of Han origin like Li Hongzhang (Viceroy of Liangguang), Liu Kunyi (Viceroy of Liangjiang), Zhang Zhidong (Viceroy of Huangguang) who entered into an agreement to insulate their own provinces of south-east China from the Boxer outspread because they were the ones who had already tasted the benefits of the Western system of trade, commerce, industry, banking and communication. With the protection of Yuan Shikai, the commander of the New Army, who avoided stopping the eight nations' march to Beijing and rather killed Boxers in Zhili and Baoding in the north, China transited into a new era of warlordism and warring states period.[113] It was a period of Han ascendency led by Yuan Shikai which became a compulsion for the Qing as well as the revolutionary leader Sun Yat-sen. Yuan became the provisional President of the Republic of China on March 10, 1912.[114] Elections for the National Assembly were won by the Guomindang. But the party was sabotaged by Yuan who got himself voted by the National Assembly as Emperor and claimed the 'Mandate of Heaven' in his favour. The new Empire of China began its function on January 1, 1916 in a costly accession ceremony.[115] But, the military governors began rebelling against this usurpation of power and he had to abandon the empire on March 22 after 88 days. He died on June 5, 1916. This left no central authority in China. The Guomindang disintegrated and the National Army fragmented into forces of competing warlords with no one like Yuan Shikai to control as their overlord. He is however credited for the Chinese currency Yuan and a modern military establishment, but his imperial ambition was his

Map 30: The Warlords Period After Qing

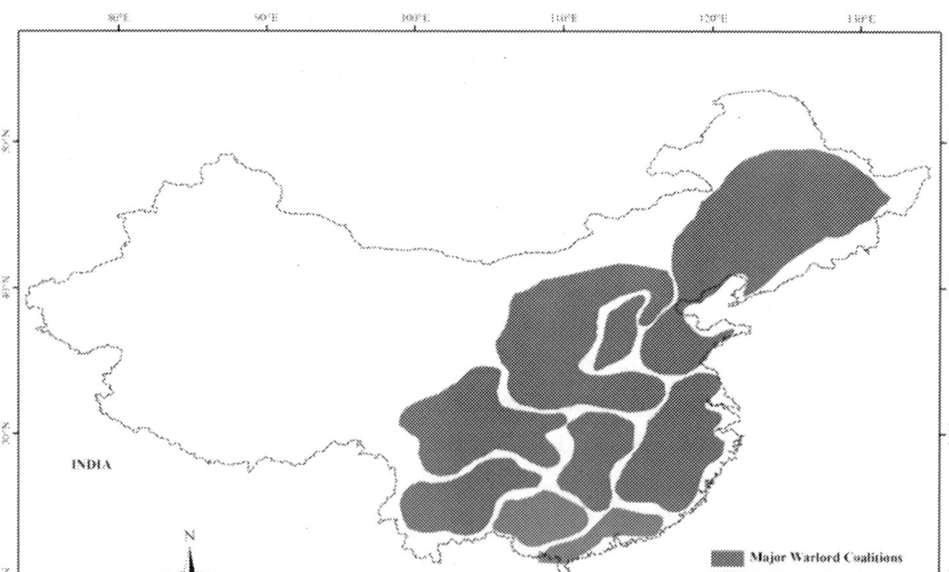

undoing, otherwise China could have well become a fully developed democracy by now.[116]

During the warlord period when there was no one to lord over them, the north–south divide of China further widened. Yuan Shikai's influence still lingered on in the north with three cliques of Yuan Shikai's old school (the Anhui cliques of General Duan Qirus, the Zhili Clique of Wu Peif and the Fenglian Clique of General Zhan Zhelin).[117] These cliques became closer to Japan and allowed Japanese influence into the north-east. In the south, the Guomindang came close to the former Soviet Union which armed its National Revolutionary Army. With the help of Chinese Communists, they established a unified Central government in China headed by Chiang Kaishek but he expelled communists from the Guomindang. Now the national government had three enemies: the Communist Party of China, the warlords mainly in the north and the Empire of Japan in the north-east. While the warlords and the communists acted in the background as conflicting forces to the nationalist consolidation, Japan became the most dangerous external force being a neighbour with expansionist designs during the

Map 31: Japanese Territories on Mainland

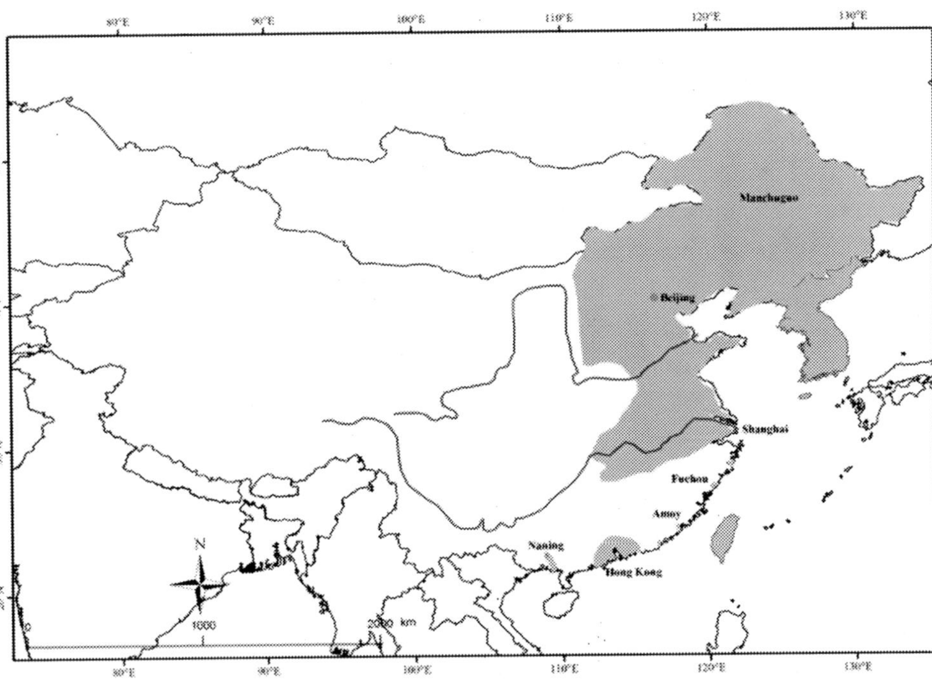

period of 1916–49 in which the European powers due to their engagement in the First and then the Second World War almost abandoned the occupation and maintenance of China as a colony which was rendered economically unviable. China was in fact lucky to have saved itself from being divided by eleven nations having a colonial territoriality in China instead of one that is Japan, during its weakest moment in the history.

The foreignness of the Manchu was exploited by the Japanese when they established the last Qing Emperor Puyi in the Manchurian puppet state of Manchuguo in 1932. Taking advantage of the internal disintegration, the Japanese reached outside Beijing (then Beiping) as China's Republican government in Nanjing remained passive to external aggression in the wake of saving itself from the Chinese communists in the south. Ultimately, Chinese resistance stiffened after December 1936 when the second Guomindang–CCP alliance against Japan was formed. The first encounter with the Japanese took place outside Beijing at the Marco Polo Bridge. Three months after, Shanghai fell to the Japanese; then took place the infamous Nanjing massacre which has never gone from the memories of the common Chinese and still haunts them as an incident of national humiliation inflicted by Japan. A puppet government led by Wangjingui was established by the empire of Japan without much control of Chinese territories.[118] In the meanwhile, the Gumonindang and communists fought over control in the areas not under Japanese control and tried to encircle each other using '*weiqi*' tactics (strategy of encirclement).[119] Despite the US efforts to bring both to reconciliation, the Guomindang established a stronghold in the urban areas and the capital retreated to Chongqing after the Japanese occupation of Nanjing. The communists became stronger among the peasants in the rural areas. However, after the Japanese attack of *USS Panay* and the Nanjing massacre, the public opinion in the West swung against Japan. While the US, the UK and France provided loan assistance to the Chinese government, Australia blocked iron ore export to Japan in 1938.[120] However, the honouring of public opinion by the US did not last for long as it began seeing economic benefits in the Japanese consumption of war munitions and restored all trade in the commercial as well as strategic material, including aircraft manufacturing tools. Great Britain even recognised the Japanese occupation of China.[121] This was a period when the Wilsonian principles of idealism manifesting themselves in the democratic representation of the people's will had taken to their zenith of achievement in the shape of the League of the Nations, and were fast being replaced by the realism of territoriality and the expansion of economic areas influenced by national interests. Hence, the geopolitical considerations changed swiftly with the changes in territoriality. Two events turned against Japan: the first was the invasion of French Indo-China (Vietnam, Laos and Cambodia) and its occupation to blockade the delivery of materials to China through the Haiphong–Yunan Railway Line, and the second was the attack on Pearl Harbour on December 7, 1941 leading to the Allied forces declaring war on Japan and seeing an opportunity of alliance for making the war of resistance against Japan, a shared war of the Allied forces. China also declared a formal war against Japan, Germany and Italy by Linsen, the President of Chinese Republic.[122] The US President Roosevelt referred the US, the UK, the former Soviet Union and China as "the Four Policemen of the world"—an unprecedented status accorded to China after hundred years of imperial occupation by these countries. In the internal geospace, Tibet and Xinjiang enjoyed greater autonomy from China due to the chaos prevailing in China, acting only when the warlords of these regions wished for China's help to ward off Russia and British India. Therefore, the former Soviet Union stopped American supplies to China through Xinjiang, being anti-Soviet. Nationally, Chiang became the Commander-in-Chief of the Allied Forces in the China theatre with General Stillwell as his Chief of Staff. But Britain was also not committed to China's cause as Japan had routed it in Burma in 1942 and China itself was not in position to extensively help the UK in Burma against Japan; thereafter, only the US was seen supporting China actually. Chiang's supporting the Quit India Movement further eroded the British support to China despite Britain being the strongest amongst the allied forces in South and East Asia.[123] Despite these consolidation efforts by Chiang Kaishek, China could defend against Japan's largest offensive of World War II on the American airbases in China and the hinterland cities to secure a rail linkup between Manchuria and Vietnam. With no coastal supply line and failure to obtain one through Xinjiang, the US pushed for the Lido Road through Burma by driving out the Japanese from North Burma by the Chinese troops attacking India and Yunnan simulteneousely.[124] China's was not an unidirectional fight against Japan during the days of the Japanese occupation of China. The former Soviet Union attacked Xinjiang in 1937 and the Chinese control was almost lost, though not recognised by Chiang, for the Soviet arms he was receiving. Chiang also had a policy to support the pro-Guommidang elements to have an influence in Vietnam and block the Vietnamese communists (Ho Chi Minh) to collaborate with the Chinese communists whom Chiang wished to wipe out. Therefore, he committed 2,00,000 Chinese troops to northern Indo-China who occupied an area north of the 16th parallel in Indo-China till 1946.[125] He also tried to engage the allied partner

France there and asked it to vacate Chinese concessions in China for the withdrawal of troops from Indo-China, subsequently in 1946.[126] But all these distractions disabled the Chinese forces' capacity to evict the Japanese. The Japanese withdrawal therefore happened unconditionally when the US attacked Japan with atom bombs and the former Soviet Union attacked them in Manchuria.

This period in China's geopolitical history is a curious case of spatial analysis. The ruling government seemed to rule its territories by selective negligence as it happened in the case of Tibet and Xinjiang and Outer Mongolia, and they were forcefully evicted by the former Soviet Union from outer Manchuria and by Japan from Korea and inner Manchuria. Another trend emerged upon the demise of the Qing regency during the republican period. Since Sun Yatsen and subsequently Chiang Kaishek ascended to power gravitated to the south with Nanjing being made as the capital, I argue that it was basically a mere manifestation of the centre of economic power leaving the centre of political power (Beijing) and moving towards the south. It was evident from the southern warlords making an association to defy Empress Dowager Cixi's decree to fight the Western powers alongside the Boxers. Sun Yatsen from a Hakka and Cantonese background from the Guangdong province, was succeeded by Chiang Kaishek from the Zhejiang province, who was from an upper-class family of salt merchants who were the leading figures of the anti-Qing, anti-Japan nationalistic movement in China and who recognised the Western virtues alongside their colonial designs. However, the north and the north-east China remained the bastion of independent-minded warlords especially the Beiyang Army warlords, the residual sympathisers of the Qing. The National Revolutionary Army of the Guomindang, therefore, had difficulty in overcoming these residual power centres in the north-east in the course of its unification drive and leaving formidable gaps in the country's defences in terms of the Manchu who became agents of Japanese imperial designs in China as Japan established Manchuguo, a puppet government, and a gateway to China for them. It emerges that the Republican government of China, either remained in control of warlords like President Yuan Shikai of the Beiyang clique or coexisted with them on a weaker footing till 1925 within the China proper (excluding Tibet, Xinjiang and Manchuria). Only when Chiang Kaishek became the Guomindang leader and raised the National Revolutionary Army with the help of the former Soviet Union (as advised by Mikhail Bordolin) that he overpowered these warlords, sweeping from the south to north in his Northern Expedition from his bastion in the south-eastern provinces of Guangdong and Guangxi and establishing a unified central government in Nanjing. However, the Chinese geospace never remained as united as it was thought to be because of conflicting forces, the nationalists of Western cultural inclination vs. the warlords of feudal inclination who were more interested in establishing some or the other imperial dynastic rule as was evident in the case of Yuan Shikai. The dynamics of the geospatial movement of forces now had taken a reverse order in the sense that the imperial regime changes that had in the past been moving from north to south were now taking place from south to north. Another clear ideological distinction which marks the north as separate from the south is that while the south became progressive with natural resources of its own and prolonged communication with the other cultures (read barbarians), the north continued with the Chinese imperial hangover. Therefore, I argue that the May 4th Movement against the Treaty of Versailles in which the territories in Shandong surrendered by Germany were transferred to Japan after the First World War, was actually a public revolt against the Beijing government still representing the Qing imperial origins and furthering own feudal designs of the warlords deriving power from the armies of the imperial and feudal origins nurtured with a greater intensity and passion in north China than in the south. It also marked the change of culture as Mao derived his inspiration for the Cultural Revolution from the May 4th Movement in which he had participated, as he says:

> "The May 4th Movement twenty years ago, marked a new stage in China's bourgeois-democratic revolution against imperialism and feudalism. The cultural reform movement which grew out of the May 4th Movement was only one of the manifestations of this revolution."[127]

The evidence of the more enlightened south against the north are the facts that the southern warlords formed a clique first to defy the order of Empress Dowager Cixi, second, the nationalist movement of Sun Yatsen found its harbour in the south and established the parallel regime in Guandong province and subsequently Chiang Kaishek also established his stronghold in the south with his capital at Nanjing from where he launched his offensive to overpower the Beijing government in the north. And the evidence does not stop at this. Even the communists also found conducive bases in the south-eastern provinces to establish their Chinese Soviet Republic, also known as Jiang Xi-Fujian Soviet within the National Republic of China in November 1931 that survived until 1937.

This north and south demarcation has always been marked by the Yangzi river historically, culturally as well as strategically. It is evident from the past narratives of geospatial movements and occupation of ancient and medieval period dynasties that Chinese nation took quite a time to extend south of the Yangzi. In the modern historical perspective during the chaos of the Warring States period and the civil war between the nationalists and the communists, the Yangzi valley and its southern territories became geo-strategically more significant for its internal geopolitics before a fully demarcated territoriality was achieved by the communist China to have the country take the shape of its modern-day map. In the second half of the last hundred years, before 1949, the nationhood evolved very fast; the changing of political ground from the barbarian Manchu to the Han-dominated national revolutionaries and communists and shifting of the power centre to the south as its geopolitical importance increased by a massive agrarian and industrial growth due to foreign influence through its coasts, despite the great dislike of the Manchu central governments.

The Xinhai revolution, which laid down the foundation of the change of governance from imperial to popular government (though not a democratic one which was the ultimate aim of Sun Yatsen) in China, started with the Wuchang uprising on the banks of the Yangzi River on October 10, 1911. When Yuan Shikai was reappointed the Commander of the New Army to fight the Revolutionary Army, though ill-equipped, the Revolutionary Army retreated south of the Yangzi, but when 14 other Chinese provinces joined the revolution, Yuan Shikai had to negotiate and compel the last Qing Emperor Puyi to abdicate power and formed the provisional Government of the Republic of China. It is immaterial whether the revolutionary Sun Yatsen or the former Qing loyalist Yuan Shikai became the President, as this revolution in the south marked the end of 2000 years of imperial rule and the beginning of the republican era in China.[128] The traditional occupation during the Republican period by the Guomindang was always interspersed and not contiguous. The territories of China were shared with the internal forces as well as external powers. First it was the Beiyang Army in the north, and then came the communists who for a varying period occupied a varying extent of territory. In 1931, they first established the Jiangxi Fujian Soviet (the seat of its Central Government) and until 1937, they occupied discontinuous territories which included the north-eastern Jiang Xi, Hunan Jiangxi, Hunan Hubei-Jiangxi, Hunan Western Hubei, Hunan Hubei Sichuan, Guizhou, Sanxi-Gansu, Sichuan-Shensi, Hubei-Henan-Anhui, Honglu and Haifeng-Lufeng Soviets. It was in fact an inception of the 'Two Chinas' which continues till today in a reverse magnificence. The communists suffixed Jiangxi, the term for administrative areas devoted as circuits during the Tang dynasty, to name a province as a unit area of administration.[129] The Chinese Soviet Republic lost its Jiangxi Soviet, the seat of Encirclement Campaigns, as the communists moved out on the famous Long March on October 16, 1934. Since the communists held some other areas like the Hubei-Henan-Shanxi Soviet, the formal dissolution of the Chinese Soviet Republic took place only on September 22, 1937 when the Communist Party formed the second united front to confront the common enemy, Japan.[130]

What is evident is the fact that the Nationalists as well as the Communists both were very comfortable in south China. In arguing so, we need to keep in mind the fact that Sun Yatsen, Chiang Kaishek and Mao Zedong all were born in the south in Guangdong, Zhejiang and Hunan provinces, respectively. In fact, Mao felt more confident to establish his first Soviet in Jiangxi in the conference held at Ruijin in the close vicinity and became the Head of State and Head of Government. In fact, Mao was inolved in a great intrigue by changing his policy to woo the peasant militia in his favour deriving the Autumn Harvest uprising in contradiction to the CPC policies. When expelled from the Hunan Provincial Committee for his military opportunism, he retreated to the Jing Gangshan city, making a self-governing state of five villages to start with, which went on to become the Chinese Soviet of 30,000 square kilometres subsequently, once he proved his might by mobilising the peasants more in the rural areas than the labourers in the urban areas.[131,132] My argument is that Mao survived the CPC onslaught on him only because he had more faith in the native region for the pragmatic experimentation which he was otherwise not allowed to carry out by CPC as it was against the Party's professed policy. Therefore, the unifying forces emerged from the South, grew in the South and overpowered the North while even during this modern period of history, when aggressors like Japan, which notwithstanding its location, colluded with the disintegrating forces in the north, made inroads into the Chinese territories and did not stop till they captured the south including Taiwan and Guangdong, because they knew where the core of China whether ethnically, economically or geopolitically lies within 'the China Proper' (broadly denoted by the Ming Dynasty China comprising of the modern-day eighteen provinces which figured symbolically as the eighteen stars on the Eighteen-Star Flag of the revolutionaries in the Wu Chang uprising and the Xinhai revolution, overthrowing the Qing dynasty).[133]

Analysis of Outer China

Having discussed the geospatial dynamics of China proper, let us turn our attention to outer China or the peripheries which were loosely held by the Qing and even more loosely held by Republican China. Discussing the outer territories of Qing

China upon its collapse, we have discussed the establishment of Manchuguo by Japan and through the Manchu territories, entering China proper from the north-east which Japan had to vacate after the Second World War. To the north of Inner Mongolia, an autonomous region of present-day China, was Outer Mongolia during the Qing period which declared independence immediately after the fall of the Qing after the Xinhai revolution. Bogd Khan was declared as the Khagan of Outer Mongolia on December 29, 1911. Mongolia was again briefly occupied by the Beiyang Army of the Republic of China in October 1919, which lasted till 1921. The reoccupation of Outer Mongolia was a design by the pro-Japanese Anhui Clique under Premier Duan Qirui who sent a separate army known as the North Western Frontier Army created out of Japanese loans known as the Nishihara loans, ostensibly to resist Russians indirectly. Xu Shuzheng, the right-hand man of the Chinese Premier, occupied Urga (now Ulan) without any resistance. It was certainly an extra-constitutional affair of the Chinese Premier outside the Ministry of the Army but was accepted and lauded by everyone in China including Sun Yatsen because that was the ways of warlordism in those days in China. As John S. Mayor says:

> "... in 1919 a Japanese influence faction in the Chinese government mounted an invasion of Outer Mongolia and forced its leader to sign a "request" to be taken over by the government of China. Japan's aim was to protect its own economic, political and military interests in North China, keeping the Russian Revolution from influencing Mongolia."[134]

However, humiliating Bogd Khan and other leaders in a ceremony by forcing to kowtow to the Chinese general and their subsequent house arrest, intensified the Mongolian efforts to seek Soviet help. Ultimately the pro-Tsar White Russian forces of Baron Ungren Sternberg captured Urga from the Chinese and restored Bogd Khan as the monarch. Close on the heels came the joint Mongolian People's Party–Soviet Red Army combine that defeated the Baron in August.[135] As the Bolsheviks won the Russian civil war, the Chinese never ventured again into Mongolia. Mongolia, after a short period of constitutional monarchy, was declared as the Mongolian People's Republic in 1924 which lasted till 1992. The People's Republic of China did recognise Mongolia as an independent country as Mongolia was a senior communist country and the first to recognise the PRC. However, Republic of China in Taiwan continued claiming Mongolia as part of its territory till 2002, where after it recognised Mongolia as an independent country. On the part of the PRC, the new-found nationalistic fervour reignited by the communist leadership of China to drum up support for one-party rule, has begun to reinvent the Chinese claim over Mongolia.[136]

How Xinjiang was captured by the Qing in an absolute totality was a method in contradiction to the Confucian philosophy of peaceful principles of filial piety and existence of others, as had been followed by their predecessors. The Zunghars, the Qirat Mongols, who were in control of Xinjiang were ordered by Qianlong Emperor to be massacred and shown no mercy barring only their women and children, during the Qing campaign between 1757–58.[137] Never before had such a genocide been carried out by any other Han Emperor of China; therefore, the subjugation was never complete either. The Qing, however, due to their policy of total destruction of the Zunghar state and its people could subjugate and physically occupy Xinjiang as part of the Chinese state.[138, 139] Since the land was now devoid of the Zunghar Mongols, the Qing sponsored settlements of millions of Han Chinese, Hui, Turkestani (Uighur), Manchu Bannermen and Kazakhs to settle there. The purpose of going back a hundred year into geospatial history is to highlight as to how the Qing, a Manchu a minority themselves in China, conquered more ethnicities, justify the new China as a multiethnic country which included more areas of other ethnic groups by now such as Manchuria, Dzungaria (including the Tarim basin) and Mongolia, proclaiming China as a multiethnic state.[140] I argue that though it was a name traditionally called as China or Zhong Guo, but in reality it was a Qing state as the expansionist tendencies during this period like never seen before, had been primarily a Manchu aspiration and not that of the Han or the Chinese. Also, it is by now an established fact that the uprising during the end of the Qing period and the taking over of China as a state by the Republicans had been the result of a majority Han rebellion against the Manchu. This was one reason why the Republican China could not effectively protect Xinjiang from its proclamation of the East Turkestan Republic (ETR) in early 1915 in the north-west of Xinjiang, notwithstanding the seeking of Soviet help by the Chinese warlord Sheng Shicai, who was seeking Soviet support for independence from China, eventually making it a virtual Soviet satelite.[141] The Nanjing government also closed its eyes towards the heavy garrisoning of Xinjiang by the Soviet troops in order to get the much needed war munitions to fight the Japanese invasion under the Sino-Soviet Non-Aggression Pact of 1937.

There are certain geospatial facts that make Xinjiang a curious case of territorial claims and counterclaims on ethnic grounds. It is a fact that the Eastern Turkic Republic was established in the upper Ili river basin in Dzungaria, mainly comprising of Turkic and Kazakh people from 1944 to 1949 but accepted an accession to the People's Republic of China as the leaders like Ehmetijan Quasim (Kasimon) were under communist influence. But the present-days claim of the Turkic people over Xinjiang seeks its roots in the establishment of the First East Turkistan Republic around the Kashgar city in the western Tarim basin, the main area of inhabitation of the Uighur on November 12, 1933.[142] There was curiously no support by the Head of the First republic Isa Yusuf Alpetkin to the establishment of the second ETR being a Russian Republic and supported Guomindang as the republic was declared against the Chinese Warlords having Soviet support. The first ETR government was expelled by February 6, 1934 and led to making the entire Xinjiang a Soviet satellite.[143] Another fact was that the Qing replaced the Zunghars with the Hui, Xibe and Han in Dzungaria, who were initially not allowed to settle in the Tarim basin, but later the Qing allowed them to do so, also due to a Turkic uprising in that region. By the end of the Qing rule, the Han were already more than thirty per cent of Xinxiang's population and it cannot be called entirely as a communist drive.[144] In fact, the Uighur basically from the Tarim basin were late arrivals to the capital city of Dzungaria, north of the Tianshan ranges. The migration, mainly after 1949, was for seeking jobs in the industrial development around Urumqi making them 12.8 per cent of the city population by 2000, despite comprising 45 percent of the total population of Xinjiang.[145] It is therefore clear that the geopolitical situation in the Central Asian region and the weakness of the Chinese central authorities in the latter half of the 19th Century and the first half of the 20th Century led to Xinjiang going under influence of Russia/Soviet Union with its design to take Xinjiang into the Soviet fold, as was done in the case of other Central Asian Republics by giving a federal structure to them to keep these states by the Bolsheviks.[146] Had it not been for the taking over of China by the communists, perhaps the geospatial picture in Xinjiang would have been different than what is it now.

As the Russians and then the Soviet influence grew in Xinjiang and they threatened Tibet from the north and the Emirate of Afghanistan from the north-west, the British Empire began encroaching from the south in 1904 in an expedition as a part of the Great Game being played between Russia and Great Britain for a greater control over Central Asia. This was followed by a period when the Qing authority had waned in Tibet after the Xinhai revolution and under the 'Three Point Agreement', the Qing forces had been expelled from Tibet. The 13th Dalai Lama who had fled to India in 1910 returned to Tibet, spurred the overtures of Yuan Shikai the Chinese Provisional President, and proclaimed Tibet as an independent nation saying:

> "During the time of Chenghis Khan and Altan Khan of Mongols, the Ming Dynasty of the Chinese, and the Qing Dynasty of the Manchu, Tibet and China cooperated on the basis of benefactor and priest relationship."[147]

On the Qing Emperor sending large number of troops, the 13th Dalai Lama said:

> "I therefore, left Lhasa with my ministers for the Indo-Tibetan border hoping to clarify to the Manchu Emperor by wire that the existing relationship between Tibet and China has been that of patron and priest and had not been based on the subordination of one to the other".[148]

He then says:

> "We are a small religious and independent nation."

And ultimately said:

> "To safeguard and maintain the independence of our country, one and all should voluntarily work hard".[149]

It therefore clearly shows the intentions and look-out of the people of Tibet about their independent mindset, supported historically. It is another matter that the Tibetan landmass that once comprised of the present-day Tibetan Autonomous Region and most parts of Sichuan, Qinghai and Gansu and some parts of Yunnan, became victim to a geopolitical 'Great Game' between Russia, Britain and China for securing more and more sphere of influence in Central Asia, despite their ethnic incongruence as well as a geo-strategic untenability of the maintenance of a state against other rivals as well as a local insurgency for independence. Therefore, despite a detailed discussion on Tibet in this regard not being part of the thesis, it can be safely said that Tibet remained independent till the annexation of its territories by the People's Republic of China in 1951 despite Russia, Britain and China trying to usurp Tibet through various expeditions and agreements like the 1907 Anglo-Russian Convention and various Shimla Agreements. Three more geopolitical realities emerge out of this discourse. One is that Tibet was caught unawares by the import of delimitations of national territories—a concept of European colonial forces, as the Tibetans understood frontiers more than boundaries as their national limits of territory. Two, the military power (China) had a comparative ease of access geographically to overpower the spiritually strong but militarily weak Tibet. Third, Tibet does have a geospatial potential of an independent state due to its location, territorial attributes and cultural linkages to other neighbouring countries and has such an opportunity in case of any change or tilt in balance of power in Asia, considering the fact that no nation-state can have its present delimitation forever.

Having come to an end of the discourse about the geospatial evolution of the Chinese nation-state many interesting influences emerge consequentially in the summing up. The first case in point is the origin of the Peking man and the romanticising about the centre of evolution of the Chinese culture around the 'Banpo Village' sites near the ancient city of Chang An (Modern Xian) in the Yellow river basin in the north, ignoring the similar fossils found near Lantian in Shaanxi and near the city of Liu Zhou in the mountains of Guangxi. The conventional historians therefore never looked beyond the Yellow river as if no other human geographical civilisation cauldron could ever exist in the other parts of today's China proper. Andrew Lawler argues that the dramatic discoveries across China in the past two decades in Manchuria in the north to the Chengdu plains in the west, and to the coastal cities in the south, reveal a host of complex and distinct ancient cultures.[150] However, recognising that the historians will always have a bias towards the eventful times and spaces for giving a historical narrative of some consequence, the northern China's central plain along the Yellow river did give such eventualities due to the intense inter-civilisational conflict between the agrarian (Chinese) and nomadic (north-west). This argument thus does justify the conventional narrative of evolution of China as a nation-state in the north. Romanticising the exclusivity of the Chinese civilisation also emanates from the confines of the northern archaeological evidence from the Yang Shao (culture) in the upper Huang He to the Luoshan culture in the east and south-east, towards the lower Chang Chiang. However, it does not credit much the contribution of the archaeological evidence of Fengshu located in the Bose basin in the Guangxi province of southern China, where the hand-axe discovered dates back to the early to the middle Pleistocene era, validating the existence of an even earlier-period civilisation of Fengshuo Dao hominines that are considered an extension of the Acheulean hominoids into the Bose basin from South Asia along the Movius Line, a theoretical line drawn across north India.[151] Even though a subsequent analysis by Wei Wang of the Guangxi Museum of Nationalities considers this archaeological evidence as an example of convergent evolution, it still demolishes the exclusivity of the Chinese civilisation as such and does hint at the movement of Early Pleistocene Hominines into the Chinese sphere, influencing the genealogy as well as the culture.[152] The archaeological finds of Sanxingdui (Three Star) near Chengdu (Sichuan) parallel to the Shang period, further consolidates the existence of an equally profound culture of the present-day Chinese realm. Therefore, the question of 'Us' and 'Them' has a good ground for a debate starting at this point.

The Geopolitical Implications

The conventional narrative of the evolution of the Chinese civilisation however is a byproduct of the geopolitical impulses, those felt in a greater intensity in the north-west than in the south-east. As the north-east became the conflict zone around the civilisational fault line between the nomadic pastoral people of the north-west and the immediate agrarian civilisation of northern China, the ruling class evolved itself out of its geopolitical experience which manifested itself in wars, retreats, defences and victories as we observe the early developments of the kingship and the state which took place in the immediate vicinity of the adversaries. The magnitude of statehood due to the primitive modes of communication, sparse population and very subsistent levels of agricultural activities can be attributed to the confinement of these political activities to the upper reaches of the Huang He. As the magnitude increased, the need for a strategic depth compelled the shifting of state activities from the west (Xian) to east Luoyang. In the later period, threats grew even from the north-east as well from the Jurchen, Silla and the Japanese. Therefore, the strategic depth was now sought in the south in the lands south of Chengjiang (Yangzi). The invasion by the Jin (Jurchen), compelling the Song to shift the capital from Kaifeng in the north to Hangzhou in the south signifies the same. It also signified the importance of the resource bowl and the trade centres in south, so far used to maintaining the political power centres in the north and the extensive canal and road transportation systems from the south to the north maintained as supply lines. The geospatial dynamic now inverted the nation-state geopolitically. To elaborate the argument, as the Huang He river valley with its tributaries was the bed of development of the Chinese civilisation from antiquity and the state developed mostly in a linear fashion from the west to east, there was hardly any contact of the statehood in the south due to the remoteness of the Yangzi valley, the adequacy of resources in the Huang He region and the limited scale of war at that time. As the demand for resources and strategic depth grew due to an increased scale of wars during the Tang Dynasty, the south was exploited. Till then, the geopolitical China had a heavier and broader north territoriality and narrow points of contact towards the south. The geopolitical significance of this territoriality can be well represented by an inverted triangle with a base along the Huang He river valley. The significance of the south increased which was pronounced by two historical events: first, the commercial and agricultural development in the south of the Yangzi and along the coast making the Southern Song the most-protected and self-sustained to withstand the onslaught of the Jin (Jurchen) from the north-west and second, Kublai Khan's attack on Southern Song from the west and south-west that forced Southern Song to submit to the Mongols in 1271. Otherwise, it became frustrating for the invaders to come from the north geostrategically. Even the Ming followed this new geostrategic pattern and consolidated themselves in the south by making Nanjing their capital. Thus, the reversal of geopolitical importance of the Chinese territories south of Yangzi became further pronounced. These changes in the patterns of geo-strategy were now most clear as the Tang can be considered as the defining period before which the dynasties first consolidated comprehensive national power in the north (the line of the Huang He), then expanded to the south. Whereas, after the Tang, the dynasties first consolidated comprehensive national power in the south (the line of Chang Jiang) and then moved northwards to expand. The geopolitical China now stood as a straight triangle with a base along the Yangzi (Chang Jiang) with the tip towards Beijing. This notion further got solidified as the threat of European imperial powers that invaded China from the south highlighted the need to defend China in the south more as the threat from the north diminished. Geostrategically, the political power centre should

Map 32: Inversion of the Chinese Core

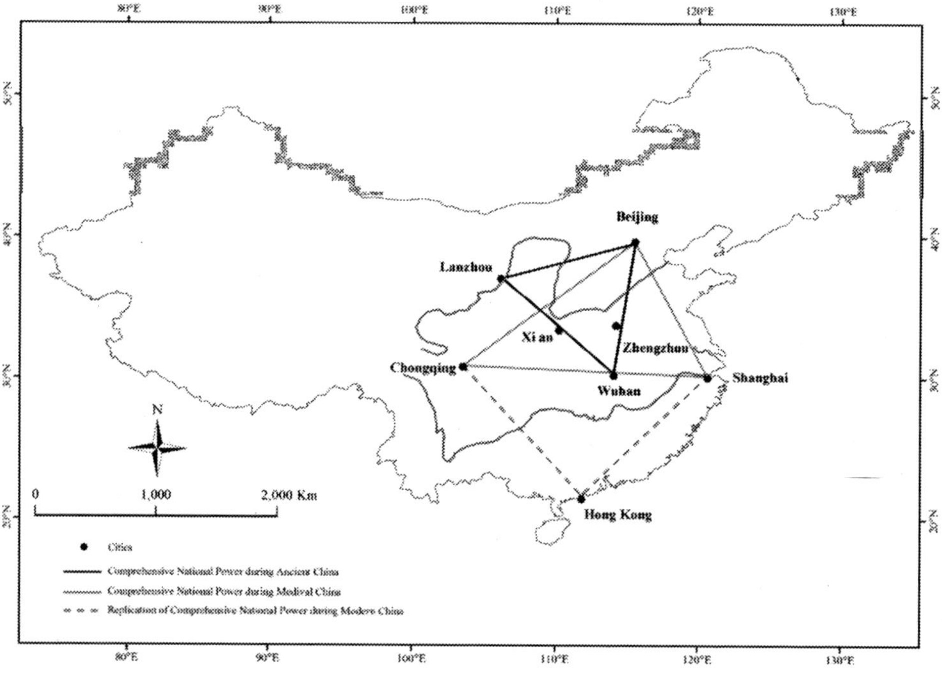

have moved to the south much earlier during the Qing period with its capital moving to the south. However, the Manchu connection to the north-east and a deeper Han antagonism prevailing in the south, perhaps, prevented the Qing to act in accordance with the geostrategic demands of that time. Although another common reason given to the successful invasions of the European colonial powers in the south-east was a sudden stoppage of marine ventures by the Ming and therefore the depletion of the naval forces in China, my argument that, if the Chinese imperial power had turned its attention the to the south and been upfront to the new waves of enemies, perhaps as per the concurrent geopolitical dynamics, it would not only have developed a potent coastal defence but could have also engaged this military–commercial forces' moves constructively. Another takeaway of this analysis is that the people in south China can be easily considered to be more communicative, assimilative and interaction-driven, making the south a fair ground for more democratic ways of internal politics and assimilation with external geopolitics.

As we posit that the geopolitical epicentre has shifted south to the Nanjing, Shanghai and Hangzhou regions as the Chinese state still remained vulnerable from that direction. During the modern era when the economic boom had taken place after 1979, the triangle with the base along Yang Zi river has again inverted itself to make the China proper complete, by including the southernmost parts in it as shown in broken lines in the map number 31. However, the other regions were either conquered by the 'Barbarians' or the external forces like the Mongols (Yuan) and the Qing (Manchu) and do not form part of traditional China proper. These far-off regions having more sense of 'Others' than 'We' with China, always excluded themselves from China at the first opportunity available to secede. Therefore, what China remained most of the times as 'China Proper' can easily be derived out of the permanence of the inclusivity of the territory in any political framework of the times, a cultural assimilation of the people of these territories and acceptance of the assimilation by its peoples and the development of the sense of 'we' which prevailed historically and exists till today. Otherwise, the politico-military assimilation or inclusion like what was carried out by Mao with regard to these peripheries still poses many geopolitical questions and imperatives for China to tackle in the future. George Friedman calls China, therefore, as an island within its own territory surrounded by inaccessible buffer zones beyond 15^0 isohyets in the north-west, the Pacific in the east and the high mountains and jungles in the south.[153] As we have seen through the historical geospatial evolution of the nation-state, China proper also gets isolated by its own territory in the west and the north-west by alien cultures besides being isolated in the rest of the directions surrounded by unfriendly nations due to historical and political reasons even across the ocean, that will be the corner-stone of our further discussions in the subsequent chapters.

NOTES

1. Starr, John Bryan, *Understanding China*, NY: Hill and Wang, 2001, p. 41.
2. Cheng, T.K,, *Prehistoric China*, Cambridge, 1959; *New Light on Prehistoric China*, Toronto: University of Toronto Press, 1996 and Chang, K.C., *The Archaeology of Ancient China*, Yale: Yale University Press, 1963 as quoted in Yi Fu Tuan, *Historical Geography of China*, NJ: Aldine Transaction, 1969. p.45.
3. Chang, P.K., 'Climatic Regions of Sichuan Province', CSPM, pp. 393-434.
4. Ibid., pp. 41-42.
5. Sen, Tansen and Victor H. Mair, *Traditional China in Asian and World History*, Association for Asian Studied (AAS) Inc. Ann Arbor, p. 17.
6. Keats, S.G., 'Home Range Size in Middle Pleistocene China and Human Dispersal Patterns in Eastern and Central Asia', *Asian Perspective*, 43 (2), 2004, pp. 227-47.
7. Cheng, T.K., *Shang Fauna and Climatic Conditions in Shang China,* Toronto: University of Toronto Press, 1960, pp. –83-87.
8. Andersson, J.G., *Children of the Yellow Earth*, NY: Macmillan, 1934.
9. Andersson, J.G., 'Prehistoric Sites in Hunnan', *Far Eastern Antiquities* Vol. 19, 1947, pp. 20-22.
10. Andersson, J.G., 'Prehistory of the Chinese', *Far Eastern Antiquities*, 1934, p. 34.
11. Cheng, op. cit., pp. 75-81 and *New Lights on Prehistoric China*, Toronto: University of Toronto Press, 1966, pp. 17-22.
12. Ibid., p. 87.
13. Chang, K.C., op. cit., pp. 77-109.
14. Liu Li, *The Chinese Neolithic Trajectories to Early States*, Cambridge: Cambridge University Press, 2004, pp. 89-93.
15. http://www.chinaknowledge.de/History/myth/prehistory-map-html, Accessed on 20 May 2014.
16. Yi-Fu Tuan, *A Historical Geography of China*, New Brunswick: Aldine Transaction, 1969, pp. 53-54.
17. Huang, Ray, *China: A Macro History*, NY: ME Sharpe Inc., 1990, p. 6.
    18. Mei, J., *Copper and Bronze Metallurgy in Late Prehistoric Xinjiang: Its Cultural Context and Relationship with Neighbouring Regions*, Oxford: Archeo Press, as quoted in Sen and Mair, op. cit., pp. 19-21.
19. Yi Fu Tuan, *A Historical Geography of China*, New Brunswick: Aldine Transaction, 1969, p. 55.
20. Chang, op. cit., pp. 150-153.
21. Shaughness, Edward L., 'Historical Perspective on Introduction of the Chariot into China', *Harvard Journal of Asiatic Studies*, 48 (1), June 1988, pp. 189-237.
22. Chauncy, Goodrich, 'Riding Astride and the Saddle in Ancient China', *Harvard Journal of Asiatic Studies*, 44 (2), 1984, pp. 279-306.

23. Huang, op. cit., p. 13.
24. Keay, John, *China*, London: Harper Press, 2009, p. 50.
25. Eberhard, W., *Social Mobility in Traditional China*, Leiden, 1962, p. 269.
26. Huang, op. cit., p. 15.
27. Shijing (trans. Arthur Waley), *The Book of Songs*, Grove Press, 1960, p. 248.
28. Huang, op. cit., pp.15-16
29. Mencius (trans. J. Legge), *The Four Books*, BK IV, Part I, Chapter 14:3, NY: Paragon Reprint Co., New York, 1966, p. 714.
30. Xu Quyun, 'The Spring and Autumn Period', in *The Cambridge History of Ancient China from the Origin of Civilization to 221 BC*, Michael, Loewe and Edward L. Shaughness, Cambridge: Cambridge University Press, pp. 545 -86 and Sen and Mair, op. cit., p. 23.
31. Huang, op. cit., pp. 22-23.
32. Mair, Victor H., *Translation and Introduction, The Art of War: Sun Zu's Military Methods*, NY: Columbia University Press, 2007, as quoted in Sen and Mair, op. cit., p. 25.
33. Huang, op. cit., p. 23-24.
34. Yi Fu Tuan, op. cit., pp. 70-72.
35. Li Feng, *Landscapes and Power in Early China*, Cambridge: Cambridge University Press, 2006, p. 286.
36. Wood, Francis, *China's First Emporer and His Teracotta Warriors*, NY: Macmillan Publishing, p. 78.
37. *Shiji*, (trans. Cavannes) in *Memoires Historique de Sema Qian*, Vol. 2, Paris 1905, p. 220 as quoted in Yi Fu Tuan, op. cit., p. 75.
38. Huang, op. cit., p.30.
39. Yi Fu Tuan, op. cit., p. 75.
40. Bodde, D., *China's First Unifier*, Brill: Lieden, 1938, pp. 116-117, 163.
41. Watson, Burton, (trans.), *Records of the Grand Historians of China, (Jia Yi Shiji)*, NY: Columbia University Press, 1961, pp. 80-82.
42. Davis, Paul K.C., *100 Decisive Battles: From Ancient Times to the Present*, NY: Oxford University Press, 2001, pp. 44-46.
43. Bielenstien, Hans, *The Bureaucracy of Han Dynasty*, Cambridge University Press, 1980, p. 105.
44. Hansen, Valerie, *The Open Empire: A History of China till 1600*, London: WW Norton & Company, 2000, p. 135.
45. de Crespigny, *A Biographical Dictionary of The Later Han to Three Kingdoms* (23-220 AD), Koninkliijk Brill: Leiden, 2007, pp. 497, 500, 592.
46. Bielenstien, Hans, 'Wang Mang: The Restoration of the Han Dynasty and the Later Han', in *The Cambridge History of China, Volume I: The Chin and Han Empires, 221 BC–AD 220*, Denis Twitchett and Michael Lowe (eds), Cambridge: Cambridge University Press, 1986.
47. de Crespigny, *A Biographical Dictionary of The Later Han to Three Kingdoms* (23-220 AD), Koninkliijk Brill: Leiden, 2007, p. 602.
48. Ibid., p. 37 and Beck Mansvelt, 'The Fall of Han', in the *Cambridge History of China: Vol I: The Chin and Han Empires*, op. cit., pp. 317-376.
49. Yi Fu Tuan, pp. 77-78.
50. Bielenstien, Hans, 'The Restoration of Han Dynasty', *Far Eastern Antiquities*, Vol. 26, 1954, p. 93.

51. Sima Qian, (trans. Burton Watson), *Shiji: Records of the Grand Historian of China*, Columbia: Columbia University Press, Vol. 2, 1961, p. 490.
52. Lao Gan, 'Population and Geography in Two Han Dynasties', in *Chinese Social History*, E Tu Zen Sun and John De Francis (eds), Washington DC: American Council of Learned Societies, 1956, p. 90.
53. Goodrich, L. Carrington, *A Short History of The Chinese People,* 3rd ed, NY: Harper, p. 39.
54. Lao Gan, op. cit., pp. –91-92.
55. Needham, J., *Science and Civilization in China*, Cambridge: Cambridge University Press, 1961, p. 183.
56. Pritchard, E.H., 'Thoughts on the Historical Development of the Population of China', *Journal of Asian Studies,* Vol. 23,1963, p. 16.
57. Belienstein, op. cit., pp. –139-141.
58. Huang, pp. 63-67.
59. Ibid., p. 75.
60. Garnet, Jacques Garnet, *A History of Chinese Civilization*, Cambridge: Cambridge University Press, Cambridge, 1972.
61. Weight, Arthur F., *The Sui Dynasty*, New York, 1978, p. 129.
62. Bielenstien, H., 'The Census of China during the Period AD 2-742', *Far Eastern Antiquities*, 1947, p. 146.
63. Bingham, W., *The Founding of Tang Dynasty,* Baltimore, 1941, pp. 14-15.
64. Roy, G.W., *The Importance of Sui and Tang Canal Systems with Regard to transportation and Communications,* Phi Theta Papers, Vol. 8, 1963, p. 38.
65. Ebrey, Patricia Buckley, Anne B. Walthall and James B. Palais, *East Asia: A Cultural Social and Political History,* Boston: Houghton Miffin, 2006, pp. 90-91.
66. Adshead, S.A.M, *Tang China: The Rise of the East in World History*, NY: Palgrave Macmillan, 2004, p. 40.
67. Pritchard, E.H., *Thoughts on the Historical Development of the Population of China, Journal of Asian Studies*, 1963, p. 17.
68. Fairbank and Goldman Merle, *China: A New History*, London: The Belknap Press of Harvard University, 2006, p. 10.
69. 'Anshi Rebellion' also known as the 'An Lushan Rebellion' was started by the Tang's own general An Lushan, and spanned over the rule of three Tang Emperors, He established his own Yang Kingdom. Though short-lived in the north of Huang He in the Pinglu, Fanyang and Hedong regions in 755 AD, it weakened Emporer Xuanzong of Tang.
70. Yumen Guan, also known as the Jade Gate, was the last check post of the Chinese empire made during the Han period and took its name from the Jade Caravan from the north-west passing through it. It was the symbol of China's effective control in the north-west along the Hexi Corridor.
71. Yi Fu Tuan, op. cit., p. 96.
72. Farris, William Wayne, *Population, Disease and Land in Early Japan between 645 – 900 AD,* Cambridge: Harvard University Press, Cambridge, 1985, p. 10.
73. Wang, Yongxing, *Draft Discussion of Early Tang Dynasty's Military Affairs History,* Beijing: Kun Lun Press, 2003, p. 91.
74. Ebrey, et al., op. cit., p.167.

75. Rossabi, Morris, *Khublai Khan: His life and Times*, Berkeley: University of California Press, 1988, p. 76.
76. Allsen, Thomas, 'The Rise of the Mongolian Empire and Mangolian Rule in China', in *Cambridge History of China: Vol. 6, Alien Regimes and Border States*, Twichett et al. (eds), op. cit., pp. 710-713.
77. Rossabi Morris, op. cit., p. 51.
78. Ibid., pp. 70-71.
79. Ray Huang, op. cit., pp. 51-53.
80. Ibid., p. 151.
81. Dillon, Michael, *China's Muslim Hui Community Migration: Settlement and Sects*, Richmond: Curzon Press, 1999, p. 208.
82. Dawa, Norbu, *China's Tibet Policy*, Richmond: Curzon Press, 2001, p. 52.
83. Van Praag and Michael C. van Walt, *The Status of Tibet: Historical Rights and Prospects in International Law*, Boulder: Westview Press, 1987, p. 11.
84. Huang, op. cit., pp. 155-156.
85. Hui Chun Hong, 'Huanming Zuxun and Jheng He's Voyages to the Western Ocean: A Summary', *Journal of Chinese Studies*, Institute of Chinese Studies, 2010, http// www.wikipedia.org/wiki/Jheng-he-file-note-huichun Hung-53. Accessed on 19 Jun 2014.
86. A Report on the book, *'Who Discovered America? The Untold History of the Peopling of the Americas,* by Gavin Menzies and Ian Hudson, by Michael Zennie in *Mail Online*, 8 October 2013, www.dailymail.co.UK/news/article-2449265/who-discovered-America-controversial-historien-Gavin-MenZies-claims-reached-new-world-first.html. Accessed on 20 Jun 2014.
87. Huang, op. cit., pp. 181-183.
88. Farquhar, David, '"Emperor as Bodhisatva" in the Governance of the Qing Empire', *Harvard Journal of Asiatic Studies*, 38 (1), 1978, pp. 5-34.
89. Zhao Gang, 'Reinventing China: Imperial Qing Ideology and the Rise of Modern Chinese National Identity in the Early Twentieth Century', *Modern China*, 32 (1), 2006, pp. 4, 7-10, 12-14.
90. The anti-Manchu element was the greatest manifestation of the Taiping rebellion.
91. Spence, Jonathan D., *The Search For Modern China*, NY: Norton, 2012, pp. 83, 86.
92. Schottenhammer, Angela, 'The East Asian Maritime World 1400-1800: Its Fabrics of Power and Dynamics of Exchanges', *East Asian Economics and Socio-cultural Studies*, Harrassowits, 2007, p. 33.
93. Kissinger, Henry, *On China*, London: Penguin Books, 2012, pp. 36-37.
94. Last lines of the English Translation of the Qianlong letter to George III (1793), www.history.uc.sb.edn/factuly/marcuse/classes/2c/texts/1792 qianlong letter george III, Accessed on 24/6/2014.
95. Maddison, Angus, *The World Economy: A Millennium Perspective*, Organisation for Economic Cooperation and Development 2006, Table B, "World Regional GDP, 20 Countries and regional totals: Appendix B, p. 26.
96. Xu Yu and John K. Fairbank (eds). *Lin Ze Xu, Moral Advice to Queen Victoria in China's Resonse to the West; A Documentary Survey 1839-1923*, Cambridge: Harvard University Press, 1979, p. 26.
97. Hans III, W. Travis and S. Frank, *The Opium Wars*. Illinois: Sourcebooks Inc., 2002, p. 20.
98. Platt, Stephen R., *Autumn in the Heavenly Kingdom: China, the West and the Epic Story of*

Taiping Civil War, 2012, p. XXII.

99. Guang Qing Liu and Richard J. Smith, 'The Military Challenge: The North West and the Coast', in *The Cambridge History of China: A Survey—Late Qing: 1800 -1911, 17 (2)*, Cambridge: Cambridge University Press, 1980, p. 202.
100. Wright, Mary Clabaugh, *The Last Stand of Chinese Conservatism: The Thongzhi Restoration, 1862-74*, pp. 196-121.
101. Xu Immanuel C. Y., *The Rise of Modern China*, 6th Edition, Oxford: Oxford University Press, 2000, p. 209.
102. Crossley, Pamela Kyle, *The Wobbling Pivot: China since 1800*, MA: Wiliey Blackwell, 2010.
103. Hunt, Lynn, Thomas R. Martin, Barbara H. Rosevdein, R. Po-Chia Hsia, *The Making of the West, People and Cultures*, Vol C, 3rd edition, Boston: Bedfords, St Martin's, 2009, pp. 712-13.
104. *New York Times*, 30 July 1894, www.query.nytimes.com/mem/archieve-tree/pdf, Accessed on 03 July 2014.
105. Ssu-Yu Teng and John K. Fairbank (eds), *China's Response to the West: A Documentary* Survey *1839-1923*, Cambridge: Harvard University Press, Cambridge, 1979, p. 70.
106. Bland J. O. P., Li Hung-Chang and Henry Holt, New York, 1917, pp. 160-61.
107. Timothy Richard, *Forty Five Years in China: Reminiscences*, Fredrick A. Stokes Company Publishers, 1916, https://archive.org/stream/fourty Years OO rechoft, Accessed on 4 July 2014.
108. Ibid., pp. 258-262.
109. Kissinger, op. cit., p. 86.
110. Cohen Paul A., *History in Three Keys: The Boxers as Events, Experience and Myth*, Coumbia: Columbia University Press, Columbia, 1997, p. 57.
111. Spence, Jonathan D., *The Search For Modern China*, NY: Norton, 2012, pp. 223-225.
112. Bicker, Robert, *Britain in China: Community Culture and Colonialism - 1900-1949*, Manchester: Manchester University Press, 1999, p. 39.
113. Jerome, Chien, *Yuan Shih-k'ai, (1859-1916)*, CA: Stanford University Press, Stanford, 1961, pp. 76-77, Source: www.books.google.co.in/books?id, Accessed on 06 July 2014.
114. Zhengyuan Fu, *Autocratic Traditions and Chinese Politics*, Cambridge: Cambridge University Press, Cambridge, 1993, pp. 153-154.
115. Spence, Jonathan D, *The Search for Modern China*, NY: WW Norton and Company, 1999, p. 278.
116. Edmund, S K Fung, *In Search of Chinese Democracy: Civil Opposition in Nationalist China* 1929-1949, NY: Cambridge University Press, 2000, p. 5.
117. www.britannica.com/EB checked/topic/*635886/warlord*, Accessed on 06 July 2014.
118. Naragoa, Li, and R. B. Cribb, *Imperial Japan and National Identities in Asia 1895-1945*, London: Routledge, 2013, p. 13.
119. Scott A. Booman, *The Protected Home: A Wei Chi's Interpretation of Maoist Revolutionary Strategy*, NY: Oxford University Press, 1969.
120. *221 Memorandum* by Mr J. Mcewan, Minister for External Affairs, 10 May 1940, Australian Government (Department of Foreign Affairs and Trade), www.dfat.gov.au/info/historical/ Hist Docs.nsf/ (look-up valume number)/3-221. Accessed on 9 July 2014.
121. US Congress, *Investigation of Concentration of Economic Power*, Hearing before the Temporary National Economic Committee, 76th Congress, 2nd session, Pt - 21 Washington, 1940,

p. 11241.

122. 'China's Declaration of war…', op. cit.
123. Huang, Ray, *Chiang Kai-shek: Diary from a Macro History Perspective, China,* Taibeshi: Time Publishing Company, 1994, pp. 299-300.
124. Ibid., p. 420.
125. Addington, Larry H., *America's War in Vietnam: A Short Narrative History*, Indiana University Press, 2000, p. 30.
126. Tennesson, op. cit., p. 41.
127. *Selected Works of Mao Zedong: The May Movements* (a commemorative article by Mao), www.marxists.org/reference/archive/mao/selected-works/volume-2/mswv2-13.htm. Accessed on 12 July 2014.
128. Li Xiaobing, *A History of the Modern Chinese Army*, Kentucky: University Press, p. 13, 26-27.
129. 'Origin of the Names of China's Provinces', *People's Daily Online*, 7 April 2004, www.people.com.cn/GB/shenghuo/1090/2435218.html. Accessed on 13 July 2014.
130. *Chinese Soviet Republic*, www.historyculture-China.com/en/34history 7366.html, Accessed on 13 July 2014.
131. Chang Jung and Jon Halliday, *Mao: The Unknown Story*, London: Jonathan Cape, 2005, Chapter 5.
132. Carter, Peter, *Mao*, London: Oxford University Press, pp. 67-68.
133. Hongwei Wang, Weiwang, Ye Tian, *Zhong Guo Lishi Juang Tang 1,* Juan 6, Min Guo, Zhong Hua Shu Ju, Xiang Gang, 2005, pp. 3-7.
134. Major, John S., *The Land and People of Mongolia,* NY: Lippincott, 1990, p. 119.
135. Sanders, Alan J.K., *Mongolia: Politics, Economies and Society*, Boulder: Lynne Reiner, 1987, pp. 16-17.
136. As the claims seen in the *Jindai Zhongguo Bainian Guochi Ditu (Maps of the country of National Humiliation of Modern China)*, Renminchubanshe, 1997.
137. Crowe, op. cit. p. 31.
138. Clarke, Michael Edmund, op. cit., p. 37.
139. Perdue, Peter C., *China Marches West: The Qing Conquest of Central Asia*. NY: Harvard University Press, 2009, p. 285.
140. Zhao, Gang, 'Reinventing China: Imperial Qing Ideology and the Rise of Modern Chinese National Identity In the Early Twentieth Century', Sage Journals, *Modern China*, 32 (1), 2006, p. 3, max.sagepub.com/content/ 32/1/3.full.pdf+html, Accessed on 16 July 2014.
141. Forbes, Andrew D. W., *Warlords and Muslims in Chinese Central Asia: A Political History of Republican Sinkiang 1911-49*, London: Cambridge University Press, 1986, p. 144.
142. Ibid., p. 174.
143. Millward, James A. and Nabijan Tursun, 'Political History and Strategies of Control' in S. Fredrick Star (ed.), *Xinjiang: China's Muslim Borderland*, NY: M. E. Sharpe, 2004, pp. 77-78.
144. Bovington, Gardner, *The Uyghurs: Strangers in Their Own Land,* NY: Columbia University Press, 2010, p. 197.
145. Hopper, Ben, and Michael Webber, *Migration, Modernisation and Ethnic Estrangement: Uyghur Migration to Urumqi, Xinjiang Uyighur Antonymous Region PRC II*, Global Oriental LTD, pp. 178-179.
146. D' Encausse, Halen Carrere, 'The Russian Revolution and Soviet Policy in Central Asia', in

Central Asia, Gavin Hambly (ed), NY; Delacorte Press, 1969, p. 230.

147. Proclamation Issued by HH the Dalai Lama XIII, *on the Eight Day of the First Month of the Water-Ox Year (1913)*, www.Tibetjustice.org/materials /tibet/tibet/html. Accessed on 23 July 2014.
148. Ibid.
149. Ibid.
150. Lawler, Andrew, 'Beyond the Yellow River: How China Became China', *Science*, 325 (5943), 21 August 2009, pp. 930-935.
151. The Movius Line is a theoretical line drawn across northern India, first proposed by the American archaeologist Hallam L. Movius in 1948 to demonstrate a technological different in the early prehistoric tool technologies between the East and the West that the old world had.
152. Wei Wang, 'Middle Pleistocene Bifaces from Fengshuo (Bose Basin Gungxi, China)', *Journal of Human Evolution*, Vol. 69, April 2014, pp. 110-122, www.sciencedirect.com/science/article/pii/50047248414000396. Accessed on 23 July 2014.
153. Friedman, George, *The Geopolitics of China: A Great Power Enclosed (Monograph)* in www.stratfor.com as quoted in www.investorsinsight.com/blogs /john-monuldins-outside-the-box/archieve/2008/06/12/the-geopolitics-of-china.aspx. Accessed on 29 July 2014.

4

Metaphysical Evolution of the Chinese Geopolity

INTRODUCTION

Understanding the Chinese geopolitical mindset is another important aspect of our discussion without which it is quite difficult to make out the imperatives which the Chinese people may derive for themselves for their future course of international relations. A detailed discussion would give a perspective for the present mindset of the people and also fathom the differences, if any, between the people and the government, especially when China is ruled by an authoritarian regime. This discourse pans the intellectual foundations of regimes' paradigms through the history of China, whether these are emanating from pure sociological, ethical and religious origins or as mix of these. The metaphysical discourse will provide the answers to many research questions which apparently do not subscribe to geospatial determinism. However, the human geographical moorings and settings for development cannot be dismissed summarily. Most of all, this discourse of the metaphysical evolution of the Chinese geopolity (and polity) also becomes one important part of the holistic narrative with a gestalt approach in order to understand the settings for the geopolitical imperatives of China and the evolution of the appropriate responses by China in the 21st Century which is the ultimate research question. Therefore, let us discuss validity and utility of this research question and subsequently make out the metaphysical perspective for the Chinese geopolitics, nuanced in greater details.

How China draws Legitimacy for its Governance? Let us begin with the question, what is the legitimacy of a political power?[1] Seymour Martin Lipset when says that legitimacy is 'the capacity of the system to engender and maintain the belief that the existing political institutions are the most appropriate ones for the society'; he is basically indicating towards the power relationship between the ruler and the ruled in terms of the people's belief.[2,3] However, the whole exercise of a regime is to ultimately impress its 'people', irrespective of its methods and to seek their approval which can be termed as legitimacy for the existence of the governance. Therefore, it is the people to be governed who are the central theme of any legitimacy and this answers our second question as to who has the authority to legitimise, and the answer is the people. However, this still leaves the question, 'what about the process? There is a whole complexity of the legitimacy business that emerges because these processes range from mystical and shamanic to authoritarian to democratic by which the people are impressed upon to give the approval to any regime. The scale begins with inducing fear and awe in the people to seek approval and ends on giving total power and freedom to elect a government. While the power scale begins with full freedom to trulers and fear of them, and ends with full freedom to the people and fear of them, the political process starts somewhere in the middle of the scale. Otherwise, the scale begins more with the shamanic and mystical processes in which the people's participation is the least, although they do give a muted approval of the ruler out of fear of different kinds induced at the beginning of the evolution of a civilisation.

China, particularly, is a peculiar case study as it, despite being the largest 'people' in the world with 4000 years of recorded history, the civilisational evolution has still not reached the end of the evolution of the governance process as the people of China still legitimise the government in a more metaphysical (to some extent even mystical) way than in a direct political way. Why it is so? Does it have a historical anchorage of metaphysics? If yes, then does this metaphysical evolution have any geospatial mooring and human geographical narrative? This discourse will try to find the answers to these questions about the legitimacy of governance for our future use in this book.

Unique or Isolationist: Is China a Victim of its Own Metaphysics? China appears the most progressive in economic terms and hopes to satisfy the ever-growing economic aspirations of its people. But as stated above, it still remains 'premature' politically. The political freedom is not commensurate with the economic empowerment of the people. However, the people still approve the regime and support it. Therefore, there is a dichotomy in these two because as Baogang Guo says, the Communist regime of today attains legitimacy by its utilitarian justification to the people, through its modernisation of economy and its redistributive and welfare policies.[4] The bigger question is that China is presently emerging from the isolationist regime of the Mao Era and as the communication between the people of China is increasing with the people of the rest of the world, how will the Communist regime tackle the realisation of this dichotomy as the communication intensifies among the Chinese people too? The awareness about other cultures and the important role of religion in the people's life is being realised, although China today manifests its isolationist tendencies in a very reflective manner in which it wishes to control the social variables, applies what the Communist regime thinks is appropriate for China and it even wishes to propagate a tailor-made religious theology as it deems fit for China.[5] However, it is not peculiar to the present regime. Traces found not only in its history but in the historical geography as well, as we have deduced in the previous chapter that how China proper rendered itself as an island geospatially. My argument is that the Bamboo Curtain was only a modern manifestation of this old-rooted geopolitically isolationist tendencies in the country's metaphysical making. What are the metaphysical foundations of these isolationist tendencies? Whether there is any linkage between this isolationist tendency and the uniqueness theory of the Chinese civilisation? And whether this uniqueness is only a metaphysical manifestation of the human geographical evolution of China proper in its geospatial dimensions? We shall seek plausible answers to all these questions in this chapter.

Will the Social Psychological Approach to Study Interstate Relations be a Correct Tool to examine the Metaphysical Evolution of Chinese Geopolitics? The metaphysical evolution of any polity can be considered as only a subset of the social and human geographical set which has a more tangible cause-and-effect relation. The metaphysical evolution is better manifested in the collective social behaviour of cultural sociology. If we consider China proper as a homogeneous civilisational society, their collective behaviour can give us a solid portent to indicate that the China proper can be taken as an area with the most intense centripetal force and the driving force of China as a nation state for the purpose of relational study with rest of China. However, since the individuals make up the society, the individuals do matter and the effective individuals matter more. This premise is truer in the case of China where whatever be the metaphysical changes, the individuals have come out as the carriers of that set of metaphysics, whether Confucianism, legalism or communism. Metaphysically, when the society bestowed the approval, it was mystically called as the 'Mandate of the Heaven'; and when the individuals who were considered the most suitable to carry out this Mandate of the Heaven, they were called the 'sage kings' and 'The Son of Heaven' who possessed desired virtues and the mandate. However, in the modern perspective, this mystic explanation falls short of the desired validity, therefore, there is certainly a need to examine these Chinese metaphysical concepts with a more descriptive accuracy for modern understanding as well as applications.

We are aware that individuals do matter in politics, as much depends upon how individuals interpret, define and represent their political environment. What actions they take is always in a context of rules and norms of political institutions. The context always changes with the feelings, passions and needs that effect prejudices, ideologies and biases. Since the individuals have mattered more in the Chinese context having all totalitarian rulers, the study of the person in a particular time and situation also becomes important and psychology offers a contingent or conditional approach to the study of political processes recognising that the contextual factors do help determine the influence that these individuals have had.[6] Therefore, in order to attain a certain degree of accuracy, the metaphysical elements will be explained more in social psychological terms then the mystical terms as we progress in our discourse.

This discourse will also avoid the bias of a missionary zeal to propagate democracy as a necessary goal for China and follow what Shannon discusses as to how every system achieves approval of its citizens for their national goals when he says:

> "In democracy, the child is taught to prize the liberties of democracy, in totalitarian state, to admire the strength and discipline of totalitarian state. In both he is taught to respect the traditions and creeds and institutions of his own country and to think it better than any other."[7]

Metaphysical Concepts of Statecraft and Geopolitics: Continuing from the last thoughts expressed in the paragraph before, searching for the modern concepts of statecraft in the Chinese antiquity will be a Western bias. Therefore, giving an adequate credit to the concepts of statecraft developed in the perspective of its own culture, its remnant influences till the modern era when a country is compelled to interact with the world at large and not allowed to remain confined to its own area of influence, being influenced by the thoughts and concepts from outside and making an assessment for the modern-day applications for their own thoughts and polity, will be the approach for this discourse. Though this discourse may appear to give a historical perspective at the beginning, the ultimate effort will be to trace the residual influences of the Chinese concepts on the modern discourses of Chinese geopolitics.

Any civilisation when it evolves, begins with some superhuman and para-psychic efforts of some individuals to exert influence on the immediate society in their desire to achieve command over the rest of them. The Chinese rulers' wisdom also followed the same route to evolve itself and traversed the path from being divine to metaphysical to philosophical to political in its mechanics. As has been discovered in the previous chapters that the Chinese civilisation has had multiple origins, I now argue here that it was unified in wisdom in the course of expansion and cultural exchanges, being in the more similar geopolitical environs than dissimilar ones, and has evolved itself now as China Proper. Therefore, these metaphysical concepts have more applications on China proper than the outer China like Tibet and Xinjiang. In the end, all these concepts are required to be seen holistically in order to create a big picture of Chinese wisdom that even persists in its modern avatar.

FROM THE 'SHAMANIC KING' TO 'SAGE KING': 'THE SON OF HEAVEN'

Mysticism has always shrouded kingship in antiquity and divine power considered to have been bestowed upon a person who was accepted as king by the social group around him. As Hocart says:

> "Perhaps there never were any Gods without Kings, or Kings without Gods. When we have discovered the origin of divine kingship, we shall know. But at present we only know that when history begins, there are Kings, the representatives of Gods."[8]

Truly said, this progression applies to all cultures in the same amount but may be in different notations. China also had a similar evolution of kingship. Therefore, let us explore whether the divine man became king, or the king became divine in the Chinese antiquity.

Shamanism is considered to be the most ancient supernatural practice to reach the altered state of consciousness in order to interact with the believed world of spirit and bring back this transcendental energy to achieve certain human aims of this world. There have been regional variations, but the spirit remains the same as that of the earliest form of religious practices. The Chinese variation comes in the form of 'Wu' (巫), a spirit medium who practised divination, prayer, sacrifice, rainmaking and healing in a tradition dating back to over 3000 years. These shamans were found in both the sexes known as Nan Wu (男 巫) and Nu Wu (女 巫). We shall debate later that how these shamans exchanged for kings in the Chinese antiquity, but it is pertinent to bring out here itself that the shamans in their pure form (as sheer spirit medium) have existed till date in almost all the cultures including the Chinese. The Sinologist Joseph Needham has brought out the existence of Shamans transliterated as Xiamen, quoting Shiji for a self-practicing Qin Shi Huang (221–210 BCE), to the modern imperial Manchu shamans known as the Shauman and Sizhu.[9]

However, the bigger question we need to discuss here is how the shamans assumed kingship. The Neolithic inhabitants of China were first to start divinatory predictions using animal shoulder bones (oracle bone) by heating them and interpreting the cracks which emerged. During the Shang period, this practice became more refined with the use of tortoises' shells being considered sacred because of their long life and having special powers in contacting the ancestors in the spiritual world.[10, 11] This attainment of wisdom by divination before and during the Shang remained confined to the upper crust of society. The oracle bone records depict words for ancestors, for guest and for king; put in that order, it indicates two things: one that the king himself received an ancestor guest in his medium (as an impersonator literally called *Shi*) and to whom the ritual offerings were made.[12] KC Chang further elaborates, quoting oracle bones, that kings directly performed as shamans and enquired the spirits about winds, rains, storms and conquests. He has also quoted inscriptions depicting the kings dancing in prayer for rains and prognosticating a dream. Thereby, concluding that the king was also a shaman is not unfounded.[13] Or else, we can safely deduce that prolific shamans became kings. However, the fall of Shang diviners as kings mitigated shamanism in being the main characteristic of a king. During the Zhou dynasty, the shamanic divination though abandoned as a qualification for the king continued to be practised for ritual divination through shells and bones and spread from the nobility to the commoners. As the divination became less reliable due to the knowledge expansion as a cause and effect derivative, the shamans were replaced by the sages and the thin line between mystical predictions through oracle bone rituals and a wisdom-based prediction through the same process, became blurred. The *Book of Changes*, a divination manual, and Confucian classics consider people possessing such wisdom as sages who had a fair knowledge of fortune and misfortune and divination—a ritual that seeks wisdom of foreknowledge that believed to have belonged to the gods. An event of ritual in the *Book of Rites* to decide the succession of a high official of the state of Wei in the 6th Century BCE exemplifies a clear shift from a pure mystical proclamation to a psychological insight-based proclamation, out of the similar rituals. The tortoise-shell oracle cracks were deciphered to say that the hint about the successor would come through the king's six sons bathing themselves after his death and coming out wearing their jade pendants. All followed, but one who refused saying that who would bathe and decorate himself with jade on this grievous occasion of a parent's death? The one who defied was declared as the heir rather than those who had followed the dictum.[14] Perhaps, the intelligence-based wisdom began to creep into the selection system of the state authority at large.

Sage King

As we have discussed earlier, the mystical powers made shamans kings, but all shamans were not kings, though the shamanic powers did become the primary attribute of a king till the Zhou period. Likewise, sagehood replaced the shamanic powers as an attribute, but all sages were not kings either. It can also be said that the shamanic powers and sageliness were concurrent attributes for a king, but when shamanism was bequeathed as the primary attribute, sageliness took prominence, and continued to be so with some exceptions like in the case of Qin, to become a king. The question 'what is sageliness' takes us to the Chinese word Wang (King) who as per the classic texts of the Warring States period was supposed to be a wise and virtuous person and as per the depiction in the oracle bones, a man having large ears, small mouth and third vertical eye *Zongmu* (纵 目). There are indications towards the sage having attributes like acute hearing (or paying heed to all that is voiced), powerful physical and spiritual vision (wisdom) and the one who speaks less (speaks only substance). The Book of Classics also uses a word *rui* (瑞) for sages, meaning profound and bright (the word included a Chinese character for sage).

To understand the domain in which the attributes of a king described above were put into use, we must now understand how the Wang (or King) was made. The oracle bones give an etymological origin of the word King (Wang), which initially depicted fire in the earth and at times, an axe. But later, it developed into a character with three horizontal lines joined by one vertical line (王). In this, the top horizontal line denoted the heavenly order, the middle one the human order and the bottom one the earthly order. The vertical line joining these three orders in a solitary effort, became the mediator cosmic man who represented all human beings in the presence of a superior heaven. With the access to the heavenly domain, the King was also termed as the 'Son of Heaven' which came into prominence during the Zhou period which was depicted by them in the Chinese characters *Tianzi* (天 子) denoting the Son of Heaven (or the son of that deity who rules the heavens).[15] Declaring the King as the Son of Heaven, had a mystical as well as religious connotation by which the Zhou in fact justified their usurping of power from the Shang, saying that the 'Son of Heaven' had the 'Mandate of Heaven' or Tian Ming (天 命), which we shall discuss later.[16] Although the sagehood related to kingship has been more mystical in ancient China during the period of the mythological Yellow Emperor, subsequently it became more meaningful and full of theocratic virtues. The scope of the king became more realistic, with a legalist paradigm coming into effect with the Qin ruler who made for himself a title '*Huangdi*' (皇 帝) usually translated as emperor. In calling so, he made himself a king of all kings and lord of lords. What is attributed to the Qin Emperor as a unifier of China actually implied the unifier of all the warring states. Although later on, there were several occasions in the Chinese history when China was fragmented, but never the subsequent unifiers were considered for this credit. In fact, as the history depicts, it was the ruthless imperial power rather than the sagely virtues of Qin that unified China. However, the historical kings continued presenting themselves as descendants from ancestors with shamanic and ascetic powers and with the so-called ability to hear the voice of the gods and to act as their mouthpiece. They jealously guarded their position as the kingship itself increasingly took on a secular role. Even Qin Shi Huang wished to continue his position till eternity—a desire he manifested in the sacrifices and the warriors' burial ground.

'ALL UNDER HEAVEN' AND 'THE MANDATE OF HEAVEN'

As we have discussed, the kingship in the Chinese metaphysical conception is that 'one man' who creates communication between the heaven and the earth with a divine authority, as the heaven has mandated upon him to do so. In this explanation, the heaven and the earth have a relational dimensionality with each other. The first dimensional derivative is from the kingship as a cosmic paradigm. The character for the word *Wang* consists of horizontal bar on the top for heaven and a parallel bar at the bottom with the humans in between as medium. Therefore, the Heaven and the Earth have always remained in a sacred astronomical relationship for the area ruled by the king as 'All Under Heaven' *Tian Xia* (天 下). The oracle bone inscriptions record the discovery of a new star (Nova) around 1300 BCE. As the ancient Chinese looked towards the Heaven above for guidance, they considered the pole star as the Emperor star and the Little Dipper nearest to the Pole Star was named as the Crown Prince, the next in line, the son of the Imperial Concubine and after that, the Empress.[17] Even the King's territory under the Heaven was considered as mirror opposite to the sky above. During the Zhou period, as the Chinese advanced in the study of the celestial bodies, movements of the sun, moon and stars, they observed the changes in the Heaven above, made predications about fortune and misfortune and distributed a territory divided into nine provinces according to the terrains and positions of the stars.[18] The capital was considered to be made right under the Pole Star and the palace facing south represented the king facing his domain, mainly towards the south, although it was not always possible to be so.[19] The figure of nine has a special place in the Chinese cosmological consciousness. The kings divided their domain into nine states; they also divided the village of the peasants into a grid of nine squares with the central square being a collective farm, the products of which were given to the king. The roots of this conception can be traced to the institution of the Bright Hall of Mingtong as mentioned in the Book of Lu (*Lu Shu*) comprised of nine rooms as the magic cells of the magic square representing, perhaps, the nine planets, in which the king moved from room to room according to the seasons in his role as the Son of Heaven and the calendar rotated accordingly to the law of the universe.[20] Even the passing of the 'Mandate of Heaven' to the heir and the capture by a new dynasty had a ritual passing the famous nine cauldrons representing the Nine Provinces *Jiushou* (九 首) that made up the country. As the legends have it, these cauldrons were made by King Yu of the Xia dynasty, were taken away by the subsequent dynasties, Shang and Zhou, and perhaps lost during the Warring States period. The figure of nine also has a significance beyond divisions and the representation of territory of 'All under Heaven'. What China calls itself is *Zhongguo* (中 国) the Middle Kingdom, and this is a further elaboration of the sacred cosmology of China's location in popular belief, to be at the centre of the earth, surrounded by nine continents beyond the seas, considering the own the divine continent or *Shenzhou* (神 州), a civilized world and the other the barbarian or primitive ones. In any case, these cauldrons or *ding ding* (鼎 鼎) became an object of rituals and instrument of legitimacy of the kings.

Before the Warring States period when the mystical rituals and explanations of the divine authority, divinations and predictions through oracle bones were practised, the orientation of the kingdom or 'All under Heaven' according to the cosmology of 'the known earth' was much more mystical. The geopolitics was played less on geostrategy and more on the cosmic beliefs and rituals. Perhaps, once the mandate was declared to have been transferred to next dynasty, it continued till the time all sorts of natural calamities went against the 'Son of Heaven' of the time and his heirs. However, these mystical notions were challenged during the Eastern Zhou and the Warring States periods and more geostrategic ideas came in as the Warring States period became a fertile ground for a 'Hundred Ideas' to flourish. The definition of 'All under Heaven' and the 'Mandate of Heaven' were challenged. The scope became more moral, humanistic, legalistic and realist.

'All Under Heaven' in the Modern Geopolitical Perspective

From the modern geopolitical perspective, it is extremely important to discuss the concept of 'All under Heaven' and examine why and how it still influences the think tanks and policymakers in China. As China calls itself the Middle Kingdom, it although does not affect the others' boundary delimitations at present, but what intrigues the geopoliticians is 'what happens if any of the interpretations of 'All under Heaven' is adopted by the policymakers of China?' In that case we certainly need to examine the various interpretations available and see each one's application to the perspective of China's internal power and external geopolitical settings.

As we have examined, up to the Zhou period, the 'All under Heaven' was more of a mystical conception corresponding to the human ability to visualise the territory right under the canopy of the sky above. The celestial beliefs were taken as a guide for the orientation of the capitals and the states. During the Warring States period, what followed was full interstate political strife and war, giving several thinkers the opportunities to study the geopolitical environment of China at that time and to redefine or reorient the old mystical concepts of the 'Sage Kings' or *sheng wang* (圣 王), 'Son of Heaven' or *tian zi* (天 子) 'All under Heaven' or *tian xia* (天 下), 'Mandate of Heaven' or *tian ming* (天 命), 'Hegemony' or *ba quan* (霸 权), etc. The Chinese thinkers recognised the richness of the repertoire of philosophy given at different periods, especially by the seven renowned ones: Laozi (老 子), Confucius (Kongfu Zi 孔 夫 子, Mencius (Meng Zi 孟 子), Xunzi (荀 子) (not Sun Zu 孙 子), Mozi (墨 子), Hanfeizi (李 斯), Shang Yang (商 鞅) and Li Si (李 斯). The revival of applications of these thoughts in the modern perspective was evident as was carried out by Luang Qichao in his '*History of Pre-Qing Political Thoughts*' in the era of the Republicans and now by Yan Xuetong in his '*Ancient Chinese Thoughts, Modern Chinese Power*'. These pre-Qing philosophers range in thoughts from moralist to hegemonist, but the application of these on the Chinese political thinking in the 20th and 21st Centuries have been selective and as per suitability of the times of the rulers, although their philosophy includes a range of subjects of human and political life. Here, we shall restrict ourselves to a few relevant areas like 'All under Heaven', mandate and legitimacy of a ruler and humane vs. hegemonic authority with a geopolitical perspective.

It has been acknowledged by sinologists like Joseph Needham that the Chinese think less in casual manner and more in a symbolic correlation. He says:

> "In coordinative thinking, conceptions are not subsumed under one another, but placed side by side in a pattern and thing influence one another not by act of mechanical causation, but by a kind of inductance...The symbolic correlations or correspondences all formed part of prior actions or impulsions of other things. They were thus parts in existential dependence upon the whole world organism."[21]

There he is basically evaluating the Chinese mindset to be more inclined towards the harmonistic thinking of Confucius rather Hanfeizi's advocacy of separate investigations of the 'Way of Heaven' and the way of human affairs. To that extent, Confucius, Mencius and Xunzi think that 'All under Heaven' is more of a moral authority than a state authority. Therefore, the 'Son of Heaven' has a different kind of role than that of the rulers of state because he represented Heaven. Confucius thought that 'All under Heaven', therefore, consists of states and therefore the states could be ruled by feudal lords, but under the observation and inspection of the 'Son of Heaven' and the rules set by him, as he says in the *Doctrine of the Mean and Harmony* that:

> "None but the Son of Heaven may determine rituals, fix measurements and decree the form of writing."[22]

The following ode sums up the Confucian conception of 'All under Heaven' and the 'Son of Heaven':

> *Under Heaven's canopy*
> *There is nowhere that is not the sage king's land;*
> *Up to the sea's shores*
> *There are none who are not the Sage King's servants.* [23]

Though Confucius believed in the universal writ of the 'Son of Heaven' over the expanse of Heaven, we need to determine the expanse of the Heaven in the context of that time. 'Up to the seashore' says all about the imagined expanse of the Heaven and perhaps nothing beyond the sea could be imagined existing under the canopy of the Heaven. Thus, we can firmly say that Confucius regarded the 'All under Heaven' as comprising the local canopy of the Heaven under which the 'Son of Heaven' ruled the states with his universal authority of a moral kind. Xunzi and Mencius both go little further to make a distinction between 'All under Heaven' and the states comprising it by saying that the moral authority and benevolence which is the essence of Confucianism may not work for the states as it works for the 'All under Heaven'. As Xunzi says:

> "The state is a small thing and a small-minded person may possess it.... A state can be held by a small-minded person but it cannot exist forever. All under Heaven is the great thing and only a sage can hold it."[24]

Mencius also says in the same spirit:

> *"There are those lacking benevolence who have acquired state;*
> *But there has never been anyone lacking benevolence*
> *Who acquired All Under Heaven.*[25]

Xunzi finally concludes by saying:

> *It is possible for a state to be stolen from others.*
> *It is possible for states to be annexed*
> *But is not possible for All under Heaven to be annexed."*[26]

The great strategist Xunzi, therefore, gives a hint for the Chinese geostrategy in the modern-day international relations to create an expanse of All under the entire sky or heaven that cannot be annexed by anyone else as there will be no one else. This will be examined in the perspective of the other schools who followed him like Hanfei Zi (韩 非 子) (280–233 BCE) who was a legalist, though a disciple of the Confucian Xun Zi, whose principles became policy for the first emperor of China, King Zheng, also called as Qin Shi Huang. Regarding the concept of 'All under Heaven' he thought that it is the power of a state writ large over all other states under the Heaven. Mozi (墨 子) (470–391 BCE) also found the power in acquiring a state and the power acquiring 'All under Heaven' the same. In fact Mozi was first to challenge Confucius to say that conformity and traditional mores is no guaranty that actions are morally right as was Hanfeizi who also said that old methods are good only for old times and new methods are required to govern new generation as human nature is dynamic and changes with times indicating to realism in governance. It was Mozi who conceptualized *Fa* (法) or model or standards first which Xunzi and Hanfeizi took to new levels of realpolitik as *Fajia* (法 家) the school of models and standards, better known as legalism.

Hanfeizi, therefore, began to apply these principles to the affairs Qin sate. It is evident when he elucidates the geopolitical advantages of the state of Qin over the other warring states responsible for acquiring the states existing 'All under Heaven'. He says:

> "The commands and ordinances, rewards and punishments of Qin, the advantages of its terrain are unlike any other state under heaven. By relying on these to gain All under Heaven, it can easily be annexed and possessed".[27]

Hanfeizi had realised the futility of the moral high ground of 'All under Heaven' and the position of the 'Son of Heaven', because during his time the high mind was not the only qualification as the desires of the people had become more materialistic; the 'Son of Heaven' had become more of a burden:

> "When men lightly relinquish the position of Son of Heaven, it is not because they are high minded but because the advantages of the post are 'slight'. When men strive for securing the government it is not because they are base but because, the power they will acquire is great."[28]

Hanfeizi thus announced the demise of moral authority, sageliness and humane authority of a king to claim the 'Mandate of Heaven' in the changing value system of the time. Therefore, the onset of a realist system of polity took its roots. However, Hanfeizi who wanted to serve the court of Qin got killed in the custody of Qin. It was the other legalist Shang Yang or Gongsun Yang (公 孙 鞅) or Lord Shang or Shang Jun (商 君) who designed the political work of Qin (秦) to make them a formidable state. Hanfei Zi and Shang Yang both were of the opinion that the past cannot teach anything as the knowledge of the past is only useful to the situation of the time and when the situation changes the human behavior also change and then, the Way must also change. Shang Yang therefore tells in the Book of Lord Shang, *Shang Jun Shu* (商 君书) a new Way (道) appropriate at the times of Qin when the people had become more knowledgeable:

> "When the people are ignorant, one can become monarch through knowledge; when the generation is knowledgeable, one can become monarch through force." (Shang Jun Shu 7:53Book of Lord Shang 7.1-7.2).

He says so because he thinks that the knowledgeable people invariably think in their own interest as "the people follow after benefit as water follows downwards", therefore, their selfishness (motivation) if used through a legal system of punishment and rewards, the state will run efficiently. Shang Yang says in his Book of Lord Shang at verse 18.2 that, in the past, those who were able to control All Under Heaven, first had to control their enemies and those who had to overcome their enemies first had to overcome their own people like the metal worker controls metal and potter controls clay. And since the people are intrinsically selfish, the ruler has to control his subject only through law (法), basically referring to punitive measures.

Therefore, what Zhuangzi considered that since family, community, state and 'All under Heaven' are different levels of a social unit, they could only be governed by different levels of political power and that 'All under Heaven' is nothing but a willing obedience to one who wins over them by extending virtues and trust—then only can he employ the political authority of 'All under Heaven, was rendered irrelevant. While Laozi's concept of 'All under Heaven' was nothing but a spiritual vessel which cannot be chased and grasped. All these became surreal conditionalities which went beyond the imagination of Qin, hence abandoned.

Having brought together the major philosophical propositions on 'All under Heaven' and how they have been acquired at different times, we notice that as the interstate relations deteriorated during the Spring and Autumn period, the philosophers of that time moved from being idealist to realist and as Qin followed what Shang Yang surmised to him, he acquired all the fragmented states by political power, totally backed by military might. He, therefore, declared himself as the first emperor of China—a new name for the Son of Heaven who had just acquired the Mandate. He was no 'sage king' and showed no benevolence to other states that came under his own sphere of 'All under Heaven' only through military defeat or by submission under coercion. He further ruled not by harmonising the heaven and earth through his humane authority, but by state power of all kinds which manifested in the form of rewards as well as punishments as per the principles of Shang Yang.[29]

Therefore, I posit three things here. One, that the domain of 'All under Heaven' was a constitution of states territorially commensurate to the corresponding perceptual imagination of the king—whatever could come under the immediate heaven over him. My second argument is that in acquiring the 'Mandate of Heaven', the means differed but the end remained the same—a writ over all states—with the means ranging from sageliness to moral authority to humane authority, and ultimately coming down to realist military power. The legal authority was backed by the power of the state which in a true sense, is the most modern means. However, the end achievement had always been the writ over the states, with a varying degree of intensity. The intensity of this holding ranged from royal domain to feudal domain to tributary states and the wasteland or barbaric lands which we shall discuss later. My third argument is that the pre-modern, modern and post-modern applications will include all of these varying means befitting the power of the state of China, ranging from benevolent to legalist to militarist force, to achieve the realist end that is influence over the ever-expanding 'All under Heaven' which needs immediate discussion.

For the sake of brevity, we shall skip the territoriality of China during the Han, Tang, Song, Yuan and Ming periods from the point of view of 'All under Heaven', but the means we must discuss as they did change with the Han after the Qin—adopting Confucian philosophy against that of Hanfeizi and Shang Yang, then followed by Taoism, Buddhism, Confucianism and Neo-Confucianism during the Tang and Ming. What is most relevant, however, is that the Qing China in its most expanded form was adopted by Revolutionary China and then the Communist China made up a thematic perception of 'All under Heaven' for unification. At the onset of the 20th Century, 'All under Heaven' was substituted with a term called 'Historic China' and the scholars in China tended to view the domain of the Qing Empire as the ultimate geographic area of historical China. Emperor Yong Zheng of Qing bragged about the vastness of Qing China that China's unification began with the Qin and its expansion went beyond the Great Wall with the Yuan, but the task was completed during his dynasty. He further said that since his dynasty had been the only one that combined China and 'the outer realm' into 'one family', therefore, he could possess an enormous territory.[30] This makes two things clear: China was never under an immediate royal as well as feudal domain of any king or emperor in terms of area what it is today, except under the barbarian rules of Yuan and Qing, and, that the Yuan China is not taken as the expanded 'All under Heaven' because the Ming China that followed was only composed of those areas which was considered actual Chinese areas against the Yuan who was considered an illegitimate occupational force. Also, other Chinese geobodies being remote in the history in the general consciousness of China, Qing China was taken as the reference point being convenient to revive the memories of people despite China being left with only half of the maximum Qing China at their demise. At the onset of Republican China, the total discourse of 'All under Heaven' was reduced to territoriality of a Geography of Humiliation (1930) which ruled over all the geopolitical arguments of the Chinese. And in that wake, receiving only half its maximum size that had been achieved by the Qing was rued. To that regard the gains of the Qing, beyond the Ming China, was neither considered expansionist nor imperialist.[31] Rather, both Republicans as well as the Communist China vowed for unification and ultimately achieved it to the largest extent possible in the realist terms of geopolitics of that time.

Now, since the boundary remains almost settled and the modern balance of power compels China to restrain from any realist political demeanour, the modern theorists and think tanks are recasting 'All under Heaven' in the most imaginative manner possible. Yan Xuetong in his modern analysis of 'Pre-Qin philosophers' does just that. The Chinese thinkers were more inclined towards Hanfeizi, Shang Yang and Qin during Mao and are now shifting towards Xunzi. There could be one primary reason that since Xunzi belonged to the Confucian school therefore, he gets more acceptance against, 'rejecting the past and overpowering the citizens and ememies alike' by Hanfeizi and Shang Yang. Second, Xunzi has discussed interstate polity and diplomacy in detail which is now being conveniently appropriated to international politics by Yan Xuetong with the support of another Chinese renowned thinker in international politics, Ye Zecheng.[32] Appropriating Xunzi's "All under Heaven" of the Warring States period to the entire world of today, they give proof of Xunzi rejecting the Jie and Zhou claim of possessing 'All under Heaven' and say that the Tang and the Wu usurped it because Xunzi had used the phrase, 'All under Heaven is the heaviest burden there is,' and that despite having the title of 'Son of Heaven', the Jie and Zhou actually did not possess 'All under Heaven'. They try to import the same sense to the modern geopolitics. The modern Chinese think tanks also liken the present day-world with the Warring States period. To put it in perspective, it is actually the change of perspective what Xunzi had and what modern Chinese strategists think it to be in 'the multipolar world' that China likes it to be called despite the US predominance and seeks a role for itself as the 'Son of Heaven'. Yan Xuetong actually takes it out of context, especially when he says that no one was actually powerful enough during the Warring States period, whose writ others could easily accept, till the Qin came to the fore. Therefore, the Zhou by inheritance had the title 'Son of Heaven' but were devoid of the writ, thus they did not control 'All under Heaven'. Secondly, 'All under Heaven' was a perspective of the China of that period and that of the modern day what Chinese think tank is witnessing today as a vacant post of the 'Son of Heaven', up for grabs.[33] But today, when the US still exists in common perception to have enough writ over the world, the Chinese think tanks' pushing this theory can only be considered as an ambition fuelled by their 'perceived old glory'.

However, it has also become a common realisation now in China that once China came out of its self-imposed exile and isolation and embraced economic liberalisation and interdependence, the political thinkers have begun to reorient and reposition pre-Qin thinkers, especially Confucius and Xunzi, and give their thoughts a world view perspective. Now 'All under Heaven' has become interchangeable with the 'World' and the hegemonic powers to the sagely attributes that a world leader country wishes to possess in order to become the 'Son of Heaven' and command the 'All under Heaven'—a Chinese desire. What Xunzi rightly calls, 'it is possible for a state to be annexed, but it is not possible for All under Heaven to be Annexed', will perhaps become the greatest lesson for China in the modern geopolitical conditions of the world.

THE GREAT DEBATE OF CHINA: HUMANE AUTHORITY VS. HEGEMONY

China, from the ancient times, has been in dilemma whether it is appropriate to rule the 'All under Heaven' with a humane authority or through the hegemony of state power. As far as acquiring the 'Mandate of Heaven' was concerned, it has always been through the benevolence of a sage king. Then why there has been a doubt about the natural means of rule, that is humane authority, to be adopted for the maintenance of the mandate? The genesis of this metaphysical change can again be traced in the development of philosophy and its transition during and between the Spring and Autumn period and the Warring States period. There were two great thinkers, Laozi and Confucius, of the Spring and Autumn period. Let us take the progression of Confucius and his disciples. Confucius always advocated principles of compassionate rules which emanated from five behaviours or *wuxing* (五 行) intrinsic to the nature of a human being that a king must possess. These have been enumerated in the *Anelects or Lunyu* (论 语) as; benevolence or *ren* (仁) righteousness or *yi* (义) rituals propriety or *li* (礼) wisdom or *zhi* (知) and trustworthy or *xin* (信). And that there was no short cuts to achieve the 'Mandate of Heaven', but to cultivate a humane authority over a long period of time was 'the Way'. Observing the chaos in society, he longed more for harmony. These principles were adopted by the Han Dynasty, much after the lifetime of Confucius when the legalists of Qin period had failed. The transition from the Spring and Autumn period to the period of Warring States was an era of decline in the role of moral norms in all walks of life including interstate relations (read foreign policy).[34]

During this period, materialistic considerations had taken over the Confucian way of harmonious methods to acquire the 'All under Heaven' and rule. No state was able to acquire the 'All under Heaven' as it was considered that 'All under

Heaven' was a humane authority rather than power, and that the humane authority was based on morality whereas power was based on state force—political, military and economic. No state had either such kind of moral authority or was accepted as such by the other states. The philosophers of the subsequent period of the Warring States though were disciples of Confucius—the great exponent of the philosophy of moral authority but began to think of the new ways that would bring more and more power and authority to the states to which they belonged. Also, as the morality among the states and its people declined, the metaphysical standards of stratagem also declined from attaining power out of morality to power attained from the militarist and legalist designs of a state. In fact, Mencius, Xunzi and Hanfeizi are the greatest examples of such gradual decline in that order. Despite being the disciples of the Confucian school of teaching, initially they developed their own theories which they thought would bring authority to their state and therefore there is a clear and gradual shift from idealism to realism and to legalism corresponding from Mencius (372–289 BCE) to Xunzi (312–238 BCE) to Hanfeizi (280–232 BCE) and ultimately Shang Yang (390-338 BCE). The ultimate result was the unification of China and its rule by brute force of a Qin Emperor, by whom Mao was greatly inspired.

Emphasis on Geopolitical Considerations

As the thinkers of the Warring States Period began to shift from humane authority to hegemony, the role of geopolitics intensified. Geographical advantages became the main consideration to plan attacks on the other states. The *Stratagem of Warring States* edited by Liu Xiang (77–8 BCE) contains such facts as part of the historical account of strategic thinking. The book frequently referred to the geographical environment of a given state and brought out the advantages or disadvantages it had with regard to the potential for victory. In one such account, Su Qin narrates the geographical advantages of the state of Qin to King Hui, by which he could gain power. Su Qin says,

> "In the stratagems of the warring state that how the state of Qin had agricultural advantages of Hubei, Sichuan and South Shanxi, that how he had the services of nomad fighters in the north, that how the East was protected by Mount Xiao and Han and the South by Mount Wu, that combined with good agriculture and immense population makes the land have strategic advantage by which he makes the states powerful and he can annex All Under Heaven."[35]

What is remarkable out here is that the philosophers and strategists had become realist and graduated from acquiring 'All under Heaven' by benevolence to the most hegemonic method of annexation, which was no more considered an oddity. In this book, there is also an instance of the geographical weakness of the state of Wei which was small, and thus the strategist Zhong Yi suggests King Xiang of Wei to make an alliance with Qin to become politically stronger, while explaining the geographical condition of the Wei State and the disadvantages it was suffering politically due to this. Therefore, the argument that as these philosophers graduated from idealism to realism of a sort, their thoughts became more determinist and ultimately it was the geographical advantage leading to geopolitical determination that led to an 'annexation' of 'All Under Heaven' instead of an acquisition by benevolence. I argue that it was the same geopolitical determination that led Mao to annex Xinjiang and Tibet, when he found himself in a relatively advantageous positioning geopolitically, thus metaphysically transiting from the Humane Authority to Hegemony in the same Confucian tradition in China. What is reversed even today is between two Confucians—namely, Mencius and Xunzi in terms of propagating and doing of polity. Mencius was a great exponent of humane authority for 'All under Heaven'. Therefore, let us first discuss Mencius. Mencius defined Humane Authority as a type of state that runs on benevolence by virtue whereas a hegemonic state pretends to be benevolent but uses force. Therefore, the one who uses benevolence to govern is called a sage king and the one who uses force is called a hegemon. In this way, the nature of the state itself changes. The state governs with the help of humane authority and therefore becomes a peaceful state, hence there is always an order, whereas the hegemonic state remains unstable and chaotic. The nature of the state depends upon the nature of the ruler who in fact reflects the collective state of mind of the people. Even in the modern perspective or in the ancient times, when the state acted, it was actually the ruler who acted. Therefore, according to Mencius, the state and the ruler are same and therefore, if the ruler applies force, he is a hegemon of a hegemonic state and if he applies benevolence, then the ruler is a sage king and his state becomes a humane authority. Thus, Mencius addresses the ruler directly and says, "King, if you should but implement benevolent governance for the people" and he also says, "if the ruler of the state likes benevolence, he will have no enemies in All under Heaven"[36]. Mencius recognised that a hegemon would have a large state by using force and a sage king a smaller one, using benevolence for governance, but his heart was never with the hegemon as he says:

> "Should you make people submit to force rather than to the heart, force will never suffice; should you make people rejoice and sincerely follow, as the seventy disciples followed Confucius?"[37]

Mencius always thought that the human mind was good and it was on this premise that he thought that the people would always submit to virtues and propounded all his axioms of state and interstate affairs accordingly. As an adherent follower of Confucius, he thought that people will follow these as the disciples followed Confucius. But as the interstate affairs developed towards the end of the Warring States period, a legalist, Hanfeizi, ironically, ridiculed the example of the same disciples who followed Confucius as he says:

> "Confucius was a good sage of the world... (But) those rejoiced in his benevolence, admired his righteousness, and were willing to be his disciples numbered only seventy...Duke Ai of Lu was an inferior ruler, yet whom no one within his boundaries did not acknowledge... (Therefore) Confucius remained a subject and Duke Ai continued to be his ruler."[38]

Hanfeizi was a direct disciple of Xunzi and can be placed at the extreme end of Chinese realism. He ridiculed Confucianism as such and therefore, Mencius also. But the seeds of this were sown, following Mencius. Let us analyse the change. Mencius, as we have discussed, did identified hegemony but never propagated it as a means and the hegemonic state as an end. Thus, Mencius has humane authority (which he recommended) and hegemony (which he did not recommend) and applied only the humane authority on the affairs of state or inter-state affairs (read international relations).

Xunzi, on the other hand, recognised these powers—humane authority, hegemony and tyranny—and felt that all three have application in different situations. Xunzi does recognise humane authority which is obtained on moral norms as he says:

> "Unlike others, his benevolence stretches to All under Heaven; his justice to All under Heaven; his authority to All under Heaven.... Relying on the authority of invincibility and a policy of winning peoples support, one can win victories without war, acquire without attacking, troops in armour are not sent out and yet All under Heaven submits. This is the man who knows the Way of leadership".[39]

This axiom starts with the writ of benevolence and ends with the word 'invincibility' and hints at the military power behind the authority of invincibility which supports the humane way. The palpable state force as a power behind winning people's support is evident. This invincibility, besides military power, also hints at the political and economic power that assumes a geopolitically invincible position for the state that wins the people's support. He believed in the invincibility of the Humane Authority, because it also derives power from the state. Xunzi thinks that once invincibility is achieved, then only the leader's personal character, sense of justice, standards and norms equal for all come into play and make him acceptable to other states or 'All under Heaven', meaning that only invincibility and only benevolence alone cannot make a world leader acceptable. This needs a balance. Therefore, Xunzi remains inferior to the use Humane Authority of Mencius.

Hegemony for Xunzi is the demonstration of predominance of the state power over the moral authority which makes the other states submit. Hegemony therefore is attained more by geostrategic superiority then benevolence. According to Xunzi, a hegemon does not win over other states by moral authority, but by strategic reliability which he attains through the hard power of geographical attributes, economic pursuits and military force. Since it is hard power, Xunzi still considers it as a lower authority than the humane authority as only hegemonic authority cannot win the trust of other states. Therefore, once the hegemon attains hard power, then only can he show benevolence. In the same chapter of Human Governance, Xunzi says that the hegemon first develops his state power by high production, careful recruitment, training and legal governance of rewards and punishments and prepares his state power well, then only he goes to save the weak and dying states; he does not annex them but assures them and wins their reliance, thus turns enemies into friends and this is the Way or the method of a hegemon.[40]

What is clear here is that the hegemon first shows the hard state power by becoming superior than showing compassion (not benevolence, as it is devoid of hard power). What Mencius termed as 'pretending' to be benevolent is the inherent shift of direction in Xunzi's philosophy and thus it requires a consistent proof of the credibility of a superior hard power, which Xunzi reflects by saying that by demonstrating his conduct as lacking all desire for annexation, 'the hegemon wins friends'.

It therefore becomes a hard and long effort, and the hegemon still only achieves reliability and does not win hearts. Therefore, the hegemon remains suspect and thus inferior to humane authority.

Xunzi felt a need for even a lower third-level power then hegemony, which is 'tyranny'. In the Humane Governance he says that if a defended city is attacked and overpowered, this creates enemies 'who hate us, increasingly wish to fight and our troops who are injured also hate us and therefore we become weak and the opponent becomes stronger'. That is the power of tyranny which is an inferior power because it is not sustainable for a long time. Another remarkable thing Xunzi says is that with the power of tyranny the tyrant may get the territory but may not get the people as the people will flee as the territory increases. Therefore, the tyrant has to defend a larger territory with the same defenders, thus he will be thinly spread and become weak. That can be said to be true when China during the Republicans annexed Tibet and Xinjiang, but could not defend.

THE APPLICATION OF HIERARCHICAL POWERS FOR CHINESE GEOPOLITICS ATTAINED THROUGH COMPREHENSIVE NATIONAL POWER: PERSPECTIVES OF THE OLD AND NEW THINKERS

It is very interesting that how Xunzi was neglected during the Han, Tang, Song and Ming periods and how his principles were revived and brought to the fore during the later Qing period and Confucius and Mencius, who were called the First and the Second Sage, were relegated to the background. While Xunzi's recognition of the three types of power gave motivation to his disciples like Hanfeizi and Li Si to propound the legalist philosophies of the state, it was a demand of the chaotic times of the later period of the Warring States. The realist hard power of tyranny became the main course for Qin ascendance and he tried to sustain 'All under Heaven' (read unification) by the power of tyranny and instead of ruling through the feudal lords, he overpowered them and brought every state under his centralised control through central army transportation system and connection of states' Great Walls. This adventure of Qin was purely based on the power of tyranny in which no other states supported, hence perished. It had gone beyond the purview of the philosophy of not only Xunzi but also Hanfeizi, as Li Si, the fellow student of Hanfeizi, became the chancellor of Qin who advised Qin Shi Huang (Ying Zheng) to use only power of tyranny. For example, it was Li Si advised King Ying Zheng to annex the state of Han to intimidate other five states to submit and unify China. When Hanfeizi, the advisor of Han came to resolve the matter diplomatically, Li Si got him arrested by convincing King Zheng that if he returns, he will tell our weaknesses and if he becomes advisor of Qin he cannot be relied. Ultimately, Li Si who envied Hanfeizi, made him commit suicide in captivity. State of Han was conquered and other five states submitted. Once unifies Li Si centralized governance through implementation of uniform standard measures, currency and language. In his over activism he went on to convince Qin Shi Huang to stop private learning, persecute freelancing scholars and destroy books of past scholars like Confucius having negative value to present state of affairs that said to have caused Burning of Books and Burying 460 Scholars or *fenshu kengru* (焚书坑儒). He also devised new cruel method of punishment Five pains or *wu xing* (五刑). Inherently legalism leads to court intrigue due to lack of faith in individuals own values. Thus, Li Si himself became cause of downfall of Qin as he along with chief eunuch Zhao Gao, conspired to kill Fusu, the choice of Qin Shi Huang after his death as he feared that Meng Tian the military general a close friend of Fusu would take his place. Hence Qin er Shi was made the king. As reversal of fate Zhao Gao who was closer to to Qin er Shi got Li Si killed by his own device 'Five Pains. United Qin therefore lasted only for fourteen years. Xunzi, in fact, had already recognised the advantages as well as the limitations of each power and asked the hegemon to become benevolent in order to win over the hearts of 'All under Heaven' that had been acquired. Hanfeizi, on the other hand, asked for a tyrant to become a hegemon for sustaining the control of 'All under Heaven', whereas Li Si perhaps advised Qin to remain an out-and-out tyrant as Julia Ching calls Qin an unabashed tyrant and that is why she says that Qin did not last for long.[41] Interestingly, Mao had great regard for Qin as well as Li Si as China considers Qin, the first unifier.

In the perspective of Confucius and Mencius, Xunzi appears as a realist but in the perspective of Hanfeizi and Li Si, Xunzi appears as a liberal philosopher who strikes a middle path. It was the geopolitical state of affairs of that time which incited the pragmatism of Xunzi and further led towards the legalism of Hanfeizi and the absolute tyranny of Li Si.

As we have seen, Xunzi says that the absolute power of tyranny cultivates more enemies than friends. Therefore, absolute power has limitations as it challenges the potential rivals to rise and encourages the tyrant and his officials to oppress by the over-use of state power. Thus, as Xunzi says, the tyranny grows weaker and loses power, and the 'All under Heaven'. While Qin considered the Confucian classics as impediments in his way to power and burnt the books and buried the scholars, the Han Dynasty that followed eventually brought them back from the ashes and established the Confucian school as state orthodoxy. Xunzi's theories, in fact, when seen in retrospect, give a very plausible and pragmatic explanation as to why Qin failed and why Han succeeded. It was evident from the Han efforts that after obtaining 'All under Heaven', they employed the verdict of Mencius on the Mandate in order to say where does it lie:

> "The people are of the utmost importance; the altars to the gods of earth and grain come next; the ruler comes last".[42]

Moving from the mystical to metaphysical levels now, it was clear that the rulers understood the heaven and the earth in order to achieve the mandate of the people. That is why Mencius was called as the Second Sage. The Han Palace Counsellor Zia Yi (200–768 BCE) was the main exponent. The emphasis on the people was also brought forward in the early Dao texts of Zhuangzi, Guanzi and Laozi. In addition, the philosopher Dong Zhong Shu (199–104 BCE) incorporated into Confucianism the theories of Zou Yan and the Naturalists' teachings that the world is an interrelated organic whole that operates according to the cosmic principles of *Yin Yang* (阴阳) and *Wu Xing* (五行) or five elements. The Han Emperor Wudi (140–87 BCE) made Confucius's classics the official teachings and the Confucian Way as the method of the Emperor. Subsequently, Daoism and Buddhism also influenced the way of the emperors of the Tang, Song and Ming.

After having a telescopic view of the intermittent period, an analysis of the pre-modern period of the Qing becomes important geopolitically. The Qing were Manchu who followed Tibetan Buddhism in private lives but conformed with Confucianism as the state's way of teaching and administration.[43] Xunzi, during this period, was relegated to the side lines. The main reason was his being a realist and the teacher of the legalists Hanfeizi and Li Si. He was discriminated against by the Confucian orthodoxy which continued to be the backbone of the Qing state policy till the late Qing period.[44] The reasons for the revival of Xunzi can be traced back to the colonial and Japanese invasions and the Taiping and Boxer Rebellion period. During this period, China had relapsed into disintegration of various sorts with the far territories of Tibet and Xinjiang acquired by the Qing, becoming independent from China. With the Qing remaining no more a potent central authority and the Confucian way having no effect on realist external powers, China had to search for a metaphysical anchorage of state polity that could match with the Western ways of hard power, colonialism and Japanese expansionist designs.

What is important here is to discuss how China during this period applied Xunzi's philosophy of state powers and how it is likely to apply the same in the future. As the values and norms deteriorated, only the hard power of materialism reigned. The realists in the Chinese political spheres were emerging in the form of republicans but in the Xunzi power hierarchy, they restricted themselves to achieve the power of the hegemon and therefore could not succeed. It was only Mao Zedong who compared himself with the first Emperor Qin and used the lowest category of power that is tyranny, and re-acquired Tibet and Xinjiang but as per

Xun Zi lost the people. What was evident through his regime was that he prepared the state power first by different internal revolutions, what was meant by the classical legalist term wherein '... to overcome the enemy had first to overcome their own people' and 'prepare well before attacking'. Mao not only prepared well before the Korean War but also before the invasion of Xinjiang and Tibet. Mao extensively began to refer to Hanfeizi, Shang Yang and Li Si and manipulated the masses for achieving his aim like the first Emperor. In this course of achieving a totalitarian control he did not consider Marxism–Leninism as philosophy of Chinese communism but merely a useful tool which had to replace the Confucian way as he said:

> "Our comrades must understand that we do not study Marxism–Leninism because it is pleasing to the eyes, or because it has some mysterious value like the doctrines of the Taoist priests who ascended Mao-Shan to learn how to subdue devils and evil spirits. Marxism–Leninism has no beauty, nor has it any mystical value. It is only extremely useful."[45]

This was the staunch realist Mao who was actually exercising the power of tyranny as per Xunzi's definition. Therefore, Chinese Communism was no different because Mao invoked the tyrant Qin along with Marxism–Leninism for its usefulness as a cover to him. In invading Xinjiang and Tibet, he used the same power. He did not invite much reprisal from the international community, because he prepared China well. What is evident from Xunzi's three powers-based interstate relations are that the varying levels of power can be used for various geopolitical dispositions. In this regard, China may be considered as having an area of influence in continuum which emanates from China proper and radiates to the circles with the apogee towards the west and the perigee towards the east, necessitating the use of these powers as they apply.

I argue that modern China has used and will use the power of tyranny in the immediate vicinity, the power of hegemony in the next immediate vicinity and the humane authority at the farthest. It will also be a balance of power versus the use of type of power, and the distance will not always be sacrosanct. As in the Stratagems of the Warring States period, the strategist Fan Ju (范雎) while suggesting King Zhao of Qin to annex Han, brings out the use of power applying Xunzi's principles of power:

> "There is nothing better for the king then to form alliance with those far off and annex those nearby. An inch gained will become the Kings Inch and foot gained the King's foot. Now to neglect this and attack a distance, is that not foolish?"[46]

There is a striking adaptation of this by Mao as he assumed power. He found Xinjiang and Tibet to be in the same category of territory which a tyrant could easily annex. Even after Mao, the policy is continuing with India as the power of tyranny is being used to nibble territories taken as extension of Tibet by China as intrusions in Pengang Tso and Galwan in Ladakh region been reported on 05 Jun 2020 and close quarter fights took place on 15/16 night at Galwan. Here the tilt in balance of power will only decide the case as was border depute settled with Russia. But unfortunately, neither Mao or Xi Jinping could not become a hegemon—nor has China till now been successful to become one, as it has not won over the people. As Xunzi says that the 'territory will be taken but people will flee' and also that 'when the hate of people of the other states against us are great, then they will want to fight us', the situation as it has emerged till now, goes by this same dictum of Xunzi. Since Xunzi thought that a morally strong king would use the power of tyranny, he suggested to annex a state first and win over the people later. He also therefore despised the people fleeing the country annexed. However, since morality is no more a quality considered for a king, the people fleeing from the territory annexed is a welcome effect, as it is found easier to consolidate further as was done by China in its policy of populating these vast territories with the Han population. Another metaphysical phenomenon that emerged is that during the Warring States period, the King and his morality was held directly responsible for the state's action. Now, since there is no King and the Head of China is the collective head of the state, the state, an inanimate authority, is not held responsible for any immoral act in the interstate relations as morality is a human quality. Therefore, it creates a buffer for the Chinese authority to sustain tyranny as it has continued in this region so far. Not discussing the nuances of application to various regions which are part of the discussion in the subsequent chapters, I argue at this stage that as a matter of geopolitical philosophy, China is likely to use the powers of humane authority, hegemony and tyranny in direct proportion to the distance from its core, from the far to near, in continuum, irrespective of the international to national geo-space subject to the power balance. Having said this, there will be other factors too, specific to geo-spaces that will come in to play as well. It is also due to globalisation that these powers may be used in the perspective of an asymmetrical sphere of influence of China over many countries. It means thereby that the power may not always be used in the hierarchical order that is tyranny, hegemony and humane authority along the growing distance from China's epicentre. In this regard, the hard power of the country itself and the influence of other powers will also play a role. Therefore, although theoretically speaking, these powers will have relevance to the distance as the stratagems bring out, in the modern global world, it may happen that China may cultivate a faraway country in Africa or South America as its tributary as a hegemon and may have to exercise humane authority closest to its borders. Therefore, there are possibilities that China using this hierarchical power may create a hierarchical order beyond its domestic sphere of influence as per the Confucian philosophy. The modern Chinese thinkers like Yan Xuetong justify it by bringing out the hierarchical order prevalent in the United Nations, the World Bank and IMF. He is not convinced with the modern perception of the international system based on equality alone and argues that a lack of hierarchy leads to the strong oppressing the weak; therefore, a combination of norms of equality and norms of hierarchy is the most suitable way.[47] Another well-rooted Chinese way we have examined is the leading state with a humane authority forming norms for interstate relations. Taking a cue from this, Yan Xuetong, comparing the contemporary theory of system of international norms, stresses on adopting a combination of both in which the leading state from its own understanding and nature can work to set the international norms. He justifies it by saying that in any case, the leading nations are doing the same, de facto. Then realising the present world perception of China as a hegemonic power, he describes hegemony as an offshoot of political power, arguing that China was already a political power that attained material power and then the hegemonic power, citing two turning points in the transformation of China's political system, first in 1949 and then in 1979. Perhaps more than anything else, he is softening the hard power element which dominates as a cause of hegemonic influence over the world starting from its neighbours. Contradicting this thought, he says how and why a country less than a population of two hundred million does not have the potential to become a world leader. In fact, here, he is only indicating the hard material power to achieve the hegemonic power first then the humane authority, which Ye Zecheng also propels by quoting the US geopolitician Nicholas John Spykman and enumerates territory, border characteristics, population, raw material, economy and technology, financial power, national homogeneity, social homogeneity, political stability and public morale as ingredients of the comprehensive national power.[48] He further goes on to group various elements into three groups—survival capacity (comprising of territory, geographic location, natural resources, climate, topography, strategic territory, population, national cohesion, nationality structure, economic power and military power, etc; developmental capacity (includes political, economic and legal institutions) and international influence (including the influence of population expansion, economic system, territory and resources), national cohesion and will power, participation in international organisation through political, economic, cultural, educational, sports, military, security and environmental activities, that are all considered to make up a rounded comprehensive national power. He also determines a level of this element as a yardstick for the nations to attain comprehensive national power for a world power status. For example, he feels that the nations greater than 50 million people only can have the potential to become world power—what Yan he pegs at two hundred million. He says:

> "In the international politics of the twenty first century, the importance of the area of territory ruled has declined as a factor in gaining world leadership, but a population of more than two hundred million does play a comprehensive role".[49]

What is clear with these examples and citations is that these Chinese political thinkers do have geopolitical and deterministic inclinations towards creating a framework of power for China to lead the world order. And if these elements are material in nature, then how can Yan Xuetong talk of political power at the base of the pyramid of hegemonic power with hard material power in the middle as an outcome of political power?[50] Yan Xuetong in this case contradicts himself in the wake of perhaps projecting China as a soft power more than a hard power, as the image China presently has is quite detrimental towards being accepted in its present form and develop as a humane authority to rule over 'All under Heaven'—the classical ambition that it nurses.

Another trend witnessed amongst the Chinese thinkers (political as well as philosophical) is that ever since China has become one of the largest economies and is now the second largest economy, they have tried hard to figure out how China can become a responsible great power. Besides what we have discussed so far, which acts as a philosophical foundation to acquire comprehensive national strength thereby achieving hegemonic power, China now wishes to undertake certain obligations and responsibilities with regard to the contemporary world.[51] We have witnessed earlier how Chinese thinkers have tried to prepare the ground for an alternative IR theory from a Chinese perspective, mainly the Chinese metaphysical percept. Zhao Ting Yang in this pursuit brought out the Tianxia theory, what he thought could be suitable for adoption by the entire world.[52] Zhao is China's renowned contemporary philosopher who insists on the need to rethink China and not keep China in its conventional mode. In proposing an 'All under Heaven' or 'Tian Xia' as an alternative philosophical framework rather than the old mould of 'All under Heaven', he says that the need for a new system arises from the failing of the world system rather of the failing of the nation states, which the present world system tried to nurture. Therefore, he strongly feels that if the interest of the entire world is emphasised instead of the interest of the nation-state or the constituents, then only can a better world order be made in the future. He finds the 'Tian Xia' philosophy a better remedy as in it, the entire world is taken as a unit, comprising of all lands under the sky, and a common choice or universal agreement is made in the hearts of all people and a political institution to ensure universal order. In this concept, Zhao has applied the archival 'All under Heaven' to the entire world geographically. Then he takes it beyond the territoriality of the world to all the people of the world, excluding none and excluding no land as well. The method he proposes is to reconstitute the world along the lines of family.[53] He therefore obliterates national interest and makes the world institution all the more important. He thinks that the international system is no more a world system because of the pulls of national interests. He also thinks that the diversity of the world can be harmonised by a strategy of common imitation and Confucian improvement, as brought out in his second book.[54]

What we can observe here is that ever since China found itself as a major world power, it is searching for a place under its own system that is metaphysically unique and different from the Western world. For this purpose, China is looking back into the future. All old philosophical and strategic thoughts and phenomena are being brought back with justifications from the past and moderations for the future. We have seen Yan Xuetong and Ye Zecheng bring back various types of powers giving meaning as per the concurrent and future perspectives for China in order to achieve hegemony or humane authority, whatever remains the need of the time. Zhao brings back the ultimate achievement an Emperor of China ever desired—ruling 'All under Heaven' or Tian Xia. 'All under Heaven' in the past also had been claimed with the most moderate means: the humane authority based on harmony between the heaven and the earth for the benefit of the people. Zhao also tries to claim by Confucian improvement, founded on a family state, as he seeks for a centralised control of a world institution of which the nation states are de-signified and the non-state actors are reorganised. Although it comes closer to the Indian philosophy of *Vasudhaiva Kutumbakam*, but with a restrictive and narrower meaning philosophically and less freedom to accept 'whatever and whoever'. In our analysis of the other thinkers we have seen that justifying the hierarchical system as against the equal status of any state big or small is on the premise that presently though not intended initially, the United States is actually influencing world geopolitics as the greatest power. If we go by the Confucian philosophy, the family system means a hierarchical system and the world institution proposed will be at the top of the hierarchy in which China visualises for it the greatest or one of the greatest roles. Another controversy would erupt is, which is the inferior culture western or the Chinese. Moreover, who will leave his values and why? Zhao's philosophical depiction also cannot be seen in isolation. What one can witness is that he is seeking collectivism through a world institution which is closer to Communism in essence.

There are other questions like. who will obtain the 'Mandate of the Heaven'? Will there be only Sage King or a Hegemon? Who will set the proverbial norms for 'All under Heaven'? Will this utopia ever be acceptable, or will it remain a mirage?

Whatever the Chinese philosophers and the IR experts try to bring out from the Chinese cultural repertoire for the sake of uniqueness, one thing is clear from its geopolitical analysis through history that China has always been a power-driven country; power that has taken different hues as the level of acceptability by the people and other states. Ranging from lowest level of tyranny to the highest level of humane authority, applications depend not merely on acceptability by the people, but also power balance. So far, since the pre-modern period till date, the world has an impression of China using lower levels of power by which it is only achieving at the most hegemony. Yes, humane authority can be achieved, but China in that case has to change to bring in more moral investment instead of hard power investment. This requires a lot of giving rather than acquiring, which is China's main stance at present. The philosophers like Zhao are though bringing in a lot of metaphysical progress in this direction but the strategic thinkers like Yan Xuetong and Ye Zicheng are the realists who would not wish to give away the advantages of the power acquired by China and correctly co-manage international relations given its present great power position alongside the US. As Ye Zecheng says:

> "...China's grand strategy is to achieve its goal is to avoid challenging the United States...let alone replace it as a global hegemon. China and the United States not only can, but in fact are, moulding new kind of great power relations.[55]

This I argue is the concurrent concern of China, but I also argue that China does have the ambition to replace the United States without bringing any bipolarity in the international order. This it can achieve but certainly not by the hard power and hegemony, but by greater acceptability which it tries to achieve through Belt and Road Initiative. As China attains confidence and moves over the present post-hegemonic system, it is not likely to leave its own nature of hegemony, as Callahan says:

> "... Proposal for a post hegemonic system often contains the seeds a new (and violent) system of inclusion and exclusion; Tian Xia presents a popular example of a new hegemony wherein imperial China's hierarchical governance is up-dated for the twenty first century."[56]

NOTES

1. Here 'political power' or 'political legitimacy' is not being used to avoid the classic Western understanding of 'governance' as an outcome of the political process of Western origin, but is being used in the context of the Chinese civilisation with its mystical moorings.
2. For further details, refer Lipset, Seymour Martin, *Political Man*, (Expanded edition), Baltimore: John Hopkins University Press, 1981.
3. Beetham, David, *The Legitimacy of Power*, NZ: Humanitas Press International Incorporation, 1999, p. 11.
4. Baogang Guo, 'Political Legitimacy and China's Transition', *Journal of Chinese Political Science*, 8 (1&2), 2003, pp. 20-21, www.academia. edu/165448/political_legitimacy_and_China's_transition. Accessed on 30 Jul 2014.
5. Saibal Gupta, 'China Wants to Evolve its Own Version of Christian Theology', *The Times of India*, 10 Aug 2014.
6. Harrman, Richard, 'Linking Theory to Evidence in International Politics', in W. Carlsanes, T. Risse and B. Simmons (eds), *Handbook of Political Science*, London: Sage, 2002, pp. 46-52.
7. Vaughan, Shannon, 'Norms are What States Make of Them: The Political Psychology of Norm Violations', *International Studies Quarterly*, Vol. 44, 2000, pp. 293-316.
8. Hocart, A.M., *Kingship*, London: Watts, 1941, p. 1.
9. Needham, Joseph and Wang Ling, *Science and Civilization in China*, Vol. 2, London: Cambridge University Press, 1954, p. 134.
10. Chang, K. C., *The Archaeology of Ancient China*, New Haven: Yale University Press, 1986, pp. 316-364.
11. Chang, K. C., *Shang Civilization*, New Haven: Yale University Press, 1980, pp. 32-33.
12. Ching, Julia, *Mysticism and Kingship in China: The Heart of Chinese Wisdom*, Cambridge: Cambridge University Press, 1997, p. 6.
13. Chang, *Art, Myth and Ritual*, pp. 46-47.
14. Loewe, Michael, *Chinese Ideas of Life and Death: Faith, Myth and Reason in the Han Period* (202 BCE – 220 BCE), London: Allen and Unwin, 1982, pp. 92-103.
15. Liu Xiang, *A Philological Inquiry in to the Traditional Chinese Understanding of Values,* Kui Kuan Publishing, 1993, pp. 18-19.
16. Ching, op. cit., p. 62.

17. Needham, Joseph, *Science and Civilization in China,* Cambridge: Cambridge University Press, 1959, Vol. 3, p. 261.
18. Ching, op. cit., p. 50.
19. Weatlay, Paul, *The Pivot of Four Quarters: A Preliminary Enquiry into the Origin and Character of Ancient Chinese City,* Chicago: University of Chicago Press, 1971, p. 443.
20. Needham, op. cit., pp. 56-58.
21. Ibid., Vol. 2, pp. 280-281.
22. Legge, James, *The Chinese Classics,* London and Oxford: Oxford University Press, 1893, Vol. I, p. 424.
23. 'Odes II, Minor Odes 6.1' in Legge, op. cit., Vol. 4, p. 360.
24. Excerpts from Xunzi 10, as quoted in Yan Xuetong, *Ancient Chinese Thoughts, Modern Chinese Power,* Princeton and Oxford: Princeton University Press, 2011, p. 46.
25. Ibid.
26. Legge, op. cit., Vol. 2, p. 483.
27. Hanfeizi, 'The First Meeting with the King of Qin' as quoted in *Ancient Chinese Thoughts Modern Chinese Power.*
28. Primary source document on selections from the Hanfeizi: 'Chapter 49, The Five Vermin', Asia for Educators, Columbia University, http://afe.asia-columbia.edu/ps/cup/hanfeizi-five-vermin-pdf, Accessed on 30 Jul 2014.
29. Stanford Encyclopedia of Philosophy, *Legalism in Chinese Philosophy,* https;//plato.stanford.edu/entries/chinese-legalism. Accessed on 25 Jun 2020.
30. Liu Xiaoyuan, *Recast All Under Heaven: Revolution War, Diplomacy and Frontier China in the 20th Century,* London and NY: The Continuum international Publishing Group 2010, p. 7.
31. Teng, Emma Jinhua, *Taiwan's Imagined Geography: Chinese Colonial Travel Writing and Pictures, 1963-1895,* Cambridge MA: Harvard University Press, 2004, p. 251.
32. Yan Xuetong, op. cit., p. 71.
33. Ibid., pp. 85-86.
34. Xu Jieling, *Chunqiu Bangjiao Yanjiu, (Interstate Relations in the Spring and Autumn Era),* Beijing: Chinese Academy of Social Sciences Press, 2004, p.129.
35. *Stratagems 3 (Qin 1) 2* adopted from quotation in Yan Xuetong, op. cit., p. 120.
36. Legge, op. cit., Vol. 2, p. 298.
37. Ibid., p. 197.
38. Watson, Burton, *Han Fei Tzu: Basic Writings,* NY: Columbia University Press, 1964, p. 102.
39. Yan Xuetong, op. cit., p. 87.
40. Ibid., p. 89.
41. Ching, op. cit., p. 248.
42. Legge, op. cit., Vol. 2.
43. Lindsay Jones (ed.), 'Chinese Religion: An Overview', in *Encyclopaedia of Religion,* 2nd Ed. Macmillan Reference Detroit, 2005, www.2.kenyon.edu.depts/depts/Religion. Accessed on 9 Jan 2014.
44. Liang, Qichao, *Xianqin Zhengzhi Sixiangshi* (A History of Pre Qin Political Thought), Tianjin: Tianjin Guji Press, 2003, pp. 117-118.
45. Mao Zedong, *Reform in Learning: The Party and Literature (1942),* in Stuart R. Schram, *The Political Thoughts of Mao Zedong,* NY: Praeger, 1963, p. 179.
46. Abstract from Stratagem 5 (Qin 3) 9, as quoted in Yan Xuetong, op. cit., pp. 129-130.

47. Yan Xuetong, op. cit., p. 213.
48. Ye Zicheng, *Inside China's Grand Strategy: The Perspective from the People's Republic*, New Delhi: KW Publisher Pvt Ltd, 2013, pp. 17-26.
49. Yan Xuetong, op. cit., p. 212.
50. Ibid.
51. Ye Zicheng, op. cit., p. 257.
52. Zhao Tingyang, *The Tianxia System: An Introduction to the Philosophy of a World institution,* Nanjing: Jiangsu, Jiaoyu Chubanshe, 2005, pp. 3-4.
53. Ibid., pp. 41-49.
54. Zhao Tingyang, *Investigations of the Bad World: Political Philosophy as the First Philosophy,* Beijing: Chubanshe, Renmin Da Xue, p. 299.
55. Ye Zecheng, 'An Analysis of the International Environment'.
56. Callahan, William, *Chinese Visions of World Order: Post Hegemonic or New Hegemonic? International Studies Review*, Vol. 10, 2008, pp. 749-761.

5

Geo-Economics:
A Driver For Chinese Geopolitics in the Era of Globalisation

INTRODUCTION

The world has come a long way from the famous aphorism of Carl Von Clausewitz that "war is continuation of politics by other means", to Daniel Bell's assertion that "economics is the continuation of war by other means". In the intervening period, the progression has been from 'war' as a method of politics to the Cold War as a method of politics by balancing power, and from the neo-mercantilism of the West and its allies to the globalisation of economics after a failure in sustenance of the Cold War by the non-mercantile socialist bloc. Thus, the economics became the main source of power and well-being of nations after 1990, i.e. the fall of the Berlin Wall. Edward Luttwak in his essay "From Geopolitics to Geo-Economics: Logic of Conflict, Grammar of Commerce", emphasised that the method of commerce is replacing the military methods by using capital power instead of firepower, civilian innovations instead of military technical advancement, and market penetration instead of area penetration and he goes on to say,

> "States are spatial entities structured to jealously delimit their own territories, will not disappear but reorient themselves towards geo-economics in order to compensate for their decaying geopolitical roles... 'geo-economics' is the best term I can think of to describe a mixture of the logic of conflict with the methods of commerce".[2]

Why Geo-Economics Appears to be Predominant Today?

Ever since the 17th Century, the European countries ventured out for mercantile purposes with the aim to buy cheap and sell dear, and followed it up with military adventures as they realised the direct benefits of occupation of cheap resources outside the European continent. History has seen Japan rising twice in the 20th Century—once before and once after the Second World War—on the back of mercantilism, first with Republican China and then the Communist China, which was watching the success from very close quarters and ultimately emulated mercantilism the whole hog in exchange for the communist philosophy to get rich as a country. The United States and Germany today are following a mercantilist agenda, leaving the ideological hangover of the Cold War period behind for staying rich and getting richer as countries. The military power no more remained as an instrument of dominance and been replaced with productive balance. And the dynamics of this productive balance has seen changes the international system with rise and fall of such powers like the Asian Tigers, the Latin American countries and Japan as the victories in such great power wars have always gone to the side with the greatest material resources, and the military overstretch has always led to a decline of a power if the resource base could not provide for it.[3]

The greatest sway of geo-economics was seen in the financial crisis of 2008–09. The most matured economies of the Eurozone like Greece, Spain and Portugal were seen defaulting in the face of the contraction of credit, lower rates of foreign investments and slower growth rates. Even economies like the US faced a downgrading of sovereign debts. During this period, the emerging markets like China with their robust domestic savings and a domestic market with great potential, kept purchasing US Treasuries and other instruments to prepare a 'War-Chest' for the commodities' purchase for the future and keep their own currencies artificially weak to have advantages in other emerging markets. China especially used its experience of 1997–98 when during the speculative attack on the Thai Baht, it extended a line of credit to support the Thai Baht and also provided a US$ 4 billion loan to other Asian economies through the IMF. China did not devalue the Renminbi, saying:

> "The Chinese government with high sense of responsibility decided not to devaluate its Renminbi, in the overall interest of maintaining stability and development in the region".[4]

In the bargain, China emerged as a great exporter to the world, whereas it remained an importer for the Southeast Asian countries, increasing the dependency of those countries on China. Curiously, a close look at the imports reveals a deepening of the dependency of these economies on China with a growing fragmentation of the cross-border production and a concurrent emergence of the global supply chain. In this emerging system of production, multi-component products like; engines, IT hardware, consumer durables, etc., are now being developed horizontally with various components being developed across multiple geographies and then assembled in China to be supplied to the West. In such a situation, South-East Asia appears to be a 'Factory' of China with two geopolitical implications: such industrialisation is faster in pace but the least resistant, and secondly, these economies have got deeply integrated with China and have become less substitutable. Naturally, these peripheral countries like Indonesia, Vietnam and Thailand took advantage of geographical proximity to become part of China's global supply chain but also became overly dependent geopolitically. Similar cases had emerged in the regions of North America and Europe. As the production line was divided across the countries in South-East Asia, the flows of intermediate and processed goods' export for final production and assembly in China grew from 6% in 1998 to 11% in 2010 and by 2014 became larger than the ASEAN exports of consumer goods to the US and EU combined.[5]

Chart 2: Exports to G2 and China by ASEAN
(% of Total Export)

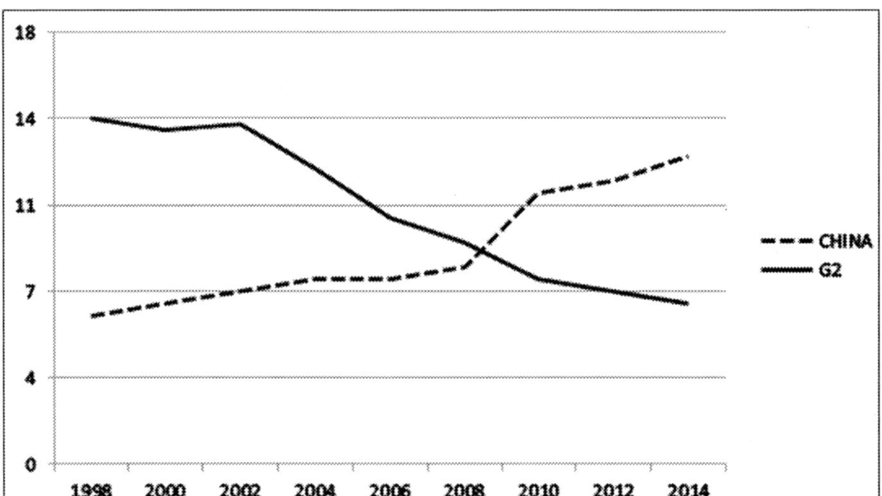

Data Source: Asian Development Bank, Asia Economic Monitor Report 2012 and ASEAN-China Trade Growth: Facts, Factors and Prospects, Forancensco Abbate & Silvia Rosina. 14 Jun 2016.

As a result, China grewn from strength to strength in mercantile efforts and ramped up its exports of merchandise to 13.5 percent of the global share. Today China does face impact of Covid pandemic but curiously reviving faster than expected causing resistance from importer countries, a burning issue needs elaborate discussion.

Chart 3: China's Share of Global Merchandise Exports: 1991-2017
(percent)

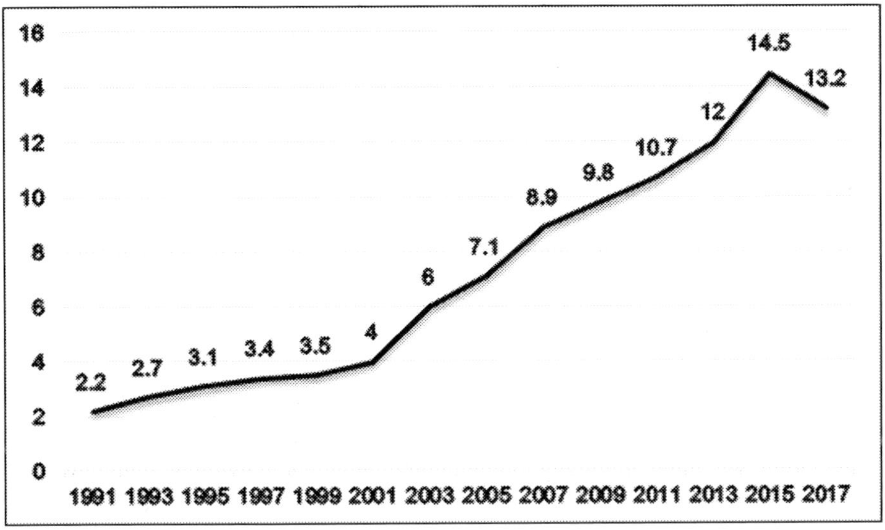

Data Source: Congressional Research Service. https://crsreports.congress.gov RL33534.2018.

The Great Debate of Geopolitics vs. Geo-economics in the Perspective of Comprehensive National Power

A great debate ensued between supporters of geopolitics and geo-economics when Edward Luttwak brought in the grammar of commerce made of the elements of GDP size and growth, trade balance, currency reserves and foreign investment as critical factors in assessing the balance of power among nations. Seemingly, it has upstaged the political clout of a hard power (read military). The emergence of globalisation after the Cold War led to a replacement of ideological rivalry with economic rivalry. New economic powerhouses have emerged to create nations based on multipolarity. If an economy does not find itself big enough to stand up to an economic competition with others, it creates a link based upon geographical proximity to stand up against rival economic powers. This interdependence has formed the European Union (EU), the North American Free Trade Agreement (NAFTA), the common market of the south (Mercosur) and of course the ASEAN, among others. Soft power has become the main tool of exposition of national power till the time war can be avoided. Over a period of time, geo-economics has become as independent a phenomena as it could.[6] Significant contributions towards this have been, one, the phenomenon of overtly rival powers not in the capacity to avoid a strategic buying of assets, like China buying the largest American debt in the form of US Treasury securities to the tune of 1.3 trillion (as of April 2014) and second, the multinational corporations (MNCs) becoming independent of their home countries in search of greener pastures and transferring even militarily significant technologies like the GM transferring the Neodymium Magnet Technology to the Chinese companies in 1995 in return for access to the Chinese auto market, and the GE entering into joint venture with the Aviation Industry Corporation of China (AVIC) and selling avionics to the state-owned commercial Air Craft Corporation of China, bringing about an observation on the security risk by the US-China Security Risk Revival Commission (USSC) which said:

> "Continued improvements in China's civil aviation capabilities enhance Chinese military aviation capabilities because of the close integration of China's commercial and military aviation sectors".[7]

Wars are also being fought between two regions for a strategic advantage over certain business sectors through the MNCs. For example, the merger of Boeing and Mc Donnell Douglas, the two largest American aerospace companies, was a strategic alliance to ward off competition from Airbus, a European Company, in 1990. The economic competition has taken this method of warfare to another level by institutionalising economic intelligence, lobbying, trade negotiations strategies and disinformation. The leaking of an unreleased investigation report of the 1980 Airbus crash (A320), incriminated the Airbus Industry and the inability to defend itself effectively by the parent company Aerospatiale, did harm the growing business demand in Asia. It was later revealed through an investigation that such internet newsgroups were created by the company's main rival Boeing.[8] Today, China is intruding other markets with its technologies like 5G which countries are not comfortable with and have begun to block such economic intrusions laced with dubious technologies to protect their pure geopolitical superiority. But such perceived techno-economic superiority emboldens countries to achieve the ultimate geopolitical aim, that is, to enhance its geo-body and increase area of influence physically and not notionally. Latest examples are the US war on Vietnam, Iraq and Afghanistan and China's intrusions in Indian territories at Galwan, Depsang, Hot Spring and Finger areas in the East Ladakh besides what it has been doing in the south China Sea, utilizing its 'perceived' advantage of economic readiness to do so. However, the physical resistance by the aggrieved nations have become overwhelming, therefore, in the present globalised context we cannot take Luttwak too seriously and start believing that war will always be fought on an economic turf only, and forget that geopolitics is a multidimensional method for a state to ultimately achieve its potentially physical power status in the world order. Thus, a necessity is felt to analyse geo-economics in the perspective of a state's desire to gain comprehensive national power through the economic means not neglecting other means in the bargain.

Geo-Economics as a Tool to Gain Comprehensive National Power

There is no denying the fact that the power projection by the states in the current international system is largely carried out through 'soft power' that refers to commercial, financial, technological and cultural means preferred over the hard power. Traditional rivalries over the control of territories have been gradually replaced by the desire to control the market spaces. However, the spatial dimension has not changed due to this economic tool. Yes, it has certainly moved more towards the control of virtual spaces, but once these virtual spaces are controlled, the 'sphere of influence' over the corresponding territory or state is always palpable and consequently evident when this influence starts effectively manifesting itself as an ally in the political sphere rendering geo-economics as a causation for geopolitical effects. Therefore, geopolitical reasoning becomes an inter-disciplinary method that takes into consideration the geographical dimension not only in its physical aspect but also in demographic, historic, cultural and economic aspects as well. While the enduring elements like geographic position and configurations of territories, languages, religions and cultures work as a constant, the fluid elements like demography, socio-political structure, alliances, strategic motivations, geo-economic considerations and technological factors only act as variables. And therefore, these variables (including geo-economics) cannot become an end in themselves which has become a trend in the modern-day strategic analysis wherein, unduly influenced by Edward Luttwak, the social scientists especially the economists, are considering geopolitics, geo-economics and geo-technology as three parallel strategies and ends in themselves,[9] as if the last two can be independent actors without having far-reaching considerations beyond the economics or technologies. The question therefore is: economics and technologies are the means to achieve what?

Therefore, there is a limit to exploiting a variable that is geo-economics at the cost of the other constants as brought out. Here, it will be pertinent to discuss the economic gains against the security considerations. Peter Lieberman raises this fundamental question in his article 'Trading with the Enemy: Security and Relative Economic Gains', asking that when do security concerns lead states to restrict economic cooperation?[10] Let us first discuss the 'relative gains' factor among the allies where security is not much of a concern. But still, we find that the US–EC (European Community) and the US–Japan economic relations in the waning years of the Cold War were played with the relative gains conflict so much so that some American strategists like Samuel P. Huntington urged for restrictions on trade with Japan in order to reduce disproportionate gains by Japan.[11] In commerce, most of the time somebody's gain is somebody's loss and the grammar of commerce hinges more on the time-tested premise of 'buy cheap and sell dear'. These two instances of stemming by the US seemingly appear to be motivated by their effects on welfare. But the question is that why they were allowed to reach the brink where they appeared to be jeopardising the welfare of the people of the United States? I take Peter Lieberman's premise as a testing standard that 'the security effects of resource dependence to those of relative gain' are always used to weigh the economic exchange between countries and argue that, as the security concerns lower and the welfare concerns rise, the allies may turn into rivals. That is what happened when threats of the Cold War receded and welfare concerns mounted, calling for the checking of the gains of allies like the EC and Japan who then turned into rivals.[12] Another inherent argument is that when the security concerns loomed large over the US, it accepted the commercial gains of the EC and Japan in exchange for relative gains in security or in other words, the US accepted adverse relative gains for security.

Having realised the relative gains' role in the relations among allies, it is now easier to understand the application of the relative gains' hypothesis among the neighbouring countries where the security concerns are more pronounced than the welfare concerns. As concerns get more and more realist, the neighbour has greater potential to turn into a rival from a competitor and an enemy from a rival and the concerns change from economic gains to security gains, thereby changing the means from commerce to military. Commercial disputes do not have as much importance in such situations as protracted antagonism due to a geographical proximity and historical grievances, because trade and military exchange cannot take place through the same border-post simultaneously. What Sanjaya Baru calls geo-economic pull and geopolitical push factors compelling strategic balancing, is reflected in India's anti-dumping taxes levied on the Chinese manufactured goods and Australia allowing a military hedging of China, stationing US troops on its soil despite China being the largest trading partner of Australia, crossing US$ 161 billion annually (July 2018 to June 2019) and China also has begun to respond by levying 80.5 per cent import duty on Australia's barley export to China. Besides, Australia is developing a joint airbase on Australia's Cocoas Islands in the Indian Ocean and strengthening strategic ties with Japan and India in a Trilateral. Australia is also likely to participate in Malabar Exercise in 2020 making it a full QUAD affair. It is clear that the security concerns are overtaking Australia's welfare concerns, and this is despite the fact that Australia does not have as much imminent threat as Japan and India have. Obviously, the argument of cultural and historical ties with the US has greater currency. The question is, why Australia then allowed China to have as much trade and commerce with it when it has to work alongside the US, Japan and India on strategic issues? The explanation can be sought from what Kenneth Waltz said:

> "In multipolar systems there are too many powers to permit any of them to draw clear and fixed line between allies and adversaries."[13]

It was a phase when China was rising and the US along with allies was engaged in the Balkans, Iraq and then, Afghanistan. China ventured out for resources and Australia saw mutually beneficial trading relations in the multipolar system after 1991 till the time it became apparent that China had some kind of hegemonic claims on the land and oceanic borders which was not as much pronounced as it has become now. In such a case where the bilateral trade with China has grown at 20 per cent in 2018-2019 and security of the nation state is not as much a concern as is economic prosperity which is more China dependent, why do countries like Australia wish to still ally with its traditional allies like the US geo-strategically? The explanation for such a divergence can be sought in the desire of a nation to accumulate comprehensive national power than a mere economic power which can have several alternatives. The same also equally applies to China when it disengages itself with Australia because China also desired a political alliance through the economic route to project its power as a world leader which seems harder to fructify post spread of Covid-19. Therefore, we shall now discuss how the desire to gather comprehensive national power by a country may make it use geo-economics as a tool for geopolitics, else it may push geo-economics to the back stage if it does not serve the purpose of becoming a country with greater comprehensive national power. The ultimate question is, when weighed on international security parameters, will China trade geo-economics for a better geopolitical position in the international relations?

GEO-ECONOMICS IN THE PERSPECTIVE OF COMPREHENSIVE NATIONAL POWER DYNAMICS

The *China Daily* in its report of December 25, 2009 brought out the comprehensive strength of 11 top nations as researched by the Chinese Academy of Social Sciences (CASS) and published in its Yellow Book of International Politics.[14] CASS considered territory, natural resources, population, economy, military, and sciences as indicators to evaluate the comprehensive national power. The report kept China at the 7th position while the US, Japan and Germany occupied the top three positions. What is pertinent to our discussion here is the fact that China as such gives due credit to comprehensive national power of which economy is just one component. The comprehensive national power has been a concept as old as Spykman who had quoted ten elements: territory, border characteristics, population, raw material, economy, technology, financial power, national homogeneity, political stability and public morale. US scholars Robert Cox and Robert H. Jackson reduced the elements to five—namely, GDP, per capita GDP, population, nuclear capability and international prestige.[15] Clearly, a trend has emerged which emphasises economy and nuclear capabilities more than any other sphere of excellence. Chinese scholars have also researched the elements of comprehensive national power well and categorised them rationally into four main components like basic power (population, resources, national cohesion), economic power (industry, agriculture, science and technology, finance and business capacity), defence power (strategic resources, technology, military and nuclear power) and diplomatic power (foreign policy, approaches to dealing with international foreign exchanges and aid). Ye Zecheng after analysing these elements gives his own categories of capacities and abilities of a nation.[16] He categorises these into three parts stacked into vertical piling one above the other. At the bottom is the survival capacity which compares basic elements like territory, geographic location, natural resources, climate, topography, strategic territory, population, national power and military power. These elements are more indicative of the inherent centripetal and centrifugal forces as determined by the nature, volume and size of these elements. For example, if greater the territory and population, greater will be the gravitational force, and the corresponding centripetal force. He also propounds that the prerequisite for becoming a world power could be a population above 50 million, a territory above 1.59 million square kilometres, a GDP among the top thirty, a per capita GDP at a PPP above US$ 3000, foreign trade and the capacity to defend its territorial integrity against any power in the world. The last capacity is an indication that a country which aspires to become a world power must be able to defend itself against any great power in its own courtyard, then only can think of venturing out to increase its area of influence. Then Ye Zecheng also talks of the Developmental Capacity comprising of political, economic and legal institutions, science and technology and human resource development, taking the per capita GDP to US$ 6000 along with the concerns for health and environment. On the top of the pile is International Influence which emanates from the expansion of the two capacities below and is manifested by a world power in its participation in international organisations, extensive role in the fields of politics, economy, trade and commerce, culture, education, sports, military security and environment.

The Chinese strategists have always been obsessed with national power calculations, whether it was Xunzi who advanced "five things" and "seven stratagems" that counted for the probability of a victory in war or during the "Warring States period", his proposal to the remaining six states to unite to make a greater comprehensive power to prevent their destruction by the Qin Hegemony. Enough evidence can be found which counted geography, economics and agricultural production, politics and military affairs in order to calculate national power and predict the outcome of an ensuing war.[17] Wu Chunqiu of the Academy of Military Science (AMS) sums up the tenor of assessment of national power by the ancient strategists by saying: "To a certain extent, the discussion of warfare in Chinese ancient literature embodies primitive, simple and unsophisticated national power thoughts." Therefore, Wu further says that "China's wise ancient strategists never advocated relying only on military power to conquer the enemy. But emphasised on combining military power with the non-military power related to war, in order to get the upper hand."[18]

In China, after Mao's regime, the comprehensive national power (CNP) or as it is called in Chinese *Zonghe Guoli* (总和 国力) became an aggregate of elements such as territory, natural resources, economic power, social conditions, domestic government, foreign policy and internal influence. These calculations were basically a directional change given by Deng Xiaoping who stated:

> "In measuring a country's national power, one must look at it comprehensively and from all sides."[19]

After the Cold War and the demise of the military power of the former USSR and its disintegration, the military power has no more remained as the main course of manifestation of national power and has been replaced with economics, science and technology and population. Therefore, power has more application in avoiding war rather than fighting a war. The same had been true for China also, as it moved from the realist Mao to the pragmatist Deng, as Deng said:

> "If at the end of the new century China attains a 'comparatively well off level' then there will be a major increase in the power restricting war. If China again goes through thirty to fifty years of construction, and comes close to level of developed countries, then at that time it will be even harder for a war to be fought (against China)." [20]

What Deng indicated were the stakes in terms of the relative gains that we have discussed earlier; they were foreseen as outweighing the territorial gains and as a less direct security threat. The resource gains since then, went beyond a powerful country's own territories and the economic gains that created wealth, became a prerequisite for a greater military power. I argue that China though insisted on a peaceful rise, however, China has never shied calculating comparative comprehensive national power of countries with its own and find its place in the geopolitical hierarchy. At the same time, China had also been careful not to miscalculate, thereby misjudging its own potential vis-à-vis the power of enemy states and allies except in case of India, which could give a wrong direction to China's own national strategic decision-making and hamper its peaceful rise. Therefore, China developed a highly quantitative method of calculation of the Comprehensive National Power (CNP) taken up formally by two agencies—namely, the Chinese Academy of Social Science (CASS) and the Academy of Military Science (AMS). Both the agencies have characteristic differences in their quantification and assessment. While the AMS team under Senior Col Huang Shuofeng gave a consistent assessment with an orthodox premise that the US will continue to slide in its CNP score and China will constantly rise, both would equal each other by 2020 which proved partially correct. Indicative is the fact that as per World Bank China's GDP (US$ 19.617 trillion) crossed US GDP(US$19.519 trillion) in PPP terms in 2014 itself. While the CASS team under Wang Songfen estimates China to remain at eight places with half the US CNP score.[21,22] It is another matter that they rated China to be at the 9th place in 2009. A detailed discussion on methodology and ranking is not the preview of this analysis. However, what is pertinent to know is that much emphasis has been given to economics and commerce for their contribution towards the accumulation of comprehensive national power. As per Huang (AMS), the system of index comprises of several subsystems like the Material Power Subsystem comprising of hard factors like natural resources, economics, science and technology and national defence and other subsystems like the spirit power subsystem, the coordinated power index subsystem and the environmental index subsystem. What is worth noting in this index system is that all easily quantifiable indices have been placed as a material power or hard power subsystem, whereas other subsystems are soft power subsystems which are not as easily quantifiable—hence, not as emphatically noticeable in their effect as the material power index. Therefore, the hard power including economics and resources becomes the mainstay of the assessment. The comprehensive National Power Index Framework by CASS brings out the economics aspect more emphatically which is present in 4 out of 8 indices like natural resources, economic activity, capability, foreign economic activity capability and science & technology capability. Further, the CASS takes the GDP as the main testing yard stick to check the validity of the CMP scores as Wang Songfen says,

> "As a comprehensive index that reflects a country's actual economic strength, GDP and CNP-are closely inter-related, and the GDP is an important component part of CNP...countries whose GDP growth is fast, also have comparatively clear strengthening of their CNP and vice versa. Accordingly, before forecasting CMP, it is essential to first observe and study the future GDP trends."[23]

It is evident that while CNP is the geopolitical strength calculation and ranking, China credits economics as most potential index that pushes geo-economic gains up against comparative security risks in order to gain more non-military geopolitical power to build its CNP. This strategy has led China to invest more and more in other countries specially in BRI projects some of which are proving to be over costing for geo-economic gains.

THE GEO-ECONOMIC POTENTIAL OF CHINA

Historically, countries have tried to obtain comprehensive national power as geopolitically disposed phenomena of summation of all-round power. The roundedness of this power always had some element lacking, which was craved in order to make the power holistic. For example, China was the world's largest economy in 1820 followed by India. But China was neither a military power nor had efficient governance that could have protected its vast territories. On the other hand, the European countries were advanced military powers seeking a better economy to be able to become a comprehensive power. Those were the days when macroeconomic elements worked more than micro-economic elements. It was considered to acquire more and more territories to collect direct revenues from the land users by the colonial powers. As the colonial powers took over these free economies through military power, the global share of these countries fell drastically. China which contributed to the world GDP by 32.9% fell to 5.2% in 1952 and mere 4.9% in 1978.[24] As colonialism designated different means of acquiring comprehensive national power that were exercised, militarism reached its zenith in the Second World War and proved its futility for the actual objective of geopolitics, that is power (whether hard or soft or a combination of both) and its sustainability. As the brute military powers could neither sustain themself nor sustain the acquired power status of the nation, it was replaced by idealism and divided into two groups: democratic capitalism and socialist collectivism. Though the outcome was manifested in the ideological Cold War, it was backed by the most advanced form of the military which could not be sustained without wealth creation found absent in the countries following socialist collectivism. Therefore, China which followed socialist collectivism met the same fate and reached the brink. But before it could collapse, Mao's demise and Deng Xiaoping's ascension to power came as a savior. Deng's comment reflects the clear compromise with Communism to create wealth first for survival, when he said:

> "Black cat, white cat, what does it matter what colour the cat is as long as it catches mice?"[25]

This quote from Deng's speech at the Communist Youth League Conference in July 1962 showed his pragmatic view of socialism which came into full bloom when he came to power in China in 1979 and opened the Chinese economy saying, "let some people get rich first" and declared before a Japanese delegation on June 30, 1984: "to uphold socialism we must eliminate poverty. Poverty is not socialism."[26] This pragmatism of Deng was the only reason why China survived, and the Soviet Union collapsed.

Growth and Size of China's Economy

Since 1979, China's GDP has grown by nearly 10% annually till 2007, meaning thereby that every eighth year, it has doubled its size.[27]At the downturn of the world economy in 2008, the Chinese GDP fell from 14.2% in 2007 to 9.6% in 2008, further going down to 9.2% in 2009 and picking up to 10.4% in 2010 before going down again. The GDP growth hovered around 7.2 (2013) to 7.3 in 2014. What is a noticeable fact is that, in the entire duration after the downturn in 2008 till July 2014, China's economy grew at a rate greater than any other economy. As a result, China was still able to beat Japan to become the second largest economy in the world in 2010.[28] This achievement was only possible because China could surpass the US to become the largest manufacturer in 2008 and become the world's largest exporter in 2010.[29]

Chart 4: Chinese Economy Overtaking Japan
(GDP Growth in US$ Billion, in Current Prices)

Data Source: World Bank Report on China in collaboration with Development Research Centre of the State Council, PRC, World Bank. 2013.

However, the International Monetary Fund assessed China's GDP to grow at an average rate of 7.0% from 2014 to 2019 which could not be maintained and in 2019 China had recorded a growth of 6.1 percent only.[30]

Chart 5: Chinese Real GDP Growth: 1979–2021
(per cent)

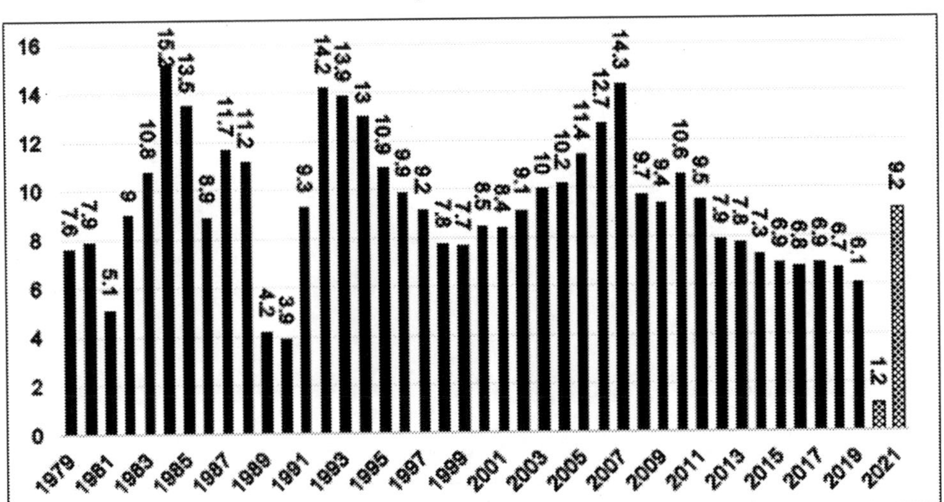

Data Source: IMF Data Mapper, https://www.imf.org/external/datamapper/NGDP_RPCH@WEO/OEMDC. Accessed on 12 August 2020.

There is a great debate in the evaluation of the actual size of China's economy—whether to evaluate the economy on a nominal exchange rate with the dollar or on the exchange rate based on purchasing power parity. While on the nominal rate of exchange, as per IMF, China's GDP in 2018 has been pegged at US$ 13.4 trillion making up the size to 65.3% of the US GDP(US$ 20.5 trillion) and per capita GDP at US$ 9,608 which was only 15.3% that of the US(US$ 62606). When evaluated on the PPP, which is 45% of the cost of goods and services in the US, the value of China's economy rose to US$ 25.3 trillion in 2018 which made it up to 120% of the US GDP of 2018. At present, China's share of global GDP on the PPP rate of exchange is 18.3%, whereas the US share is 15.3%. Thus, China had already crossed the US GDP in PPP terms in 2014. Evaluating China's economy in terms of the per capita GDP in 2018, it stood at US$ 9608—just 18% of Japan and 15.3% of the US. At the PPP exchange rate, per capita GDP then jumps to 18,110 or say 28.9% of the per capita GDP of the US. Now in 2020 per capita GDP has just crossed $10000 ($10276) mark on nominal rates as per China's National Bureau of Statistics and therefore has lot of money to spare for investment abroad.[31] However, the GDP growth rate was estimated to go down to 5.8% by 2022 as per estimation before pandemic. In terms of Gross National Income or GNI, a tool used by the World Bank which is an indicator of

Chart 6: China Overtaking US Economy

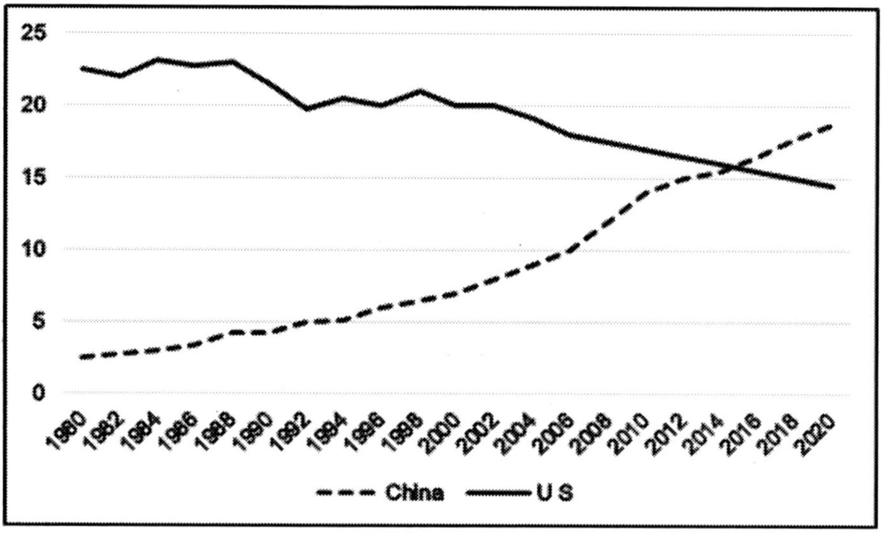

Data Source: IMF Data Mapper, https://www.imf.org/external/datamapper/NGDP_RPCH@WEO/OEMDC. Accessed on 12 August 2020.

the living standards and which China would like to give out to every citizen in order to sustain the legitimacy of the one-party government, China has moved from low middle income economy in 1997 to upper middle income economy in 2010. At present China as per World Bank is still 38.7% below the high-income economy and it is estimated that China will be able to achieve it by 2025.

But now there is a catch with the onset of Covid-19 Pandemic. The growth rate of Chinese economy was recorded by the World Bank at 6.1% in 2019 which was lowest in last 29 year. Coupled with pandemic leading to huge contraction in the economies worldwide, China also suffered a contraction of 6.8% year on year in the first quarter of 2020 but then grew by 3.2% in the second quarter surprising the world. However, as per IMF, although China is expected to grow by just 1.2 percent in the year 2020, but then estimated to grow at the rate of 9.2 percent in the year 2021. This has led to the world, especially the US, looking at China suspiciously for, first allowing Corona virus to spread and then controlling it faster than any other country and exporting goods and services while the world has come to stand still. The effects of this new situation have to be discussed for its geopolitical ramifications.

Distinguishable Characteristics of China's Economy

Despite apparently too much opening up of the economy, China was able control the economy from the slump of 2008 because China could invest through its instruments as deemed fit geo-economically unlike the US instruments (MNCs) which have become free from the US geo-economic interest in search of profit. There are three instruments of this geo-economic control in the China's economy. The first instrument has been the historical tendency of the high rate of savings. In 1979, domestic savings were 32% of the GDP which constantly increased to 53% of GDP in 2010 which in turn led to more investment. This high investment led to GDP growth, whereas in the households, domestic consumption declined as a share of the GDP. If calculated on a year-on-year rate of increase of consumption, it grew at the rate of 9.7% till 2012, but declined to 7.2% from 2013, whereas fixed assets investment grew by 20%. Though better than India and Brazil, the investment still contributed 53.9 per cent of the GDP, whereas the total consumption contributed 45.2% of the GDP.[32] Compared to the global level of 65% and the developed Western Economies level of 70%, the consumption is still very less in China. This less domestic consumption has led to over-investment in the manufacturing sector for which the IMF warned China of the accumulation of wasted resources and nonperforming assets, leading to China's industrial

Chart 7: Composition of China's GDP by End Use (2017 Estimates)
(as share of GDP in per cent and world rank)

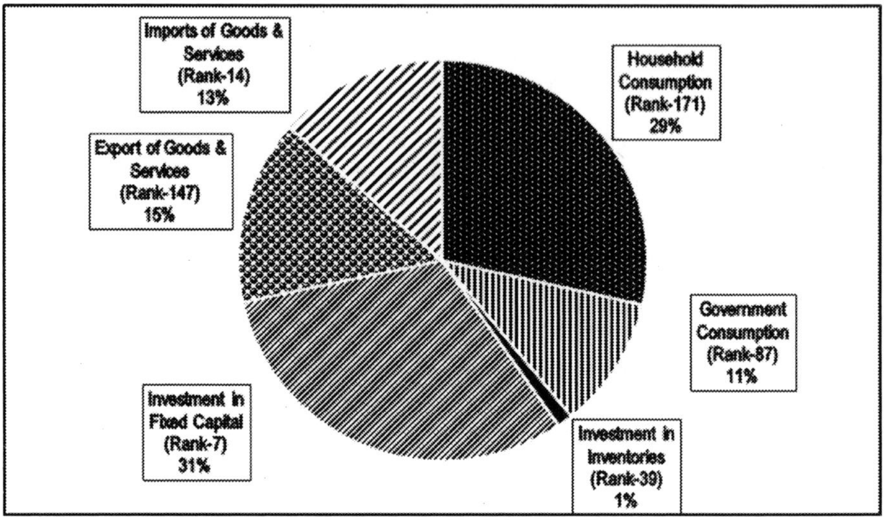

Data Source: CIA World Fact Book and other Sources: 2020

Chart 8: Composition of GDP by Sector: 2010-2019
(as share of GDP in per cent)

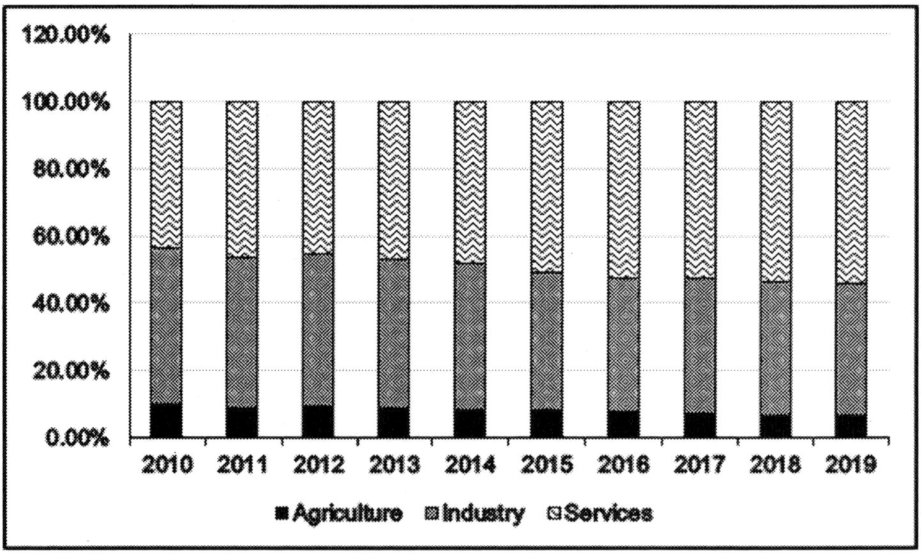

Data Source: National Bureau of Statistics of China at stats.gov.cn, released in Feb 2020.

overcapacity and deceleration in exports.[33] However, China still continues with greater investments than consumption, leading to huge savings of the State Owned Enterprises (SOE) utilised as the second instrument and investing through state-owned banks utilized as the third instrument, dominating the investments and to exercise total indirect control! The graphs below show the composition of China's GDP by end use as well as sector of origin. It is clear that the China is still far behind in consuption ranking 171 in the world and very high on fixed capital investment at rank 7, proving lack of market orientation which is nowhere closer to developed economies. On the other hand seeing the graph on GDP by sector of origin, internally China is progressively moving towards greater dependance on service sector and lesser dependance on agriculture and industrial sector, a sign of developed economy.

State Capitalism

As China emulated the Soviet system of socialist, planned economy, the Communist Party of China demolished the market economy developed in the period prior to 1949. Till 1979, all economic activities were carried out by SOEs which accounted for an 84 per cent of the total investments in the industrial fixed assets. These SOEs had become white elephants and loss-making enterprises. But after three phases of reforms and after the establishment of the State Assets Supervision and Administration Commission (SASAC), a quasi-governmental ministerial level agency directly working under the State Council to oversee the management of the SOEs, they have now been turned into a smart instrument of capital investment and control while formally being recognised as an investor in 2008, SASAC holds shares on behalf of the state in these SOEs. The SASAC in 2003 became a holding company for 196 central SOEs selected by the government as China's National Champions had become global companies of the future. With mergers and closures, this number has been reduced to 117.[33] These SOEs through the SASAC became the world's largest controlling shareholders by holding 40 per cent of nonfinancial assets, 60 per cent of sales and 70 per cent of the profits of China by 2013 reforms. What is significant to note here is that even despite China pledging to promote mixed ownership in order to diversify the shareholding of SOEs in these reforms in 2013, they did not allow any loss of control over the key SOEs vital for national security as the then Huang Shu, the Vice Chairman of the SASAC said in a press conference, "absolute majority share can be held by State Owned Capital for SOEs in major industries and key fields that are the life-blood of the economy."[34]

Mechanism of the control is by appointment of the top positions and constant evaluation of their performance in 54 keys controlled SOEs including the Chairman of the Board of Directors, Chief Executive Officer and party secretary, by the Control Organisation Department (COD) of CCP. This is how any Chinese involvement in foreign ventures through these SOEs is directly controlled by the Central Party Leadership.[35] The Chinese government leverages the advantages to SOEs vis-à-vis private players, especially the foreign MNCs, by various measures like tax reductions and exemptions, direct subsidisation, providing low-cost capital from state-controlled banks, granting exclusive rights, captive equity enabling transferring of control to any private person, favourable access to raw materials and inputs, protection by government procurement, etc. Through these means, rival companies always find themselves going up in bidding against these Chinese National Champions. These SOEs therefore are not always considered as an instrument of business but an instrument of resource acquisition, technology transfer and market capture, regardless of cost.[36]

But the business environment have changed. And therefore, the present Vice-Chairman of SASAC Mr Ren Hongbin is dynamically bringing in vital reforms to reduce notority of these SOEs and bring some transperancy for better better international recognition. These reforms have primarily emphasised on mixed

Chart 9: Comparison of SOEs in Fortune Global 500

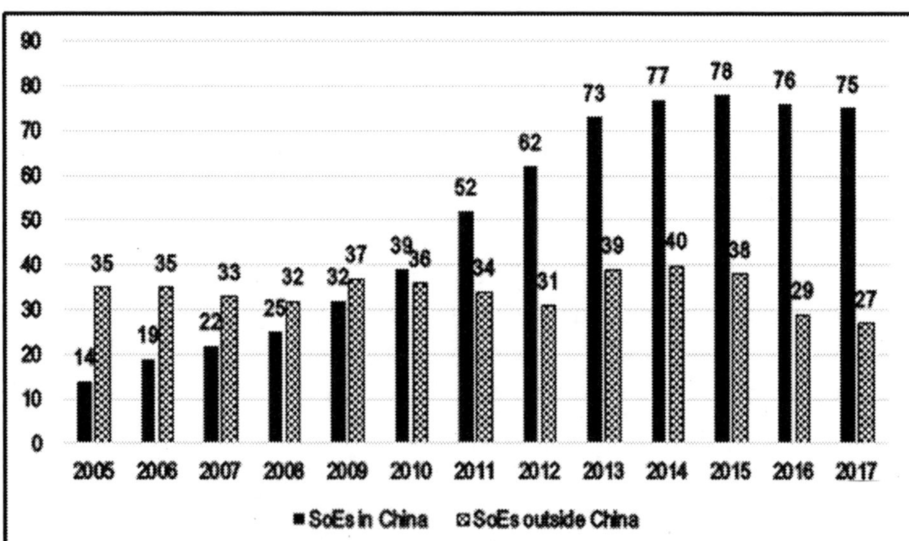

Source: Elsevier, China Journal of Accounting Research 2019.

ownership to make them compatible with multinational companies. As a result in 2017 revenues of Fortune Global 500 SOEs reached to US$ 6.1 trillion amounting to 22% of total revenue of US$ 27.7 trillion, while 75 of the 102 FG500 SOEs were from China. The figure below shows proportion of Chinese SOEs in relation to all SOEs in the FG500 list.[37]

Therefore, there are arguments against the lack of efficacy of the SOEs of China as well with a question that if these are inefficient entities, how are they contributing so much to the growth rate of China? In the last 20 years total assets managed by the SOEs have increased by 1.39 times, sales by 5.6 times and net income by 321.34 times, which only demonstrates operational efficiency.[38] Besides, they help in undertaking corporate social responsibility, bring social stability through employment creation and still be a tool in the hands for capital mobilisation to garner advantage against multinational companies having corporate governance. Therefore, they can be called unique entities between 'for profit' and 'not for profit' organisation as a remanence of communist system.

Monopoly over Capital and Credit Market by the State-Owned Commercial Banks (SOCB)

Chinese SOCBs provide 75 per cent of the national capital as against 50 per cent in other developing countries and 20 per cent in the developed countries. Yet, bank lending is largely inaccessible to Chinese individuals and private small to medium size enterprises because they mainly service government-directed projects and SOEs. This creates not only a monopolistic advantage against the Chinese domestic private enterprises but also creates a Chinese SOEs and SOCBs nexus against the foreign MNCs in domestic as well as private foreign enterprises in the foreign markets. With the backing of the People's Bank of China (PBOC), China's Central Bank has set a quota for the Five State-Owned Policy Banks: the Agricultural Development Bank of China, the Bank of China, the Industrial and Commercial Bank of China, the China Construction Bank and the Bank of Communication along with other state-owned commercial banks that hold sway over the total assets of China. A diagram below gives the true picture of how state-owned Banks dominate China's banking assets.

Chart 10: Share of Financial Assets by Bank Types: 2019

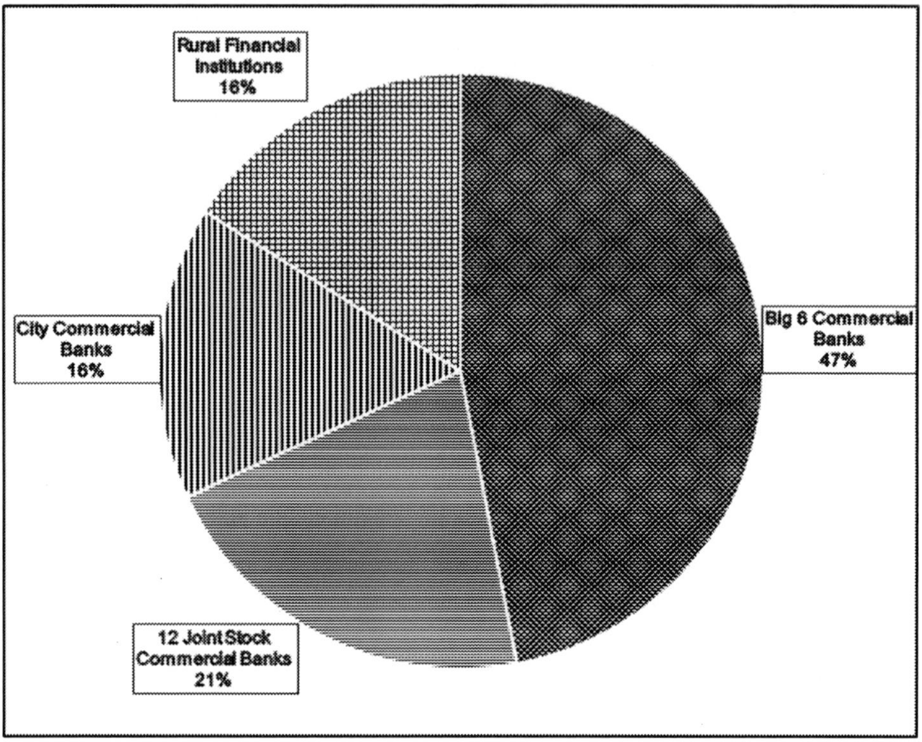

Source: US China Economic Security Review Commission Report 2020.

This lethal combination of SOEs, SOCBs and Policy Banks are the most potent tools in the hands of the PRC to develop China's economy through macroeconomic stimuli, secure resources and economic interests abroad. They will continue protecting the strategic industries and give advantage to China's private and state-owned enterprises through capital allocation at the lowest interest rates. Despite the strongest representation by the US against China to declare the SOEs as Public Bodies and impose an out-of-country benchmark on the Chinese Public Bodies doing commercial activities abroad, the WTO ruling has failed to bring in a level-playing field between the MNCs working in China and abroad and the Chinese SOEs backed by the SOCBs working in China and abroad due to gaps in the regulations. This advantage can only be reduced either by drastic reforms and transparency in the banking system in China or by filling the gaps in WTO rules—else, China will continue using these tools for geo-economic hegemony.

China's Wage Advantage and Manufacturing

China had huge advantage of wages and volume of labour. Riding on these factors, Deng Xiaoping brought in an economic revolution. However, as the economy grew, the wage advantage eroded as these wages grew at the rate of 11.4% from 2000 to 2013. It became double the wages in Mexico and 68% higher than Vietnam in 2013. As per the American Chamber of Commerce, the rising labour cost is one of the main factors that is causing a loss of competitive edge for China. The excess supply of labour that stood at 150 million was likely to fall by 30 million by end of 2020 as per the IMF due to the changing age profile of the Chinese labour caused by the One Child Policy.[37] Evident is the fact that overall labour force(16 to 59 years old) has just slightly expanded from 789 million in 2012 to 807 million in 2016.[39] To keep the wages low companies operating in China are adopting ulterior means to maintain their wage advantage specially in manufacturing sector. For example; employment of college graduates as interns for work of a regular employee for low stipend, using comprehensive working hours system to reduce overtime, outsourcing labour as agency workers instead of direct employment to avoid many financial obligations and deployment of robots at mass scale are some of these means. Although these means are being used to

Chart 11: Average Monthly Wages in China and Selected ASEAN Countries: 2001-2016
(US Dollars)

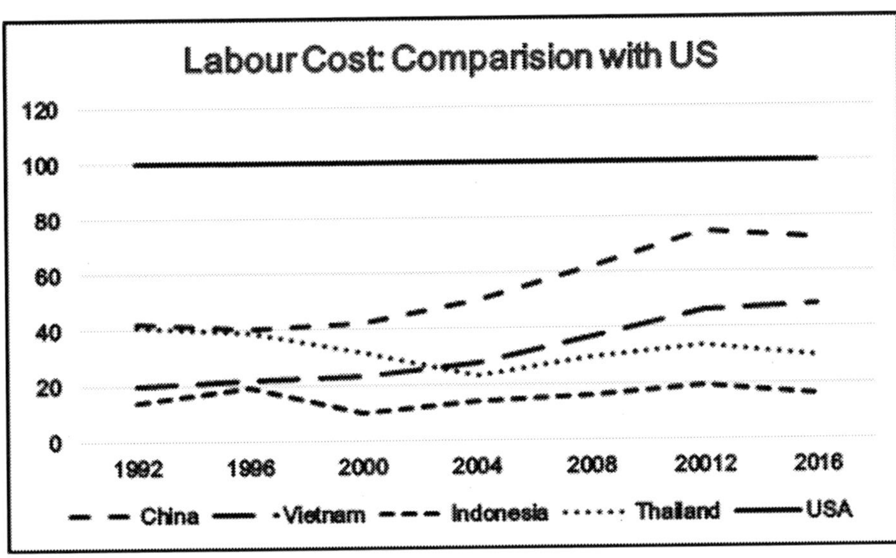

Source: Based on Data from Economist Intelligence Unit, Congressional Research Service, US Labour cost of producing one unit of output (the US index being 100)

circumvent the labour law of 2008 (amended in 2013) but benefits of such means are not going to bring any long-lasting cost reduction to industrial production. The Chinese government is therefore focusing to offset this imminent disadvantage by boosting the nation's innovation and production levels. The graph below also gives the trend in erosion of the Chinese labour advantage.

For now at least, this wage advantage coupled with extremely liberal policies to invite FDI and set up manufacturing units in the coastal zones followed by the interiors, still enabling China sustain as the world's largest manufacturer. As per this has already played a greater role in the contribution to the GDP of China (30%) compared to Japan (12.3%) and the US (18.7%). China became first in manufacturing and will continue to challenge the competitive edge of the United States, Germany and Japan in the 21st Century. However, the contribution of industry is reducing due to the reduction of wage advantages from highest 46% (2010) of the GDP to 39% (2019) of the GDP.[40]

Foreign Direct Investment Profiling of China

Having understood the mechanism of financial and asset control system of China especially for outbound investment, we analyse how China uses the FDI outflows for geo-economic purposes. Though this is a complex phenomenon, China learnt its lesson by attracting FDI inflows and subsequently used the outflows of FDI to serve its national economic interests. Therefore, here we shall discuss both inflows and outflows to evaluate the Chinese financial power in the perspective of a controlled fiscal regime. From 1979 with an 'Open Door Policy' till 1992, China's conscious approach towards reforms was a very cautious effort of first experimenting in a region, then applying all over, termed as 'crossing the stream while touching the stones'. It was not until the famous visit of Deng Xiaoping to the Southern Coast that forced Jiang Zemin to adopt further liberalisation and opening of the coastal areas to Foreign Direct Investment and private entrepreneurship. Thereafter, China has come a long way in terms of the inward flow of FDI by establishing High Technology Development and Free Trade Zones besides Special Economic Zones and Economic and Trade Development Zones established initially, especially made for Foreign Invested Enterprises (FIEs). There were 445 FIEs registered in China in 2010 which employed 55.2 million workers.[41] FIEs accounted for just 2.3% in 1990 and then rose to 35.9% in 2003 and then fell to 25.9% in 2011 as domestic inputs in the industrial output increased. However, the FIEs remained a major contributor to Chinese exports by 47.3% and imports by 44.8% in 2013. The FIEs have had a major contribution in

China's high-tech exports contributing to 82% in 2010. The export orientation of FDI was further evident by the share of wholly owned foreign MNCs not in a joint venture with Chinese firms, contributing to 67% in 2010. The UN data shows the flow of FDI in China steadily rising from just 2 billion in 1985 to 124 billion US dollars in 2013.[42] Further, the figure below shows the fall of FDI net in-flow BoP and rise in net out-flow BoP crossing each other in the year 2015-16 when China invested abroad more than it recieved. This trend started immediately after BRI was taken up by China in 2013 and matured by 2016 when adopted in the Chinese constitution along with strong internal surpulses available with China for investment abroad. The graphs below showing the Annual FDI outflow/inflow validates the argument. As after 2013, the main focus of investment has been on infrastructure projects through BRI, causing investments overseas going up by 49.3% in 2016. But seeing the over all trend, the investment overseas have now dropped to by 13.6% year on year as per Moody's and It is going to slow further down due to risk around the world increasing, one caused by the US-China trade war and the second due to countries resisting BRI-projects for unfavourable conditionalities.[43] This trend has now got more eccentuated by the COVID pandemic causing trust deficit towards China.

Chart 12: Annual FDI In Flow & Out Flow China: 2007-2019 in Current US$ (Bn)

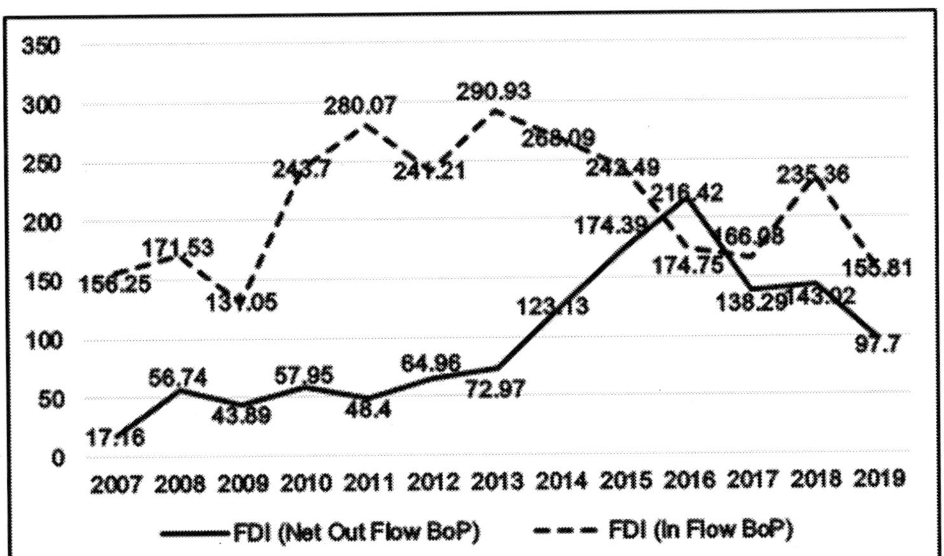

Data Source: World Bank https://data.worldbank.org/indicator/BX.KLT.DINV.WD.GD.ZS?locations=CN. 02 August 2020.

Chart 13: Annual FDI In Flow & Out Flow China: 2007-2019
(% of GDP)

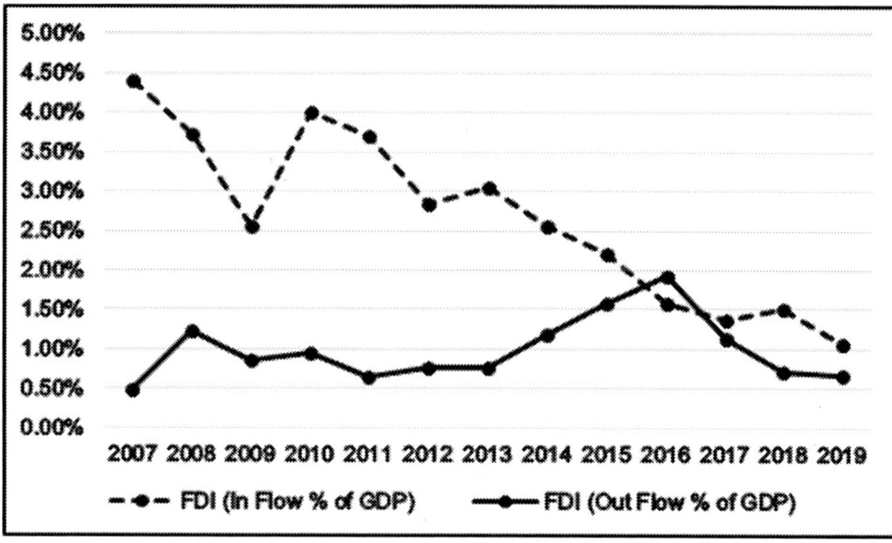

Data Source: World Bank. https://data.worldbank.org/indicator/BX.KLT.DINV.WD.GD.ZS?locations=CN. 02 August 2020.

China has been among the largest recipients of FDI in 2013. As per the UNCTAD World Investment Report, a survey based on 174 validated MNCs revealed China to be the most favoured destination and host economy for their business and investments in 2012–2014. As a result of the positive outlook of China, the country had become the second largest recipient of the global FDI inflow after the US. Armed with such investments and the export-oriented commerce, the Chinese foreign exchange has been climbing up all the time, making it a country having the biggest foreign exchange reserves. China has climbed from the lowest USD 2,262 million in 1980 when the economy had not yet opened, up to USD 3.85 trillion 2014.[44] The graph below shows the meteoric rise in the foreign exchange reserves of China, especially after 1998, peaking in 2014 and then sliding down to basically accommodate industrial production overheating. Nevertheless, it has never gone down below 3 trillion mark as it stands at 3.12 trillion in 2019.

With such surplus money, China has become bold since 2000, when it adopted a "global" strategy and directed SOEs to invest overseas. China also invested in the low-yielding assets like US securities especially during the global slowdown in 2008. China also launched the China Investment Corporation (CIC) in September

Chart 14: Foreign Reserves Minus Gold in Current US$

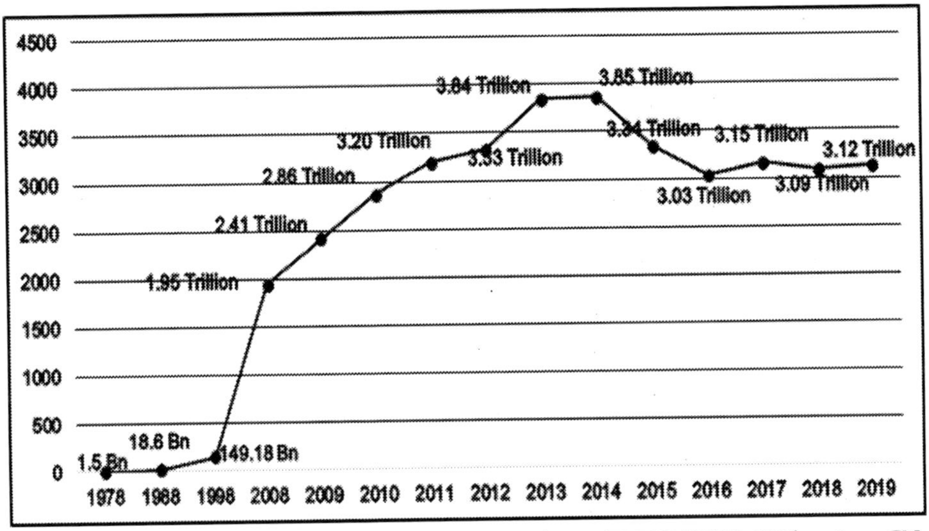

Data Source: World Bank. https://data.worldbank.org/indicator/FI.RES.TOTL.CD?locations=CN. 02 August 2020.

2007 to make more market-oriented profitable investments of its foreign exchange assets. These investments are made through three subsidiaries, CIC International, CIC Capital Corporation and Central Hujin Investment Limited. CIC has now become the largest sovereign wealth fund with a fund of more than USD 940.6 billion as per its Annual Report released on 20 Sep 2019.[45] The report also talks about "Hujin Model" through which Central Hujin owns 40% of the total central state owned capital.

The main investments have been the companies extracting natural resources such as oil and minerals, necessary to sustain China's rapid economic growth. The other companies are those which can help technology transfer, management skills and bring good branding for the Chinese firms so that the Chinese firms can become international brands themselves. The acquisition of the IBM Corporation by Lenovo in April 2005 has been an action in this direction only. Besides this, the investment in Africa, South America, the Middle East and the Central Asian Republics has been the main geo-economic instrument to expand its area of influence over smaller countries.

CHINA'S STRATEGIC INVESTMENTS TO SECURE OWN NATURAL RESOURCES

The economic might of China manifests itself the most in its investments to secure natural resources. As we have discussed, the Chinese companies, mostly the government backed SOEs, have engaged themselves in acquisition of equity stakes in the resource companies abroad, extending soft loans to mining and petroleum investors in return for long-term procurement contracts. As the overall scenario emerges, China entered into special relationship with Angola and Nigeria in 2004 and 2006, taking equity stakes in the major producers. The CNOOC invested in Angola and Nigeria for the assured benefit of equity in terms of the share of production on terms comparable to other co-owners. The Chinese SOEs like CNPC, CNOOC, CHINAALCO, Sinopec, etc., have taken stakes in the independent producers of natural resources in the countries like Sudan's GNOC and Petrodar the operating company, Australians' West Shelf Ventures, Kazakhstan's Petrokazakhstan, Australia's bauxite projects, Iran's Yadavaran Oil Field, South Pars Gas fields and Azadegan Gasfield and many other joint ventures. In addition, China has also entered into the field of foreign natural resources through the direct granting of loans by the Chinese banks to the producers. For example, the China Development Bank gave loans to Rusneft and Transneft of Russia; loans were given through Chinese SOEs to the producers. Similarly, the Sinopec gave loan to Petrobras (Brazil) in order to secure resources through purchase agreements to service these loans. These examples reveal the multipronged strategy of China to secure resources from abroad. In a broader sense, these strategies do control the international resource market. Alarmed by the Chinese ploy, other mining companies and buyers in the commodity market have stared at reinvesting in the new sites in Vietnam, Kazakhstan, Sudan, Canada and other places, despite the environmental concerns. The Chinese dominance in the resource market and the geopolitical concerns thereof, is best exemplified in the world energy market where China wishes to remain secure by any means in the foreseeable future saving their own resources. We shall discuss these phenomena in some detail here.

CHINA'S ENERGY GEOPOLITICS

The question of energy geopolitics emanates from the unreasonable demand that cannot be balanced with the supplies. China's appetite for energy has been growing at exponential rates. And in order to bring the entire billion of population out of the middle-income trap of an economic growth, China is likely to consume more energy at an incomparable rate of increase with any development country. During its developing stage, China's energy consumption figures over the years reveal that it overtook the US in 2009 while its energy consumption was just half of the US in 2000. According to the International Energy Agency projections that came during 2008, taking the same year as the baseline, China will account for 35% of total increase in the energy demand by 2035. The argument of population-sapping energy comes very true when by 2035, China will start consuming 70% more energy than the US despite each Chinese still consuming less than half of what an American consumes.[46]

With regard to oil consumption, China again stood at the second position after the US at 10667 thousand barrels per day (BPD) in 2013 that went up to 14055 thousand BPD in 2019 and will reach up to 16900 thousand BPD by 2035. To meet this demand, China produced just 4246 thousand million BPD in 2014 out of 24.4 million BPD of proven capacity at that time.[47] Therefore, China has a huge gap between its oil production and consumption which it continuously tries to match. But the production level strangely went down to 3798 thousand BPD in 2019 which shows China's intention to hoard own oil and buy cheaper as they get.[48]

Chart 15: China's Oil Production and Consumption: 1979-2019
(Thousand Barrels Per Day)

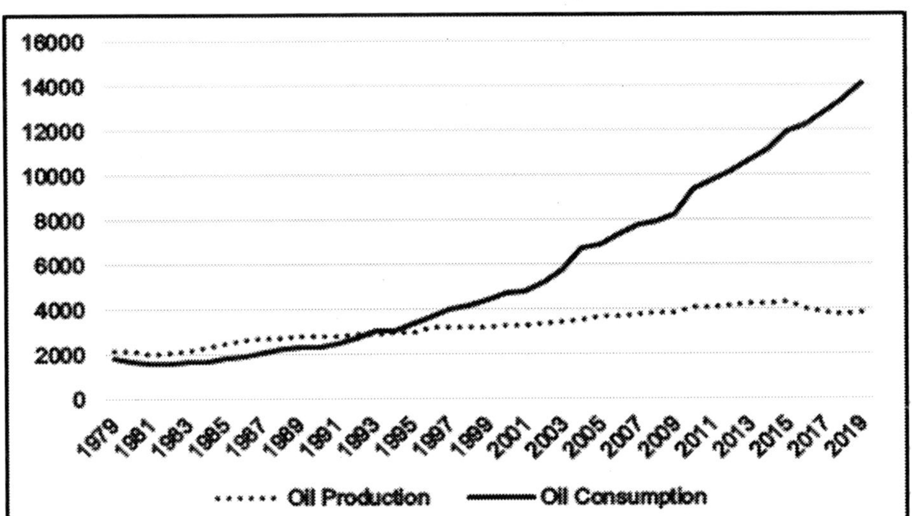

Data Source: BP, Statistical Review of World Energy: 2019, https://www.bp.com/en/global/corporate/energy-economics/statistical-review-of-world-energy.html. Accessed 06 August 2020.

China became a net oil importer (import minus export) from 1993. The imports grew from 632 thousand bpd in 1997 to 5.8 million bpd in 2013 and reached to 6.6 million bpd by the end of 2014.[49] That was more than the net oil imports of the US which stood at 5.5 million bpd of oil.[50] However, there has been tremendous change in the profile of oil importing countries post the US withdrawl from Iraq. The net import of the US in 2019 was just 0.6 MBD equivalent of 03 % of total consumption, while in 2005 it was 60%. This was because the US produced 19.25 MBD and consumed 20.46 MBD of oil in 2019. Therefore, the share of petroleum (including crude oil) imports from OPEC-has drastically declined from 70% in 1977 to 18% in 2019.[51] The main reason of this trend is because the US imports of crude oil has become more of comodity for proccess and sale. This has left the oil fields of the world open for China to explore. Differance between net oil imoprts of China and the US in the figures below ampiefies the direction, the oil geopolitics going to take.

Chart 16: Top Ten Annual Net Oil Importers: 2019 (In Bn US$)

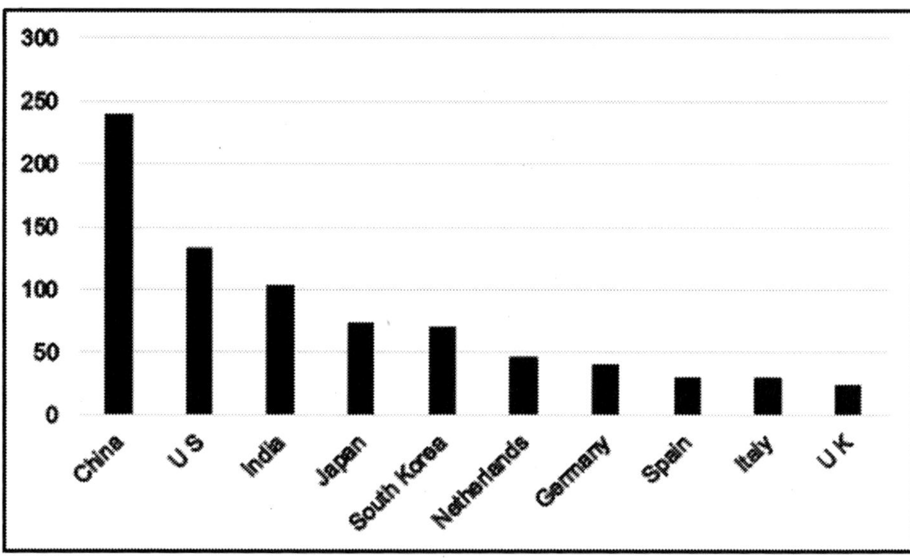

Data Source: World's Top Exports, http://www.worldstopexports.com/crude-oil-imports-by-country/ Accessed 21 August 2020.

Chart 17: Top Fifteen Crude Oil Suppliers to China: In Bn US$ (2019)

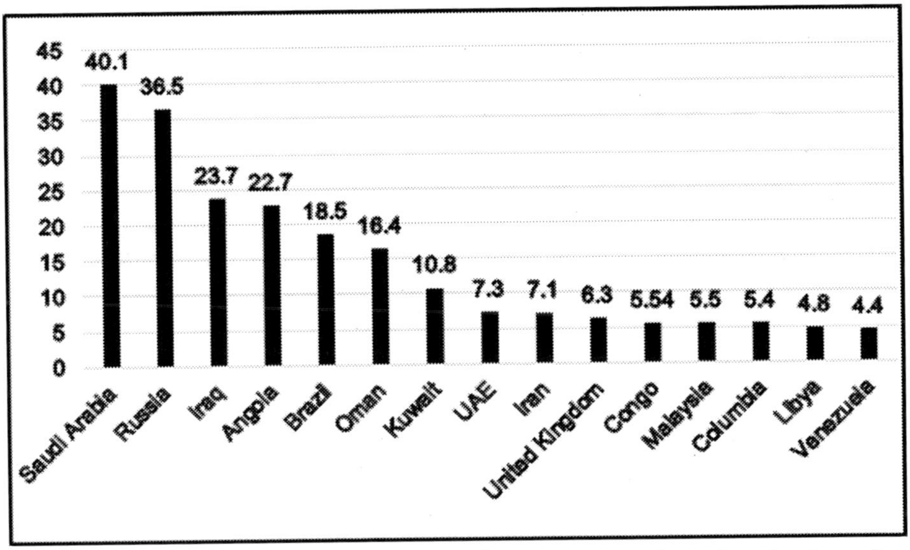

Data Source: World's Top Exports, http://www.worldstopexports.com/top-15-crude-oil-suppliers-to-china/. 21 Accessed July 2020.

A graph as shown below gives the correct picture.[53]

Chart 18: China's Gas Production and Consumption: 1979-2019

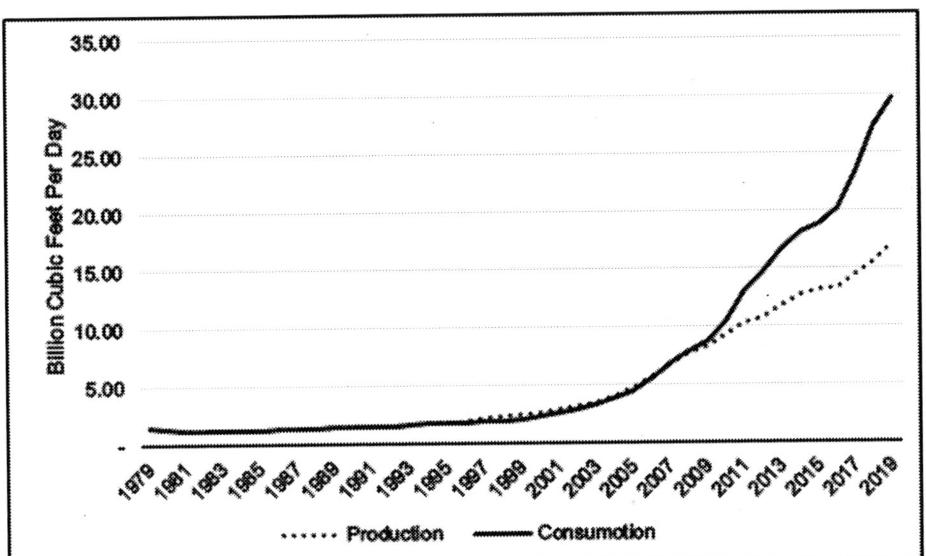

Data Source: BP, Statistical Review of World Energy: 2019, https://www.bp.com/en/global/corporate/energy-economics/statistical-review-of-world-energy.html. Accessed 06 August 2020.

Natural gas is another energy source that drives China's foreign policy and has geopolitical implications in the future. China though derives only 4% of its present energy requirements, the natural gas extraction through conventional and non-conventional sources and its impact have great geo-economic significance due to the fact that the demand of gas as a non-pollutant source of energy in China is going to assume greater importance. As per the *Oil and Gas Journal*, China as on June 2014 had 155 trillion cubic feet (TCF) of proven gas reserves, one of which produces only 3.8 TFC which is likely to rise to 4.2 TFC in 2020 and 10.1 TFC by 2040 as per the EIA. As far as the demand is concerned, it is likely to rise to 7–8 TFC in 2020 and to about 17 TFC by 2040.[52] Therefore, as the consumption rises, the gap with production increases which as it stands, looks starkly at the meagre reserves of natural gas that China has. The yawning gap that is going to be created in the natural gas supplies and demand or consumption as foreseen by 2040 has already reflected in the Chinese strategy to secure more than the procured liquefied natural gas through its SOEs and policy banks' investments and acquisition of rights abroad.

The future of energy security is said to be in the extraction of Shale Gas. EIA estimates the shale gas source of China to be at 1,115 TFC—the largest in the world. However, China's Ministry of Land and Resources pegs it at 883 TFC. The majority of the reserves lie in the Tarim and Sichuan basins. China aims to produce 2,100 BFC by the end of 2020. However, despite China's vast shale gas reserves, the production remains a geological challenge and a technological nightmare. Therefore, China is trying to rope in firms like Shell in partnership with Sinopec and CONOCO. However, the US has the advantage of technology that is going to become its trump card in the next twenty years.[53] China's efforts to bring technologies for extraction of shale gas from the US is going to be the next big challenge for China. If successfully acquired, these two giants may no more remain energy dependent on the Middle East, Russia and Central Asia, as much as China is today. Therefore, the geopolitical fallouts are serious and critical and will be discussed in detail in the next chapter.

The main portion of China's energy generation and consumption comes from coal. We are not discussing this source in as much details as its volume because the maximum sourcing is done domestically and does not have much geopolitical implications because of the lack of overdependence on foreign sources. However, the emission and pollution in China does have a great concern, for which, China would have to change the course of its energy usage as the pollution through coal has become alarming. The similar trend is seen in the graph below to some extent.

However as per projection by the EIA, represented in the next graph the carbon emission record of China at maximum can only plateau and not reduce.

Chart 19: Change in Energy Consumption Pattern in China

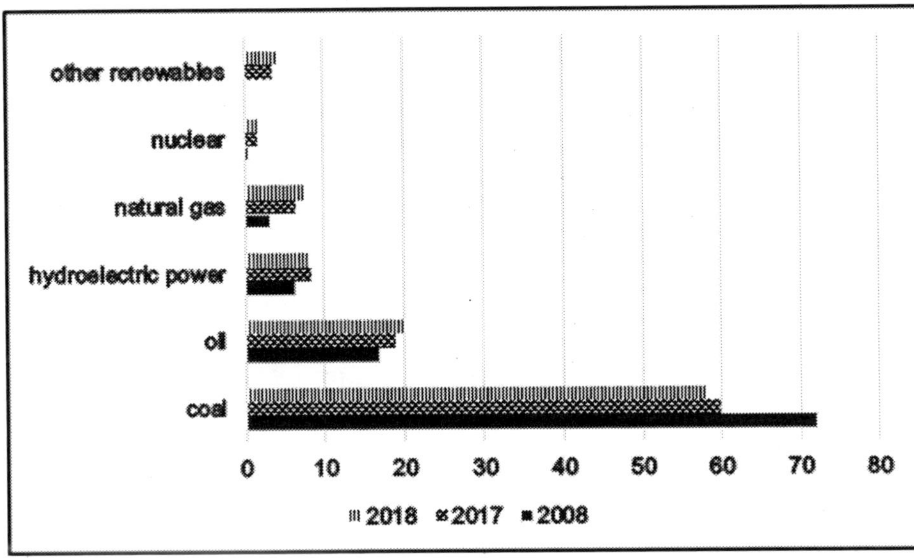

Data Source: BP Statistical Review: 2019. https://www.bp.com/content/dam/bp/business-sites/en/global/corporate/pdfs/energy-economics/statistical-review/bp-stats-review-2019-china-insights.pdf Accessed on 08 August 2020.

Chart 20: Global Energy-Related Carbon Dioxide Emissions Outlook

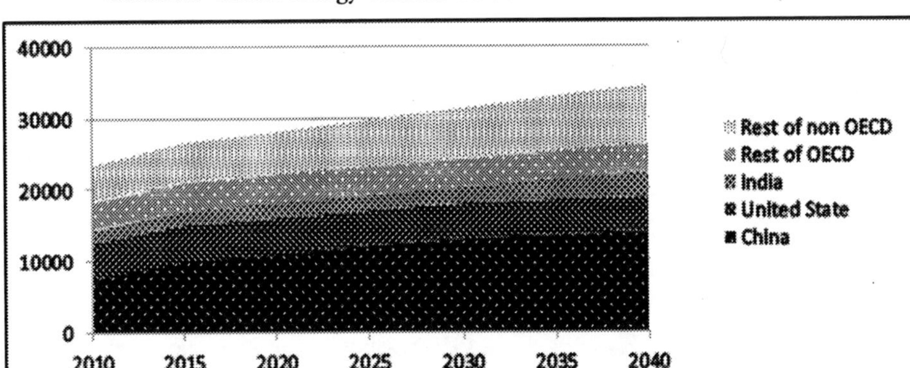

Data Source: U.S Energy Information Administration, International Energy, Outlook, 2013

OTHER EMERGING GEO-ECONOMIC VARIABLES

As discussed in the past, the US government, under Trump Administration, has initiated a trade war on the world at large and China in particular under "America First" policy professed during the election campaign and laid out in the 2018 and 2019 Trade Policy Agenda.[54] In the wake of struggle to have parity in tariff, the US government has taken several measures like, withdrawal of Trans-Pacific Partnership (TPP), asking for more favourable tariff in North American Free Trade Agreement (NAFTA) involving Mexico and Canada and Korea US Free Trade Agreement (KORUS) involving South Korea besides being critical of close allies like EU, Japan and India. However, his main target being China, to reduce huge trade deficit, the US in 2017 tried to compel China to purchase additional US$ 200 Billion of American goods and services by 2021. But the agreement failed because China demanded greater access to US market and recognition to Belt and Road Initiative which the US declined. Hence, punitive tariff on estimated US$550 Billion of Chinese products were imposed in 2019 which China tries to retaliate with similar tariff on US goods mainly agricultural goods. Both the countries are hurt but the war goes on. The situation got further accentuated with the US and allies (Australia) alleging China for Corona Virus spread. As per Moody's Analytics September 2019 report, the trade war de-escalation has only 15% probability and has cost .3% contraction in the US GDP with 300,000 job loss while the loss to China in exports to the US goes down to estimated 10%.[55]

Corona virus pandemic started in December 2019 in Wuhan, China. Thereafter, world economy (GDP) has been estimated to contract by 5.2% in 2020 and if things improve, GDP is going to grow by 4.2% with a caveat to a worst-case scenario wherein contraction would continue to persist if no remedies to Corona virus found.[56] In such a situation, China has claimed to have overcome the pandemic with just 84951 cases and 4634 deaths by 23 August having only 422 active cases. While the world is reeling with innumerable deaths, China is enjoying early recovery from pandemic and sliding economy as well. As brought out earlier China with after a slump from 6.8% of GDP in the first quarter of 2020 and registered a 3.2% growth in the second quarter. But no one believes the Chinese figures of pandemic cases and deaths being the most populous country while the economic upswing can be believed for exploitation of situation by shipping medical supplies being main component of export. The World Bank predicts a 7% shrink in the GDP of major economies, an overall shrink of world economy by 5.2% in 2020 and a most optimistic recovery of 4.2% in 2021.[57]

This has become an opportunity in calamity for China which major powers would like to deny to China, more so when IMF has predicted 9.2% growth in GDP for China in 2021.

Therefore, another trend which has caught up is relocation of foreign owned industries from China. Although, it appears as if the trend is owing to the recent Covid spread from China and vocal measures taken by the US and Australia, but the real reason lies in the trade war between the US and China starting in 2017, whereafter, the tariff laid by the US made the products dearer and companies, even the Chinese, have planned relocate or have already relocated to avoid increased taxes to goods shipped to the US from China. Even to some extent it can be traced to even earlier times when some of the companies planned to move because of the labour costs. Now the questions are; how severe is this trend? where are they moving to and who is losing/gaining? As per Nikkei Asian Review, 50 Global Companies planned exodus from China including the US, Japanese, Taiwanese as well as Chinese global manufacturers to relocate 15% to 30% of production.[58] The major beneficiaries have been Vietnam, Thailand, Taiwan, Mexico and India besides Japan taking majority of its companies back to Japan. The American Chamber of Commerce estimates that approximately 40% of 250 big firms would move out their production facilities from China. However, the Chinese Ministry of Commerce paints the picture as a normal result of market mechanisms confined to few "outward-oriented low-value -added foreign-invested enterprises", but that is only an expression for consumption of outside world or putting up a brave front.[59] For now China is recording increase in overseas orders but in long term perspective, actually the Chinese Ministry of Commerce must be estimating the ramifications realistically.

The FinTech revolution in China is another geo-economic tool to leverage world economy at least in the underdeveloped markets. China with a share of 47% share of global digital retail sales, all domestic at present, is gaining tremendous experience by embedding into financial and non-financial services and next generation services like blockchain and artificial intelligence services.[60] Three companies, Baidu, Alibaba and Tencent are spearheading the revolution with many subsidiaries in tow. These companies are leapfrogging from retail e-commerce to wealth management, insurance and private banking as well. Their investment majorly comes from domestic state-owned banks and private investors, but the heavy volume of domestic market also entices foreign direct investors as Chinese FinTech companies received more than eight billion dollars in 2015-2016. The next natural ambition of these FinTech companies is, entry into global market.

Although the developed markets will be little hard to enter, but these Chinese Companies will certainly explore the developing markets where resistance from government is less. Therefore, like investments in BRI projects, these Fintech Companies could likely become a tool for financial influence on smaller economies. To gain these economic access and reach, export of 5G of technology with cheaper 5G mobile phones, is certainly going to prove great carrier for Chinese FinTech companies to proliferate majority of these countries. China is offering its 5G services along with Bei Dou Navigational Satellite Systems (BDS) to the countries as an alternative to GPS navigation system for free.[61] Therefore, high speed cheaper communication with locational services will place China in highly advantageous plane for not only its commercial services but also allow to have access to all strategic data and locations making China all pervasive like the US is today.

In all, China is looking at itself in the 21st Century as a great economic superpower with only few negative elements. All these geo-economics conditions will necessitate certain imperatives which China has to tie over in order to become a global superpower. We shall discuss these geo-economic imperatives also along with other geopolitical imperatives emanating for China in the 21st Century. Not all economic powers can become a global superpower, till they back up these economic assets with an IR philosophy that makes the geo-economic conduct predictable, non-hegemonic and plausible. The applications of these philosophies along with the geo-economic assets are totally governed by the geopolitical situations of the concurrent times. But at the bottom of it all, the IR policy depends upon the metaphysical moorings of the countries governing population, manifested in the government either by the democratic processes or by the popular fervour, constantly gauged by an autocratic government in order to justify its authority in China. I argue that the geopolitical application of the geo-economic ascendance will be manifested in the creation of Tributary States; a concept well entrenched in the Chinese political philosophy with a modified application compelled by geostrategic choices or lack of them. Therefore, as a probable policy choice that may govern Chinese geopolitics in the 21st Century, the concept of tributary state in the modern perspective deserves a discussion here.

GEOECONOMICS AS A TOOL TO CREATE A TRIBUTARY SYSTEM IN THE ASYMMETRIC WORLD

The tributary system of China or *Cefeng Tizhi* (册封体制) was a traditional system of managing foreign relations in which by usual practice, foreign peoples would be granted trade and contact with China provided the ruler of the country or the ruler's emissary demonstrated their subservience to the Chinese emperor by personally bearing him tribute. This was a fact in the times of China securing its position as a Middle Kingdom in the sphere of 'All under Heaven' or Tianxia as perceived by it under the limitation of the means of communication at that time. Having the 'Mandate of Heaven' or *Tianming* as discussed earlier, the 'Son of Heaven' would seek the barbarians or the peripheral inferior civilisations to be allowed to come in contact and 'be reformed'. It was a hierarchical system of relations with the neighbours near and the countries far, which were always considered inferior. The system reached its apogee during the Ming Dynasty (1368–1644) when due to Zheng He's maritime expedition during early 1400, the embassies, beside the countries with contiguous land boundaries, from the areas such as Bengal, Sri Lanka, Sumatra, Java and faraway places like the eastern coast of Africa arrived in Beijing to pay tribute and in turn were allowed to trade with China. However, as the communications increased, contact with the faraway Western European countries was also established. To say that when these merchants were authorised to conduct trade with the far eastern regions in general that included China as well and offered gifts on arrival to the Emperor of China as they did to other countries to seek permission for trading, necessarily conveyed their political subjugation to the Chinese Emperor and conceded their position as a tributary state in the Chinese perception. There was an asymmetry in status—certainly not as it was always conceived in the Chinese perception. The asymmetry had existed from the earlier days; Japan, a neighbour, became a tributary for a brief period that ended in 1549. Korea in the east and Vietnam and Burma in the south were considered proper tributary states, which existed in the historical consciousness of Chinese minds as such. However, even these three were not always under Chinese influence as given out in the Confucian morality as applicable for relationship between China and a tributary state. The relation with these less ambitious neighbours were maintained in a manner that created an equilibrium against the most aggressive forces in the north and west to which China at times paid tribute itself.[58,59]

An independent historical examination of these tributary relations hints more towards a persistence of economic and commercial relations which were sustained better than the political relations between the two states. Zhou Fengyan concedes that it is basically the equilibrium or the balance of the power with the neighbours achieved in the regional framework when China has not always been in a superior position with respect to its neighbours to exercise the tributary relation system.

For example, during the early Han period, the western Han and the Xiongnu represented a bipolar system. The Southern Song and the Jin in the north could be considered in a bipolar order. The Northern Song, Liao, Western Xia and Jin could be characterised into a multipolar system.[62] Therefore, what can fairly be arrived at as a conclusive application of the tributary system is that it has a predominant economic consideration for achieving geopolitical equilibrium to pacify some in order to conserve power so that the other dominant enemies or competitors could be controlled well. A second inference could be drawn is that as the communications developed, the concept of tributary system went well beyond China's immediate neighbourhood and therefore in the modern perspective of globalisation and communication explosion, the tributary system, if China wishes to explore and exercise as its mechanics of development of relations, can be used in the most novel ways in the asymmetry that has emerged because of the non-existence of distance as a barrier and the existence of closeness as a barrier.

Applying Zhou's theory of equilibrium, let us first examine why the tributary system with most of the periphery states has failed. The tributary system had two basic premises: one that China is in a better position of power compared to the countries on the peripheries. The second premise is that to maintain the stability of its own power, the Chinese foreign policy will be defensive in nature. Zhou says that as the power distribution becomes asymmetric in the neighbouring countries, a strategic interaction may take place between China and its neighbouring countries in any of the following combinations.[63]

Chart 21: China's Combination of Types of Interaction with Peripheral State

		Peripheral States	
		Harassment	Submission
China	Conciliation	A	B
	Punitive Expedition	C	D

If we explain the present combination, due to the prevailing territorial disputes, almost all neighbours of China are in a combination of harassment versus punitive expedition. However, who is harassing and who is taking punitive measure is a matter of dispute. Thus, the situation is tense without any doubt. Therefore, my premise that **the closeness is a barrier and cause for friction, but distance is not,** is proved by the fact that the relations do not remain that of tributary states, despite most of the countries having massive investments in China and vice versa. Hence, the political agenda does overpower the economic agenda. So, my argument is that the tributary system in the Chinese sense as a form of interstate relations can be successfully applied only where the geopolitical risks are absent. Otherwise, in the era of globalisation, the asymmetry of power distribution can be present in the immediate neighbourhood as the relation is maintained with a power located as far away as can be imagined. Japan–US and Taiwan–US are good examples of this argument.

However, as the Chinese think tanks have developed a penchant for the application of the concept of interstate relations from their own ancient thoughts, their ability to moderate the concept of tributary system within the modern perspective is likely to be applied to the countries far away where there are no political risks and only geo-economics gains. This situation will have both China and the probable tributary in a win–win situation. As the countries far and wide with no political baggage will gain commerce with China, China will gain international prestige by mustering as many admirers as possible as the distances no more matter. This will enable China to show to the world that not every country is an enemy. Fairbank's observation that 'the tribute system had prestige value in the government system of China where prestige was an all-important tool of government', still proves true.[64]

As China brings out its own concepts of the Chinese world order and assumes a greater position of power, the so-called Westphalian order dissolves and will be filled by the tributary system which will start at the peripheries of the world with respect to distance from China; for example, in the continent of South America, provided these countries do not come under the direct influence of the US, i.e. if the US strengthens ties with these countries as per its policy of containment against China and ameliorates relations with countries of South America. Similar cases are already evident in the African continent which is having a waning power influence of the erstwhile colonial powers of Europe and has no economic attention of the US as well. Therefore, China will use its economic might to bring as many far-away countries under its influence as possible and use them in the forums like the UN and others to show its strength as a contending world power, for example, Sri Lanka against India. This is going to be the Chinese strategy of geo economic encirclement of the world power and not mere India It will be at its best as during the peaceful economic rise, China will be well on its path to have comprehensive national power by the support of tributary states.

NOTES

1. Bell, Daniel, *Germany: The Enduring Fear of Dissent*, 1990, Vol 37.
2. Luttwak, Edward N., 'From Geopolitics to Geo-Economics: Logic of Conflict, Grammar of Commerce', *National Interest*, Summer, 1990, pp. 17-23, www. dtci.mil/dtic /scanipii, Accessed on 8 Sep 2014.
3. Kennedy, Paul, *The Rise and Fall of The Great Powers*, NY: Random House, 1987, pp. 438-439.
4. *Pro-Active Policies by China in Response to Asian Financial Crisis*, http:www.finprc.gov.cn/mfa_eng/ziliao_665539/3602_665543/3604_665547/t18037. shtml, Accessed on Sep 2014.
5. Asian Development Bank, *Asian Economic Integration Monitor Report (July 2012)*, http://www.adb.org/publication/asian-economicintegration-moniter- July – 2012. Accessed on 09 Sep 2014. ASEAN-China Trade Growth: Facts, Factors and Prospects. Forancensco Abbate & Silvia Rosina14 JUN 2016- 14 JUN, 2016T.
6. Morrison, Wayne M., 'China's *Economic Rise: History, Trends, Challenges and Implications for the United States*', Congressional Research Service Report, 21 Aug 2018, p. 1.
7. Kapoor, Devesh and Manik Suri, 'Geo-Economics vs Geopolitics: Implications for Asia and the US Australia Alliance', 21 Aug 2012, pp. 3-4, http:// asiapacific.anu.edn.au/researchschool/emerging_asia/papers/kapursuri_final.pdf, Accessed on 12 May 2014.
8. Guisnel, Jean, *Guerres Dans le Cyberspace la Decouverte*, Paris, 1997, pp. 231-232.
9. Khanna, Parag, 'Introductory Thoughts', a paper presented in the session, *Understanding Geo–Economics and Strategy*, in the IISS summer conference on 'A New Era of Geo Economics: Assessing the Interplay of Economics and Political Risk', 23-25 March 2012, New Delhi.
10. Liberman, Peter, *'Trading with the Enemy: Security and Relative Economic Gains'*, International Security, 2 (1), 1996, pp. 147-175.
11. Huntington, Samuel P., *'Why International Primacy Matters'*, International Security, 17 (4), 1993, p. 81.
12. Gowa. Joan and Edward D. Mansfield, *'Power Politics and International Trade'*, American Political Science Review, 87 (2), 1993, pp. 408-42
13. Waltz, Kenneth, *Theory of International Politics*, NY: Random House, 1979, p. 168.
14. "Yellow Book' Ranks China 7th in Overall Strength', *China Daily*, 25 Dec 2009, http://www.chinadaily.com.cn/world/2009_12/25/content_9228213.htm, Accessed on 9 Nov 2014.
15. Spykman, Nicholas John, *The Geography of Peace*, NY: Harcourt Brace, 1944, and a Discussion by Huang Shuofeng, *New Theory of overall National Strength*, China Social Science Press, Beijing, 1999, p. 8.
16. Ye Zecheng, *Inside China's Grand Strategy: The Perspective from the Peoples Republic*, New Delhi: KW Publishers Pvt Ltd, 2013, pp. 18-30.
17. Chai Yuqiu, *Moulue Jia (Strategist)*, Beijing: Lan Tian Chubanshe, 1996, p. 511.
18. Wu Chunqiu, *Guangyi Da Zhanlue (Grand Strategy)*, Beijing: Shishi Chubanshe, 1995, p. 98.
19. Deng Xiaoping, quoted in Renmin Ribao (*People's Daily*), 26 Feb 1990, as quoted in *Huang Shuofeng Zhong He Guidi Lun (on Comprehensive National Power*), Beijing: Zhongguo Shehui Kexue Chubanshe, 1992, p. 7.

20. Zhu Liangyin and Meng Renzhong, '*Deng Xiaoping Zonghe Guoli Sixiang Yanjiu' (A Study on Deng Xiaoping's Comprehensive National Power Thought)* in *Xin Shiqi Junshi Jingli Lilun Yanjiu* (Studies of Modern Era Military Economic Theory), Li Lin and Jhao Qinxuan (eds), Beijing: Jun Shi Kexue Chubanshe, 1995, p. 42.
21. Huang Shuofeng, op. cit., pp. 220-221.
22. Wang Songfen (ed.), *Shijie Zhuyao Guojia Zong He Guoli Bijiao Yanjiu (Comparative Studies of the Comprehensive National Power of the World's Major Nations)*, Changsha: Hunan Chubanshe, 1996, p. 434.
23. Ibid., pp. 432-433.
24. Estimates based on the Organisation of Economic Cooperation and Development (OECD), *Chinese Economic Performance in the Long Run 1910–2030,* by Angus Madison, OECD, 2007.
25. Deng Xiaoping, *Excerpt from a Speech at the Communist Youth League Conference,* 7 July 1962, www.chinadaily.com.cn/china/2014–08/20/content _18453523.htm.
26. Ibid.
27. Morrison, op. cit.
28. 'China 2030: Building a Modern, Harmonious and Creative Society', A World Bank Report in Collaboration with Development Research Centre of the State Council, The People's Republic of China, World Bank, Washington, DL 2013, P-5
29. Ibid.
30. IMF Data Mapper, https://www.imf.org/external/datamapper/NGDP_RPCH@WEO/OEMDC. Accessed on 12 August 2020.
31. Economic Times, Jan 17 2020, *China's Per Capita GDP crosses US$10000 mark for the first Time*, https://economictimes.indiatimes.com/news/international/business/chinas-per-capita-gdp-crosses-usd-10000-mark-for-the-first-time/articleshow/73329871.cms. Accessed on 23 July 2020
32. 'USCC Annual Report 2013 to Congress' by US-China Economic and Security Review Commission, Nov 2013, pp. 50-51, www.uscc.gov/annual_report/2030annual_congress, Accessed on 14 Sep 2014.
33. Houng Lee, Murtaza Sayed and Liu Xueyan, *'China's Path to Consumer Based Growth: Reorienting Investment and Enhancing Efficiency*', IMF Working Paper 13/83 (March), Washington, 2013, p. 20, http://www.imf.org/ external/bubs/ft/wp/20131383. Pdf, Accessed on 14 Sep 2014.
34. Press Conference report. http://www.sasac.gov.cn/11296330/index.html, Accessed on 18 Sep 2014.
35. Ming Du, *'China's State Capitalism and World Trade Law'*, International and Comparative Law Quarterly, 63 (02), April 2014, www.economist.com/news/finance and economics, Accessed on 18 Sep 2014.
36 'China's Economy: Perverse Advantage', *The Economist*, Shanghai, 27 Apr 2013, www.economist.com/news/finance and economics, Accessed on 18 Sep 2014.
37. Karen Jingrong Lin, Xiaoyan Lu, Junsheng Zhang, Ying Zheng, *State-Owned Enterprises in China: A Review of 40 Years of Research and Practise,* https://reader.elsevier.com/reader/sd/pii/S1755309119300437...A5E740A5BB6443EA6B002C4587612A2D9243E9DE77D6082E81358C21EA. Accessed 14 Aug 2020.
38. Ibid.
39. China Labour Bulletin, Employment and Wages, 15 July 2019. https://clb.org.hk/content/employment-and-wages. Accessed 18 August 2020.

40. Ibid.
41. Deloitte, 'The Next Wave of Industry Ignite Chinese Growth Momentum', 10 Sep 2014, http://www.deloite.com/view/zh-cn/cn/pressroom/pr/33409805d5 8410vgn/vcm30000034 56f70/RCRD.htm. Accessed on 20 Sep 2014.
42. China 2012 Statistical Year Book and UN data, United Nations.
43. CNBC, Why Chinese overseas investment growth is set to slow further, https://www.cnbc.com/2019/08/21/moodys-chinese-overseas-i6frastructure-investment-growth-to-slow.html. Accessed 15 August 2020.
44. World Bank. https://data.worldbank.org/indicator/FI.RES.TOTL.CD?locations=CN. Accessed on 02 August 2020.
45. Zhag Rui, *China's Sovereign Wealth Fund releases Annual Report,* http://www.china.org.cn/business/2019-09/23/content_75237120.htm. Accessed on 15 August 2020.
46. International Energy Agency World Energy Outlook 2012, London, 2012, http://www.iea.org/newsroomandevents/speeches/weo_launch.pdf, Accessed on 25 Aug 2014.
47. US Energy Information Administration, 'China', pp. 3-4, http://www.eia. gov/countries/analysisbriefs/china/china.pdf. Accessed on 25 Aug 2014.
48. B P, Statistical Review of World Energy: 2019, https://www.bp.com/en/global/corporate/energy-economics/statistical-review-of-world-energy.html. Accessed 06 August 2020.
49. US Energy Information Administration, 'China', pp. 3-4, http://www.eia. gov/countries/analysisbriefs/china/china.pdf, Accessed on 25 Aug 2014.
50. Ibid., p. 4. And http://www.eia.gov/countries/analysisbriefs/china/images/top_ten_oil importers.png, Accessed on 25 Aug 2014.
51. U.S. Energy Information Administration, Oil Imports and Exports, https://www.eia.gov/energyexplained/oil-and-petroleum-products/imports-and-exports.php. Accessed 03 August 2020.
52. US Energy Information Administration, 'China 2014', http://www. eia.gov/countries/analysisbriefs /china/china.pdf., Accessed on 25 Aug 2014.
53. Nye, Joseph, 'Shale Gas is America Geopolitical Trump Card', *Wall Street Journal,* http://online.wsj.com/articles/joseph_nye_shale_gas_is_americas_ geopolitical_ trump_card_140226 6367, Accessed on 02 Sep 2014.
54. Federartion of German Industries (BDI), "America First"- U.S. Trade Policy under President Donald Trump. https://english.bdi.eu/article/news/america-first-u-s-trade-policy-under-president-donald-trump/. Accessed on 23 August 2020.
55. Moody's Analytics, Mark Zandi, Jesse Rogers and Maria Cosma, Trade War Chicken: The Tariffs and the Damage Done, https://www.moodysanalytics.com/-/media/article/2019/trade-war-chicken.pdf. Accessed on 23 August 2020.
56. The World Bank, The Global Economic Outlook During the COVID-19 Pandemic: A Changed World, https://www.worldbank.org/en/news/feature/2020/06/08/the-global-economic-outlook-during-the-covid-19-pandemic-a-changed-world.
57. Ibid.
58. Nikkei Asian Review, Nikkei Staff writers,China Scrambles to stem Manufacturing Exodusas 50 Comapanies Leave, https://asia.nikkei.com/Economy/Trade-war/China-scrambles-to-stem-manufacturing-exodus-as-50-companies-leave. Accessed on 23 August 2020.
59. The Diplomat, Dingding Chen and Yu Xia, Amanufacturing Exodus in China - Fact or Fiction? https://thediplomat.com/2019/12/a-manufacturing-exodus-in-china-fact-or-fiction/. Accessed

on 24 August 2020.

60. Sachin Mittal, James Lloyd, The Rise of FinTech in China: Redefining Financial Sevices, A Collaborative Report by DBS & EY, Nov 2016. PP 6-7.

61. 5G, BeiDou integrate to become Key Infrastructure: Expert, Jun 30 2020, The State Council, The People's Republic of China, http://english.www.gov.cn/news/topnews/202006/30/content_WS5efa921ac6d05a0f8970665f.html. Accessed on 25 August 2020.

62. Zhou Fangyin, 'Equilibrium Analysis of The Tributary System', *The Chinese Journal of International Politics*, Vol. 4, 2014, pp. 147-178, http://cjip.oxford journals.org, Accessed on 31 Jul 2014.

63. Ibid, pp. 151-152.

64. Fairbank, John K., 'Tributary Trade and China's Relations with The West', *Far Eastern Quarterly*, 1(2), 1942, p. 135.

6

Geopolitical Imperatives and a Response Model for China

INTRODUCTION

China is a geopolitical behemoth. As it grew in size, the geopolitical imperatives also became gradually complex. We have seen how China had grown as a nation state historically and where does it stand today as a country. Now, it is only appropriate to identify China's geopolitical imperatives in the perspective of concurrent internal as well as external advantages and limitations that its geostrategic situations have. China has such contiguity in the geopolitical layout that it compels us to see the Chinese external geopolitical imperatives as an expression of its internal geopolitical imperatives. Therefore, while discussing these imperatives **an inside-out approach** has been adopted. As we discuss the imperatives, I am sanguine that a clear linkage between the domestic and external imperatives can be established.

There are several drivers that have caused this set of geopolitical imperatives. Foremost are the historical drivers, which predispose the Chinese geography and the strategic thinking that we see today and work behind the popular choices that the Chinese state is forced to adopt. Historical reasons pervade China's thinking in all spheres today—whether, territorial, ethnic, linguistic, military, economic, cultural or global. The decision-making is further made inherently unidirectional by the one-party rule which has to invoke these factors time and again to seek the approval of the people whose mindset is well rooted in these factors. In such a case, it is seen that the assumed modern ideological plank does not work for long and the people find refuge in the old cultural and social principles and values as it gives them a kind of comfort zone that they consider their own. For example, the communist principles and values failed in the former USSR and other communist-bloc countries, but communism in China finds an easy replacement with state capitalism: the Confucian way of life, Xunzi's strategic thinking and nationalism which otherwise have no place in communism.

In the light of all the above, what remains non-exchangeable is the geography and its elements that act as stimuli to the responses that emanate from the human geographical layout of the surface, resources and the political geography of the neighbourhood and the world. The critical examination of coherence and cohesiveness of human geographical factors have led to, as we have already discussed, the distinctions made by the geopoliticians for China into China proper and Outer China, based upon historical dispositions of China's geographies. This distinction also indicates the geopolitical dimensions as well as the intensity of the centrifugal forces. When Friedman calls China proper an island, we do have to take the notice of this internal dimension while analysing the geopolitical imperatives.[1] The internal geopolitical dimensions of China have far-reaching ramifications on the international relations of as well as global geopolitics of China, which cannot be seen in the enclosed sphere of only immediate frontiers of China and its security as brought out by Friedman. Rather, the internal geopolitical conditions have an outreach beyond the Chinese political borders of today, having global economic and political dimensions with direct ramifications on China's world power status. Therefore, the approach to identifying the Chinese geopolitical imperatives in this chapter will be contiguous in nature with the inside-out analysis, beginning with the internal geopolitical regions going towards the geopolitical region beyond, to cover the entire globe; all the perceptible elements of geopolitics will be discussed with their possible influence over China's internal policies as well as external affairs.

The foundation of this argument of contiguity is laid in the fact that the Chinese state boundaries are one of the latest adaptations of the Westphalian concept of state with equal rights and sovereignty within the demarcated boundary through military means by Mao. Before that, the hierarchical concept of "All under Heaven" was the principle of rule for China as **the 'Middle Kingdom'** with its vassals and tributaries around it. The 100-year period before Mao, was the period in which China learnt the concept of state and sovereignty with fixed boundaries the hardest way due to the ingress of Western colonial powers, and infamously called the period as **the Century of Humiliation**. The latest annexations and consolidation of loosely held frontiers and inclusion of erstwhile tributaries have not yet matured as part of the Chinese sovereignty and with these areas of inclusion still having old interstate as well cultural linkages with the other sovereign states beyond the Chinese political boundaries, reflect themselves in rebellions, human right and boundary disputes dictating political risks. On the other hand, the economic dimensions of these areas have led China to think even beyond the precipice of its boundary line and compel China to weigh the economic losses of holding on to them against the imminent political gains. It also heavily weighs on China's world power projection. Beside all these risks and gains, China has a peculiar problem of satisfying its domestic constituents for a kind of tacit approval of its actions by balancing it against the nationalistic fervour through which the one-party government has also constantly tried to attain legitimacy of its governance in the absence of a democratic process. Therefore, in this discourse of geopolitical imperatives, the methods of identification and analyses of the imperatives will be based on the criteria of economic gains versus geopolitical risks in the framework of interconnected elements across a contiguous geo-space and the bargaining framework of the two-level games as evolved by Robert Putman.[2]

As Robert Putman puts across the idea of pushes of international pressures and the domestics pulls in determination of international relations as a path to be traded as brought out in his article, "Diplomacy and Domestic Politics: The Logic of Two-Level Games". It applies the most in the case of China as against a democratic country where to a large extent once a mandate given, authorises the government of the day to take a decision in the larger interest of the nation. Therefore, violent reactions against a purported national interest brought forth in a democratic country remains muted as compared to a despotic regime for two reasons; the public once realises that it has chosen the government of the day then shares the responsibility of a wrong policy and the second, that it has choice to eject the government out of power in the next term.

Two other test criteria, geopolitical risks and geo-economics gains define the line of advantage. Along with these, the Chinese strategic mindset composed of the metaphysical elements as discussed in the previous chapters will always have to be borne in mind to evaluate the geopolitical situation for China and determine the imperatives that guide the future course of responses. As explained earlier, the approach to evaluation of Chinese geopolitical imperatives has been holistic. Effort has been to see the big picture first and then derive the imperatives for China without losing credibility for generalisation. Analysis has been carried out with sound inputs in all aspects of the Chinese geo-body's interrelation to the world in general and the regions in particular, estimating gains and losses for China in the short term and in the long term, in one spatial domain as against the other, from the perspective that it would serve China's ultimate national interest. This drawing of a holistic picture is a modern researcher's necessity as David Shaumbaugh finds in the academic profession, a growing tendency to "**know more and more about less and less...has allowed us to know more about the trees it has, not necessarily to better understanding of the forest (that is China)**".[3]

THE CONCENTRATION OF COMPREHESIVE NATIONAL POWER AND ITS IMPLICATIONS

Comprehensive national power is comprised of several elements which according to various scholars differ as per the approach to the calculations and emphasis given as we have discussed in the previous chapter. However, it is very obvious now that China has tremendous capabilities to become the world's leading power. What we intend discussing here is the fact that how these CNP resources are distributed across China and analyse these concentrated or sparse distribution of recourses with the premise that a greater density of resource concentration will reflect a greater concentration of the comprehension of national power. These concentrations therefore will also depict the power centre which may vary from the political centre (not the political power centre).[4] Therefore, for the purpose of discussion of the distribution, we must take more generic forms of these resources; for example we take the distribution of GDP on PPP as a distribution of economic resources along with the distribution of capital investment, distribution of natural resources indicated by arable land, water and ores and energy resources; human resources, by distribution of population, knowledge and technology resources by more use of computers, registration of patents and publication of scientific journals or concentration of education and research facilities. The government resources are to be seen not in terms of the location of national government, but in terms of locations of the fiscal spending of the central government including the current and capital and spending on public undertaking and organisations. This reflects the spatial distribution of national power. And the distribution pattern of military apparatus and its concentrations, reflect the intensity of the need felt to safeguard the regions of these valuable resources of the nation against external threats. Most of these elements can be best understood with the help of distributional maps and imagery superimposition, which can then clearly depict the distribution of national power, its centres of concentration as well as the areas of alienation where the centrifugal forces are working stronger due to a lesser concentration of the CNP.

The regional disparity and the study of its causes in China lead us to an inevitable geographical determinism. I posit that even the market forces follow the geographically advantageous disposition of a location in any country. Like, why south east China was allowed to develop first was due to its closeness to the ocean routes for export and an easy capital from Hong Kong and Taiwan. Another factor which has worked in China is the core–periphery model established by Krugman, wherein the monopolistically competitive manufacturing sectors and competitive agricultural sectors tried to seek an equilibrium of development after a see-saw battle in development with its possession of mobile skilled labour and immobile unskilled labour wherein surpluses could move to and fro from each sectors.[5] Even in the controlled policymaking mechanism of communist China, the geographical distribution of resources (capital, labour and transport) compelled the south-eastern provinces to grow first and then the industries moved to the agricultural hinterland to tap the immobile labour. The household registration system or Hu Khou in China gives good indication of labour mobility. Several studies have been carried out using New Economic Geography (NEG) model of Krugman to see causes of this labour mobility and it has been found that the foremost determinant of labour mobility are market access, population and arable land which created agglomeration of industries and labour.[6] This equilibrium seeking dynamics between the agglomeration and dispersion of labour forces has determined the equilibrium in distribution of firms. However, the caveat is that this interregional integration has still not reached an equal intensity beyond China proper that has already been brought out earlier based on historical geographic factors. Another factor we need to account for is the in-hospitability of the far west, its geographical distance from the already developed east and south-east China and the 'alien' races inhabiting these areas.

This, as posited earlier, integrates the areas with these attributes with the initial industrialised coastal zones and has created a core in China. This identification of core is an outcome of balance between agglomeration and the spreading forces and the evidence ahead would further bring out the more pronounced core–periphery outcome for China. The core has been created first with the agglomerations bounded by the line joining three municipalities of Beijing, Shanghai and Chongqing as the cardinal points. In the previous chapter, it has been discussed how historically, the Chinese core within China proper was in the shape of an inverted triangle bounded by cardinal points of cities: Xian,

Chang An and Luoyang, generally aligned along the Wei river and the Yellow river with the central plains of the Yellow river being the main cradle of the core. Hypothetically speaking, the tip of the inverted triangle touched the Yangzi river at the confluence of the Han and Yangzi rivers or the city of Wuchang. The same is represented by the black solid inverted triangle in the map below. That was the time when all economic activities (primarily agricultural) took place in the north along the Yellow river and there was hardly any economic gain or geopolitical risk perceived in the south-east. All geopolitical threats emanated from the northern and western land borders and it was a period of land communication and the political power centre was also therefore commensurate. By the Qing period, the economic activities gravitated towards the south. And by the end of the 18th Century, due to the development of the oceanic communication system, geopolitical threats began to emanate in the south in a relatively greater force as the time passed by. Thus, the inverted core triangle had straightened itself in terms of the concentration of comprehensive national power. Though the symbolic political power centre remained in the north, the political strengths were drawn from the south. I posit this on the basis of the contention that the more economically potent regions of the south tried to break away from the Qing imperialism as their Han manifestation, like Yuan Shikai, who first became a Republican president and later declared himself as emperor in 1905. It was in the Yangzi basin where the nationalists as well as the communists gathered their political mandate first and with that moral authority marched towards the north through their expeditions and long marches, respectively. This contention of the politico-economic power has further consolidated itself in the south along the base of the triangle coinciding with the Yangzi river basin as represented in the map by solid red triangle. The position of the core of China is now considered as settled we further realise that the core does not derive any additional CNP strength from the north. It rather gets the economic strength from further down south as Shenzhen becomes the second most valuable economic centre after Shanghai, hence the supplementary CNP concentration zone is going further south in an inverted triangle represented by broken red line in the map below. Now the all the three triangles together make up China Proper which clearly have internal geopolitical dynamics as well. Therefore, let us first discuss China proper and China's peripheries purely on the basis of a concentration of the comprehensive national power elements. Considering that the per capita GDP productivity will be a good indicator, if the distribution of the provincial productivity is mapped, it would give a fair indication of the concentration of resources in China and allows us to see the Chinese core, China proper and peripheral China clearly. As the orientation of geopolitical risk is concerned, the deployment of the PLA Army, Navy and Air Force indicates the intensity of perceived dangers which can be considered to be directly proportional to the intensity of force deployment. If the force deployment is superimposed upon the map of concentration of resources, makes the picture clearer. Coupled with the factors of what China calls the first and second chain islands, China does not have the freedom of an open sea in the east and south-east. Therefore, the geopolitical risks are very intense as well as closest to the resource-intense areas of south-east China. As the resource concentration thins out towards the northeast, the risk also thins out comparatively. It can be better understood in a cognitive depiction through concentric elliptical circles considering that the gap between the rings express the intensity of resources (read CNP) versus geopolitical risks as given in the figure below.

Map 33: CNP Ripples: The Concentration shows Geo-Strategic Risks

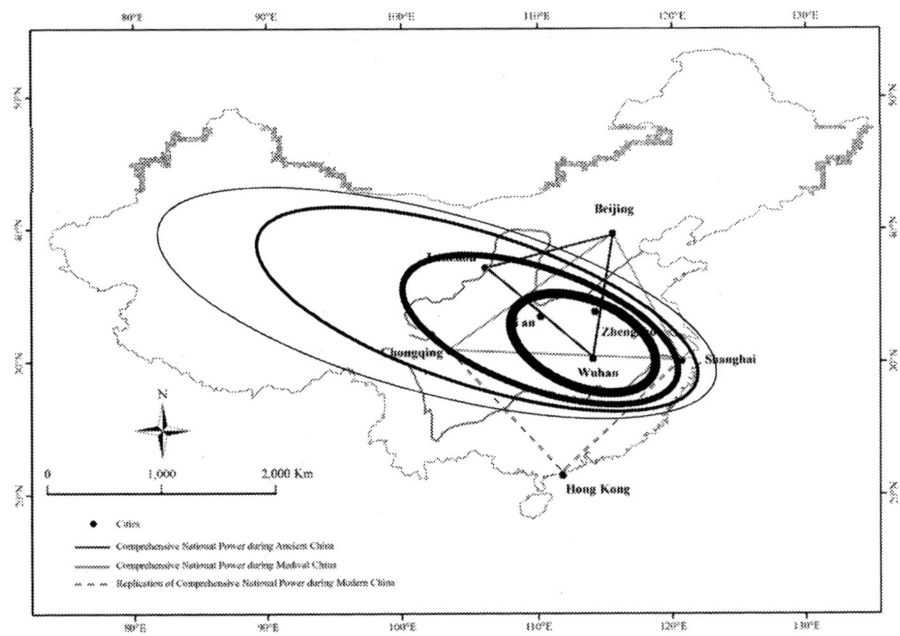

Now, the imperative for China is clearly drawn for paying more attention towards the south-east in the light of gains versus risks analysis and to decide whether to deal with it with power or diplomacy. For the internal dynamics of China Proper, China has an internal political imperative to handle the south-east keeping in mind the facts that the revolutions have gained strength from these regions whenever the symbolic power centres in the north have failed to match the political aspirations of these regions, fired by economic independence and more frequent communication with the outside world. Taiwan, Hong Kong and Macao are the new gateways to fuel fresh political aspirations which may ignite the mainland in the south-east as well as the adjacent rich regions. Hong Kong particularly has shown such aspirations explicitly, which has become an ideological imperative for China to deal with, started in 2014, the demonstrators continued their protest for the right to vote in the Umbrella Revolution, mainly carried out by students.[7,8] Though the Chinese government tried to factionalise the protestors and not use force, in the backdrop of the Tiananmen incident of 1989, it did not use force to cull the unrest fearing international condemnation. That mind set was suitable for those times when China was growing at very fast pace and the any hedging by western countries and media would have led to unaffordable economic losses. Now, after the US-China trade war began and the corona pandemic has already caused downturn in economies, China has become bold in its dealing with the issue as a situation of geopolitical flux has emerged where a rejig of alliances is taking place. Use of force as well as changing the status of self-rule for Hong Kong promised by China till 2047 is being infringed by bringing in regulations like Fugitive Offender and Mutual Legal Assistance in Criminal Matters Legislation(Amendment) Bill in Jun 2019 which will allow China to take any alleged offender to mainland for trial jeopardizing the independence of judiciary of Hong Kong. This has again led to massive protests and has even influenced election results in Taiwan where Democratic Progressive Party which follows the path of independence from China won the 2020 elections. Now it becomes imperative for China to deal with such sentiments of disintegration. Till now China has only tried to forcibly work to bridge the gap that existed in the 'one nation two government' system to fully integrate Hong Kong and has also become coercive towards Taiwan as well. Both issues now seam interlinked and have instigated the US and UK to push for fulfilment of obligations of treaty on transfer of Hong Kong and independence of Taiwan.

GEOPOLITICAL IMPERATIVES IN WESTERN CHINA

Though the geopolitical remoteness of western China begins from Gansu, Qinghai and Sichuan because these provinces have a sizeable population of the non-Han races of the west, mainly Tibetan Buddhists and Uighur and Hui Muslims, but politically, only Xinjiang and Tibet are considered formally different from the rest of the Chinese provinces, being designated as the Xinjiang Uighur Autonomous

Region and the Tibet Autonomous Region as part of the five autonomous regions within the PRC; the others being Inner Mongolia, Ningxia and Guangxi. These two autonomous regions are further alienated due to their recent accessions, independence movements and linkages beyond their borders with other countries, whether formally or informally, in order to get energy for their movements from cultural similarities. However, there is a clear distinction between the Tibetan movement and Xinjiang because while the Tibetan independence movement is being taken up on a political level through the Tibetan government-in-exile and the charismatic leader and Noble Peace Prize recipient, the 14th Dalai Lama, the Xinjiang movement is primarily based on the militant activities it carries out against the Han people and the Chinese establishment. Xinjiang and Tibet are spread over a vast area of 1.6 million sq kilometres and 1.2 million kilometres, respectively. However, both have distinct values geopolitically. While Tibet has the Himalayan watershed as the defining line and an inhospitable boundary with India, Xinjiang has no such impediments and gives China an access route to Central Asia, Europe, the Middle East and their energy resources. It has also been the main Silk Route for China's trade from antiquity, whether as part of its dominion or otherwise. Due to these distinctions, China has different geopolitical imperatives for Tibet and Xinjiang.

Xinjiang: An Alternative Window to the West

The first impression one gets of Xinjiang is of the Uyghur nationalist movement fuelled by pan Turkism and Islamism; the ideologies reflected in various terrorist attacks. The not-so-latest being the knife attacks on March 1, 2014 at the Kunming Railway station and on April 30, 2014 at the Urumqi railway station to oppose the visit of Xi Jinping and the May 6, 2014 attack at the Guangzhou railway station, besides the bombings carried out by the separatists at other occasions. The genesis of this separatist movement lies in the fact that Xinjiang was never ruled by China continuously and that the Uyghur even founded their short-lived independent Islamic Republic of East Turkistan from 1933 to 1934. Subsequently, the former Soviet Union continued to fuel the separatism of the Uyghur through its Central Asian provinces and established the second East Turkestan Republic which was only incorporated into the Peoples Republic of China in 1949 by the Chinese communist regime. The former Soviet Union had continued supporting such separatist movements in China through its funding of the East Turkistan People's Revolutionary Party (ETPRP) and the United Revolutionary Front of East Turkestan (URFET). The Chinese government considers the East Turkistan

Islamic Movement (ETIM), the East Turkistan Liberation Organisation (ETLO) and the Uyghur Liberation Organisation, beside the URFET as the most violent separatist organisations.[9] However, unlike other democratic countries like India where the accommodation of differences and identity issues are given freedom, the authoritarian government in China deals with the separatists with a "Strike Hard" Policy on the Muslims interloping with Xinjiang's Islamic neighbours and the Middle East, which had taken wing due to Deng Xiaoping's limited return to religious tolerance allowing the hajj and visits to their religious places within China. However, the Uyghurs increasingly brought considerably secular areas like Turpan under the fundamentalist influence.[10] Since then, the terrorist activities have not ceased to take place. In the knife attack and bomb blast in a police station and government offices in the Sache county (also known as Yarkand among the Uyghur) of the Xinjiang province on July 28, 2014, 96 people including 37 civilians and 59 terrorist died, which the Chinese government took a long time to confirm.[11] In a swift trials, a court in Xinjiang's Kashgar Prefecture sentenced 12 people to death, giving various punishments to a total of 58 people.[12] That is why Xinjiang has become so important for China in such a backdrop of the alienation of its people and a distance from the mainland. However, the foremost agenda for China in the 21st Century is to become a developed country and the resources that Xinjiang holds can be the singular reason as to why China cannot afford to set Xinjiang free in the foreseeable future, besides using it as buffer to the terrorism coming to China proper.[13] The abundance of natural resources of Xinjiang begins with a 68 million hectare land available for cultivation and forestry. Out of the 122 types of minerals discovered, iron ore accounts for 730 million tonnes and other rare earths like neodymium essential for green technologies like wind turbines are found in abundance. Besides, Xinjiang holds 38 per cent of the coal reserves and 25 per cent of the petroleum and natural gas reserves of China.[14] The Tarim basin of Xinjiang holds an estimated 40% of China's 25.08 trillion cubic meters of exploitable shale gas—the world's largest and the future of energy, which can change the energy geopolitics of the world.[15] It still holds equal to, if not more, value as a modern trade route, especially when the oceanic routes in the East China and South China sea remain enclosed and seem claustrophobic to the Chinese geopolitics. Therefore, as an alternative access to the Middle East and Europe through Xinjiang, it is imperative for China to not only keep the land in its possession but keep it well and peaceful in order to assure a safe passage of trade and commerce. The most important trade through this Silk Route is the import of oil and gas through pipelines from the reserves of the Central Asian republics as well as the Middle East and Caspian Sea. Therefore, China knows very well that the value of the land far exceeds the value of its people and while the demography can be changed, the resources of the land cannot—all the more so when such vast and thinly populated areas can also act as risk-free testing grounds for nuclear arsenal and missiles. Now it is clear that China has a two-fold aim for retaining the land; one is the resources of Xinjiang and the second, an alternative transit route to the west. However, the hostile Uyghur play spoilsport by their demand of independence and following violent means to achieve it. China is trying to meet this challenge by two methods: first, by bringing in a demographic change in Xinjiang through various sponsored as well as direct organisational immigration and secondly, by constructively engaging the Muslim neighbourhood of the Central Asian republics in order to check and contain any possible support to the Uyghur separatists from across the border. The first method of overpowering the land mass through demographic measures has been carried out by Han settlements and the ever-increasing farmer settlements of Xinjiang Production and Construction Corps (XPCC) established in 1954. For this purpose, even today, China despite the communist rule, draws its policies from the ancient practices and philosophies. For example, the Tuntian agro-colonial system was first evolved by Cao Wei, later known as Emperor Lin of Wei, during the Three Kingdom period (more famously known as Cao Cao) who resolved the problem of migration from war zones by settling the people into new tracts of land, in turn enhancing production. Later, this system was turn into military households during the Jin, Yuan and Mongol periods. This was adopted by the Ming and later the Qing (the original Jin or Jurchen), as a garrison of peace-time agriculturists who would become soldiers during war with an allocation of a vast tract of land for sustenance. The same policy was adopted by China in 1954 in order to create ***bingtuan*** or soldiers' settlements in Xinjiang, interspersed among the Uyghur as isolated colonies of the XPCC. The aim of the XPCC is overtly pronounced in the government white paper which says:

> "In October 1954, the Central People's Government ordered most of PLA units in Xinjiang to be transferred to local civilian work by the unit and be reported from setups of national defence forces to form a production and construction corps whose mission were to carry out both production and military duties and cultivate and guard border areas."[16]

So, distinct characters of this enterprise separated this ***bingtuan*** from the old ***juntuan*** (military settlements). The first distinction is the deployment pattern and the second is its half-demilitarisation. Today, there are 14 divisions having

176 regimental and stock-breeding farms with 70,600 square kilometres under their administration, having more than 4,400 industrial construction, transport and other commercial enterprises with a population of 27,01,400 accounting for 11.9% of Xinjiang's total population.[17] The Chinese government accepts the XPCC to be part of the four-in-one joint defence system in Xinjiang with the local troops, armed police, local militias along with their own on-duty militia to fight against the threat of the 'three forces: separatists, religious extremists and terrorist'. The white paper likens the XPCC to an "embedded type" system because of its communication and interaction with the local people, especially the Uyghur which is also capable of military action instantaneously. Beside this, the Han migration also took place on a formal basis to develop Xinjiang's infrastructure and natural resource extraction industries like oil, gas and cotton comprising 95 per cent in the technical workforce and a majority in the government administrative and managerial jobs through the state.[18] Besides these systematic and orchestrated efforts of the Chinese administration to increase the proportion of the Han Chinese in the region dominated by Muslims, a self-initiated migration of the Han Chinese has taken over the sponsored migration since 1980, the beginning of reforms. Therefore, since 1980, the percentage of the Han and the Uyghur which was 6.2 and 82.7 per cent respectively, has changed to approximately 41 and 51 per cent respectively, with the remaining made up of other nationalities.[19] The other trend that has been noticed is a concentration of the Han in northern Xinjiang, especially in the largest cities of Urumqi, Karamay and Shihezi and the Uyghur in the south, especially in the Tarim basin, who have tended to move from several areas of south to the urban areas of north and the Han are now moving to the south for oil and gas exploitation, the southern centres of national resources, with the new establishments of the XPCC.[20] Considering the oppressive role of XPCC the the Office of Foreign Asset Control (OFAC) of the US has banned two officials, Sun Jinlung, the former Political Commissar of XPCC and Peng Jiarui, the Deputy Party Secretary and Commander of the XPCC for the purpose of cutting off any access to the US and Western financial market and transaction in dollars or the US goods and services.[21] This migration of the Han population is a well-designed effort towards the strategic dominance of Han over the resources of Xinjiang, causing drastic inequalities between the Uyghur and Han. The Uyghur are not only facing fierce competition from the Han in the government and public sector employment, but are facing a fierce competition from the Han immigrants from the other provinces, primarily Sichuan, Gansu, Shanxi and Henan, who are better skilled and protected by the relaxed policies of the Hu Kou system which works

against the rural Uyghur who migrate to the urban centres for employment in a situation wherein they are treated at par with the immigrants from other states. They are more disadvantaged on factors like the Chinese language, skills, weak social network, work ethics, culture or religion. One such example is the prohibition from display of religious markers by the government, public institutions and public enterprises. Therefore, many Uyghur view the Chinese as colonisers and this perception of China among the Uyghur does not help in keeping Xinjiang a safe passage to approach Eurasia as an alternative route. However, in the long run, it does help China to cross over the critical mass of the Uyghur population to legitimise claim over the territories of Xinjiang backed by a majority Han population which is most likely to become so in the future.

However, in following this policy China violates the human rights which is going to become an impediment in pursuing smooth international relations. Indoctrination being the main tool of communism China has detained approximately 1.5 million Uyghurs in indoctrination (China calls them re-education camps) which invited massive backlash from international community.[22] Although, the direct terrorist action by Uyghur militant organisations have already ceased but the China paranoid by information that during 2014-16 the Uyghurs did fight alongside the Al-Qaeda and the Islamic State terrorists, a preventive action has been taken to curate the probable militants by, setting up of these camps for detention and re-education and participation in antiterrorist activities abroad, especially in the Middle East and the South West Asia. However, the friendly Islamic countries like Turkey have begun to criticize China's Uyghur policy. Therefore, China has to fight the west and balance the Islamic nations which is going to be a tricky task.

LEVERAGING THE INFLUENCE OVER CENTRAL ASIA AND BEYOND, THROUGH THE SCO

Having discussed China's internal strategies to contain Islamic Terrorism and overpower alien territories demographically, we will now discuss China's strategic imperative to cut off support from the Islamic Central Asian republics. China's strategy so far has been to constructively engage these governments, thereby not only clamping any state support but also cultivating the authority to ask them to cap any support to the extremist demands in Xinjiang, if extended through non-state actors. Russia and China, being victims of similar extremist threats, in order to support these initiatives from the Muslim-populated CAR countries, created the Shanghai Cooperative Organisation (SCO) in 2001 to fight the "three evils"—ethnic separatism, religion extremism and terrorism—with China, Russia, Kyrgyzstan, Kazakhstan, Tajikistan, and Uzbekistan as it members and Afghanistan, India, Mongolia and Pakistan as observes, leading to a membership to India and Pakistan in 2017. The SCO has been able to ward off US dominance in the region post-1991 collapse of the Soviet Union. However, China has gone beyond the SCO's brief and has invested heavily to displace the US and Russia in the CAR as it knows well that it is only the over-dependence of the Central Asian countries on China and the subsequent lack of any substantial geo-economic alternative that will influence them to insulate any support for the Islamic separatists of Xinjiang. China also finds the autocratic regimes of these countries easier to work with as it never discusses any domestic political affairs with them. China knows the importance of Central Asia and therefore, initiated diplomatic actions at the highest level bilaterally much before the inception of the SCO. Chinese Prime Minister Li Peng visited these countries in 1994 and President Jiang Zemin visited in 1996. Going beyond the SCO brief, President Hu Jintao inaugurated a gas pipeline in 2009 in Turkmenistan which was attended by the presidents of Kazakhstan and Uzbekistan, through which the pipeline runs. These actions were parallel to those of the SCO at bilateral or multilateral levels, without involving Russia. The immediate gains of the Chinese influence over the Central Asia are an energy resource acquisition and a market for Chinese manufacturing.

Taking cue from the past, Xi Jinping, the Chinese President visited four of CAR countries for 10 days, before the SCO Summit meeting on September 13, 2013. It was evident that Xi Jinping made more fruitful a visit at bilateral levels. The main emphasis was on oil and natural gas and the consolidation of trade and the New Silk Road Economic Belt. Xi Jinping inaugurated the world's second largest gas field production facilities at Galkynysh in Turkmenistan, developed by the Chinese National Petroleum Company (CNPC). Turkmenistan now exports more gas to China than Russia, which is planned to go to up to 65 billion cubic metres by end of 2020.[23] A new gas pipeline for transportation is likely to run through Uzbekistan and Galkynysh to China. In Kazakhstan, Xi sealed the deal to buy 8.33 per cent shares of the Kashgar oilfields, preventing a possible sale to an Indian oil company—the second such effort to keep India at bay from the Kazakh oil field after the failure of the ONGC in August 2005 to buy Petrol Kazakistan.[24] China also sealed a deal to transit 38 billion cubic metres of Gazprom Gas annually in a tight market situation where Europe was trying hard to diversify its gas imports in the wake of the Ukraine crisis. And China having access to

Central Asia, made Russia sell gas to China cheaper by one-third, thus working unfavourably for Russia for the fear of being shut out of the Chinese gas market when the European market is also drying.[25] Such disadvantaged deals evoked more fears for Russia in the coming future then the bonhomie of the SCO as the Chinese trade with Central Asia has also surpassed that of Russia. Russia did try to stymie the Chinese growth with the finalisation of the Eurasian Economic Union or EEU with Kazakhstan and Belarus with a common currency and unified parliament and more subsidies from Russia, but the effects are not likely to last long against the Chinese economic onslaught. As China's trade share increases, the EEU and Russia feel the pinch. Xi Jinping during his visit to inaugurate the Nazarbayev English University in Astana, pressed for creation of the Silk Road Economic Belt in order to counter the likely advantages of the EEU. However, with such fierce competition over Central Asia, China is actually losing the sphere of influence beyond Central Asia, that is, the market of the EU and Russia and the reach towards the Middle East and the Caspian. Regardless, Xi ran a parallel diplomatic bonhomie at a bilateral and even a multilateral level, going far beyond what the SCO platform could provide him. Clearly, the 'Bishkek Declaration' reflected more of Russia's concerns like Syria and Afghanistan, but for Xi Jinping, it was the wooing of Central Asia. The visit of Xi Jinping during the 2013 Summit was an economic blitzkrieg what Martha Brill Olcott calls 'a ten days' victory lap'. The 2014 SCO Summit meeting at Dushanbe, Tajikistan, held on September 11 and 12 was a time to remind the Central Asian countries of the perceptible returns of these investments that was expected when Xi Jinping called for the SCO to "focus on combating religion-involved extremism and internet extremism". China also showed its intention to expand the area of influence of SCO to Afghanistan in order to 'turn Afghanistan into a country with genuine peace and stability with an Afghan-led, Afghan-owned reconciliation and reconstruction process devoid of the US and the NATO.[26] However, it is easier said than done. Although China more than Russia, has realised the confined ambit of Islamic religious terrorism fanning out of the Afghanistan–Pakistan border and the Middle East, especially Iraq and Syria, and has cleared SCO's procedural hurdles to involve new members like India, Pakistan and Iran. And Afghanistan, with China emphatically wanting to tie up with it for containing terrorism to China, is not even an observer state, neither it is likely to be on board as its umbilical cord will remain un-severed with the US and NATO for a long time to come. Another country bordering Afghanistan, Turkmenistan, is not a SCO observer or member. China has also made a short of condition to include China in SAARC in exchange for India's membership to the SCO. Therefore, it can be fairly concluded that the SCO is forced to cover the ground beyond its capacity to control. Of the two main countries, primarily China has realised the long-term futility of the SCO to achieve its primary aim, that is, to contain Islamic terrorism coming to its soil, despite all the investment. Therefore, this will be the greatest geopolitical imperative for China in Central Asia, as it has invested heavily there in the hope of tangible returns.

The Chinese geopolitical imperatives, therefore, in its west, are not only contiguous to the internal geopolitics of Xinjiang but also short term and long term in nature. In the immediate future, China can look towards Central Asia for favourable regimes that would address its security issues; going back to the Chinese philosophy of interstate relations, there is a clear trend in the Chinese intensity of activities to develop these countries into China's tributary states in its classical sense. In order to achieve that aim, China has graduated from economic investment to intellectual investment in order to bring about a common perception to the problems of international affairs, whether economic or political. For example, besides announcing 30,000 scholarships for SCO students to study in China over the next ten years, Xi Jinping offered to have 10,000 students and teachers at Confucian Institutes in Central Asia, opened by China in the universities. China has also opened China Halls—cultural centres to educate the local people about the Chinese culture and Confucian values. This hyper-cultural propaganda actually manifests the intrinsic dissimilarities between the two worlds i.e. China and the Central Asia (to which Xinjiang is closest culturally, overpowered by China through the Han settlers). This is the biggest challenge of China which goes beyond the immediate argument of Central Asia's economic over dependence of China. Therefore, the conflict between the unfavourable culture of China and its favourable economic overtures is palpable all-over Central Asia. A PhD candidate at Tajikistan brings out these factors—comparing the Indian and Chinese cultures as he says that the university libraries that China has established in Tajikistan remain bereft of visitors, whereas people love to go to the Indian Cultural Centre in the Indian Embassy as they find the Chinese cuisine, language and music strange, whereas they drool over Indian music, films and language because of the similarities. He also brings out that the Chinese remain aloof due to the language barrier, eating habits and inhibitions.[27] Therefore, the cultural charm of India is there to stay for long. Therefore, for China there is always a danger in terms of the local ethnic and cultural support that the Uyghur of Xinjiang have in these countries. The deeper support on the people-to-people level is prominent in

Kyrgyzstan, Kazakhstan and Uzbekistan due to their own Uyghur population and it is latent in Tajikistan and Turkmenistan. Organisations such as the Ittipak have an active presence in preserving the Uyghur culture and rights along with the Turkistan Islamic Party and the Islamic Movement of Uzbekistan, which claimed the bomb blast at the Karachi airport in 2014, have overtly supported the freedom of Xinjiang.[28] Therefore, China's short-term imperative remains the protection and preservation of the present governments in order to keep the hostile elements at bay so that the Uyghur movement does not get material and moral support of any outside government. This also seems to be in favour of the present autocratic regimes of Central Asia which are collaborating for now, but the future is always suspect, more so in the wake of the transnational Islamic movement and terrorism, as seen in the case of the ISIS in Iraq and Syria.

The long-term geopolitical imperatives for China emerge from two sources: one is the Chinese attitude towards its present dominance and upstaging of Russia and US influence, as General Lin Yazhon of the PLA once said:

> "Central Asia is the thickest piece of cake given to modern Chinese by the heaven".[29]

Coupled with the influx of Chinese contractors, labourers, military elements and businessmen who buy land and properties but remain aloof due to cultural differences and lack of spontaneous communication, the alienation at the people-to-people level is ever increasing and developing into Sino-phobia—a cause for attacks on Chinese workers.[30] As the local population finds that no tangible direct benefits like employment ensues to them and that these Chinese projects rather deplete the national resources like the farmlands leased to the Chinese people and firms which also directly affect them, it has resorted to the looting of Chinese businesses and even an overthrow of the government in Kyrgyzstan and protests in Almaty, Kazakhstan, and at other places. China's policy of no-strings attached offers of aid and investment and non-interference in internal matter takes a nosedive because of the attitude behind these investments that shows, when it actually translates on ground.

Another geopolitical imperative which the Chinese face in the long term is that Central Asia is becoming a breeding ground for a sub-set of new Cold War with China (because the main Cold War is already being fought in the Indo-Pacific), wherein the US and EU are slowly being evicted from the businesses as well as the existing military clout, which so far they enjoyed in the wake of the NATO's war against terrorism, fought in Afghanistan. The mistrust is so palpable that the US State Department believed that China was even trying bribe the Kyrgyz movement to evict the US from that country, as was revealed in the release of the Wikileaks. This phenomenon is taking a great momentum. Russia staking claim over eastern Ukraine by aiding the separatists, was even ready for a direct military intrusion, thus faced sanctions by the US and European Union, which was a sort of counterbalanced through a SCO military exercise conducted in China's Inner Mongolia involving China, Russia, Kazakhstan, Kyrgyzstan and Tajikistan in August 2014. Sensing these fallouts, the Soviet leader Mikhail Gorbachev who had pulled down the curtain on the US–Soviet cold war commenting on the 25th anniversary of the fall of the Berlin Wall on November 8, 2014 had already said:

> "The world is on the brink of a new cold war. Someone even saying that its already begun."[31]

Gorbachev apportioned the major blame on the US for its 'triumphalism' to resolve conflicts to a logical end. Nevertheless, the ground reality today is that Russia loves the SCO military exercise at this point in time and is able to demonstrate successfully that Russia and China together with the Central Asian countries in tow, can rise against the NATO firepower. However, there are two glitches which remain unanswered. Firstly, are the Central Asian countries getting sucked into this 'Great Game' being played out by the major powers and secondly, does China itself like to face the US-led NATO in the forthcoming sub-set of 'Cold War' which could become a war of attrition for its economic progress and proclaimed peaceful rise, as China has yet not risen enough to satisfy its people who are still at the bottom of the progress ladder? As far as the first glitch is concerned, the cracks have already showed as Uzbekistan once refused to take part in the SCO military exercise. Even Kazakhstan has vehemently invited the US to invest in the country in order to show neutrality. The latest effort from the US in the region has been the 5+1 (5 CAR + 1 US) meeting in Feb 2020. China, on the other hand, though leading the exercise to give the SCO a shape of a strong security organization which is benefitting Russia more than China, thus jeopardising China's rise in the region. Therefore, China has had its own 5+1 meeting in the month of July 2020 to garner political support in Central Asia in the face of post COVID-19 diplomatic backlash, with rapid medical supplies and economic help when majority are blaming China for the world shut down. Therefore, the greater imperative for China will be how to win over the great game emerging in the region with US too emerging as a player besides Russia and still achieve a safe secure alternative business route in the west through Xinjiang and Central Asia, besides containing and eradicating terrorism in Xinjiang and the rest of China.

GEOPOLITICAL IMPERATIVES IN TIBET AND THE INDIAN SUBCONTINENT

Evoking Friedman to say that China is an Island, is again a good postulate to explain the Chinese geopolitical linkages with Tibet. As explained in the beginning, Tibet forms China's other south-west and the thinning of the spread of the Chinese comprehensive national power has caused the dominance of centrifugal forces in Tibet, as expressed by the ever-widening gaps between the concentric circles of the core–periphery axiom. This thinning of the Chinese comprehensive national power has been historically endowed spatially. That is why there is a geospatial transition zone existing today with a scant but effective Tibetan population in the state of Qinghai, Gansu, Sichuan and Hunan what the Tibetan government-in-exile claims as greater Tibet. However, the controversy and disputes not being the focus of this study, we shall only bring out the geopolitical importance of Tibet for China's geopolitical linkages with the regions beyond Tibet and the geopolitical imperatives in the concurrent situation.

In our study of the geopolitical evolution of the Chinese nation-state of today, we have brought out that how the Chinese nation-state remained confined to China Proper. Tibet was first brought under the control of the Yuan Dynasty with a form of suzerainty and not sovereignty and was ceded during the Ming who loved to remain confined to their national boundaries of China Proper consolidated Great Wall in the west with a final outpost Jiayuguan in Gansu Province at the end of Hexi corridor and even disallowed any venture into the sea after Zheng He's famous voyages. But China continues to claim a continuum of Chinese sovereignty over Tibet ever since the Yuan, which is misplaced. These claims and counterclaims however denote only one thing that the Tibetans could not be assimilated well into China so far. They are different and fall into the categories of the 'Others'. The 'Other' has always been those, as our study brings out, whom China fought off in the west and the north and whom they called as nomadic barbarians since antiquity. The Chinese agrarian civilisation always fought them over the control of the land in China Proper till the times of the Yuan, the nomad Mongolians, actually succeeded. My argument is that even the Manchu or the Jurchen were themselves semi-nomads of the north-east who were the last imperial rulers before the republican and the communist revolution which in fact was a Han uprising against the Manchu rule of external power. The other aspect of the formation of a nation-state which is politically accepted today is the recent analytics of the Westphalian concept which our national consciousness accepts. Therefore, two different cultures may develop a 'totally distinctive national consciousness', more so when they are geographically far apart with the least mixing of cultures as was the case with Tibet as there no regular trade route existed between China and India through it due to natural barriers. Juxtaposed with Xinjiang, we can further understand the comparative lack of assimilation with Tibet and China. My other argument is that the delineation of a nation-state's boundaries in Asia(excluding areas east of Pamir) and Africa was an outcome of colonisation, which somehow could not take place in the same intensity in China despite 11 countries invading China from sea and the Great Game played between Russia and Great Britain in Xinjiang and Tibet. The geopolitical picture would have been different had the British persisted with their Tibetan expeditions. Therefore, the declaration of independence (not even conceding suzerainty, what to talk of sovereignty) by the 13th Dalai Lama was the culmination of the 'other' nature of Tibet which could only be subjugated by the military expedition of Mao in 1950.

The other centrifugal force is the religio-social nationhood of Tibet which is an alien concept in China today. Although Buddhism came to Tibet from Central Asia, it later directly connected with Nepal and India in its spiritual endeavours. The 13th Dalai Lama while making the proclamation of independence of Tibet invoked his allegiance to India after fleeing to India due to Chinese oppression. The 14th Dalai also fled to India while in distress. On both the occasions, the physical proximity to India and its being the land of the Buddha proved to be a natural harbour for a strategic withdrawal of the Dalai Lama and the Tibetan people. The fact that Tibet was and remained an independent entity was evident from the fact that a tripartite convention in Shimla not only had Tibet as an independent member in the negotiations but also that after the failure of the negotiations, with the Chinese plenipotentiary Evan Chen backing out on the final signing, there resulted a bilateral agreement between India and Tibet, with the latter granting concession of vast tracts of land to India.[32] This affinity of the Tibetan authorities could not have been demonstrated without an existing religio-social affinity between the two countries i.e. Tibet and India. In the modern times, Tibet with its Buddhist culture, influenced even the Chinese officials of Tibet to pay respect to the Dalai Lama, causing a retribution against such officials by the Communist Party's Central Commission for Discipline Inspection.[33] Evidence of such independence of Tibet from China could be found in the recognition of the Chinese themselves. Mao himself recognised this in 1931 when he, as a leading author of the Constitution of the first Chinese Republic, gave out the following stipulations for the national minorities of China:

> "The soviet government of China recognises the right of self-determination of the national minorities of China, their right to complete separation from China and to the formation of an independent state for each national minority. All Mongolians, Tibetans, Mao, Yao, Koreans and others living on the territory of China shall enjoy the full right of self-determination i.e. they may either join the union of Chinese soviets or secede from it and from their own state, as they may prefer".[34]

May be, this was the time when Mao was more under the influence of the former Soviet Union and the Communist International, but it was certainly a recognition of the independence of Tibet which had been brought under Chinese suzerainty by the Qing in the past by force. But Mao forgot these tenets of Marxism in order to compete with the nationalist revolutionaries who had been defying the Manchu rule but also reasserting their territoriality in the backdrop of the Qing granting concessions to the colonial powers. Ironically, it was the Qing Empire's territorial domain of 1820 during the Zhaqing Emperor that the nationalists made their claims. Such ambitions were ministered in the maps of national humiliation projected from time to time. One such map of 1930 was widely circulated that showed the lost territories in a darker shade—those that had declared themselves independent and were yet to be reclaimed.[35] In fact, Tibet and Xinjiang have been victims of that territorial grandiose of China. Fortunately for Mongolia, Soviet Russia's protection prevented Communist China to reclaim it and it still haunts the Chinese that the Mongolian nation-state is so formalised that they can no more assimilate it militarily. However, China did succeed to usurp inner Mongolia, which is now an autonomous region of China, but Tibet had a failed attempt of occupation from the British and Soviets during the Great Game, thus, became an easy victim when Mao came to power.

Being a communist regime, China since Mao, had always had religion and culture as a challenge to their political philosophy. Any nationalism emerging out of these, has been considered a force against the state, whether Islamic nationalism or Buddhist nationalism which have stood out so far, especially when China was a Buddhist theological state in the past during Thang period. Inside China, even such religious overtones like the Falun Gong (Dharma Wheel Practice) a combination of meditation and 'Qi Gong' (life energy cultivation) practices mainly derived from Buddhism in north-east China with a few teachings incorporated from Taoism and Confucianism, suffered a heavy crackdown.[36] China in the same spirit had not allowed Buddhism in Tibet and the adjoining provinces to be practised, which some experts call as cultural genocide.[37] Tibet does have a direct linkage with India in terms of the philosophical as well as theological origins of Buddhism. And unfortunately for China, it is also surrounded by Myanmar, Thailand, Cambodia, Vietnam, Japan and South Korea having a sizeable Buddhist population, directly affecting the mindset of the Chinese people. Therefore, China has been worried about the moral and monetary support to the Tibetan cause epitomised by HH, the 14th Dalai Lama Shering Gyatso and his government in exile located at McLeodganj, Dharamshala, in India. This gives the Tibetan people still residing in Tibet a strategic depth which is likely to nag China for the years to come. China thus, has deployed a policy to control the Buddhist practices under the government supervision and diktat. Such policies have been resented by the Tibetan people in China. 2008 was a watershed in the Tibetan uprising which was supported by the Uyighur activist Rebiya Kadeer in a statement.[38] There were a total of 344 protests in the Tibet Autonomous Region (TAR) (76), Qinghai (61) and Sichuan (166), Gansu (37) Hunan (2) and Beijing (2) causing the deaths of 227 Tibetans, out of which 107 had been shot dead, 23 died due to torture and malnutrition, 2 were executed besides 6,810 arrested.[39] China took this uprising as an action fomented by the Dalai Lama and the West to stall the torch-bearing and lighting ceremony as well as creating an anticlimax to the successful completion of the Beijing Olympics which was considered an event for redeeming its honour suffered during the 100 Years Of National Humiliation (*baman guchi*)[40,41] Sixteen policemen were also injured in a terrorist attack in Xinjiang four days before the Olympics, but surprisingly the separatist cause of Uyighur did not garner as much support as the Tibetan cause did. This is due a basic deference between the two. While the Tibetan protests were peaceful and death was inflicted upon the Tibetan people themselves by the Chinese authorities or by self-immolation by the protestors, the Xinjiang Uyighur have always been resorting to violent means of terrorist attacks based on a pronounced methodology of Islamic terrorism of which the world at large has been a victim. The second reason is that the Tibetan people and the authority, even the CTA, has somewhat resolved to accept more religious and administrative autonomy, rather than full independence. The official website of the Dalai Lama, www.dalailama.com, clearly pronounces the middle way approach which clearly says:

> "The Tibetan people do not accept the present status of Tibet under the Peoples' Republic of China. At the same time, they did not seek independence for Tibet which is a historical fact. Treading the middle path in between these two, lies the policy and means to achieve genuine autonomy for all Tibetans living in the three traditional provinces of Tibet within the framework of the People's Republic of China".[42]

This policy pronouncement does offer an opportunity to China to resolve the issue but there are other geo-strategic imperatives which China thinks it must achieve. The foremost is the Tibetan Plateau being key to the water ecosystem of Asia, besides being a repository of mineral and timber which China would like to control. Giving a religious, cultural and administrative autonomy may not serve that purpose which can only be achieved through a total control of the land as Brahma Chellaney, a renowned strategic thinker of India, says:

> "Indeed, the plateau plays a triple role: it is Asia's main freshwater repository, largest water supplier, and principal rainmaker. But Tibet is rich in more than just water; it also holds other resources of immense strategic value... It is a treasure trove of minerals, including precious metals and the so-called rare-earth elements".[43]

The other geopolitical imperative for China comes from the border dispute with India. China considers it logical to reclaim all the presumably Tibetan territories before the 1951 invasion and occupation of Tibet. The two main bones of contention are Aksai Chin and Arunachal Pradesh. Aksai Chin is primarily a dispute in the state of Jammu and Kashmir over the Indian claim of territories of Aksai Chin as per the Johnson Line of 1865 in commensuration with the erstwhile territories of Jammu and Kashmir along the Kunlun range and with the northern-most point being Hazi Langar and not the McCartney Macdonald lines of 1899 which the Chinese accepted until 1959 when Chou En Lai presented a new line of claim once the Chinese made the Xinjiang–Tibet road in 1957 and established posts much inside this line. In fact, any of these lines remained largely unoccupied except for one post established by the Maharaja of Jammu at Shaidullah, north of the Kunlun and an occasional patrolling up to Hazi Langar before the occupation by Chinese forces going up to 1958.[44] Today, the Chinese are sitting even closer after the 1962 war. The other dispute is the famous McMahon Line which was accepted by the Tibetan authorities as appended to the Shimla Convention of July 3, 1914, initialled as a tripartite draft but subsequently becoming a bilateral agreement once China refused to sign.[45] China also did not recognise the declaration of its independence by Tibet. However, the McMahon line was first published by the Survey of India in 1938 in the map which included the Tawang tract as per the agreement.

Strategically, this lack of timely delineation and occupation in Jammu & Kashmir as well as Arunachal Pradesh by India gave China a window of opportunity to look south-west of the Himalayas into Arunachal Pradesh. However, this aim cannot be achieved as long as elements of Buddhist separatists and sympathisers dominate the Tibetan space. Edward Wong, reporting from Lhasa in July 2010, reflected upon the process adopted by the Chinese to undo it, very well.

> "They come by new high-altitude trains, four a day, cruising 1,200 miles past snow-capped mountains and they come by Military truck convoy, lumbering across the roof of the word. These Chinese workers, investors, merchants, teachers and soldiers are pouring into remote Tibet. After the violence that ravaged this region in 2008, China's aim is to make Tibet wealthier – and more Chinese."[46]

Chinese government planned to invest 21.4 billion dollars by 2016 in a series of infrastructure projects including railways, airports and hydropower plants.[47] Out of these projects, the Shigaste railway line was inaugurated on Aug 16, 2014 much ahead of schedule.[48] What is significant is that Shigaste being the seat of the Panchen Lama who has been installed by the Chinese, is being highlighted to underline the Dalai Lama's influence over the Tibetan people. China has planned to build 1,300 kilometres of railways and 1,10,000 km of roadways by 2020.[49] This is factually nothing but an over-speeding of the Sinicisation of Tibet. What is most damaging of the Sinicisation efforts is the control over the monasteries when the Party Secretary of TAR declared the posting of government or the party officials in all monasteries permanently and even in some cases, a senior ranking official as per the Human Rights Watch. Beside, more than two million Tibetans have been resettled by the government in the so-called 'socialist villages', and a Communist Party official has also been assigned to each village to keep watch by living with them, which is causing more resentment among the Tibetan people.[50,51] China's pressure on weaker nations like Nepal is such that it has banned the political activities of the Tibetans in exile under the obligation of aid and infrastructure projects.

As the Dalai Lama rightly said in a foreword to a book on Tibet by John Heath:

> "Although new generation of Tibetans may feel patriotic about Tibet, the fact that they have been born and brought up in a Chinese culture means their sense of their Tibetan Identity will have altered."[52]

It is already coming true as Tibet is being transformed into a favourable Chinese territory even extended to Nepal, in order to make it a springboard of launch attacks on India for territorial acquisition as the territorial reclamation is also a ploy to redeem from national humiliation and a method to achieve legitimacy for the Communist Party to continue ruling. As the Dalai Lama has declared that there will be no more heirs to his seat, the vacuum thus created, augers well for the Chinese where they can plant their own Dalai Lama. There will also be an absence of a central motivating figure for the independence movement of Tibet. As the Tibetan landmass is being consolidated, it is further being used to go across to Nepal as highlighted by the Chinese stands to build a rail track through a tunnel under the Everest.[53] China's ambitions to reclaim Nepal as its tributary state is also clear with the investments it makes in the infrastructure projects and becomes the largest foreign investor in Nepal, beating India in 2014. However, a natural ally is determined by human geographical constructs and not by trying too hard to reach out as is being done by China. This was proved beyond any doubt to the people of Nepal when they received rescue and relief within hours on the same day when a massive earthquake hit the country. China was found lagging behind India.[54] It was nothing but Nepal's geographical and cultural closeness that mattered more than the geopolitical overtures that China is trying to create. Therefore, the imperative in Nepal for China is going to be more like working in the backyard of India geopolitically, rather than out staging India and reaching out through Nepal to India—the new market and an Asian power centre. For now, with China through Nepal is escalating the situation against India with support to Nepal on their claims on Kalapani, Limpiyadhura and Lipulekhon on the northwestern border adjacent to China but ultimately theses could prove to be measures to tame India in the long run to access their market the main imperative.

IMPERATIVES IN THE INDIAN OCEAN

As we have discussed earlier, in the light of the Chinese efforts to reach out to the Indian Ocean through continental routes from South Asia, it is relevant to discuss the long term imperatives for China in the Indian Ocean in the 21st Century. As we have already deduced that China's strategic assets are concentrated in Southeast China, it compels the Chinese to concentrate effectively on the Pacific Ocean. However, the protection of the Sea Lanes of Communication (SLOCS) along the Indian Ocean also becomes the next important imperative. The Chinese response in this wake has been to influence the Indian Ocean Region (IOR) countries commercially with militaristic overtones in order to contend the existing US naval power and geographically advantaged Indian naval power which is expanding to pursue its 'Look East' policy.

As we have already analysed, there is a naval expansion of China to become a blue water navy in order to conduct a far-sea defence as China is 'protecting natural maritime rights and interests' with 'armed forces providing reliable support for China's interests overseas'. This militarist strategy has been further accentuated in the IOR by the docking of a submarine Changzheng-2 and a warship Chang Xing Dao on October 31, 2014 in Sri Lanka and with India raising concerns over it.[55] However, though not in the same league of intensity as with Nepal, India certainly does have geopolitical and cultural advantages in Sri Lanka vis-à-vis China. This was initially expressed in the change from the India-hostile Rajapaksa government to the India-friendly Sirisena government in Sri Lanka which assured a non-military use of Chinese developed facilities and signed a civil military nuclear deal during Indian Prime Minister Modi's visit to Sri Lanka in February 2015.[56] However, due to massive infight in the two national parties, the United National Party (UNP) and the Srilankan Freedom Party (SLFP), the younger brother of Mahinda Rajapaksa, Gotabaya Rajapaksa won the presidential election in 2019 and Mahinda Rajapaksa's Sri Lanka Podujana Party won the parliament elections in August 2020 with two third majority giving China its space back in Sri Lanka. It is well understood that the use of the Gwadar Port and Pakistan's land route to Xinjiang does not invite as much comparison with the Indian strategic involvement in Pakistan barring geostrategic apprehension, but the development and use of facilities in Nepal, Myanmar and Sri Lanka does invite contestation between India and China in the backdrop of the US conceptual framework of the Chinese 'String of Pearls' around India and the Chinese conceptual framework of the 'Maritime Silk Route'. While the US is still entrenched in the Indian Ocean ever since the Cold War period and has further strengthened its position to strategically translate its Indo-Pacific concept on waters, China can only deploy ten warships, one attack submarine and one replenishment ship in the Indian Ocean without jeopardising its security and strategic concerns in the North China Sea and South China Sea. Compounded with India cooperating with the US in the Indian Ocean Region, it would be pretty difficult for China to sustain the presently overbearing naval posturing. Meanwhile, China would consolidate its land routes to Indian Ocean. However, out of the two routes, Gwadar–Xinjiang and Myanmar–Yunnan, the first one does have the potential to develop into an uninterrupted military base and a safe corridor to China, albeit with a longer detour to China Proper. Other 'pearls in the string' surrounding India like Maldives, Sri Lanka, Bangladesh and Myanmar are not likely to develop without a balancing act either by the host country or by China itself. An outright power dominance in the Indian Ocean is not an option for China—neither do the Chinese think tanks envisage so in the long run, especially in the eventuality of India becoming a more effective naval power with a backing of the US to an extent that the US outsources its power play to India having the greatest geographical advantage in the Indian Ocean. Such thoughts have already started occurring to the Chinese think tanks that never recognise the existence of any String of Pearl theory in the Chinese geopolitical dictionary nor advance any military designs to achieve hegemony in the IOR. Rather, they propagate a harmonious sea approach towards the Indian Ocean and desire to engage the US and India—the other powers with the advantages of early entrenchment and better geographical location—and create a space for China within this setup to safeguard its economic interests in the IOR. However, China does think about a possible Indian independent strategic role in the IOR where China would like to woo India for its sea route protection. Though this is not going to materialise without any accommodation of the Indian interests on the border issues and Pakistan, still with this aim, China had been thinking in the past about normalisation of relations with a view that India in the future may become more assertive with its growing power and may think independent of the US policies on the IOR and on the Indo-Pacific.[57] A Princeton Professor and a highly influential member of an international relations think tank in China, Wang Zisi, thinks that wooing India is a good option in the long run.[58] However it is going to be at a cost of a lot of relaxation in the present stand of China on the border issues and Tibet which will only be possible if China tries to change the perceptions of the IOR littoral countries which is going to be an arduous task, considering the domestic jingoism towards China not being enough assertive, aggressive and proactive in using its power in South Asia and on India. The case in point was the relief work in Nepal during the Apr earthquake where the PLA got flak from the media in China for not acting swiftly and mobilising military for the relief work as India had done. One Chinese defence spokesman Gang Yansheng, defended the sending of civilian resources instead of the military for relief, saying it was decided by various factors.[59] This "various factors" term expresses that China did realise its geopolitical limitations—the great distance from its resource core, the cultural and linguistic barriers and the recentness of its investments, whether economic or cultural in Nepal which did not inculcate enough courage in the Chinese government to mobilise the military for rescue and relief as they were not sure of the Nepalese reactions. After all, linkages with India ever since the existence of both countries and 28,000 plus Nepalese soldiers working in the Indian Army and more than 150,000 Indian military pensioners can never be overtaken by the geopolitical overreach of recent nature by China successfully. This is an example which is likely to be replicated in other littoral countries where India is better entrenched historically. Therefore, China's most important imperative in South Asia and the IOR will be to first recognise India's importance and pave methods to co-exist not only peacefully but with a friendly approach in order to secure a resource flow to China and a goods and services flow to China's markets in Africa and Europe because no other new-found silk route can ever take that volume of transportation as the Indian Ocean Region can. More so, because India is proactively involving itself in taking measures for its better control over the IOR through forums like the Indian Ocean Rim Association for Regional Cooperation (IOR-ARC) and the projection of its naval power through the India Ocean Naval Symposium with the US backing it as an invitee.[60]

THE EAST AND SOUTH CHINA SEAS AND CHINA'S IMPERATIVES

In our discussions in the previous chapters we brought out certain geopolitical facts which require being reiterated for the perspective in which we are going to decipher the geopolitical imperative for China in the 21st Century. The foremost is our deduction that China is an enclosed civilisation by virtue of its own doing, that in the west it has amassed a more than a forty per cent size which was not historically its own and the oceans in the east and south-east, which were never its own due to the Chinese's own inhibition to venture deep into the oceans historically. The second is result of the mindset of considering anyone coming from the north-west and from the sea as barbarians. The third geopolitical fact is that Japan never conceded a tributary status to China, and therefore, remained a rival since antiquity as and a country, 'causing humiliation to China in those '100 years of humiliation'. The fourth important one is that China has realised the importance of the industrial revolution and the resource crunch resulting from the fact that it had to feed nineteen per cent of the world's population.

The fifth and the most important deduction we made out was that there is the most intense concentration of resources as well as the population of China proper in the south-eastern part of China and the greatest threats are coming from the littoral countries of the East and South China Seas, thereby creating a huge geostrategic compression of the concentric circles representing a ratio between the geo-economic gains vs. geopolitical risks in the South China.

Therefore, my argument is that it is the handiwork of these circumstances and the logic of the compression of these geostrategic concentric circles that has compelled China to microscope its strategic expansion activities in the East and South China Seas at faster pace compared to the other areas like the north-west and the south-west, thereby causing more geostrategic frictions as well as attritions in the East and South China Seas. Since the conditions as discussed earlier are interlinked, the geopolitical imperatives will also be discussed in continuum.

The East China Sea

Let us first examine the economic gains from the point of disputes in the East China Sea. The main dispute in the area are the counterclaims of China and Japan over four oil and natural gas fields and the Senkaku Islands (for Japan) or the Diaoyu Islands (for China) in the close proximity of Chinese mainland, Okinawa and Taiwan. Besides historical reasons, the dispute mainly arises from the interpretation and application of the Geneva Convention on the Continental Shelf and the UN Convention on the Law of Seas (UNCLOS). China applies both the laws in tandem, first claiming that the continental shelf of China extends up to the Okinawa trough which is favourable to China. On the other hand, Japan exercises the UNCLOS on the EEZ and considers the median point as the limit of the special economic zone as the total width of East China Sea is only 360 nautical miles and does not permit each country to have 200 nautical miles as EEZ as per convention. It implies that the four oil and gas fields (with Chinese names/Japanese names) Longjing/Asunaro, Chunxiao/Shirakaba, Duanqiao/Kusunoki and Tianwaitian/Kashi remain just outside the Japanese claimed EEZ, whereas well within the Chinese-claimed extended continental shelf. China started the operation of the oil fields in 2006. However, Japan realised that these oil wells have the potential to draw out the gas from underground stretches in the areas claimed by Japan. The total reserves have been estimated to be the tune of 7.063 Trillion Cubic Feet (TCF).[61]

Another famous bone of contention is a group of eight uninhabited islands (Senkaku/Diaoyu) and rocks in the East China Sea in a total area of 7.59 km, offering rich fishing grounds and potential oil and gas reserves. The dispute rose with the US transfer of administration of these islands to Japan in 1971 under the Okinawa reversion deal which was under the US trusteeship. China contends that it should have been attached to Taiwan and not Okinawa by the US, as they have been part of that entity administratively. The islands attracted the attention of both the countries with Japan in 1969 commissioning geological studies to explore the oil and gas reserves. This prompted China to lay claims over these Islands. The US Energy Information Administration estimates about 200 million barrels of oil reserves in the East China Sea, mostly in the Okinawa trough, whereas Chinese sources claim it to be somewhere between 70 to 160 billion barrels of oil, and thus these Islands become crucial to the control of these oil and natural gas fields.[62] These islands do help Japan to claim the above mentioned oil and gas fields if these islands be considered for their own continental shelf and EEZ.

The third dispute in the East China Sea is between China and South Korea over Socorta Rock, a submerged reef on which South Korea has constructed a scientific research station which China has objected to as a breach of EEZ rights.

What has further compounded the gravity of the East China Sea is the establishment of the overlapping Air Defence Identification Zones by China in November 2013 covering these Islands to which Japan declared that it would ignore the identification process laid down by China as Japan considers it as 'unilateral escalation'. Further, the US also declared that these islands do come under the umbrella of the security alliance of 1960 with Japan meaning thereby that China should expect a US intervention in case of any military action is taken by China against Japan over these isles.[63]

Map 34: Areas of Dispute in the East China Sea

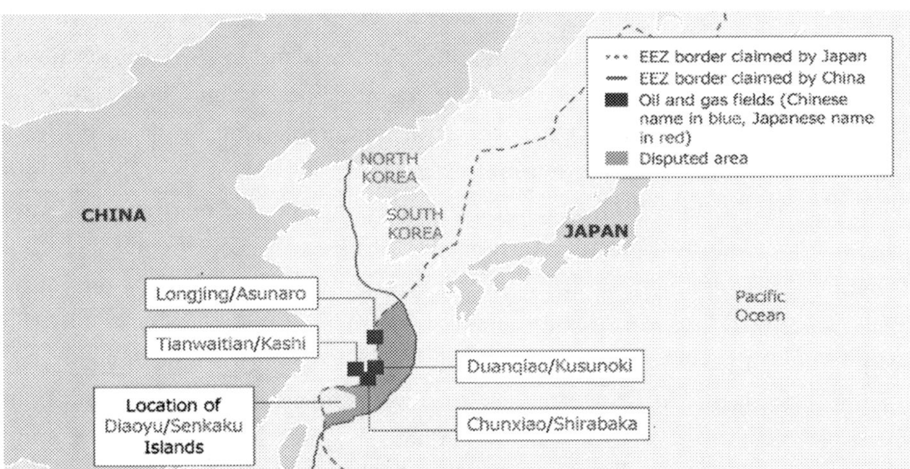

Source: The US Energy Information Administration.

South China Sea

As we have seen that in the East China Sea, the main problems are between China and Japan but in the South China Sea the main problem generates from China's territorial water claims over almost the entire South China Sea through its U-shaped Nine Dash Line officially drawn on a Chinese map in 1947 by the then Chinese Nationalist Government and later adopted and proclaimed by Zhou Enlai as a "traditional maritime boundary line" that enclosed Pratas Islands, the Paracel's Islands, the Macclesfield Bank, and the Spartly Islands.[64] The disputes arise from the fact that the UNCLOS or any international law does not govern the maritime historic rights. However, the territorial claims over these islands may stand for an argument within the international law, but a further claim of territorial waters does not. Besides, this is a 'beyond the comprehension claims' of China; there are conflicts over the overlapping maritime zones generated from the mainland of all other littoral countries and over some littoral countries claiming maritime zones of the uninhabited Islands of the Parcels and Spartly while others not recognize these claims. What is important to notice here is that while other countries' claims generate a dispute between one and one or one and some and negotiable within the ambit of the UNCLOS, China's Nine Dashed U-shaped line claim generates a one-to-all dispute. Thus, China appears most antagonistic than the others in the South China Sea. Why China is most outrageous in its approach to the South China Sea may be based upon two reasons. The first is that the waters within the Nine Dashed (or dotted) line as per China has an estimated reserves of 125 billion barrels of oil and 500 trillion cubic feet of natural gas in undiscovered resources.[65] It could be that China puts an exaggerated stake to highlight the importance of its claims over the South China Sea as its territorial waters. But the way China as a latecomer to Spartley Island in 1988 has reclaimed submerged reefs and low tide elevations, it was anticipated that China was going to drastically alter the character of these uninhabitable features to turn into a shape and size that fulfils the requirements of Article 121 of the UNCLOS of being able to "sustain human habitation or economic life of their own" and subsequently claim fully entitled territorial seas, EEZs and continental shelves of its own.[66] This apprehension has come true as China has developed a prefecture level "Shansha City" on Woody island of Paracels with Nansha as District headquarters on Fiery Cross Reef, resettled small fishing community, all civic amenities and facility of cruise for tourists to visit from mainland. In addition, in Spartly Islands, in the last six years China has reclaimed huge land mass around several reef sand atolls where military facilities including 3000-meter-long runway,

Map 35: The Areas of Dispute in the South China Sea

Source: https://www.bbc.com/news/world-asia-53344449

naval berths, hangers, missile silos and radar sites etc have been built up.[67] Therefore, the situation is escalated. Historically, there is a US military commitment towards the Japanese defence including that of disputed islands and waters and there is also a US defence commitment towards the Philippines under an enhanced defence cooperation agreement signed on April 28, 2014 in Manila during the former President Obama's visit to the Philippines which allows US to further construct new facilities and upgrade the old ones in the Philippines, the defence ties getting intensified is viewed by China as a confirmation of their apprehension "that the US Pivot into the Asia-Pacific is about trying to contain China".[68]

Taiwan and China

Taiwan and China are in a peculiar political position wherein ever since 1971, when Taiwan (or the Republic of China) lost its UN seat to PRC or the Mainland China, the countries have started deserting Taiwan and try not to formalise any relations with it by allowing the formal attendance of any international forum on their soil. However, the de-recognition of the Republic of China (ROC) has still not daunted it. As the Kuo Min Tang (KMT) dreamt to rule a united China as a republic, the pro-independence elements gained ground in Taiwan seeing no future to such dreams but getting sucked into the communist folds as the PRC is now too strong to mend ways to become a democracy. However, the Taiwanese dream stands on the defence shield provided by the US under the US–ROC Mutual Defence Treaty Signed in late 1954. Though diluted politically by recognising the PRC, but still holds good on the defence aspect through a US domestic law called the Taiwan Relations Act (TRA) governing the US–Taiwan relations after 1979 in an informal way after the Carter Administration terminated the 1954 treaty. The TRA provisions worry the PRC much beyond the general comprehension of the US–Taiwan relations despite Taiwan being de-recognised of its independent state status by the US because the TRA preamble says that the US would consider "any effort to determine the future of Taiwan by other than peaceful means, including by boycotts or embargoes, threat to the peace and security of the Western Pacific area and a grave concern to the United States;...the United States will make available to Taiwan such defence articles and defence services in such quantity as may be necessary to enable Taiwan to maintain a sufficient self-defence capability."[69] With onset of the US trade war and contestations on Corona Pandemic, the US Congress has enacted a law on 26th March 2020, "Taiwan Allies International Protection and Enhancement Initiative (TAIPEI) Act of 2019" which not only increases the scope of the US relations with Taiwan but also encourages other countries and international organisations to initiate and strengthen their ties with Taiwan enraging China.

Having analysed three flashpoint, we can easily conclude that in the event of any eventuality of strife in the East China Sea and the South China Sea, there are enough reasons for the US to get involved under the deferent bilateral treaties and the US domestic laws. Thus, it creates a balance of power situation in the Western Pacific where China is having an immense military advantage over other littoral countries. A scenario may emerge wherein China may engage into a duel on a one-to-one basis and have a strategic victory, but China is not likely to confront those directly who have a military backing from the US. However, even a duel with those countries not having the US backing may not be an option for China for the reasons of the economic risks that will ensue in the form of the oil and cargo supply lines getting hampered which would affect China the most. The Chinese aggressiveness, however, by eschewing legal challenges at the international tribunals to creating new islands out of dredged sand and establishment of Air Identification Defence Zones and by seeming ready for eyeball-to-eyeball military confrontations, appears more determined to turn South China Sea into a Chinese lake. This, backed by the economic pressure of increasing trade deficits with smaller territorial economies (for example, the Philippines reported a 12.4% increase of exports to China in 2014 increasing the trade deficit by an increase of 35% imports from China over the last year with Vietnam also recording an 18.9% increase in imports from China[70]) may have for the while compelled a truce and a non-effectiveness of the US defensive shield over the Philippines. It was certainly a tactical victory for China wherein the other claimants did not jeopardise the Chinese economic interests for being more dependent on China and rather compensating for the loss of any, as in case of Vietnam reimbursed and rebuilt China's factories damaged by the anti-China protests in 2012. However, there are strategic imperatives too which China is required to address in order to rise peacefully. The first imperative is the concentration of domestic industries and commercial investments on the coastal lines of the East and South China Seas which being the heaviest, may cause the heaviest damages to China. The second is the inflow of inputs to these industries which actually empowers China to create a favourable economic ascendency over the littoral countries at a tactical level when the supply chain gets choked if China continues to take its present tactical efforts to the brink of a breaking point. Third, counter-balancing the US security umbrellas to South Korea, Japan, Taiwan, the Philippines, Thailand and Australia does create an unfavourable imperative which cannot be balanced with a heavy naval investment by China alone. Fourth, Japan is the strongest military opposition and if China happens to face Japan it cannot face others in the South China Sea at the same time. Now a new resolve building up among the member countries to address the maritime issues of South China Sea at the ASEAN forum collectively, is going to isolate China if started. Also realizing that Chinese PLA from its mainland may be a potent force at home, Quad has taken leadership role through naval exercise in the South China Sea to contain China. Thus, it is imperative for China not to open both the East and South China fronts at the same time. Fifth, despite seeking access to the western and southern corridors, the resistance of geography cannot allow as smooth flow of the volume as the trade routes of South and East China Seas. Sixth, what happens if the littoral countries diversify their investments to more secure regions and upcoming economies like India in South Asia, and to ASEAN? Therefore, the most conclusive imperative is how much tactical risks China can take in order to jeopardise its own geopolitical survival. Hence, China would be compelled to see reason in the international law and the institutions for dispute settlement and make sense of its own philosophy to use these international governance organisations to influence the decision in its favour as much as possible through peaceful means. China may transform the East and South China Seas into Chinese lakes, but ultimately, lakes being surrounded by land (in this case land mass of other countries) don't provide access to economic oceans.

CHINESE GEOPOLITICAL IMPERATIVES IN AFRICA

The African continent had been an European continent in terms of their colonial occupation. During the Cold War period, though the countries began to attain independence, they were never really free as the exploitation of resources by these colonial powers continued because of their deep-rooted investments and patronage of the political powers that ruled these countries. During this period, the African countries also suffered from the lack of any specific foreign policy in the geopolitical scheme of the US-led West which gave China a lot of empty space to sneak in. Not that China did not have any geopolitical design for Africa—but for the exploitation of the same resources, China had a four-fold advantage over the West. First, the growing resentment among the African rulers and public for the West being the old imperial masters and the exploiters which Nietzsche calls 'ressentiment' turning from a noble "yes saying" to a reactionary "No saying".[71] The imports of the application of ressentiment to our research situation has been well articulated by Max Schelar which applies very well to the collective African sentiment as to why China became successful to sneak in a way that has paved its way to become an econo-colonial master of Africa today.

"The formal structure of "ressentiment" expression is always the same: 'A' is affirmed, valued and praised not for its own intrinsic quality, but with unverbalized intention of denying, devaluing and denigrating 'B'. 'A' is played off against 'B'."[72]

In this replace, 'A' with China and 'B' with the 'all colonial masters', and one would better understand the reasons for the current Chinese dominance in Africa.

The second reason is the timing of the booming of the Chinese economy, enabling it to spare its resources for investment in order to satiate its immense resource hunger at home. Third, there is a cheaper industrial conversion of natural resources into goods in China as compared to the West and fourth, which is the most important one, is the lack of any initial geopolitical design or ideological attachments because of which China's likes or dislikes whether to a despotic or democratic government, purely depend on its ease of business.

The most sure-footed China's venturing into Africa began with Jiang Zemin's six countries' visit in 1996 giving an official shape to the so far bilateral interactions by announcing a creation of the Forum on China Africa Cooperation (FOCAC) at the African Union headquarters in Addis Ababa, Ethiopia. China, ever since, has taken the required initiatives to occupy the investment spaces which no other country, even the past colonial occupiers from Europe, have ventured to. Here is a picture of these, which have been drawn on the basis of a variety of sources.[73] By 2013, the China–Africa trade reached US$ 210 billion with a year-on-year growth of 5–9 per cent, surpassing the US in 2009 in order to become the largest. While the exports to Africa reached US$ 93 billion and the imports reached US$ 117 billion, up by 8.8% and 3.7% respectively, indicating a heavier natural resource import by China from Africa while exports to Africa were not finding enough market as yet. It is evident from the fact that in 2011, more than 80% of the imports were in crude oil, raw materials and other resources. One of the fields where China has invested heavily is the Engineering, Procurement and Constructions (EPC) which other countries have not invested in as much. China's share in these infrastructural development ventures in Africa was 44.8% in 2012. Compare this with the US investments—a mere 4.7% in the same year, and one would realise the long-lasting impression China is going to create in the minds of the African people as a powerful geopolitical player. Another field of investment is foreign aid by China, of which by the year-end of 2009, 45.7% share was provided to Africa. However, all these investments of China in Africa only accounted for 4.3 % of its global total, the majority of which went to Asia (60.9%), Latin America (16%) and Europe (11.1%). This also in a subtle way indicates the geopolitical emphasis and priorities of China. It also indicates that China is yet to find Africa as a geopolitical leverage though it has begun thinking of militarily occupying the choke points to the supply lines. The case in point is China establishing a military base in the strategic port of Djibouti to which Djibouti's President Ismail Omar Guellah has said that China is "welcome".[74] To assuage Djibouti, China has already invested over US$ 9 billion to improve ports, airports and railway lines to the landlocked Ethiopia and says that it is willing to do more.[75] That willingness to do more has already translated on ground. China has commissioned Doraleh Port, Africa's deepest and biggest handling 90% of Ethiopian trade being a land locked country through Chinese made Djibouti-Ethiopia (Addis Ababa) railway. China is also constructing 48.2 square kilometre Djibouti International Free Trade Zone (DIFTZ) occupying 10% of Djibouti Land. [76] The infrastructure is going to leverage Chinese trade of eight members East African bloc named Inter Governmental Authority on Development (IGAD) and consolidate their political support through infrastructure of Djibouti. Djibouti has also become lynchpin with data services provided to all the neighbours by Chinese built and maintained internet and communication systems. However, presently majority of the capacity is being used for Chinese goods and services, but it will always be in the interest of China to keep the viability of projects afloat to justify its heavy military presence in the Djibouti, a choke point to Red Sea and Suez, bringing it to the level Singapore and Dubai is the ultimate aim of China. Therefore, Djibouti's place in Chinese Scheme of things is going to be very different than any other African nations for purely geopolitical reasons. Besides Djibouti, rest of Africa also today appears China's own backyard—a cultivation ground for compensating the resource crunch back home and a prospecting ground for the Chinese over-population. This fact is evident with over 20 million Chinese flooding Africa today through China's major EPC investments in resource-rich countries like Nigeria, Algeria, Angola, Ethiopia, Uganda, Ghana, Cameroon, Republic of Chad, Sudan and Niger, and creating farming settlements for the Chinese in Mozambique and Zambia. That is the reason why Africa is now termed as China's second continent.[77] Because China is offloading its own population burden in Africa today, there are also instances of conflict between the local people and Chinese migrants. As Howard W. French, a veteran American reporter with a Ghanaian wife who is based in China and Africa both and reports for the *New York Times* says, this more than 20 million estimated Chinese Diaspora is mostly due to immigration for most of the menial jobs and prospecting at personal rather than governmental initiatives. However, these Chinese do not mix so well with the government officials and Mr French says that while there is a growing charm between the Chinese and the African people, there is greater hobnobbing with rulers like the presidents of Angola and Zimbabwe, causing harm to environment dispossessing powerless landholders, flouting local rules, fuelling corruption, dumping cheap and shoddy goods and most of all, empowering awful governments.[78] The Chinese State Ethnic Commission though has taken contingence of such conflicts in Africa, the steps taken do not affect the freelancing ethnic Chinese as desired as these elements abuse the freedom after coming from the stringent Chinese environment.

Due to the above overpowering factors which are more visible, the Chinese involvement in Africa appears greater than any other country. However, it is interesting to learn that while 80% of the African export to China is in the natural resources, still the overall percentage of export of the energy resources to China does not support the exaggerated impression that we all have. Taking the example of the oil export to China, as per the US Energy information Administration (EIA), China imported 22% of Sub-Saharan oil, while the US imported 13% (due to an overall drop in imports of oil after large scale shale gas fracking) and the Europe 28% in 2012. Out of the North African oil, Europe imported more than 70%, China 12% and the US 4%. It means that the West still has most of the resources while the US share is declining because it does not need the African oil as much. China is instead consuming other resources like timber, cotton and agricultural products more than any other country.[79]

It is clear from these facts that Africa is a continent marginally relevant from the geopolitical point of view as North Africa controls the Mediterranean passage and the Hormuz Strait. What have proved relevant historically are the African resources which continued to be exploited as ever, only that the mechanics have changed. Mackinder also relegated the African continent to be part of the Outer Insular crescent. Only the Northern Saharan belt had some relevance in his maps of 1904 and 1919. Such territories do suit the Chinese ambitions of creating tributary states which can be achieved through the Chinese benevolence first, that then could be turned into hegemony more of an economic rather than of the military kind. Of course, the economic look of hegemony would then justify a little bit of strong-arm tactics wherever needed in order to support the favourable governments. China has laid claims of natural linkage with the African continent through its 'Belt and Road' initiative, citing historic links with Africa through 15 century Zheng He's voyages as described in the previous chapters, as was proclaimed by Xi Jinping during his speech at the Nazarbayev University in Astana, Kazakhstan. This strategy to cultivate more and more countries through rail and road developments will only consolidate the ideological cultivation of more and more tributary states in a modern perspective through an economic dependence on China. This desire is going to be China's prime imperative in the 21st Century. This imperative also stands to test our hypothesis as correct, that China will engage the countries farther from its core more through economic means compared to those closer to its core. The African aspirations with China are also equally well founded ideologically as the Chairperson of the African Union Commission, Dr Nkosazana Dlamin Zuma said while welcoming Li Keqiang on his visit to the headquarters at Addis Ababa on May 5, 2014:

> "This strategic and unique relationship is an expression of a long, deep and enduring solidarity between Africa and China. It was built in the long wake of Africa's struggles against colonialism and foreign domination and Africa's pursuit for self-determination, freedom, justice, peace and prosperity."[80]

The market of Africa is growing in this bargain which China also has an eye on and has already made a great impact by flooding the African market having a growing and conscious middle class, with its cheap goods that is within the purchasing power of the majority of Africans. Seeing such high visibility of China in Africa, the US-led West has also woken up and stepped up investment. In 2012, the US, the UK and France invested $178.2 billion while the BRIC countries totalled $67.7 billion, of which China's share of FDI was only US$ 27.7.[81] However, China though having a totally different approach of investment at the grassroots level and at the private and SOE levels in contractual terms which have already crossed US$ 200 billion worth of trade as discussed before, the geopolitical hedging of China in Africa by the US has already started. But the basic difference will be counting efficacy of western aid vs Chinese loans. Despite all the hue and cry made against the debt trap and counting the benefits of aid, the historical fact is that the free money of aid has made African rulers as well systems more corrupt as the market driven profitability factor has always been missing. My argument is that comparatively, the loans will work better as all the governments and citizenry will be watching the Chinese loans more closely and the governments will be care full not to lose sovereignty of their governance. With this assured, if they are able to raise infrastructure through Chinese money which no other country can match, I am sure, more often than not, the market will take care of the correctness of investments by China. The fate of the neo Chinese raised infrastructure, therefore, is not going to be that of Tazara railroad between Tanzanian port of Dar-Es-Salaam to the copper mines of Zambia, built by Mao in 1970s spending an aid of more than 500 Million dollars as an indication of China's early independent resolve to bid for Africa in face of the US and Soviet Union during the Cold War. Therefore, China in the long run is going to have the greatest and deepest influence on the majority of the African countries; it will be able to use them in its favour in the international organisations, working as a new form of tributary countries, provided the Chinese Diaspora assimilates well with local people and keeps away from local wars and terrorism.

In the end, we can derive three geopolitical imperatives for China in Africa. One is that China has to come up with the US-led West's hedging being carried out through higher investments which come with lesser or no immigrants compared to China. Two, China if invests more and more, the imports from Africa will need greater security of the passage of its imports through the Indian Ocean routes and South China Sea for which I argue that China has to follow the principle of amelioration rather than intimidation that is being pursued today especially in the South China Sea, as the economic risk versus geopolitical gain will increase day by day. Third, China has to offset the negativities of the immigrant Chinese in the African countries which will, if not now, then after about 10 years, compel the African authorities to balance it out with other investments like those from Europe, US and India. My argument is that the African countries will not allow the economic dependence on China to turn into economic slavery. Hence, China still requires a balanced approach, despite having the initial advantages. In this regard, the Confucian benevolence will be a more helpful principle to China than the Xunzi principle of winning the enemy without war but by mere intimidation, because Africa is not an enemy of China yet and China must not allow it to turn into one, especially against the competitive investments from the West and India.

GEOPOLITICAL IMPERATIVES IN LATIN AMERICA

China looks towards Latin America and the Caribbean through the Pacific Ocean which is by far considered as the US's Ocean. China also recognises the US hedging through the first and the second chains of Islands. Thus, geo-strategically the access remains under the control of the US. However, these kinds of control do not become active unless there is an outright war. Hence, so long as the international laws of the sea protect the countries' access to one another for commercial purposes, they can carry out their power projection through economic and commercial means, so does China, vis-à-vis the US in Latin America. China does have a tendency to appropriate its rights invoking some obscure historical narrative. Similar exercises have been done with Americas, as brought out earlier.

The Latin American countries otherwise have been following the US with regard to their policy towards China as was evident from the late recognition by these countries which came about only after the visit of the US President Nixon to China. Still, these countries remained passive towards China till the visit of Chinese President Hu Jindao to Brazil, Argentina, Chile and Cuba in 2004, in which he promised an investment of US$100 billion in the next 10 years. This was the beginning of the Latin American countries' swaying towards China.[82] The influence of China on the Latin American countries accentuated the deals like the US$10 billion credit to an oil company like Petrobras for 2,00,000 barrels a day of crude oil for ten years in return. This credit was equal to all the approved financing by the Inter American Bank in 2008.[83] This clearly showed an increasing lack of interest from the US which ultimately was recognised by Obama who admitted during his visit to Latin America by saying that 'at times the US took this region for granted' according to the *Latin American Herald Tribune*. This concern has been evident from the fact that the direct investments from the US firms have fallen by almost 20% since 2011, creating a gap which is being fill by China most willingly and now the trade with China has gone up from US$40 billion in 2004 to 260 billion in 2013 with a pledge by the Chinese President Xi Jinping to take it to 500 billion by 2024.[84,85] Xi, during his visit to BRICS and CELAC (China-Latin America and the Caribbean) summits between July 14–23, 2014, proposed two things that showed his intentions of a counter-pivot to the US pivot in Asia being established in Latin America. One, a proposal of "1+3+6 framework" which included US$ 250 billion as investment within 10 years and the local currency swap in bilateral trade as key measures and the second, the construction of the Two-Ocean Railways to connect the Pacific and Atlantic Oceans over a stretch of 5,300 km at a cost of more than ten billion dollars. The matter took a concrete shape during Li Keqiang's discussions with Peruvian President Olanta Humala as well as the Brazilian President.[86,87]

China had timed its investments in the Latin America and the Caribbean very well. It was the time of populist Left-leaning governments being elected to power which have been hostile towards the US policies at large. To name a few, Hugo Chavez in Venezuela (1998), Lula Da Silva in Brazil (2002), Nester Kirchener in Argentina (2003), Tabare Vaques in Uruguay (2004) and Euo Morales in Bolivia (2005). The most stunning win of David Ortega in Nicaragua further reflected the US hold on Latin America as ceasing. Therefore, the Chinese investments have reached to US$ 130 Bn in 2019 with 56% in energy projects and 28% going to metal and mining. No one in LAC mind exploitation of natural resources as much as the US because they offer what they have, and they have what China needs. Therefore, it is a mutually beneficial business resulting political influence of China as an added outcome.

It is considered by a US think tank that China has made an ingress into the American backyard which was considered so, ever since US President James

Monroe issued a doctrine in 1823 stating that any efforts by outsiders (meant at that time by the European colonial powers) to colonise land and any such interventions in North and South America would be considered as an act of intervention. However, the situation changed to the extent that the US had to welcome the Chinese influence over Latin America and Caribbean (LAC) in a sugar-coated statement issued by the spokesperson of the US Embassy in Argentina. This is despite the fact that China backs Argentina's claim over the Falklands/ Malvinas archipelago as a return favour for Argentina's support for China's claims over Taiwan and the islands in the South China Sea.[88]

What is different from China's African clamour is that in Latin America, China comes in direct confrontation with the US riding on the beleaguered administrations in various countries trying to balance it out while enticing China more and more. China, though, seeks to secure its trade and commerce, there are certain measures like the Two Ocean Railways that are already being propositioned as the Chinese answer to the US-controlled Panama Canal. Such strategic overtures have certainly alarmed the US. Though the US seeks to constructively cooperate with China to get into the skin of the Chinese long-term objectives. As recommended in the US-China Economic and Security Review Commission report, China has to ensure more stable and internationally valid engagements with these countries to avoid opening a new front with the US.[89] An impression has already been created that China has embarked upon a well-planned US$ 210 billion aid to enhance its policy of pivot to Latin America, focusing on a multifaceted military approach.[90] China has a suitable geopolitical environment at present in South America as the US influence is waning. However, the LAC is still a US backyard where the US is still the number one trading partner.[91] Despite the fact, the CELAC (Community of Latin American and Caribbean States) instead of going to Washington went to China for the first formal conference.[92] It therefore becomes imperative for China to look at Latin America in a long term-perspective and not offend the US in its backyard for now. Perhaps China is doing the same by the investing in infrastructure development and lending a helping hand to floundering economics like Venezuela. Creating a reputation of a benevolent country far from the mainland with the countries having no border baggage will be a good ploy in the LAC in order to muster more and more supporting countries for a power projection against the US in the UN and elsewhere. The outcome is evident. The tread between China and Latin America has gone up from US$ 17 Bn in 2002 to US$ 315 Bn in 2019 which China aims to take it to US$ 500 Bn in next 10 years.[93] This fillip to trade has sole credit to US withdrawal from

Trans-Pacific Partnership (TPP) free-tread agreement (FTA) in January 2017 under the US First policy of President Trump. Besides China has huge investments in communication systems in 16 countries in the region and building deep seaports controlling the strategic nerve systems of these countries.

IMPERATIVES AFTER THE SHALE GAS REVOLUTION

In the entire discussion on power projection dynamics, China is squarely appearing to contend with the US as a world power. China's deepening interest in any continent, whether Africa or Latin America, poises China before the US. The US on its part though does have the advantage of an early economic and political investment in these countries backed by the European countries, but the interest of US is seen as waning. The primary reason for such diminishing US interests is the domestic shale oil and gas production and reducing dependence on the OPEC oil. Out of these, the US is reducing imports from the countries not politically favourable to it. Thus, the creation of such a void in North Africa as well as the Latin American countries is filled by China for cheaper oil and gas acquisitions through long term investments. A similar case with Russia was witnessed when China signed a US$ 400 billion deal in May 2014 for Russia to supply China with 38 billion cubic metres of natural gas annually for three decades.[94] The analysts say that it was an event of a geopolitical turnaround, not favourable to the US. But Joseph S. Nye Jr says, in that the shale gas boom is a bigger turnaround that liberates the US from encumbrances of procuring oil and gas from potentially dangerous zones of supply.[95] Taking cue from the same facts, I argue that the US may or may not now engage with the oil-producing regions for causes like non-proliferation, protection of Israel, human rights and counter-terrorism. Had oil been an urgency for the US, its geopolitical engagement of the highest levels could be assured as has been the case ten years before. This shale gas boom in the US, therefore, has created a geopolitical space for China where China can turn into the biggest buyer of oil and in the bargain have a key political role greater than the US till the time the Chinese master shale oil and gas fracking and reduce oil and gas imports. This phase of Chinese engagement with the oil and gas-producing nations drastically make them China-dependent, with India following China. It is therefore imperative for China to consolidate this relationship and leverage it for geopolitical purposes against the US. In the long run, China will also maximise its own shale oil and gas potential with production as China is having the third largest shale oil reserves and the largest shale gas reserves.[96]It will therefore, be imperative upon China to continue engaging these nations through commodity imports and infrastructure development and management. Despite China having mastered the shale oil and gas technologies and having already mainstreamed the shale oil and gas output to contribute major portion of domestic production to consumption, is actually now will save the reserves for cheaper imports available due to drastic fall oil and gas prices caused by the net US imports going down to 3% of consumption. Thus, what is considered an advantage to the US will actually become advantageous to China. During the Covid-19 Pandemic though Chinese demand has also gone down, since crude oil prices have gone below US$ 50 per barrel, China taking advantage of the crisis has doubled the speed of piling up reserve storage.[97] Therefore, whether in short term or long term, China will capture the oil market leveraging its geopolitical position in the world.

THE MIDDLE INCOME TRAP AND ITS GEOPOLITICAL IMPERATIVES

The economists fear for Chinese economy to slow down as witnessed in the GDP growth to stay at 7.1 percent with India marching ahead with 7.5.[98] As discussed in the previous chapter, it is imminent that the Chinese growth over the medium term will continue to be sluggish, partly because the working-age population will lose the advantage of low-cost labour but maintain itself because of easy adoption of technology. Buoying the economy to cross the upper income levels ($12,500 per capita GDP) will need out-of-box reforms and steps like stepping up innovations, carrying out financial deregulation to fund only profit-making SOEs and private ventures to boost the economy, land reforms to lease for longer terms for sustainable investment in housing and agriculture, sustainable use of natural resources, etc.[99]

The middle-income trap has an empirical backing evident from the Latin American and the Middle East countries reaching a middle-income status in the 1960s and 1970s but remaining there ever since. For China, offsetting the future population disadvantages and the per capita lesser resources will reflect on China's geopolitical imperatives and power projection in the 21st Century. If we believe the Chinese Finance Minister Lou Jiwei's apprehension of China's chances of falling into the dreaded 'middle income trap', the threat can be considered realistic and thus compelling China to get tied down more and more with the outside world.[100] As Mr Lou, suggested one of the measures to reduce farm subsidy and import farm produce, will tie down China's geopolitical freedom, that too when the Chinese FM himself accepts that 'many Chinese have this war mentality and believe the country's food security will be endangered if war breaks out.'[101] As we have already discussed that how China is investing heavily in farms abroad and importing farm goods, the steps to obviate this problem are in the right direction but with a catch. It also intensifies the vitalities of the ocean routes of the Indian Ocean, the South China Sea and the Pacific which are geopolitically going to remain under the control of the littoral countries and the US. Therefore, it becomes imperative for China to make the environment conducive and to curb the war mentality as underlined by Mr Lou, which is presently overpowering the decision-making authorities in Chinese foreign affairs establishments.

Another geopolitical imperative emerges from the industrial overcapacity resulting from the 2009 stimulus package that the Chinese government owned financial institutions infused post-2008 recession.[102] Coupled with rising labour costs which reached US$ 495 per week in 2011, China needs to take its production lines to countries like the Philippines, Indonesia and India for cheaper production in order to come out of the middle income trap and arrest the unrest that may brew out of slackening productivity growth and sales abroad. This compels China more than any other country to remain a normal country which rises peacefully. The economic risk is therefore going to be always more than the geopolitical gains for China that will compel it abandoning an aggressive military policy in the long term around its neighbourhood. The greatest example was seen in China's aggressive military posturing on Doklam issue with India which defused unexpectedly fast without any real military action against India.

IMPERATIVES EMERGING OUT OF LEADERSHIP CRISIS DURING THE COVID-19 PANDEMIC

The spread of Corona virus in China and from China to the entire globe has put Chinese leadership in a tight spot. Chinese citizens in the initial stages of the spread in around Wuhan were flummoxed due to lack of information and later the entire world suffered due to lack of any early information or warning. The method of control of pandemic in China has also raised multitude of questions as other countries are still not able to fathom out the extent and magnitude of the problem. Role of WHO has also been put under scanner and the member countries led by the US and Australia have demanded probe into the spread. This has put Xi Jinping's leadership under severe pressure, more so because the power has been centralized to him and with no one else to blame, his position has become very vulnerable. In a well-researched article Michael D Swaine holds the political masters responsible for the lack of early reporting of bad news by lower level officials for fear of criticism and punishment.[103] Example is the silencing Dr Li Wenliang the ophthalmologist who first broke the news of severity of the virus and possible human to human transmission on Weibo to be one like SARS and warned his colleagues to be careful. Later he died of Corona virus himself. It was not before 20 January 2020 that the virus and its severity was recognised by National Health Commission experts announced to the press that the virus was spreading from human to human contact, a news that was already viral on social media in China. The death of Dr Li Wenliang generated a public uproar for feedonm of expression. Further, a virologist from Hong Kong School of Public Health, Li Meng Yan, who has defected to the US has claimed in a paper published in an open access repository Zenote that the virus originated in a Wuhan laboratory in six months.[104] She also claimed that the story of virus spreading from Wuhan wet market is a smoke screen. While the newspapers have carried the conspiracy theory the scientific community and medical journal like Lancet have been very careful. All said, the image of China has already been sullied, may not be because of so called origin from Institute of Virology lab in Wuhan but certainly for the fact that China has had history of origin of viruses like SARS in 2002 from Yunnan, H1N7 avian influenza (Bird Flu) 2017 from Shanghai, H5N1 (Bird Flu) in 1996 from Hong Kong, Hong Kong Flu in 1968, Asian Flu from Guizhou in 1957 and reading the history Smithsonian Mag in 2017 asked readers whether China was a 'Ground Zero' for the next pandemic?[105] With such background it is imperative for the Chinese Communist regime to improve country's image to become a responsible world leader if not the second-best world power.

During the pandemic a situation has emerged where China has been declared a winner over the pandemic while all other countries are either bleeding with loss of lives and doom of economies or nursing their wounds. China is already on its path to recovery of economy after having declared to have conquered pandemic. No new cases were reported for the first time as early as 19 March 2020. Even the WHO heavily praised Chinese efforts and called upon all nations to follow China. China then began to supply masks and medical equipment considered to have won the hearts of those suffering, diplomatically. While the poor authoritarian nations have taken it for benevolence, richer and capable democracies have not been able to take the design for a default or a naïve intent. It is rather being propagated by Chinese media as powerful ability of the current political system to rally organise, mobilise, appeal and act. However, imperative for China is its responsibility towards international community for had there been an open society or media or freedom of expression, Dr Li Wenliang's alarm would have saved nations going to the brink of disaster and rather would have established China as a responsible nation. China's upward economic mobility is more being taken as exploitation of pandemic. The opening of fronts of territorial claims and strife is also being considered as ruthless exploitation of situation doing no good to China in the long term.

A GRADUAL FREEDOM TO ITS PEOPLE: A GEOPOLITICAL COMPULSION

Any discussion on the freedom in China takes a turn towards the perspective of freedom as the US-led West lays as a norm that any country must abide by. In their enthusiasm, the West goes on to interfere and try bringing a country from authoriterianism to democracy in such a haste that so far it has always resulted into chaos. The Western debate on liberties in China results into how democracy can be brought into China. However, China is not as much a fragile regime as the West would like it to be and neither is a West-motivated 'Arab Spring' kind of revolution possible to be instigated. China is a well-organised system where the people themselves are more traditionalist/ conformists than modern/ democratic (read Westernised). They do believe in a centrality of authority and as we have discussed in Chapters Three and Four, they have never experienced any kind of democracy before the communists as well, as was in the case of India where republics existed as early as the 6th Century in the form of *Sanghas* and *Ganas*. At the most, the Chinese people have witnessed liberties in the form of Humane Authority of Confucius during the Han period. However, 'Authority' and all its forms and connotations have always been at the prime position for how the Chinese people understand governance. Therefore, the rude authority in governance has always been accepted involuntarily, and the people are more accustomed to having a system and regulating their likes or dislikes through such systems. They also cherish the hierarchical system of governance and society which they consider essential for good order in public lives. This is the basic reason the communist 'authority' lives on in China while it failed everywhere else. The issue of discussion here therefore is, then, when the Chinese people do cherish authority, why do they need liberties and what are the compulsions that force the Chinese Communist Party to grant them?

One of the greatest reasons is the sustenance of its huge population that could not be possible with the inadequate domestic resources that China has. Mao's failure showed as to how the insulation from the world could not work because China did need the resources of the outside world. Deng Xiaoping showed how liberalising the economy and opening up to the outside world could remedy this problem of sustenance to a large extent. And now the middle-income trap and the slowing down of economy coupled with a retarding population, needs a totally different approach to satisfy citizens in the medium term in order to achieve the long-term objective of getting into the higher income group of the world.

Considering that the communists do have the desire to stay and that the Chinese people do have a desire to avoid chaos at any cost, there are only two reasons why 'authority' will gradually appear to be liberating. One, the openness to the world for economic pursuits whether sponsored by the Chinese government or the private persons, has brought a sense of comparison with the outside world in all walks of lives in China. Second, the collective desire of the Chinese people to be a central player in the world geopolitics, which is a position taken for granted in the Chinese psyche since ancient times, has now transformed as an ambition to become the world's leading power in their collective consciousness. These two reasons I see as complementing each other more than conflicting. The awareness about the world at large is teaching China the new 'way' to govern which includes how regulated liberties are enjoyed in the best democracies. On the other hand, in order to reach among the higher income group countries, China needs a fair amount of time with its people in the medium term. Therefore, both the reasons are complementing each other to accelerate liberties as a geopolitical imperative.

China has already marched ahead in private liberty like commerce and life choices like dress code and fashion, but the political liberties and collective civil liberties remain curtailed and a red line still remain drawn.[106] However, it will be impractical to seek political liberties ahead of other civil liberties in China in the perspective China historically presents for itself as discussed before. In this regard China does consider Hong Kong's civil liberties movement a case of 'the more you have the more you want'.

My argument is that China will regulate freedom also, and in that wake, it will move from economic liberties, to religious ones and perhaps graduate to political liberties within the Party as a measure to avoid chaos, resolve economic woes, and constantly seek people's approval of its legitimacy. My argument does have a partial support in Samuel Gregg, the Director of Research at Action Institute, who says:

> "Once you grant liberty in one area, it's hard to preclude freedom from spreading to other spheres. Economic liberty, for instance, requires and encourages how people think and choose freely. Without this, entrepreneurship is impossible. It's challenging, however, to limit this reflection and choosing to only economic questions. People start asking social questions, and yes, religious questions. And many Chinese have decided Christianity is the answer to their religious pondering."[107]

I do differ with Gregg on one count that is his eagerness to highlight Christianity as a natural choice for the Westernising Chinese, which can if replaced with Buddhism, looks more natural and spontaneous as China's religion of majority. However, the fundamentals of his quote cannot be different. Another argument is the order in which China will see the civil liberties coming to them. Having studied the processes of nation-state evolution, metaphysical upbringing of the people and the economic risks involved, an out-and-out democratic revolution no one wishes to jump to. The majority of the people or the authorities, will not dare to take up a chance with such a risky proposition, in China. Therefore, it can be safely deduced that the next bouts of reforms will come in the private ownership of assets, one-child norm, religious freedom and some freedom in the Party's democracy, in that order. These reforms and liberties will be used by the Chinese Communist Party to release pressure on its economic performance to achieve prosperity for all.

A RESPONSE MODEL

As the discourse on the Chinese geopolitics has progressed, a methodical expression of direction for the Chinese response to geopolitical imperatives does emerge in its natural course which can be encapsulated into a formula. Before that, there are several conditions that have emerged to guide China for any such response. The major geopolitical conditions that emerged from this discourse need enumeration given as under:

(a) China's comprehensive national power was initially concentrated towards the north within the Huang He valley.
(b) In the medieval period, the concentration shifted towards the south in the valley of the Chang Jiang river.
(c) This concentration of national power replicated itself further south (not shifted itself) during the modern period.
(d) The political centre still remains in the traditional north, whereas the political power is derived from the south-east.

(e) Therefore, geo-economic risks are most concentrated towards the south-east as is the concentration of the centripetal forces making it the Chinese Core.

(f) The north-west does not have the concentration of national power elements as much, therefore has lesser geo-economic risks but more concentration of centrifugal forces which is further accentuated due to the cultural divide.

(g) Therefore, in the regions of Tibet, Xinjiang and beyond, geopolitical gains are more than the geo-economic risks as compared to south-east China and beyond.

(h) However, where China does not have any geopolitical risk (like border issues), the geo-economic gains bring geopolitical gains as well, creating a win–win situation. Such conditions emerge more and more away from the border where China can create economic dependencies and use them for geopolitical support.

(j) Except for the immediate border, the world is becoming more and more asymmetric in terms of friend-and-foe relations due to globalisation and communication and information outreach. Therefore, the sphere of influence is expanding from regional to global.

(k) The Chinese metaphysical upbringing of the policymakers' provisions for different types of political powers like benevolence, hegemony and tyranny are to be used as per the need in order to achieve geopolitical gains in a realist world of today.

The above postulates have emerged out of the evolutionary analysis of the geographical, historical, geopolitical and geo-economic facts and leads us to deductively formulate a response model which can be spelt out as the following:

> That the response to a geopolitical imperative (or a problem) by China will be a factor of the spatial distribution of the Chinese domestic production (or CNP), the centripetal and centrifugal forces and the distance of an adversary or admirer from its core.

The generic response emanating out of the above model can also be spelt out as under:

(a) The military response or power of tyranny is more likely to be used within the national boundary in the west and north from the core and beyond than the east and south, due to lesser geo-economic risks and more geopolitical gains.

(b) The greater the distance from the Chinese core, a country will invite more economic response (benevolence) to a problem.

(c) Closer to the core, an adversary will invite more hegemonic response (largely military) subject to the corresponding geo-economic risks versus the geopolitical gains.

Therefore, the above deductive logic will set a pattern and terms for response by China to its geopolitical imperatives.

NOTES

1. George Friedman, *Stratfor*, 15 June 2008, p. 2.
2. Putman, Robert D., 'Diplomacy and Domestic Politics: The Logic of Two-level Games', *International Organization*, 1988, 42 (3), pp. 423-460.
3. Shambaugh, David, *China Goes Global: The Partial Power*, NY: Oxford University, 2013.
4. Considering that more the concentration of the CNP Resources, the greater is the representation of their interests in the organs of political decision-making (which could have reflected more directly in a democratic setup).
5. Krugman, P., 'Increasing Returns and Economic Geography', *Journal of Political Economy*, 1999, pp. 483-499, and Krugman P., *Geography and Trade*, Cambridge, Massachusetts: MIT Press,.
6. Bosker, Martin, Steven Brakman, Harry Garretsen and March Schramin, 'The New Economic Geography of Prefecture Cities in China: The Relevance of Market Access and Labour Mobility for Agglomeration', April 2010, http:// www.researchgate.net/publication/22857260, Accessed On 7 Oct 2014.
7. *Times of India*, New Delhi, 1 and 2 October 2014.
8. Protestors covered themselves with umbrellas against the tear gas, thus the nickname "umbrella revolution".
9. Ogden, Suzanne, 'Inoculation against Terrorism in China', in, *Democratic Development and Political Terrorism: The Global Perspective*, Williams J. Crotty (ed.), Michigan: North Eastern University Press, 2005, pp. 227-254.
10. Millward, James, *Violent Separatism in Xinjiang: A Critical Assessment*, East West Centre of Foreign Studies, 2004, p. 6.
11. Bochm, Dana Carver, 'China's Failed War on Terror: Fanning the Flames of Uighur Separatist Violence', *Berkeley Journal of Middle Eastern and Island Law*, Volume 2, Article 3, 2009, p. 91.
12. Rauhala, Emily, 'China Now Says Almost 100 were Killed in Xinjiang Violence', *Time*, http/ /time.com/3078381/china-xinjiang-violence-shache-yarkand, Accessed on 10 Oct 2014.
13. '12 Sentenced To Death Over Xinjiang Violence', Beijing, 13 Oct 2014. http/ www.news.xinjiang–net.com/english/china/2014-10/13/C-133713584.htm, Accessed on 14 Oct 2014.
14. 'Xinjiang Natural Resources', http//www.china.org cn.english/ material/ 139230.htm, Accessed on 14 Oct 2014.
15. 'China Seen Outspending US Drillers to Chase Shale-Gas-Boom', http://www.bloomberg.com/ news/2014-05-29/htm, Accessed on 02 Sep 2014.

16. 'White Paper on 60th Anniversary of XPCC Dated 08 Aug 2014', http://www.china.org.cn/chinese/2014-10/08/content_33702216_6.htm, Accessed on 15 Oct 2014.
17. Ibid.
18. Iredale, Roby R, Naran Bilik, Wangsu, Fei Gou and Caroline Hoy, *Contemporary Monitory Migration: Education and Ethnicity in China,* Cheltenham: Edward Elgar Publishing, 2001.
19. Howell, Anthony and C. Cindy Fan, 'Migration and Inequality in Xinjiang: A Survey of Han and Uyghur Migrants in Urumqi', *The Eurasian Geography And Economics*, 52 (1), LA: Bellwether Publishing, 2011, pp. 119-139.
20. Ibid.
21. The U.S. Department of Treasury, T*reasury Sanctions Entity and Officials Pursuant to Global Magnitsky Human Rights Executive Orders,* 31 July 2020. https://home.treasury.gov/news/press-releases/sm1073. Accessed on 07 August 2020.
22. Sheena, Myunghee and Emir, *Understanding China's 'Preventive Repression' in Xinjiang.* Brookings,04 March 2020. https://www.brookings.edu/blog/order-from-chaos/2020/03/04/understanding-chinas-preventive-repression-in-xinjiang/ . accessed on 07 September 2020.
23. Olcott, Martha Bill, 'China's Unmatched Influence in Central Asia', Carnegie Endowment for International Peace, 18 September 2013, Source: http//carnegiendorment.org/2013/09/18/china's_unmatched_influence_in_central_asia. Accessed On 14 Oct 2014.
24. Moran, Theodore H., 'China's Strategy to Secure National Resources: Risks, Dangers and Opportunities', Peterson Institute of International Economics, 2010, bookstore.piie.com/book-store/572k.html. Accessed On 04 Nov 2014.
25. Casey, Michel, 'Central Asia is China's Backyard not Russia's', *The Moscow Times*, 24 June 2014, http://www.themoscow.times.com/opinion/article _/central_asia_is_china's_backyard_not_russia's/502470/html. Accessed On 04 Nov 2014.
26. Tiezzi, Shannon, 'The New Improved Shanghai Cooperation Organisation', *The Diplomat*, 13 September 2014, http://www.thediplomeat.com/2014/09/the-new-improved shangai-cooperation-organisation. Accessed on 07 Nov 2014.
27. Majidi, Umedjon, 'Tajik Views of the Dragon and the Elephant in Dushanbe', 13 October 2014, http://chinacentralasia.com/2014/10/13/tajik-views-of-the-dragon-and -the-elephant-in-dushanbe. Accessed on 8 Nov 2014
28. Lain, Sarah, 'China's Strategic Presence in Central Asia', 20 October 2014, http.//chinacentralasia.com/2014/10/20/china-stratgic-presence-in-central-asia/, Accessed on 8 Nov 2014.
29. Kucera, Joshua, 'China's Relations in Asia-Pacific: Central Asia', *The Diplomat*, 10 February 2011, http://thediplomat.com/central-asia/, Accessed on 8 Nov 2014.
30. Lain, op. cit.
31. Kucera, op. cit.
30. 'World is on Brink of New Cold War Warns Gorbachev', *Sunday Times of India*, Pune, 09 November 2014, p. 11.
32. Bhardwaj, Atul, 'British Wiles in Tibet', *Frontline*, 03 Oct 2014, pp. 64-66.
33. Gupta, Saibal, 'Beijing to Punish Dalai Supporters', *Times of India*, 6 Nov 2014, p. 13.
34. Norbu, Dawa, 'Tibet: The Road Ahead', *Riders*, pp. XIII-XIV.
35. Callahan, William A., *China: The Pessoptimist Nation*, Oxford: Oxford University Press, 2010, pp. 102-104.
36. Annual Report, 2008, Congressional Executive Commission on China.

37. Katoch, Lt Gen Prakash, 'China's War on Buddhism: Tibetan Strategic Depth', Indian Defence Review.net, 21 Mar 2014, http://www.indiandefencere view.com/spotlights/chinaswar-on-buddhism-tibetanstategic-depth/ Accessed on 10 Nov 2014.
38. Ibid.
39. Department of Information and International Relations, 'Central Tibetan Administration Report on 2008 Uprising in Tibet: Chronology and Analysis', Dharmashala, India, 2010, pp. 168-169.
40. For the chronology of events and the international support that the Tibetan uprising garnered see 'Tibetan Uprising and 2008, Beijing Olympics: A Chronology', 7 Aug 2008, http://www.idsa.in./chronology/tibetan-uprising-and-the-2000-beijing-olympics.html. Accessed on 14 Nov 2014.
41. Callahan, op. cit.
42. 'His Holiness's Middle Way Approach for Resolving the Issue of Tibet', Messages of HH the Dalai Lama, http://dalailama.com/message/middle-way-approach. Accessed on 14 Nov 2014.
43. Chellaney, Brahma, *Water: Asia's New Battle Ground,* New Delhi: Harper Collins Publishers India's and the India Today Group, 2011, p. 95.
44. Guruswami, Mohan, 'The Great India-China Game', 23 June 2003, http://rediff.com/news/2003/20spec.htm. Accessed on 15 Nov 2014.
45. Guruswami, Mohan, *The Battle for the Border*, 23 Jun 2003, http://rediff.com/news/2003/20spec.htm. Accessed on 15 Nov 2014.
46. Wong, Edward, 'China's Money and Migration Pour into Tibet', *The New York Times.*
47. 'China to Invest 21 Bn in Tibet Projects: Xinhua', *Reuters*, 20 July 2011, http://www.uk reuters.com/article/2011/07/20/idukL3E7IK39020110720. Accessed on 15 Nov 2014.
48. 'Lhasa-Shigaste Railway to open on Saturday', *China Daily*, 15 August 2014, www.chinadaily.com.cn/china/2014-08/15/content-18314858.htm.
49. Haidar, Suhasini, 'China Inaugurates New Rail line in Tibet', *The Hindu*, http://www.thehindu.com/news/international/new-raillineintibet-toboost-tradeacrossborders/articles6369931.ece. Accessed on 15 Nov 2014.
50. Halton, Celina, 'China Resettles two Million Tibetans Say Human Right Watch, BBC', Beijing, www.bbc.com/news/world-asia-china-23081653. Accessed on 15 Nov 2014.
51. Sharma, Gopal, *Reuters*, 01 Apr 2014, www.reuters.com/article/2014/4/1/us-nepal-china-tibet. Accessed on 15 Nov 2014.
52. The Dalai Lama in his Foreword in Heath, John, *Tibet and China in The Twenty First Century*, London: SAQI, 2005, p. 9.
53. Siddique, Haroon and Jason Burke, 'China May Build Rail Tunnel Under Mount Everest, State Media Reports', Guardian.com, New Delhi, 9 April, 2014. Source: www.thegaurdian.com, Accessed on 29 Apr 2015.
54. Bagchi, Indrani, 'India Scores on Aid Diplomacy, China Lags', *The Times Of India,* Pune, 29 April 2015, p. 9.
55. *Reuters*, 'Chinese Submarines Docks in Sri Lanka, Despite Indian Concern', 2 November 2014, www.in.reuters.com, Accessed on 30 Apr 2015.
56. *The Diplomat*, 'A New Era for India, Sri Lanka Relations?' 26 Feb 2015, http://the diplomat.com/2015/02/a-newerafor-india-shrilanka-relations. Accessed on 30 Apr 2015.
57. Kaplan, Robert D., 'China is unfolding Indian Ocean Strategy', Centre for A New American Strategy, 11 February 2014, http://cnas.org/content/china's_unfolding _indianocean_strategy.

Accessed on 30 Apr 2015.

58. Ibid.
59. 'China got on Backfoot: PLA gets Flak over India's Swift Rescue Operations' *Times of India*, 1 May 2015, Pune, p. 12.
60. Indian Ocean Naval Symposium–2014, www.ions.gov.in/content /indian-ocean-naval-symposium-2014. Accessed on 03 May 2015.
61. Cohen, Dave, 'A Glimpse of our Geopolitical Future: The East and South China Seas', http:/ / www.theoildrum.com/story/2006/3/14/192717/219, Accessed on 02 May 2015.
62. The US Energy Information Administration, 'Unresolved Territorial and Maritime Claims Continue to Hinder Exploration and Development in The East China Sea', 17 September 2014, www.eia.gov/countries/analysis briefs/east-china-sea/pdf. Accessed on 08 May 2015.
63. *BBC*, 'How Uninhabited Islands Soured China-Japan Ties', www.bbc.com/news/world-asia.pacifc-11341139, Accessed on 08 May 2015.
64. Hong Nong, 'Interpreting The U Shape Line in South China Sea', www.chinafocus.com/ peace-security, Accessed on 09 May 2015.
65. Lan-Anh T, Naceyen, 'The Quest for Effective Ocean Management In The South China Sea', 16th Asian Security Conference: 2014, New Delhi, 20 Feb 2014.
66. Tran Truong Thuy, 'Construction in South China Sea: A Comparative View', www.amti.csis.org/ construction-in-the-south-china-sea-a-comparativeview. Accessed on 10 May 2015.
67. BBC report, South China Sea: What's Chin's Plan for it's 'Great Wall of Sand'? 14 July 2020. https://www.bbc.com/news/world-asia-53344449. Accessed on 11 September 2020.
68. Talev, Margeret and Phil Mattingly, 'US Philippines Sign Defence Pact Amid China Tensions', 28 April 2014, www.bloomberg.com/news/articles/2014-04-27/philippinestosign-defence-deal-with-us-amid-chinatensions, Accessed on 10 May 2015.
69. *Taiwan Relations Act: Public Law, 96th Congress*, January 1979, http://www.ait.org.tw/en/ aboutait/tra/. Accessed on 11 May 2015.
70. Nicolas, Jenny, 'Trade goes on as Usual in the South China Sea, www.realclearworld.com/ article/2015 /01//28-trade-goes-on-as-usual-in-the-south-china-sea-110939.html Accessed on 11 May 2015.
71. Nietzsche, Frederick, (trans. By Mandemarie Clark & Alain J Swensen), *On the Genealogy of Morality*, Indianapolis: Hackett Publishing Company, 1988, p. XXIX.
72. Schelar, Max and W. Holdhiem, NY: Free Press of Glencoe,, 1961, p. 64.
73. The data on Chinese investments has been adopted from an assortment of sources to include www.brooking.edu; Frontier Service Group (FSG), A Business Consultancy Service and www.people.cn, etc., for an unbiased assessment avoiding totally US sources.
74. Michel, Arseneault, 'Somaliland: Djibouti to host 'Historic' Chinese Military Base in the horn of Africa', *Somaliland Sun*, 15 May 2015, Somaliland–sun.com. Accessed On 15 May 2015.
75. 'China Willing to do More in Horn of Africa: Beijing', *Economic Times*, Source: www.india times.com/news/international/world-news/. Accessed on 11 May 2015.
76. Xinhua News. Chinese Engagement in Djibouti's Economic transformation in Nutshell, 10/ 1/2020. http://www.xinhuanet.com/english/2020-01/10/c_138694414.htm. Accessed on 12 September 2020.
77. French, Howard W., *China's Second Continent: How a Million Migrants are Building a New Empire in Africa*, NY: Alfred A. Knopf, 2014.

78. It is a summary of the various narrations and experiences as given in the book cited above.
79. Bratingam, Deberah, 'How Much of Africa's Oil is going to China', *China in Africa: The Real Story*, 4 Nov 2014, www.chinaafricarealstory.com, Accessed On 16 May 2015.
80. Experts from the statement of the Chairperson of AUC, Dr Nkosazana Dlamimo Zuma, on the occasion of the visit of the Chinese Premier Li Keqiang, www.au.int/in/default/files/statement-of-the-chair-person-on-the-visit-of-Chinese-premier-5-May-2014-ppt. Accessed on 17 May 2015.
81. Stevis, Matina, 'Foreign Investments in Africa, Seen At Record $ 80 Billion in 2014, Report Shows', *Wall Street Journal*, http://www.wsj.com/articles. Accessed on 17 May 2015.
82. China Research Centre, 'China's Growing Presence in Latin America: Implications for US', http//www.chinacenter.net/, Accessed on 9 Mar 2014.
83. Ibid.
84. Lafargue, Francois, 'China's Presence in Latin America', http://www.chinaperspectives.revues.org/3053, Accessed on 9 March 2014.
85. Siow, Maria, 'China-Latin America Ties Raise Concerns', 19 April 2015, www.channelnews asia.com, Accessed on 7 Jun 2015.
86. Swaine, Michael D., 'Xi Jinping's Trip to Latin America', 5 September 2014 in www.carnegie-endowment.org/2014/0905/xi-jinping-july-2014-trip-to-latin-america, Accessed on 18 May 2015.
87. 'China, Peru and Brazil Mull Amazon Railway', 23 May 2015 www.bbc.com/news/world-latin-america-32858944. Accessed on 18 May 2015.
88. Lahrichi, Kamilia 'China's Growing Military Sway In Latin America', *Asia Sentinel*, 04 August 2014, www.asiasentirel.com/politics/china-military-sway-in-latin-america, Accessed on 09 Jun 2015
89. Brandt, Jon, Nicole Adams, Christina Dinh, Devin Kleinfield-Hayes, Andrew Tuck, Derek Hottle, Nav Aujla, Kristen Kaufman, Wanlin Ren, 'Chinese Engagement in Latin America and the Caribbean: Implications for US Foreign Policy', www.american.edu/sis/usfp/upload/chinese_engagement_in_au.uscongress-final-pdfdec2012, Accessed on 10 Jun 2015.
90. Rosenthal, Terence, 'China's Pivot to Latin America', *Right Side News*, 06 September 2013, www.rightsidenews.com Accessed on 10 Jun 2015.
91. Gillespie, Patrick, 'China's Big Chess Move against the US: Latin America', 04 Mar 2014, www.money.cnn.com/2015/03/04/news/economy/china-latin-america. relastion-united-state/ , Accessed on 10 Jun 2015.
92. Ibid.
93. Congressional Research Service, China's Engagement with Latin American and the Caribbean. https://fas.org/sgp/crs/row/IF10982.pdf. Accessed on13/09/2020.
94. Nye Jr, Joseph S., 'Shale Gas is America's Geopolitical Trump Card', *The Wall Street Journal*, 8 June 2014, Source: www.wsj.com/article/joseph-nye-shalegas-is-americas-geopolitical-trump-card-140226637. Accessed on 11 Jun 2015.
95. Ibid.
96. US Energy Information Administration, Analysis & Projection, 'Technically Recoverable Shale Oil and Shale Gas Resources: An Assessment of 137 Shale Formations in 41 Countries Outside The United States', http://www.eia-gov/analysis/studies/worldshalegas/, Accessed on 27 September 2014.
97. Russel, Reuters, China doubled its crude oil storage inflows during coronavirus demand hit,

20April 2020. https://energy.economictimes.indiatimes.com/news/oil-and-gas/opinion-china-doubled-crude-oil-storage-inflows-during-coronavirus-demand-hit-says-russell/75252060. Accessed on 14 September 2020.

98. Forecast Table, *World Bank*, http://worldbank.org/en/publication/ economic-prospect/summary_table, Accessed on 12 Jun 2015.

99. OECD, 'The Peoples Republic of China: Avoiding Middle-Income Trap, Policies for Sustained and Inclusive Growth', www.oecd.org/china-brochure-eng-september-2013.pdf, Accessed on 13 Jun 2015.

100. Cai, Peter, 'How China can Avoid the Middle Income Trap', *China Spectator* 28 April 2015, www.bussinessspectator.com.au/print/959706, Accessed on 13 Jun 2015.

101. Ibid.

102. Sweeny, Pete, 'Productivity goes Negative as China Slips Towards Middle Income Trap: Study', *Reuters*, 29 August 2014, www.reuters.com/article/ 2014/08/29/us-china-productivity, Accessed on 14 Jun 2015.

103. Michael D. Swine, Chinese Crises Decision Making the Covid-19 Pandemic Part One: The Domestic Component. China Leadership Monitor. 01June 2020. https://www.prcleader.org/swaine. Accessed on 15 September 2020.

104. New York Post, Chinese virologist posts report claiming COVID-19 was made in Wuhan lab, 14 September 2020. https://nypost.com/2020/09/14/chinese-virologist-posts-report-claiming-covid-19-was-made-in-wuhan-lab/. Accessed on 15 September 2020.

105. OpIndia, Here are 5 other deadly diseases apart from the Wuhan Coronavirus that originated from China, 7 April 2020. https://www.opindia.com/2020/04/5-china-epidemics-deadly-viruses-avian-flu-influenza-sars-coronavirus/. Accessed on 15 September 2020.

106. *BBC News*, 'China: How Much Freedom do its People Have?' 9 Dec 2010. www.bbc.com/news/world_asia_pacific_11949981. Accessed on 15 Jun 2014.

107. Quoted in Edward Trancik, 'Will free Markets Bring Religious Freedom to China?' *Action Institute Power Blog*, www.blog.action.org/achieves/70729, Accessed on 15 Jun 2015.

7
Conclusion

The effort in this book has been to bring out a rounded appreciation of almost all aspects of Chinese geopolitics. These aspects have been discussed as chapters and each chapter gives us certain derivatives. China has been introduced in its concurrent international perspective emerging out of geospatial evolution and its metaphysical as well as geo-economic setting in order to derive geopolitical imperatives holistically. Once the geopolitical imperatives were identified, it became easier to create the model for geo-strategic responses by China. The model gets continuously tested during all these discourses and establishes that China remains committed to its realist designs and will behave in a fashion that would suit its national objectives. To conclude, the reflections of the model can be discussed as the highlights of China's character and ongoing activities of geopolitical nature being pursued by China.

CHINA PROPER: A MULTI-ETHNIC MILIEU

To say that China is a Han country, is not an anthropological phenomenon as much as a cultural phenomenon. In our study we have established that ever since the Neolithic age, the existence of a multiethnic occupation of space in China proper was evident. Subsequently, the inclusion of the Jin, Yuan and Qing (Jurchen) and their seamless assimilation into the Han culture gives us a macro-level historical evidence of a multiethnic milieu. China is otherwise considered as a country that has developed out of a Han Core in the Huang, He valley in the north. As the study brings out, during the medieval period, the Chinese core shifted to the

Chang Jiang river valley where the population of different anthropological origins already existed. When this core triangle further replicated down south and up to Hong Kong during the modern period, it further assimilated into its folds the Cantonese culture and races of different ancestries. Therefore, the Han is more of a concept which does not have an anthropological sanctity.

CULTURAL DIVERSITY IN THE CHINESE GEO-BODY AND THE CNP CONCENTRATION

China is considered as a well-integrated nation; however, it is more owing to the fact that the internal divisions do not surface as often as they do in an open society or a democratic country. In reality, the Chinese geo-body remains confined to the east of 150 Isohyets. The geopolitical discourse on this issue in various chapters has proved it beyond doubt that the Chinese autonomous regions are not mere administrative regions but a different set of geopolitical realities due to their cultural divide between the nomadic and agrarian dispositions. Therefore, a great emphasis on this fact has to be laid and geopolitical experts have to start their assessment of the geopolitical imperatives for China right from the very boundaries of China Proper. China itself does consider this reality as the deployment patterns of the PLA suggest that the Chinese are more inclined to protect this geo-body of China Proper from their adversaries and in this regard, the external adversaries begin from immediately beyond the borders of this realm of China Proper in the South China Sea, East China Sea, Xinjiang and Tibet.

The other factor for compulsion of the Chinese protection of this region is the concentration of the comprehensive national power elements as brought out in the evolutionary study of the Chinese nation-state and how the CNP triangle in the north inverted its concentration to the south and then replicated itself to further south, thereby creating the present-day geo-body of China Proper. On the other hand, while the autonomous regions with their sparse population produce more than what they consume and are a reservoir of natural resources, it leads us to designate the Autonomous Regions as Resource Zones and China Proper as the Consuming Zone. It also, therefore, pronounces well as to who is exploiting whom.

Within China proper, the designated power centre is not commensurate with the actual power centre. Through this study, it has been made amply clear that how the concentration of comprehensive national power elements and their intensity shifted from the north to the south and therefore, how the new political movements, whether republican or communist, took roots in the south despite the designated political power centre remaining in Beijing in the north. This incongruence still persists as was evident with the pro-democratic movements in Hong Kong, and therefore concludes that the winds of change will continue to come from South-East China while the centrifugal forces will still work towards disintegration in western China. Therefore, the one-party Chinese government will have to deal with two dilemmas—one from the south-east coming out of centripetal forces not conforming to the communist regime and other from the north-west coming out of centrifugal forces. It is a strange but valid geopolitical dynamic that too-much concentration of CNP elements in a region makes the citizens of that area confident to wield their power with a moral authority that would surpass on occasions, the communist party's legitimacy to govern.

SILK ROAD ECONOMIC BELT INITIATIVE VERSUS THE IOR TRADE ROUTE FOR CHINA

As we have already discussed how China has taken up the One Belt One Road as its own project and has been negotiating at bilateral levels for their execution which raises suspicion in several countries like India because, though worked out on multi-lateral and bilateral levels both, these initiatives have implications for the countries in the vicinities. The clear example is China's Maritime Silk Road initiative being termed by the US as String of Pearls for India and this perception has been echoed by the Indian security experts in the same tone. Thus, now, China realising the opposition to such new ventures, has tried to cast away apprehensions by bringing out a document, 'Vision and Action on Jointly Building Silk Road Economic Belt and 21st Century Maritime Silk Road' on March 28, 2015, issued by the National Development Reform Commission (NDRC).[1] The document gives out a lot in terms of the new realisation about the geopolitical realities working against such an obtrusive initiative. Firstly, China has realised the susceptibilities of the old traditional Silk Road for its two limitations: one, that the Islamic belt is prone to extremism and disruption in the future in support of the Uyghurs of Xinjiang and two, the total land route is frictional in terms of freight carriage and cannot be ever equated with the sea lanes of communication for the volumes that can be transported economically. Therefore, Xi Jinping has turned towards the ocean routes, which has not been as prominent a trade route for China traditionally as the land-based old Silk Route has been in the past. In the ocean, there are two partial and one full ocean routes—the sea route up to the Gwadar port in Pakistan: the sea route up to the Kyaukpyu port in Myanmar and the ocean route through the Malacca strait. All this runs through the Indian Ocean. These ocean routes will be considered more secure in the future because the IOR is surrounded by stable democratic countries, barring a few until China becomes aversive to these democracies. While the Central Asian Republics, Afghanistan, Iran and Iraq which adjoin the Silk Road Economic Belt remain volatile, they are likely to be more volatile in the future for the safety of land based silk route. Thus, this policy document brings out a more inclusive approach of jointly building 'the Belt and Road'. However, there are two things that are very 'Chinese' in the perception of dealing with this matter. One is that China is unilaterally initiating all the actions like establishing a Silk Road Fund or asking other organisations to cooperate, coordinate and contribute for the Belt and Road establishment and the second is that China while asking for a country to open, keeps its baggage of bilateral strife intact and asks a minor player in the region to play a major role; for example, to open the Belt and Road through South Asia, the document calls upon Nepal to open borders with Tibet but does not make a mention of the major player India making the route to come to a dead end in Nepal. It just shows how such bilateral conflicts will not allow much progress for this magnum opus to be successful.

The other argument is that China has vigorously invented the Maritime Silk Road to offset the risks of the Belt through Central Asia and its sluggish volumes of transportation. Therefore, the Indian Ocean Region remains vital to China for its economic growth. This is the reason why China announced alternative routes to the Malacca strait through the Indian Ocean, like a multimodal transportation through Pakistan and Myanmar much before the Belt and Road initiative was announced in 2013 and a plan to develop a canal link through Kra Isthmus in Thailand to directly connect South China Sea to Andaman Sea avoiding 1200 nautical miles of detour through Malacca Straight. Its thin economic viability is still being debated in the perspective of geopolitical upheavals and security concerns in the Thai territories south of canal infested by Islamic separatists. In encouraging Thailand to build this canal with readiness to invest US$ 25 bn China is however, trying to stitch together such bilateral initiatives into a multilateral Belt and Road in order to safeguard the passage of its resources from across the world to China. On the other hand, because of no relenting on the bilateral disputes by China, the success of the Belt and Road remains a distant dream. In all this, what has emerged is how the IOR becomes even more important for China and the uneasiness among the Chinese about India's geostrategically commanding position due its imposing geographical location which was evident in China objecting to the Indian Ocean to be understood as India's backyard.[2] China, however, cannot wish away the geographical realities and has to recognise India's role in keeping the IOR peaceful and conducive for the smooth passage of its commerce. This, in my argument, is going to prove as a leverage to India in balancing against its disadvantageous position on Tibet and the other border issues in the north. Evident is the fact that any passage from the east has to go through Indian controlled waters whether from Malacca Straight or proposed Kra Canal (now called Thai Canal). As India has already begun to build and upgrade INS Kohassa in the north Andamans and Campbell strip at Nicobar into a full-fledged fighter bases, will leave no respite to China from avoiding choking. Further, the development of Agatti air strip in Lakshadweep into a fighter base will have both island groups work as aircraft carriers while Indian Navy dominating ocean routes on Nine Degree Channel from Lakshadweep and Six Degree and Ten Degree Channels from Andaman and Nicobar, the seize will be complete. This is strategic poise which still does not discount the US presence in Diego Garcia.

THE *TIAN XIA* ('ALL UNDER HEAVEN') AND *GONG GUO* (TRIBUTARY STATE) SYSTEMS ARE EASIER TO INTERPRET AND ACTUALISE TODAY

One of the conclusions of this study is that China is trying to invoke its old philosophers for redefining the types of powers, governance and interstate relations in order to create a new international system based on a hierarchical authority. In this effort, what is going to be implemented first is the Chinese concept of 'All Under Heaven'. This has become only possible because of the globalisation and informationisation of the earth and its business environment. Therefore, the spheres of influence of any country can be felt all over the world as every aspect of statehood remains interconnected globally. China assumes that since it will have the greatest power concentration within as well as outside it, China will be able to play the most influential role on the globe and thus be able to rule 'All Under Heaven', maybe through humane authority.

The other concept of exerting the sphere of influence for China has been by creating tributary states across the globe. However, with the dispute on the immediate land and ocean borders, it is least likely that China will garner support to create a true tributary state in the close vicinity. But in the globalised state of the asymmetric world, the making of a tributary system has changed its dynamics as there is no need to have a contiguous boundary in order to create a tributary state. My argument is that now in the globalised environment, communication need not move in a linear fashion and has become a Knight's move like on a chessboard and can leap, hop and jump ignoring the strife-stricken countries to create economic dependencies of China which is a modern interpretation of a tributary state. Therefore, with these two methods, China seems to have planned to become the most influential country in any world organisation, mustering the political support of such countries which will increase in number by the day in the long term. It will be a parallel strategy to the economic rise which can be considered to have reached only half-way in terms of the domestic population's satisfaction. Therefore, the so-called desire of 'peaceful rise' is not devoid of its desire of 'expansion of geopolitical sphere of influence'. It is only the strategic poise of China which is presently taking an indirect route far away from its borders. Therefore, China will always remain pro globalization although it may appear to have been looking inward by giving its economy a fillip through domestic consumption route during the recovery phase post Covid-19 Pandemic.

BUYBACK LEGITIMACY TO ONE-PARTY GOVERNMENT

The above arguments lead us to another conclusion that the only way to stay in power for China's Communist party is to buy out its legitimacy through making its people affluent. It may not be as rich as the US in terms of per capita GDP, but certainly has to be in the category of a developed nation. This domestic compulsion forces China to rise peacefully. China, therefore, makes friends away from borders and does rattle but does not escalate strife with its foes on its border. However, it does give timely reminders of its claims so as to keep and maintain a track of claims to be settled later when it becomes all-powerful. Therefore, its present strategy of going global first than local, works well on domestic as well as international fronts. For the domestic consumption, the Chinese government appears as working hard to muster resources for its people from abroad and the intermittent reminders of its claims on the borders to keep the people charged with nationalistic fervour to pardon a delay in making them prosper. On the international front, China appears peaceful on a majority of fronts away from the borders, while on its borders, it carries out a power play to remind the others of its potential to be the future superpower. However, the only drawback may be the insufficient natural resources that would not keep up with its huge demand of the population, which would compel China to always look out for resources and remain peaceful in mid-term.

CHINA CREATING A TRANS-CONTINENTAL ASYMMETRIC LEBENSRAUM FOR ACHIEVING AUTARKY

This lack of resources leads us to conclude that China will always remain dependent for resources on all the continents. Even the human resources, on whom its economic progress rode, will no more be an advantage as discussed in the previous chapters. Therefore, going global for sucking in resources is a compulsion for China. Once the huge population becomes an increasingly old-age burden, China will need to outsource its manufacturing, using others' human resources. Inadevertantly, China is also following the US way to economic progress if not political and geopolitical, where the China will become dependent on global market more and more.

In the globalised economic environment, therefore, China is appearing to create its 'autarky' through a global 'lebensraum'. The only difference it has from the classic concept of Haushofer is that it was a contiguous expansion of own space to create autarky, whereas the modern Chinese expansion is an asymmetric lebensraum and derived out of geo-economic means rather than the military means, in order to achieve autarky. Coupled with the concept of 'All Under Heaven' the Tributary States system in the global environment has become its tool to expand its economic sphere of influence and subsequently, turn this into a politico-military sphere of influence.

GEOSTRATEGIC RISKS IN THE EAST VERSUS RISKS IN THE WEST OF CHINA PROPER

As geopolitical risks versus the geo-economic gains have been discussed separately in the previous chapters, it will be wise to make a comparison here to draw out an inference as to which side of the Chinese border is likely to see military escalations in the 21st Century. It is clear that the sea routes through the South China Sea will always have more strategic significance to China than any other. It was evident in the policy directions in the White Paper "China's Military strategy" issued on May 26, 2015 which clearly indicates the new bias towards developing a new blue water navy, bringing out four "critical security domains", namely—the ocean, outer space, cyber space and nuclear force.[3] It clearly gives out that 80 per cent of the resource traffic flowing into China through the sea route needs protection through a policy of "active defence". China under the pretension of its active defence policy has created Naval Outposts on artificially developed isles and tries to acquire the deepest point of occupation on the Nine Dash Line. No such stake seems to exist in the west except on the Tibet issue and the related border issues with India. However, it is posited that more stakes for China mean a less probability of even a localised war in the eastern and southern oceans. However, the same is not the case with the Indo-China border where a local confrontation may erupt because China perceives the least economic risk there. This perception is a short-term perspective. In the long term when China raises its economic stakes in South Asia with the Belt and Road as well as the economic corridors through Pakistan and Myanmar, the economic gains versus geo-strategic risks are going to adversely turn for China, provided India not only makes China deeply invest in India but India also invests deeply in neighbouring Sri Lanka, Bangladesh and Myanmar so that these countries think hard before acting as the tributary states of China. In that case, it is likely that China would weigh the economic pros and cons more deliberately. It will also depend on whether how much leverage is given to India in the SCO and if India finds a position as at least the third-most important power in the organisation, the situation may become more amenable for both countries. Most of all, it will be very difficult for China to offset the benefits of trade surplus with India in exchange for small territorial gains in the foreseeable future. This phenomenon was well demonstrated by China in the hasty diffusion of Doklam border issue with India in 2017 and later in the East Ladakh where India dug it's heals to force China to either come to war or retract its advances on the LAC in 2020. But taking the matter too far will have severe geopolitical consequences for China. In that case, seeing the Indian disinvestments measures taken up against China in response to no withdrawal of Chinese troops from the Eastern Ladakh, in absence of any alternative market in South Asia, will have further reduced the economic risk for China to plan a limited war with India. However, if economic major powers start investing in India, China will be forced to geopolitically compete with India and not the US in real sense as India will be provided a shield of protection for these investments and will become a frontline nation which China must avoid if it wishes to become a true world power.

THE WORLD VS REST OF THE WORLD: A POST PANDEMIC PERSPECTIVE

In the Modelski's model of world leaders, the US has had its first cycle of leadership in the 20th century with Soviet Union as its challenger and by the end of the century there was no one to challenge. In the first 15 years of the 21st century there was no one to challenge either. Then has emerged China out of the "Peaceful Rise" to challenge the US. The mode of power projection for China has been geoeconomic in the entire evolution of China so far, however, now during the pandemic, China has begun to manifest itself militarily as well. The reasons for this are not unilateral. As explained, the seeds sown in the trade war between China and the US but the standoff was accentuated due to China not been able to meet its international obligations of forewarning the world of the impending threats of Corona virus and timely check on its spread.

Therefore, the traditional world order led by the US has begun to take punitive measures against the emerging challenger China justifying their actions against 'the culprit' China as the perpetrator of the pandemic. In the pandemic, China has given an opportunity to the traditional world to consolidate its ranks which was otherwise appearing scattered and now compelled to move towards protectionism, going against their own professed and propagated liberalisation. In the challenge against the traditional world, China does not appear to be alone but supported by some of the rest of the world countries where China has heavily invested during its 'Peaceful Rise', while the traditional world is made of the developed or developing democracies which existed as a group during and after the Cold War with a few new inclusions and exclusions. To call the traditional world as 'The World' and the remaining as 'Rest of the World' will be appropriate, because while the traditional world is still having a dominant leader in the US, the rest of the world is not yet resolute to identify with an emerging leader i.e. China. Hence the real cold war is yet not on as the second power centre is yet to establish itself. Hence, my argument is that the situation in the world will remain volatile for some time as options for limited wars are on the horizon and will remain so for at list a decade till either China as centres of power achieve actual geopolitical balance through military means with the US and not mere geoeconomics means, or China succumbs to its economic deprivations caused by the traditional world.

Let us first analyse how the traditional world has consolidated itself which will give a benchmark for examining potential of 'the other' power to standup for a cold war to begin. As geo-economic activities gravitated towards China and South East Asia and the European countries organized themselves into a confederation, the classical 'West' slowly began to exclude the US and include a lot of East European countries in its fold. With the Cold War with Soviet Union dissipated and Russia, losing its economic potential to back its military power, appeared to join China through the SCO after Warsaw Pact got disbanded and the Collective Security Treaty Organisation (CSTO) losing its relevance. Hence there was hardly any economic compulsions on European Union countries specially the NATO members to follow the US as leader. As explained earlier, the 'America First' policy of president Trump accelerated the alienation. Thus, for economic and mercantile reasons, all the allies of 'the West' began to work independently with China. The greatest example has been Italy having heavy investments and take over from China, one of the reasons of inflow of Chinese investors and workers who contributed to faster spread of Corona Virus in Italy. Italy signed the BRI agreement and China invested heavily in the Italian brand market taking the total value trade to US$ 48.25 billion.[4] Similarly, Germany showed independence from the US in many affairs it deals with China, not towing line of the US trade policies of restrictions and protections with China. Some experts say that China having controlled the pandemic and on the path to recovery of its economy, thought to have arrived geopolitically as well having achieved the geoeconomics ascendency over the US. China, having heated the situation in the South China Sea with active naval exercises, regulation of marine traffic and fishing and intrusions in the East Ladakh on the India-China borders in the Covid environment, has given chance to the US led allies to reorganise and re-concede the US leadership in against China. The lead has been taken by the countries of Indo-Pacific where even country like India having heavy stakes in Russia is finding difficult to stick to multilateralism and shown desire to consolidate the Quad with active participation in the naval exercises in the South China Sea. The inhibitions of all the four members of the Quad coming together dissipated and the 24th edition of Malabar Naval Exercise was under taken in November 2020 which US Naval Institute News in its communique on 20 Oct 2020 said that with Australian Navy taking part for the first time, Quad represented not only a military counter to China but also a diplomatic and economic one too.[5] The shimmers went down the very spine of the geostrategic thinking in China with member countries making ASEAN a platform to voice their collective concerns against China in the South China Sea. Further, the US moving in the direction of consolidating the countries around China, China felt a geopolitical noose around it which was reflected in the statement given by the Chinese Foreign Minister Wang Yi calling Quad an Indo Pacific NATO while wooing Malaysia with COVID Vaccine during his visit to ASEAN countries in Oct 2020. This was a spontaneous and strong reaction from China which was given in reaction to a question by a journalist. The European Union may have appeared disintegrated but the old NATO members except Turkey are realigning with the US. Turkey seemingly aligning with China for Turkey President Erdogan seeking leadership in the Islamic World upstaging Saudi Arabia, the US ally.

At this juncture, Samuel P Huntington's 'The Clash of Civilisations' has tentatively started taking shape but in some what modified form. As propounded by Huntington, the Islamic world and the Confucian Civilisation (China) along with Slovic Orthodox world of Eurasia (led by Russia) appearing to come along to fight against the dominance of the US led European West, a predominantly Catholic/Protestant Christian culture. But in my opinion, these are the temporary groupings of transitional nature. It is understood without much pondering that neither the entire Islamic world is together against the West nor the entire Christian world is against the Islamic and the Confucian civilisation at present. Rather, the old-world charm of the West is still intact because during the strife in Syria the Muslim refugees at individual levels did seek asylum in the Western European democracies and were accepted whole heartedly until they did not manifest some elements of terroristic trouble. Hardly anyone sought refuse in Russia or any other Slavic or Confucian civilisation countries. Similarly, at states' level, it may be appearing that Slavic-Orthodox countries are together against the West, but the individual aspirations may be divergent and seeking western liberties. Therefore, examining on the theoretical tenets of Huntington even, it is quite unlikely that the Rest of the World will consolidate itself against the World in the long term.

Thus, the concept of the Rest of the World has arrived wherein, the countries forming up alongside China are not the ones who had been mainstreaming the geopolitics in the twentieth century. They are those fringe countries of the twentieth century which have found some geopolitical voices in China through the BRI funding but, have also conceded their geopolitical choices and options calculating that China will someday stand up to the US and its allies and will be able to safeguard their long-term geopolitical interests as well. However, the numerical value is of very low order because majorities of weak economies are seeking favours from China and are ready to accept a position of tributary states till the time it is financially beneficial to them, therefore, not adding much power to China or 'the rest of the world' as there is no ideological moorings of opposite kind as it had happened during the Cold War. This loose grouping as has emerged, also has potentially many other weaknesses. For example, will Russia, a military power in itself with largest nuclear weapons in the world, accept leadership of the other power to be i.e. China if we even hypothetically conclude that the cold war between China and the US has started trading its course? Therefore, I argue that Russia and China will have a competition to occupy the position of the second power against the US. Though, presently the South China Sea has become the zone of contest for the US and China, but the Middle East, the Balkans and the

East Europe will become area of power projection between the US and Russia while the Central Asia will become the area of power projection for Russia and China. Therefore, the actual contest or latent jostling for the second power will actually be between China and Russia. The fault line between these two countries is that while Russia is a capable military power but is economically too weak to challenge the US, China is more of an economic power and yet to become capable military power worthy of challenging the US militarily. Because the US has both the capabilities, Russia and China are likely to remain the second rung powers. If considered the value of other European countries both in terms of economic as well as military capabilities, they add great value to the US led power calculus. Independently also, there are many like France, the UK and Germany those can be considered better comprehensive powers who can stand before China and Russia not discounting Japan that can independently stand before China in terms comprehensive power of economy as well as military for a theatre specific war in the East China Sea.

There is a further consolidation of strength around the world's leading power, the US, through Quad. What appeared to be a hesitant participation by some of the Quad members like India and Australia has dissipated during the COVID. What also appeared to be an overreaction by the Trump administration in hyper activating Quad, has gone a step further during the Biden administration. In a virtual Quad summit conducted on 12 March 2021 the quad had put up a plan to tackle COVID-19, climate change and supporting each other on critical technologies changing perception of becoming a mere security bloc. It means that the core group of Quad has realised that to contain China it is important to become an economic and commercial alternative of China in the Indo-Pacific as well. The first flagship plan implemented is production of Jonson & Jonson single dose vaccine production in India, with the US and Japan providing finances and Australia taking care of logistics and will be distributed in the ASEAN states and the wider Indo pacific region. Raising the level of interaction of Quad members from foreign ministers to head of states has been significant and 'historic' as called by each head of state in their respective statements. However, the boldest step has been full attendance in the Malabar Exercise in 2020 which has posed Quad as a military forum. Also, when the joint statement declared to "collaborate, including in maritime security, to meet challenges to the rules based maritime order in the East and South China Seas", an utterly worried China is a natural outcome.

A FUTURISTIC ASSESSMENT

The detailed analysis of domestic Chinese geopolitics, especially that of China proper, tells us that China draws its power from its own south and particularly, the south-east. There are regional disparities in China proper itself that are being addressed by the Chinese government adequately. However, the positioning of the autonomous regions of Tibet, Xinjiang and Inner Mongolia are different in this regard. China thinks of these territories without their original ethnicity. Therefore, this internal strife is going to remain as such as Xunzi himself says that 'when a victory is achieved our troops become tired, whereas the enemy is motivated to counterattack with a sense of revenge'. Therefore, ethnic minorities of these regions will wait for appropriate time to counterattack if they remain motivated. China, however, realising this problem, finds a solution in making these territories ethnically Chinese, as it became evident as we have already discussed the changing demography in these areas in detail.

There are certain other domestic areas where such tactics of altering the ethnic patterns will not work. For example, Taiwan and Hong Kong are two areas where China is likely to deploy a different strategy. As was discussed before that the wind of change will blow from the south-east, it is expected that Taiwan would not like to join China under its present one-party government or even the arrangements of 'one nation two system' specially after seeing the fate of Hong Kong. If at all China was serious about the annexation of Taiwan, has lost an opportunity when the US becomes self-serving and lost its vigour to protect the Taiwan for a brief period during the Obama regime, and as was evident, the US showed its progressive aversion to power projection against China on the Taiwan front. Now the posturing of the US has diametrically changed and will be followed up vigorously being the Congressional law. Therefore, China can annex Taiwan only when it musters enough support through various regional initiatives to make Asia stand stronger against the West with China as its leader or the US lets its guard against Taiwan down coupled with Taiwan further becomming a country of marginalised sovereignty in the international forums which suits China well. Evidence shows that China does have a desire to 'unify' Taiwan, as it was reported that all mock military drills were continuously carried out on how to annex Taiwan in a recent exercise.[6] China may not do so in the immediate future but certainly will keep such intentions and claims alive for its near-border ambitions by such acts. As has been propounded theoretically in the various discourses before that China will follow the types of powers like humane authority, hegemonic authority and tyranny from the far to near in that order in an asymmetrical pattern because it will need the support of strife-neutral countries of the far-away continents in order to justify its more realist power play closer to its borders in order to achieve these long-nursed territorial aims in the same spirit of Xunzi when he says, 'There is nothing better for the king then to form alliance with those far off and annex those nearby'.[7] And also, Fan Sui's maxim stands equally true that, 'an inch gained will become the king's inch and a foot gained will be the king's foot'.

May be, not in the same magnitude, but certainly, such an act will be followed up when the power of the alliances formed will become hugely overbearing and such military action may not be necessary, especially when the powers behind such territories are not able to put up resistance. Till then, China will keep continuing the micro-level encroachments or nibbling as in the case of India and the East and South China Seas, considering that 'an inch gained will become the king's inch'. And about 'a foot gained,' China will wait for its global geopolitical position to become strong enough to support such actions. This is an assessment of the midterm Chinese geopolitics.

Then, what happens in the long term? Will China be accepted as a world's leading power by the end of the 21st Century? It is certainly not possible with the present geo-strategic behaviour. The basic motivating factor behind the current geostrategic behaviour has been the sentiments of 'hundred years of humiliation' which has been kept alive in the minds of the Chinese. This has now become a burden on China. The other factor which has become a geopolitical burden is the aim of communist dispensation to regain territories as per maps of Qing and oceans as per Jheng He Voyages during the Ming. Whether it was Indian. Nevertheless, it also indicates China's intellectual unrealism on geopolitical front when it tries to keep military and commercial objectives going with any country on parallel tracks. However, with the evidence presented in the discourses before with regards to use of the hierarchical power system by China, the lowest and the meanest power of tyranny will always be applied starting immediately beyond the China proper within its own political boundary, where the centrifugal forces present a conflict with the centripetal forces. It is also expected that this strategy will continue till the dissident powers are dissipated in these territories. As China goes beyond its political boundaries, the middle level of power, that is, hegemony, will be used. This use of power will remain exclusive in use against those countries having territorial disputes. This power use will be asymmetric, and the quantum will also be decided as per the economic risks versus the geostrategic gains. The power of benevolence or humane authority will be kept in reserve for those countries mostly far away from China and not having allegiance to the rival blocs. China will, in this direction, keep engaging the smaller countries with the least international standing but contributing tremendously to the resource as well as geopolitical needs of China.

All the above geopolitical strategies to engage the world will remain cogent only till the time CPC holds onto the power efficiently and the cracks do not emerge owing to a failure to bring prosperity to its people in the medium term or say, by 2040. However, as a matter of strategy, China may be forced to allow some religious freedom if the authorities realise that dissatisfaction on the economic front can be safely contained with 'Faith'. There are already signs of such tendencies creeping into Chinese life where the Chinese are covertly practicing faith, especially Buddhism, in order to cope up with their day-to-day frustrations. As the Dalai Lama says that more than 400 million people practise Buddhism in China that includes members of the military as well, the danger for the present-day Chinese mindset is that a further growth in these numbers may give the Dalai Lama and the Tibetans 'a real chance'.[6] But, it is not in terms of this Tibet-centric danger that we are discussing this openness, but the changing mindset and temperament of the people which will compel the Chinese authorities to give not only room to its people but also to practise internal party democracy, faith and spirituality. As the Chinese actor Wang Baoqing said during the Shanghai International Film Festival in July 2015, that "if you grow up like I did, in an environment in China which has belief, then you will know about Buddhism and you will know about India."[9]

What it underlines is the fact that spirituality and practising faiths and beliefs is a common sight in China in the private spheres of its people. It also indicates a greater cultural inclusivity to come about in the future. When the number of such people grows in China, such inclusive-minded people will reach to the top political sphere of influence and therefore the geopolitical thinking of China will also change. In the long term therefore, it will open China to the world with its more acceptability of the 'other's point of view'. And then only, the time will come when China can replace the US as world leader as desired by the Modelski's model of power cycle.

NOTES

1. http.Mriew. Xinhuanet.com english/ 2015. 03/28/C-134105435.htm Accessed on 25 Jul 2015.
2. Statement of Senior Capt Zhao Yi, Associate Professor, Institute of Strategy at National Defence University, Beijing, http://www.timesofindia. indiatimes.com/india/china-says-india-must-not-think-of-indian-ocean-as-its-backyard/article/47899583.cms. Accessed on: 25 July 2015.
3. 'China's Military Strategy', a white paper issued on 26 May 2015 by the State Council Information Office, http:IInews.xinghuanet.com/english/2015-5/26/c_134272293.htm Accessed on 25 July 2015.
4. China Daily, China-Italy Deal a Milestone in Cooperation, https://www.chinadaily.com.cn/a/201903/26/WS5c99657aa3104842260b2792.html. Accessed on 20 September 2020.
5. USNI News, 20 Oct 2020, Australia to Join U.S., India, Japan for Malabar 2020in High-End Malabar Exercise of 'The Quad'. https://news.usni.org/2020/10/20/australia-to-join-u-s-india-japan-for-malabar-2020-in-high-end-naval-exercise-of-the-quad. Accessed on 06 November 2020.
6. 'PLA Training to Storm Taiwan's Prez Palace: Video Aired by China's State Channel show Military Exercise at Buildings Replica', Time Global, *Times of India*, 26 July 2015.
7. As in Chapter 4 note 46.
8. Jyoti Malhotra, 'The Monk in the Middle', *India Today*, July 13, 2015, p. 34.
9. Ananth Krishnan, 'Passage to India', *India Today*, July 13, 2015, p. 110.

Index

*